Optical Computing Hardware

Optical Computing

Editor:

Sing H. Lee
University of California—San Diego
San Diego, California

Editorial Advisory Board:

R. A. Athale
George Mason University
Fairfax, Virginia

P. Bruce Berra
Syracuse University
Syracuse, New York

H. John Caulfield
Alabama A&M University
Normal, Alabama

Jack Cederquist
ERIM
Ann Arbor, Michigan

Uzi Efron
Hughes Research Laboratory
Malibu, California

Arthur Fisher
Naval Research Laboratory
Washington D.C.

Lee Giles
NEC Research Institute
Princeton, New Jersey

Adolf W. Lohmann
University of Erlangen—Nürnberg
Federal Republic of Germany

John A. Neff
University of Colorado
Boulder, Colorado

Demitri Psaltis
California Institute of Technology
Pasadena, California

William T. Rhodes
Georgia Institute of Technology
Atlanta, Georgia

Alexander A. Sawchuk
University of Southern California
Los Angeles, California

Armand R. Tanguay, Jr.
University of Southern California
Los Angeles, California

Wilfred Veldkamp
MIT Lincoln Laboratory
Lexington, Massachusetts

Cardinal Warde
Massachusetts Institute of Technology
Cambridge, Massachusetts

Pochi Yeh
University of California
Santa Barbara, California

Optical Computing Hardware

Jürgen Jahns
AT&T Bell Laboratories
Holmdel, New Jersey

Sing H. Lee
University of California—San Diego
San Diego, California

ACADEMIC PRESS, INC.
Harcourt Brace & Company, Publishers

Boston   San Diego   New York
London   Sydney   Tokyo   Toronto

This book is printed on acid-free paper. ∞

Copyright © 1994 by AT&T and Academic Press, Inc.
All rights reserved.
No part of this publication may be reproduced or
transmitted in any form or by any means, electronic
or mechanical, including photocopy, recording, or
any information storage and retrieval system, without
permission in writing from the publisher.

ACADEMIC PRESS, INC.
1250 Sixth Avenue, San Diego, CA 92101-4311

United Kingdom Edition published by
ACADEMIC PRESS LIMITED
24–28 Oval Road, London NW1 7DX

Library of Congress Cataloging-in-Publication Data
Optical computing hardware / [edited by] Jürgen Jahns, Sing Lee.
     p.   cm.—(Optical computing)
  Includes bibliographical references and index.
  ISBN 0-12-379995-3 (alk. paper)
  1. Computers—Optical equipment. 2. Optical data processing.
  3. Computers, Optical. I. Jahns, Jürgen, date–. II. Lee, S. H.
(Sing H.), date–. III. Series: Optical computing (Boston, Mass.)
  TK7895.O6O67 1994
  621.39′1—dc20   93-9230
                                                                                            CIP

Printed in the United States of America
93 94 95 96 97 BB 9 8 7 6 5 4 3 2 1

Contents

CONTRIBUTORS ix
PREFACE xi

Chapter 1: Architectural Considerations for Optical Computing and Photonic Switching
T. J. Cloonan

1. High-Performance Processing Systems of the Future 1
2. A Model for System-Level Packaging 7
3. Fundamentals of Free-Space Digital Optics 10
4. A System Example 36
5. Conclusion 39
   References 41

Chapter 2: Self-Electro-Optic Effect Devices for Optical Information Processing
Anthony L. Lentine

1. Introduction to Electroabsorption and SEEDs 45
2. Surface Normal Quantum Well Modulators 48
3. Self-Electro-Optic Effect Devices 51
4. Smart Pixels 64
5. Conclusion 69
   References 70

Chapter 3: Vertical-to-Surface Transmission Electrophotonic Devices
Kenichi Kasahara

1. Introduction 73
2. VSTEP Concept and Motivations 74
3. LED-Mode p-n-p-n VSTEP 75

4. Laser-Mode Vertical Cavity VSTEP 78
5. Ultimate Performance Possibility 88
6. VSTEP Applications 91
7. Developing Applications Technologies 93
8. Conclusion 96
   References 96

Chapter 4: Microlaser Devices for Optical Computing
J. L. Jewell and G. R. Olbright

1. Introduction 99
2. Optical Interconnects 100
3. Optical Logic Devices 103
4. Ultrasmall Microlasers 107
5. Conclusion 111
   References 112

Chapter 5: Physics of Planar Microlenses
Masahiro Oikawa and Kenjiro Hamanaka

1. Introduction 113
2. Planar Microlenses 115
3. Characterization of Planar Microlenses 123
4. Planar Microlenses with Swelled Structures 131
5. Conclusion 136
   References 136

Chapter 6: Diffractive Optical Elements for Optical Computers
Jürgen Jahns

1. Introduction 137
2. Fabrication of Diffractive Optical Elements 139
3. Theory of Diffractive Optical Elements 148
4. Applications of Diffractive Micro-Optics 154
5. Conclusion 162
   References 165

Chapter 7: Diffractive Microlenses Fabricated by Electron-Beam Lithography
Teruhiro Shiono

1. Introduction 169
2. Basic Theory of Diffractive Microlenses 170
3. Fabrication by Electron-Beam Lithography 180
4. Optical Measurements 187
5. Conclusion 191
   References 191

Chapter 8: Parallel Optical Interconnections
D. E. Smith, M. J. Murdocca, and T. W. Stone

1. Optical Considerations in Free-Space Parallel Interconnects 193
2. Interconnects 201
3. Architectural Considerations 213
4. Designing with Imperfect Arrays 220
   References 224

Chapter 9: Multiple Beamsplitters
Norbert Streibl

1. Introduction 227
2. Applications 228
3. Panopticon 228
4. Performance Parameters 229
5. Image Plane Beamsplitters 231
6. Fresnel Plan Beamsplitters 234
7. Fourier Plane Beamsplitters 237
8. Beam Shaping 243
9. Noise 244
10. Chromatic Errors 244
11. Irregular Geometries 245
12. Conclusion 246
    References 247

Chapter 10: Photorefractive Optical Interconnects
Arthur E. Chiou

1. Introduction 249
2. Classification of Optical Interconnections 251
3. Photorefractive Effect 256
4. Interconnections Based on Passive Holographic Storage in
   Photorefractive Media 270
5. Interconnections Based on Photorefractive Energy Coupling 273
6. Interconnections Based on Photorefractive Phase Conjugation 279
7. Conclusion 282
   References 282

Chapter 11: Three-Dimensional Optical Storage Memory by Means of Two-Photon Interaction
A. S. Dvornikov, S. Esener, and P. M. Rentzepis

1. Introduction 287
2. Persistent Hole Burning 297
3. Two-Photon Processes 293
4. Writing and Reading of Information in 3-D Space 297
5. 3-D Memory Materials 304
6. Sample Preparation and Spectra 309
7. Stability of Written Form 313
8. Stabilization of the Written Form 316
9. Fatigue 319
10. Dependence of Stability on Polymer Host 321
11. Conclusion 322
    References 325

INDEX 327

Contributors

Numbers in parentheses indicate the pages on which the authors' contributions begin.

Arthur E. Chiou (249), Science Center, Rockwell International Corporation, 1049 Camino Dos Rios, P.O. Box 1085, Thousand Oaks, CA 91358

Thomas J. Cloonan (1), AT&T Bell Laboratories, Room 2F-233, 200 Park Plaza, Naperville, IL 60657

Alexander S. Dvornikov (287), Department of Chemistry, University of California, Irvine, Irvine, CA 92717

Sadik Esener (287), Department of Electrical and Computer Engineering, University of California, San Diego, La Jolla, CA 92093-0407

Kenjiro Hamanaka (113), Tsukuba Research Laboratory, Nippon Sheet Glass Co., Ltd., 5-4 Tokodai, Tsukuba City, Ibaraki Pref, 300-26, Japan

Jürgen Jahns (137), AT&T Bell Laboratories, Room 4G-524, 101 Crawfords Corner Road, Holmdel, NJ 07733-3030

Jack L. Jewell (79), Photonics Research Inc., 2402 Clover Basin Drive, Suite A, Longmont, CO 80503

Kenichi Kasahara (73), Opto-Electronics Research Laboratories, NEC Corporation, 34, Miyukigaoka, Tsukuba, Ibaraki, 305 Japan

Anthony L. Lentine (45), AT&T Bell Laboratories, Room 2F-229, 200 Park Plaza, Naperville, IL 60566-7033

Miles J. Murdocca (193), Rutgers University, Department of Computer Science, New Brunswick, NJ 08903

Mashara Oikawa (113), Fiber Optics Division, Nippon Sheet Glass Co., Ltd, Shinbashi Sumitomo Building, 5-11-3 Shimbashi Minatoku, Tokyo, 105 Japan

Gregory R. Olbright (99), Photonics Research Inc., 2402 Clover Basin Drive, Suite A, Longmont, CO 80503

Peter M. Rentzepis (287), Professor of Chemistry, University of California, Irvine, Irvine, CA 92717

Teruhiro Shiono (169), Matsushita Electric Industrial Co., Ltd., Central Research Laboratory, 3-15, Yagumo-Nakamachi, Moriguchi, Osaka 570, Japan

Donald E. Smith (193), Rutgers University, Department of Computer Science, New Brunswick, NJ 08903

Thomas S. Stone (193), Rutgers University, Department of Computer Science, New Brunswick, NJ 08903

Norbert Streibl (227), Robert-Bosch GmbH, Abt. ZWP, Robert-Bosch-Platz 1, Gerlingen Schillerhohe, W-7000 Stuttgart, Germany

Preface

The speed of today's high-performance electronic computers is increasingly limited by the number and bandwidth of the interconnections and by data storage and retrieval rates rather than by processing power. Optics, with its inherent parallelism and three-dimensional interconnection capabilities, can offer interesting solutions to help alleviate these limitations. Applying optics to computing is an emerging technology and many significant advances have been made during the past couple of years in the development of optical computing hardware. The goal of this volume is to review the progress and describe their status.

The selection of the topics for the different chapters was influenced by the two application areas on which we focus in this volume: high-performance computing and high-throughput photonic switching. These two applications require the use of fast logic device arrays, for which only semiconductor-based devices are currently available. Devices for other areas of optical computing such as neural networks, which do not require high-speed operations, are not included in this volume.

The volume starts with a chapter giving a system overview and contains ten other chapters that describe the recent research in optoelectronic devices, microoptics, optical interconnections, and optical memory.

System overview: Chapter 1 defines the requirements on hardware from a system perspective, i.e., it provides the reader with an overview of the various parts required to build an optical computer: devices, interconnections, packaging, architectures. An example of a free-space optical photonic switching system is presented.

Optoelectronic devices: The self-electro-optic effect device (SEED), the vertical-to-surface transmission electrophotonic device (VSTEP), and vertical-cavity surface-emitting microlasers (VCSEL) are presented in Chapters 2, 3, and 4. The chapters explain the basic principles of the devices and their operation either as logic devices or for optical interconnection applications.

Micro-optics: Chapter 5 describes the planar optical microlens as an example of a refractive microlens of the gradient-index type. Diffractive optical elements are also discussed. Chapter 6 explains fundamentals and a few applications of diffractive optics for interconnections and integrated microoptic packaging. Chapter 7 features an advanced way of fabricating diffractive optics by means of direct electron-beam lithography.

Optical interconnections: The large temporal and spatial bandwidth of optical signals is one of the major assets of optics for computing applications. Parallel optical interconnections based on multistage interconnection networks and architectural considerations for optical computing are described in Chapter 8. A specific interconnection application, i.e., the generation of two-dimensional spot arrays, is presented in Chapter 9. Chapter 10 discusses the use of reconfigurable interconnects based on the use of photorefractive materials and holographic storage.

Optical memory: Chapter 11 describes a technique for writing and reading optically in parallel from a three-dimensional matrix by means of two-photon interaction in photochromic organic materials.

Although optical digital computing is not yet a mature technology, the development of hardware components may be useful to other, more near-term applications, such as optical interconnections for VLSI systems or optoelectronic sensors. It is important to note that optoelectronics and micro-optics are built on the same technology base as electronics. For example, the use of lithography and etching techniques has become as common in the manufacturing of microlenses as it is for the fabrication of gallium arsenide optoelectronic devices. The technological compatibility between optoelectronics, micro-optics, and electronics may be one key to making optical technology more acceptable to computer manufacturers than it has been in the past.

Another important consideration that concerns the practicability or manufacturability of computing systems that use optics is optoelectronic integration and packaging. Without suitable means of building optoelectronic systems in a compact and reliable way, it will be hard to introduce optics as a technology of the future. The difficulty of the task becomes obvious from the requirements that optical systems have to satisfy in terms of alignment precision. To overcome this difficulty, packaging considerations must be included as part of the hardware design.

Based on these thoughts, the chapters for this volume were selected. We hope that the reader will find this book a useful source for information and reference.

ACKNOWLEDGMENT

We would like to express our gratitude to the authors for using precious personal time to write their contributions. Furthermore, we would like to thank Kathleen Tibbetts and Robert Kaplan from Academic Press for their support and valuable assistance throughout the publication process.

Jürgen Jahns and Sing H. Lee

Chapter 1
Architectural Considerations for Optical Computing and Photonic Switching

T. J. CLOONAN

AT&T Bell Laboratories
200 Park Plaza
Naperville, IL 60566

1. High-Performance Processing Systems of the Future 1
   1.1 Fundamental Components in Computing Systems 3
   1.2 Fundamental Components in Telecommunication Systems 3
   1.3 Interconnection and Packaging Problems in Processing Systems 4
2. A Model for System-Level Packaging 7
3. Fundamentals of Free-Space Digital Optics 10
   3.1 Planar Device Arrays 12
   3.2 Three-Dimensional Optical Interconnections 21
   3.3 Limitations of Free-Space Digital Optics 34
4. A System Example 36
5. Conclusion 39
   References 41

1. High-Performance Processing Systems of the Future

Research into the use of free-space digital optics for interconnections and packaging during the past two decades has produced many promising results by combining and coordinating the efforts of researchers, scientists, and engineers from a wide variety of backgrounds. These many backgrounds include classical optics, lens design, diffractive optics, holography, optomechanics, laser design, device physics, semiconductor device fabrication, high-speed electronics design, advanced electronics packaging, thermodynamics and thermal packaging, digital logic design, and system architectures.

The driving force behind this coordinated research effort comes from the demanding requirements being created by the system engineers of today who are designing the processing systems of tomorrow. In particular, the future requirements for two specific types of processing systems are beginning to greatly outpace the evolving capabilities of the standard interconnection and packaging technologies that will be available to implement these future systems. These two rapidly growing processing systems are (1) high-performance computing systems and (2) high-throughput telecommunication switching systems.

These two different types of processing systems exhibit many similarities. For example, computing systems are beginning to rely more heavily on parallel processing techniques to provide their functionality. As a result, interconnection networks are oftentimes used to provide the connections between the multiple processors and between processors and shared memories [Fig. 1(a)]. At the same time, telecommunication networks are beginning to be used more frequently to carry packet-oriented data, and the nodes in the self-routing packet-switching networks are being designed with more functionality to route these packets. As a result, the packet-switching networks are beginning to resemble parallel processing systems with small processors (nodes) connected by links [Fig. 1(b)]. In addition, as the data rates in both computing systems and telecommunication systems continually increase, designers are adding registers within the data paths to provide global synchronization of the data signals on different data paths. As a result, both systems are beginning to resemble the simple pipelined processor model shown in Fig. 1(c), where stages of combinational logic are sandwiched between synchronizing latches yielding a long pipeline of processing logic. Nevertheless, some basic differences still exist between computing systems and telecommunication systems, and these basic differences are outlined in the following sections.

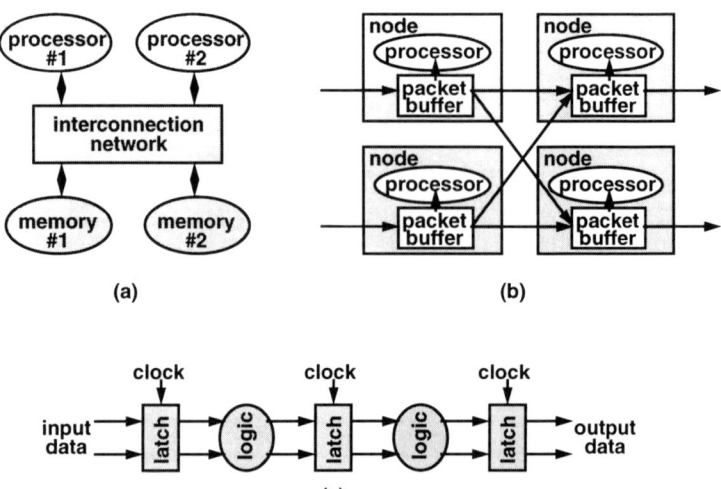

Figure 1. Typical processing systems: (a) parallel computer, (b) packet-switching network, and (c) pipelined processor.

Architectural Considerations for Optical Computing and Photonic Switching

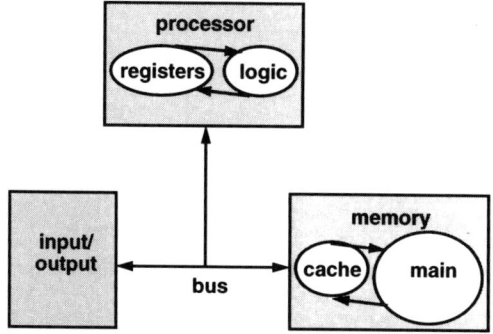

Figure 2. Fundamental components in computing systems.

1.1 Fundamental Components in Computing Systems

In general, any computing system must contain at least three fundamental components: a processing element, a memory, and an input/output interface (Fig. 2). The processing element typically contains combinational logic to implement the desired arithmetic operations, and it also contains registers to store intermediate results. Since data are often repeatedly routed between the registers and the combinational logic in a manner reminiscent of classical finite state machines, feedback loops are generally an inherent part of computing systems (Stone 1980). The registers in the processing element are usually filled with data that were initially stored in the memory, and the results of mathematical operations can then be stored in the memory for future access or for retrieval by the system user. The memory is often divided into two functional units to improve the average processing rate. A small cache memory with a very fast access time holds data that are accessed quite frequently, while a larger main memory with slower access times holds most of the other data. The input/output interface within the system provides a means for the user to communicate with the computing system, and it also provides a means for the system to send pertinent information regarding the internal system status to the user.

1.2 Fundamental Components in Telecommunication Systems

A telecommunication system can be divided into two distinct subsystems: the transmission facility and the switching system. The transmission facility provides a physical connection for signals to be transported over relatively long distances (ranging from hundreds of meters to thousands of kilometers depending on the particular application). This physical connection can be provided by metallic cables, microwave towers, or optical fibers. The transmission facility must also provide the hardware needed to amplify and regenerate the transmitted signals as

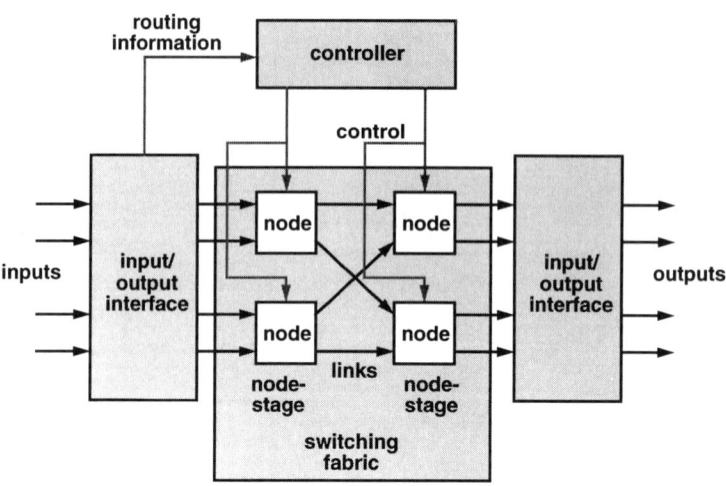

Figure 3. Fundamental components in switching networks.

they are distorted and attenuated by the propagation along the imperfect channel. The actual routing of the signals along the desired path is accomplished by the switching system, which receives signals from multiple transmission links and steers the signals to the desired output transmission link based on control signals sent to the switching system. A typical multistage interconnection network that could be used in a switching system is shown in Fig. 3. This system is comprised of four fundamental components: a controller, a pair of input/output interfaces, a set of nodes, and a set of connecting links. The input/output interfaces provide conditioning of the signals (such as bit synchronization, extraction of routing information, etc.) between the transmission facility and the switching network. Extracted routing information is sent to the controller, which determines the network path through which the signals must be routed. The controller then sends commands to the nodes, indicating how they should steer the signals, and the node hardware must actively guide the signals as directed. The links between adjacent node stages provide the passive connections that carry the signals from stage to stage. Thus, unlike the data in a computing system, the data in a switching system only flows through the stages in a feed-forward fashion, which tends to ease some of the system-level requirements within the switching system.

1.3 Interconnection and Packaging Problems in Processing Systems

High-performance computing systems and high-throughput telecommunication systems will share many common attributes in the future. For example, both of these processing systems will undoubtedly require very high data rates (50 Mbps to 1 Gbps) to be passed on the signal traces between functional units. (A functional unit can be defined as an integrated circuit chip, a multichip module, a printed circuit board, a card shelf, or an entire electronic frame.) High-performance computer systems will require these data rates as the speeds of processors and cache memories are continually increased. High-throughput telecommunication systems will require these data rates as future communication networks begin to carry high-definition video signals, video-conferencing signals, CAD/CAM and medical imaging information, and high-speed computer data signals in addition to the voice traffic they transport today. [In anticipation of these changes, new transmission line formats such as the Synchronous Digital Hierarchy (SDH) and Synchronous Optical Network (SONET) are already being standardized and developed to carry these higher data rates (Davidson and Muller 1991).] Future computing and telecommunication systems will also attempt to capitalize on the high degrees of integration that will become possible within the different functional units as the gate count within integrated circuit chips continues to increase. Empirical formulas, such as Rent's rule, give an indication of the number of pinouts that may be required as the gate count within an integrated circuit chip increases. According to Rent's rule, the number of pinouts P required for an integrated circuit chip with G logic gates is described by:

$$P = k(G)^{1/c}, \qquad (1)$$

where k is a constant that depends on the amount of sharing (multiplexing) on chip pinouts ($k = 2.5$ for high-performance applications and 0.5 for low-performance applications) and c is another constant whose values are typically between 1.5 and 3.0 ($c = 1.79$ is typical for high-performance systems) (Rymaszewski and Tummala 1989). Typical pinout requirements for high-performance processing systems are plotted as a function of the gate count in integrated circuit chips in Fig. 4. Since the gate count of VLSI circuit chips is rapidly moving from

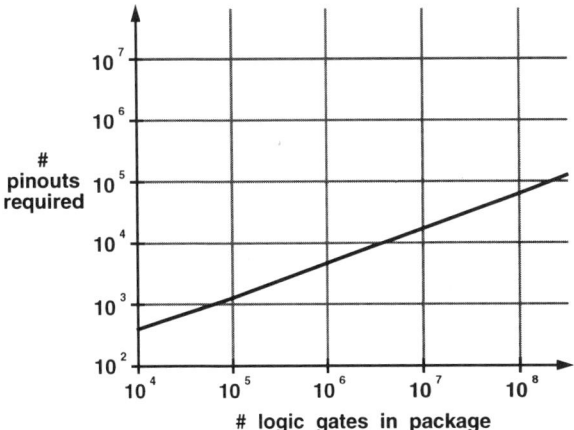

Figure 4. Pinout requirements for device packages in high-performance processing systems ($k = 2.5$, $c = 1.79$).

the tens and hundreds of thousands toward the million mark, it is very likely that future processing systems will also require high degrees of connectivity (many pinouts) between their functional units (Johnson 1990).

The hardware design engineers who are presented with the challenge of designing the high-performance computers and high-throughput telecommunication equipment of the future will undoubtedly find that a large number of the design problems they will encounter fall under the category of "packaging and interconnections." In fact, high-speed digital circuit designers that have been using emitter-coupled logic and GaAs logic have been encountering these packaging and interconnection problems for years, because they have oftentimes used clock frequencies in excess of 100 MHz. As "medium-speed" digital circuit designers begin to use advanced transistor-transistor logic, advanced complementary metal-oxide semiconductor (CMOS) logic, and advanced Bi-CMOS logic in their medium-speed circuit board designs, the clock frequencies in their designs have rapidly climbed toward the 50- and 100-MHz rates. More importantly, the signal transition (rise and fall) times in their designs have rapidly dropped below the 1.0-ns interval, producing signals with a frequency content in excess of 100 MHz. Thus, even medium-speed digital circuit designers are beginning to encounter packaging and interconnection problems.

As a result of these trends, all digital circuit designers are entering a new era in which the interconnections between the active devices can no longer be considered as perfect conductors with zero delay and no effect on the shape of the signal's waveform. Designers of future systems must be aware of the analog nature of their digital designs, planning for the effects of undesired packaging parasitics (capacitance and inductance in package interconnections). These undesired effects include the following:

1. high-power requirements for drivers of capacitive loads and the resulting thermal management problems of removing the generated heat
2. signal distortion due to dispersion (interconnection delay that varies with frequency)
3. signal distortion due to interconnection attenuation that varies with frequency
4. signal distortion due to capacitive crosstalk coupled from signals on neighboring traces
5. signal distortion due to inductive crosstalk coupled from signals on neighboring traces
6. signal distortion due to noise caused by inductive and resistive voltage drops in the bias and ground lines
7. signal distortion due to reflections and ringing when transmission line characteristic impedances are not properly matched

Architectural Considerations for Optical Computing and Photonic Switching

8. signal distortion due to source impedances, load impedances, and characteristic impedances that vary with frequency (causing unavoidable reflections)
9. skew (variations in the delay between different waveforms on different paths) in signal and clock traces that lead to synchronization problems
10. high sensitivity to electromagnetic interference (EMI)
11. the inherent propagation delay within signal traces (which can limit the clock rate in a system with unterminated transmission lines and can limit the processing rate of computer systems if the processor is idled while waiting for data in the processor/memory feed-back loop).

The cumulative problems caused by all of these electronic interconnection effects make it very difficult for digital circuit board designers to decrease their clock cycle times below approximately 10 ns, even though some of the high-speed logic families used on the boards have transistors that can switch in tens of picoseconds (Tsang 1991). Unfortunately, all of these problems will only be exacerbated by the higher number of package pinouts and the higher data rates that will undoubtedly be required in future processing systems.

2. A Model for System-Level Packaging

Since all of the undesired effects listed in Section 1.3 are a direct result of the packaging and interconnection issues within the system design, an understanding of the key topics in device packaging will be essential for future system designers. In general, designers must be concerned with three important attributes related to device packaging: (1) managing the waveform integrity of power, clock, and data signals that flow into and out of the package (predominantly an electromagnetic field theory problem), (2) managing the electrical power dissipation and flow of heat into and out of the package (predominantly an electrical and thermodynamic problem), and (3) managing the thermal and mechanical integrity of the materials that bind the components within the structural package (predominantly a thermodynamic and material science problem). Failure to satisfy the system-level requirements in any of these three packaging areas can result in a catastrophic system failure. For example, if signals arrive at a receiver device with too much noise due to crosstalk or transmission line reflections, then system data will be lost. If the power dissipated in the package exceeds the heat removal rate, then the package will overheat and the semiconductor devices will no longer operate correctly. If temperature variations across the device package cause two connected substrates to expand at different rates, then the connections between the substrates can be severed. All of these problems must be avoided through the use of appropriate packaging and interconnection design techniques.

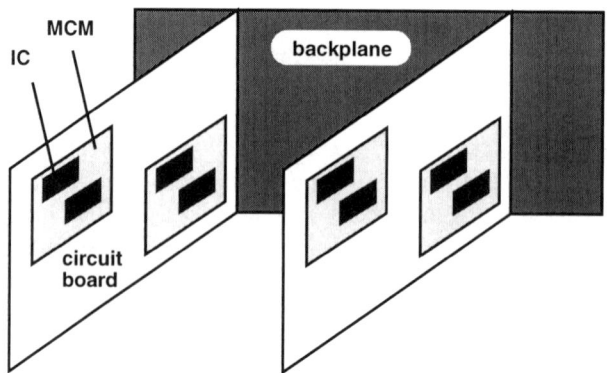

Figure 5. Typical packaging arrangement in high-performance processing systems.

Since any evolutionary solution to the packaging and interconnection design problem must build on the packaging and interconnection techniques that are standard in today's high-performance systems, it is important to gain familiarity with the packaging and interconnection hierarchy that is typically used today. Figure 5 illustrates a typical packaging arrangement for current high-performance systems. Within this arrangement, logic gates within an integrated circuit semiconductor dice (IC) are typically connected to other logic gates on the same IC using metallic traces or polysilicon traces within the substrate. Several ICs are mounted on multichip modules (MCMs), which can be fabricated using ceramic or silicon substrates. The MCMs are positioned on printed circuit boards, and the printed circuit boards are typically held in place by a slotted card cage. Connections between the circuit boards are normally provided through a backplane. All of these connections are confined within the plane of the substrate (IC, MCM, circuit board, or back-plane) through which the data signals are permitted to flow.

The interconnections between different levels within the packaging hierarchy can have far-reaching effects on the architecture of a large-scale system, because the pinout limitations will oftentimes dictate the manner in which a system is partitioned. As a result, it would be beneficial to consider the pinout limitations for each of the interconnection levels within the packaging hierarchy of Fig. 5. Defining limits for a technology is always a difficult task, because ongoing research is always pushing those limits toward new extremes. Nevertheless, if the standard interconnection technologies available in 1990 are used for the basis of comparison, interesting results are obtained.

For interconnections between logic gates within a single IC, the limits are a function of (1) the resolution limits of the lithographic techniques being used to create the traces and (2) the number of interconnection levels being used. Although the number of connections permitted between logic gates on an IC chip can become a problem in a complicated design, the on-chip connection capabilities provided by metallic or polysilicon traces are usually sufficient for most system designs. For interconnections between the semiconductor IC and the MCM, perimeter wire-bonding, tape-automated bonding (TAB), and flip-chip solder bump bonding are the three chip attach methods of choice (Markstein 1991). Wire-bonding techniques are limited to approximately 225 connections per IC, while TAB techniques are limited to about 300 connections per IC. Laboratory prototypes based on flip-chip solder bump bonding have yielded approximately 16,000 connections per chip, but the crosstalk between these closely positioned connections must be carefully controlled and the long-term reliability of these small bonds must also be studied (Koopman, Reiley, and Totta 1989a). For interconnections between the MCM and the printed circuit board, perimeter wire-bonding or TAB is often used to connect to a metallic lead frame, which can be mounted within a pin grid array package and inserted into a socket on the printed circuit board. Since the perimeter of a MCM is larger than the perimeter of a chip, these techniques can yield as many as 400 connections per MCM (Johnson 1990). The interconnections between the printed circuit board and the backplane are typically provided by a pin grid on one edge of the board. This technique can typically provide up to 1000 connections per circuit board.

When one compares the number of connections currently provided within the various hierarchy layers to the number of required connections predicted for future systems by the plot in Fig. 4, it becomes clear that current packaging technologies will not be adequate for the high-performance computing systems and high-throughput telecommunication systems of the future. Even with the moderate increases in pinout capabilities that will be provided by ongoing research, the pinout limitations of current packaging technologies will still probably be inadequate for future processing systems. In addition, the bandwidth limitations on current packaging technologies may also make them undesirable for future processing systems.

Researchers are actively working to solve these interconnection and packaging problems on many different fronts, and it is very likely that future designs will incorporate and combine results from many of these different research efforts to produce cost-effective systems that satisfy the demanding design requirements. These research efforts include work on advanced electronic packaging technologies, such as flip-chip solder bump bonding, wafer-scale integration, and 3-D device packaging (Koopman, Reiley, and Totta 1989b; Stopper 1990; Schroen 1990). Other work is being carried out in guided-wave photonic technologies, such as time-division multiplexing, wavelength-division multiplexing, directional coupler routing, and parallel connectivity on fibers and waveguides (Hinton 1990; Hartman et al. 1989; Prucnal, Santoro, and Sehgal 1986; Glance *et al.* 1988; Kogelnik and Schmidt 1976; Novotny *et al.* 1991). Another area of active research is centered around the technology of interest within this book. In its most fundamental form, free-space digital optics is merely another interconnection and packaging technology that may offer powerful solutions to many of the problems within high-performance processing systems. It will be shown that free-space digital optics can be used to provide interconnections at most of the levels within the packaging hierarchy (gate to gate, IC to IC, MCM to MCM, and board to board). As a result, free-space digital optics promises to augment and enhance the capabilities of many digital electronic systems. High-performance processing systems of the future will still make ample use of interconnections based on metallic traces, but the availability of free-space digital optics will give circuit designers an alternative choice when selecting an appropriate packaging and interconnection scheme. This alternative scheme can be useful in many system applications that have two fundamental requirements: (1) a large number of interconnections between system components and (2) very high bandwidths within those interconnections.

3. Fundamentals of Free-Space Digital Optics

Free-space digital optics is an emerging interconnection and packaging technology that promises to help high-speed electronic circuit designers overcome many of the potential problems that plague electronic systems. Instead of relying on metallic traces to guide the signals between active logic devices, a system based on free-space digital optics uses beams of light propagating orthogonal to the plane of the device substrates to carry the information signals between the active logic devices (Fig. 6). These information signal beams can be routed between the device substrates using many different types of optical components (such as refractive lenses, mirrors, beamsplitters, holographic interconnection elements, diffractive lenses, microlenses, microfabricated reflective prism arrays, etc.). As a

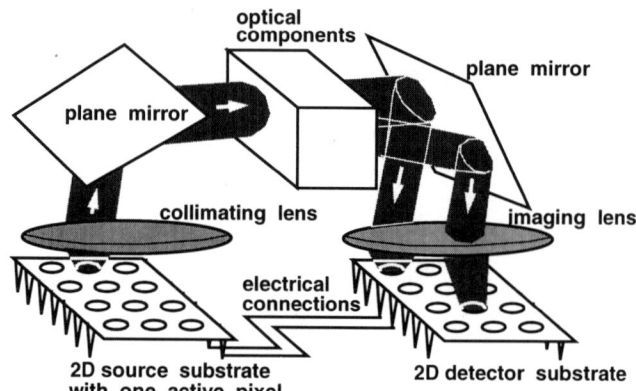

Figure 6. Packaging and interconnections based on free-space digital optics.

result, the signal beams are not confined within a waveguide material, but are instead propagated through "free space" (vacuum, air, and glass).

The binary signals in a free-space digital optical system can be encoded using any one of several encoding techniques. A common technique encodes the binary information within the irradiance of the propagating light beams. Thus, a logical "1" can be represented by a bright, high-power beam, and a logical "0" can be represented by a dim, low-power beam. Lasers or optical modulators in the source device substrate must be able to create these optical signals based on inputs from the electronics within the source device substrate, and receivers in the receiving device substrate must be able to detect these optical signals and convert them into electrical outputs that can drive the electronics in the receiving device substrate. As a result, large-scale systems can be created in which optical signals are used to provide connectivity between "islands" of electronics (Midwinter 1988a, 1988b; Midwinter and Taylor 1990). The ideal complexity level for the electronics located on these islands is still being researched, but proposals range from very little electronics ("all-optical" systems based on optical logic devices) to high degrees of electronics (electronic systems that use optical interconnections sparingly) (Krishnamoorthy et al. 1992; Kiamilev et al. 1991; Cloonan et al. 1993).

Regardless of the electronic complexity level, the use of free-space digital optics for device connectivity may offer several benefits over other approaches based on metallic traces, because it eliminates the undesired electrical parasitics (capacitance and inductance) that burden metallic-based systems. It can also take advantage of the two-dimensional imaging capabilities of optics. The potential benefits of a system based on free-space digital optics include the following:

1. higher interconnection densities (also known as parallelism)
2. higher packing densities of gates on integrated circuit chips
3. lower power dissipation and easier thermal management of systems that require high data rates and high interconnection densities
4. less signal dispersion than comparable electronic schemes
5. easier (less expensive) impedance matching of transmission lines using antireflection coatings
6. less signal distortion
7. higher interconnection bandwidths
8. less signal crosstalk
9. grater immunity to EMI
10. lower signal and clock skew
11. the opportunity to explore new, more efficient architectures that can capitalize on the flexibility offered by the higher interconnection densities.

A more detailed description of each of these potential benefits will be given as the topics are addressed throughout the remainder of this chapter.

In general, any system based on free-space digital optics is comprised of two types of functional components: (1) planar, two-dimensional device arrays that can detect, process, and create the optical signal beams, and (2) three-dimensional interconnection hardware that can appropriately route the optical signal beams from one planar device array to another (Fig. 6).

3.1 Planar Device Arrays

Many different types of planar device arrays are being developed and researched for use within systems based on free-space digital optics. These device technologies include nonlinear Fabry-Pérot devices (Smith 1986; Jewell, Rushford, and Gibbs 1984), VSTEP devices (Hara *et al.* 1989), DOES devices (Taylor *et al.* 1989), S-SEED devices (Lentine *et al.* 1989), microlaser devices (Jewell *et al.* 1990), and ferroelectric liquid-crystal devices (McKnight, Vass, and Sillitto 1989). Several of these device types are discussed in detail in subsequent chapters. However, before these devices are discussed, it would be beneficial to create a general framework into which these different devices can be categorized.

3.1.1 Device Array Types

At a minimum, each device within a planar device array must provide the capabilities of the three basic functional blocks shown in Fig. 7. These functional

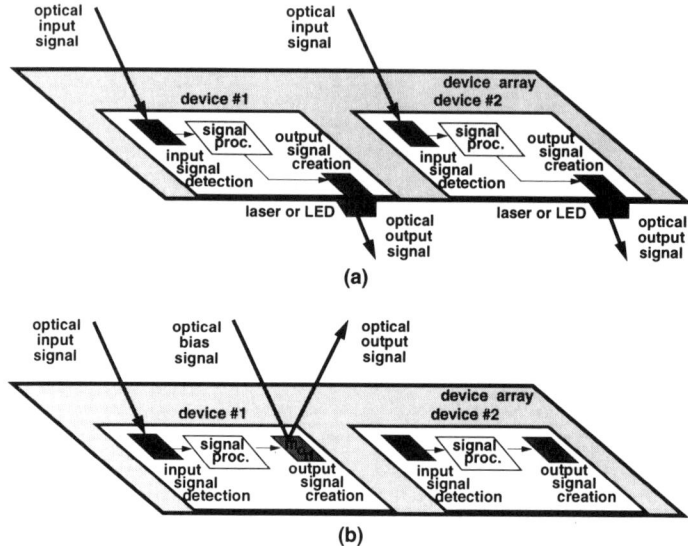

Figure 7. Functionality within 2-D device arrays: (a) two-sided array with active sources and (b) one-sided array with modulators.

blocks include the input signal detection block, the signal processing block, and the output signal creation block. Usually, input signal detection implies the use of an optical-to-electronic converter (such as a photodiode), an amplifier, and a thresholding decision circuit to determine the binary value of the incoming signal. Clock extraction may also be required to provide a clock for any synchronizing latches in the signal processing block. The signal processing block may contain many different forms of digital logic to implement the required computing or switching functions. The output signal creation block can be implemented as an active source, such as a laser or light-emitting diode (LED) in Fig. 7(a), or it can be implemented as a passive modulator that can absorb or transmit the optical bias beam that must be generated in an external light source [Fig. 7(b)]. In either case, the digital signal created by the output signal creation block is a modified version of the input signal whose power level has been regenerated, whose timing has been resynchronized, and whose optical signal quality has been restored.

The various functional blocks described in the previous paragraph can be physically combined in many different ways. At one extreme, all three functional blocks are implemented within the same physical structure, making it virtually impossible to separate the operation of the three functions. This type of device is often called an *optical logic device,* because optical inputs and optical outputs seem to merge toward and emanate from the same spatial locations. The functionality within the signal processing block of an optical logic device is usually limited to a simple Boolean function such as a NAND gate or a NOR gate. At the other extreme, all three functional blocks are spatially separated on the device array, and the separate logic within the signal processing block (which can be implemented in Si or GaAs) will usually permit more complicated functions to be provided than is possible with a single optical logic device. As a result, this more functional device is often called a *smart pixel* (Hinton 1988).

All planar device arrays can also be categorized according to the manner in which the optical signal beams can be routed into and out of the device substrate. Two-sided device arrays [Fig. 7(a)] permit beams to be routed into and out of both sides of the device array, while one-sided device arrays [Fig. 7(b)] only permit signals to be routed into and out of one side of the device array. Two-sided arrays may simplify the optics required to route signals between device arrays by giving the designer more degrees of freedom, but they also may result in a more complicated packaging problem when attempting to remove the dissipated heat from the device array.

Whether a device array is implementing a computing function or a switching function, there is typically some form of control signal that tells the signal processing block how to process the data. This control signal can be derived from an optical source (on another device array) or from an electronic trace routed onto the optical device array. If the latter approach is used, the optical device array is actually a hybrid array, containing both electronic and optical pinouts.

The simplest type of hybrid array is a spatial light modulator (SLM), which passes the optical input signal if the electronic control signal is enabled, and absorbs the optical input signal if the electronic control signal is disabled. Oftentimes, a SLM will also provide a means of latching the electronic control signal within the hybrid array. A simple telecommunication switching application of a SLM is shown in Fig. 8, where an $N = 4$ input, $N = 4$ output crossbar switch is implemented. The two-sided SLM for this particular application must have N^2 pixels (windows) arranged in an $N \times N$ array, and each pixel must be individually controllable so that it can be made transparent or opaque. By horizontally fanning out each input across a row of the SLM and by vertically fanning in the outputs from the SLM columns to create the output signals, the connections for a crossbar switch are obtained (Goodman, Dias, and Woody 1978; Dias et al. 1988; Sawchuk et al. 1987). A transmitting pixel in row I, column J, will provide a connection from input I to output J. The hardware shown in Fig. 8 can also be used for computing applications. In particular, the hardware can implement an analog vector-matrix multiplier if the transmittances of the SLM pixels can be set to gray-scale levels by the electronic control signals. The gray-scale transmittance levels should correspond to the analog values of the matrix elements, and the analog irradiance levels of the input signals should correspond to the analog values of the input vector elements. The resulting analog irradiance levels at the system output will represent the analog values of the output vector, which is the vector-matrix product of the input vector with the SLM matrix. Whether implementing a crossbar switch or a vector-matrix multiplier, the fan-out and fan-in operations in Fig. 8 can be implemented quite effectively using free-space optics, because simple imaging systems based on cylindrical lenses can be used to provide the required beam-steering operations.

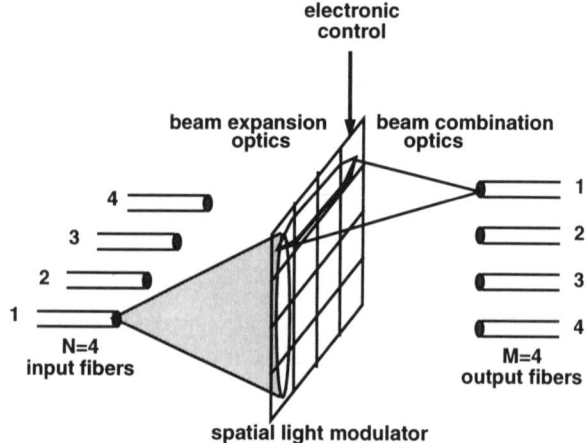

Figure 8. SLM-based crossbar switching network and vector-matrix multiplier.

3.1.2 Device Design Considerations

When selecting an appropriate device technology for a particular system application, the device operating characteristics must be analyzed very carefully. For example, the system designer must always be concerned with the maximum switching speed of the device. In a hybrid device array containing both electrical and optical pinouts, the electrical switching speed and the optical switching speed must both be determined. The designer must also determine the amount of optical power required to switch the device at the desired speed. Most device models have a photodetector in the input signal detection block with a specified responsivity S [Fig. 9(a)]. The responsivity describes the amount of photocurrent I that is generated as a function of the optical input power P. Typically, this photocurrent will charge up the capacitance C of the device to a switching voltage δV. The amount of time δT required to switch the device is given by:

$$\delta T = C\delta V/I = C\delta V/(SP). \qquad (2)$$

From this equation, the required optical power P for a given switching speed can typically be calculated. The total optical power required to drive X devices within a single device array is therefore given by XP, and the designer must guarantee that sufficient power can be supplied by the optical source and that sufficient cooling can be provided to remove this dissipated heat from the device array.

Another important device characteristic that must be known is the maximum optical power rating for the optical device. For example, many optical modulators

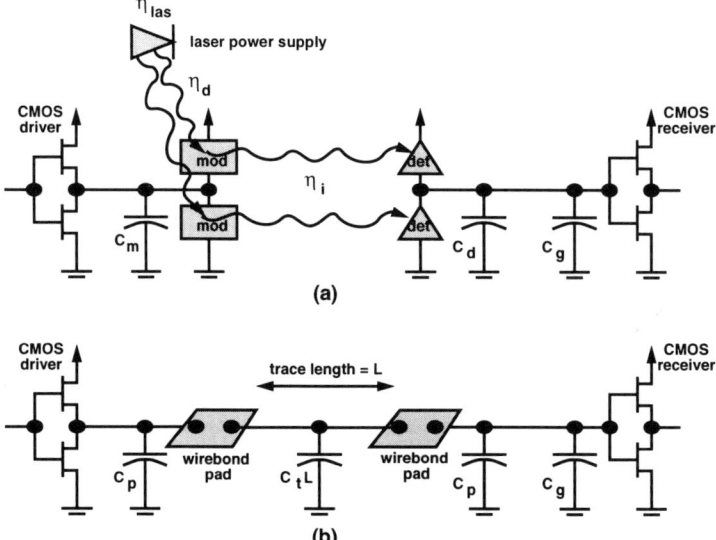

Figure 9. Circuit models: (a) IC-to-IC interconnections with free-space digital optics and (b) IC-to-IC connections with metallic traces.

will saturate when they attempt to modulate an optical beam with a very high irradiance, so in many system designs, the maximum switching speed will be limited by this maximum power rating. System designers must also be concerned about the fan-out and fan-in limitations of the devices within a system. Fan-out (the number of distinct device inputs that the output from a single device can drive) is typically limited by the required switching speed and the related minimum power requirements in the receiving device array. A large fan-out requires the optical signal to be subdivided and the amount of optical power P arriving at each receiving device is decreased, so from Eq. (2), the switching time δT is increased and the maximum switching speed is decreased.

Fan-in (the number of distinct device outputs that can drive a single device input) is typically limited by the effective signal-to-noise ratio at the input of the receiving device, which in turn is limited by the contrast ratio at the output of the source device and variations in signal intensities. For example, if a modulator device has an output contrast ratio of 5:1, then a logical 1 output from the device might be given by $0.5P_{in} \pm \epsilon$ and a logical 0 output from the device would be given by $0.1P_{in} \pm \epsilon$ (where P_{in} is the nominal input power probing the state of the modulator). If the receiving device in the next stage is trying to perform an F-input OR gate function, it should be clear that the presence or absence of a single 1 input is more difficult to detect as the fan-in F is increased, because the noise created by the other $(F - 1)$ 0 inputs will also increase (Stirk and Psaltis 1991). Noise created by other sources (such as laser power supply fluctuations) must also be considered when a potential device is being evaluated.

In addition to these specific device-related issues, the many interdependencies between the device array and the other hardware components must also be considered within a complete system design. For example, the operating wavelength of a device will affect the design of the system imaging optics as well as the selection of an optical power supply (laser or LED). Device tolerances to wavelength fluctuations will often determine whether the wavelength stability of a particular optical power supply is sufficient for the system application. In addition, the power supply must also satisfy the system power requirements and must offer sufficient operating lifetimes to be useful with the device arrays. Once component lifetimes are known, overall system reliability, availability, and maintainability can be analyzed, and redundant hardware can be added to the architecture to increase the fault tolerance and satisfy the system requirements. Another set of interdependencies between the device array and the system hardware is found in the resolution and field of view (FOV) on the system imaging optics. The resolution requirements of an imaging system are typically determined by the size of the device windows into which the light beams must be directed. Smaller device windows are desirable, because they have lower capacitances, and according to Eq. (2), they can be switched at higher rates. However, smaller device windows also require optics with higher resolutions, which will usually lead to much higher system costs. In addition, smaller device windows will also decrease the margin of error that is permitted when the light beams are directed into the windows during system alignment. Unfortunately, this will decrease the manufacturing tolerances on the optics and the optomechanical mounts, and it will also make the optics and optomechanical mounts more sensitive to temperature variations and thermal expansion.

If the number of devices within the device array is increased or if the substrate area used by a single device within the device array is increased (which might be done to accommodate additional complexity and functionality within the signal processing block or to lower the power density on the substrate), then the area of the entire device array will be increased, and the imaging optics (lenses, polarizing beamsplitters, waveplates, etc.) will have to operate over a larger FOV and a larger field angle. Increasing the requirements on the FOV will usually increase the cost of the imaging optics, and there are often technological limits beyond which the FOV can no longer be increased without major changes to the system design. Optical problems associated with high resolutions and large FOVs will be discussed in more detail in the section on interconnections, Section 3.2.

3.1.3 Architectural Advantages Offered by Optical Device Arrays

The use of planar device arrays and free-space digital optics can offer several system-level benefits over device packaging technologies that use metallic traces to guide signals into and out of the device substrate. For example, a single metallic bonding pad for wirebond attachment is typically a square whose side lengths can exceed 100 μm. Optical logic devices (such as S-SEEDs) can be fabricated on center-to-center spacings as small as 20 μm with device windows on the order of 5 μm in diameter (Lentine *et al.* 1989), so in the area of a single electrical pinout, an array of optical logic devices can have as many as 25 optical pinouts. As the optical FOV continues to increase on optical components, typical device arrays in future applications might have dimensions of the order of 1 to 10 mm, so with optical pinouts spaced on 20-μm centers, these device arrays should be able to support 2500 to 250,000 pinouts. [Prototype systems can already image over 1.28 mm × 1.28 mm fields of view with 3-μm resolution, so these systems can currently support 4096 optical pinouts spaced on 20-μm centers (McCormick *et al.* 1991).] This high interconnection density is often described as the parallelism of free-space digital optics, and it may help solve many of the problems caused by package pinout limitations in future systems. In addition to this increased interconnection density, arrays of optical logic devices can also offer higher packing densities for the logic gates, because the metallic traces running to bonding pads at the perimeter of the electronic device substrate are not needed in the optical device substrate, so more of the substrate area is available for active logic devices.

The use of optical device arrays and free-space digital optics in place of electronic device substrates and metallic traces can also lead to a substantial decrease in the overall system power dissipation and can ease the thermal management problems within the device substrate. In a system based on metallic traces, the amount of power dissipated as a logical signal is transmitted from one IC to another is usually a primary source of heat within the IC. In fact, in low-power logic families (such as CMOSs) the output drivers that must charge up the capacitances of the traces between two ICs are often the largest contributors to the overall IC power consumption (Bakoglu 1990).

An analysis of the power consumption for IC-to-IC interconnections based on metallic traces and the power consumption for IC-to-IC interconnections based on free-space digital optics may help illustrate this fact. Consider the amount of power required to transmit a digital signal from the output of a CMOS driver circuit on one IC to the input of a CMOS receiver circuit on another IC. Figure 9(a) shows a lumped-parameter circuit model for the interconnection based on free-space digital optics. This interconnection requires the CMOS driver circuitry, the laser power supply, the free-space power supply delivery system, the modulator, the free-space interconnection channel, the photodetector, and the CMOS receiver circuitry. For this interconnection, it can be shown (Feldman et al. 1988; Goodman 1989; Miller 1989; Lentine et al. 1989) that the average amount of optical power dissipated within a single device containing one differential detector and one differential modulator (assuming the worst-case situation of a 1010 NRZ bit stream) is given by:

$$P_{d+m} = V_{th}(C_d + C_g)/(0.25\delta TS) + (1/\eta_i)V_{th}(C_d + C_g)/(0.25\delta TS) \\ + V_m{}^2 C_m/[(2)(0.25\delta T)]. \quad (3)$$

This equation assumes the use of differential optical signals, a differential modulator with infinite contrast ratio, each modulator containing a pair of components with a switching voltage of V_m and each with capacitance $0.5C_m$, a pair of photodetectors each with capacitance $0.5C_d$ and responsivity S, a pair of FETs each with gate capacitance $0.5C_g$ and threshold voltage V_{th}, an optical interconnection with efficiency η_i, a bit period of δT, and switching required to be completed within 25% of the bit period. The first term in the equation describes the optical power dissipated in the receiving device's photodetector (which is receiving a differential signal), the second term describes the optical power dissipated in the source device's output modulator (which is absorbing the power supply beam to create a dim output beam), and the third term describes the electrical power required for the CMOS output FETs to drive the capacitance of the modulator circuit. The total amount of electrical power that must be supplied for this single differential, optical interconnection (including the power driving the CMOS output FET and the power driving the laser power supply) is given by:

$$P_{eo} = [2/(\eta_{las}\eta_d\eta_i)]V_{th}(C_d + C_g)/(0.25\delta TS) + V_m{}^2 C_m/[(2)(0.25\delta T)], \quad (4)$$

where η_{las} is the electrical-to-optical conversion efficiency of the laser power supply, and η_d is the efficiency of the optical power supply's delivery system. Here, the first term describes the electrical power drawn by the laser, and the second term describes the electrical power drawn by the CMOS output driver. Through the analysis of system prototypes, typical values for these parameters have been derived as follows: $C_d = C_m = 40$ fF; $S = 0.5$ A/W; $C_g = 20$ fF, which includes the routing traces to the gate; $V_{th} = V_m = 1$ V, $\eta_i = 0.2$, which accounts for 1% Fresnel reflections from about 30 optical interfaces and the 80% efficiency of a 1 × 3 holographic element; $\eta_{las} = 0.25$; and $\eta_d = 0.48$, which accounts for 1% Fresnel reflections from about 30 optical interfaces and the 65% efficiency of a spot array generating hologram. Assuming a bit rate of 100 Mbps ($\delta T = 10$ ns), the amount of heat-generating power dissipated in a single device on the chip [Eq. (3)] is 296 µW, and the total amount of electrical power that must be supplied to the connection [Eq. (4)] is ≈4 mW.

Figure 9(b) shows a lumped-parameter circuit model for the same interconnection based on metallic traces. This interconnection requires the CMOS driver circuitry, the unterminated interconnection trace and wirebond pads, and the CMOS receiver circuitry. For this interconnection, it can be shown (Feldman *et al.* 1988; Goodman 1989; Miller 1989; Lentine *et al.* 1989) that the average amount of optical power dissipated within the drain-to-source resistances of the driver field effect transistors (FETs) (assuming the worst-case situation of a 1010 NRZ bit stream) is given by:

$$P_e = V_{th}^2(C_t L + 2C_p + C_g)/[(2)(0.25\delta T)]. \quad (5)$$

This equation assumes the use of a single-ended electrical signal, a pair of receiver FETs each with gate capacitance $0.5 C_g$ and threshold voltage V_{th}, an interconnection trace with length L and with a capacitance per unit length defined by C_t, a pair of wirebond pads each with capacitance C_p, a bit period of δT, and switching required to be completed within 25% of the bit period. The average power defined within Eq. (5) is also the amount of electrical power that must be supplied to the system by the power supply to drive this single electrical interconnection.

Typical values for the parameters in Eq. (5) have been derived assuming the connections are routed through a MCM (Goodman 1989; Nordin 1992): $C_t = 100$ fF/mm; $C_p = 150$ fF, assuming a 100-µm bonding pad; $C_g = 20$ fF; and $V_{th} = 1$ V. Assuming a bit rate of 100 Mbps ($\delta T = 10$ ns), the amount of heat-generating power dissipated in the FETs of a single driver circuit is a function of the interconnection trace length L, and it is plotted in Fig. 10 along with the values of P_{d+m} and P_{eo} from the earlier optical analysis. The plot of P_e levels off at 20 mW for trace lengths greater than 60 mm, because it is assumed that for 100-Mbps data rates, the interconnection must be treated as a transmission line for these lengths. A terminating resistor ($R_{term} = 50$ Ω) can be added to the end of the line to prevent undesired reflections. As a result, the worst-case power dissipation (for a continuous NRZ bit stream of logical 1's) is given by $P_{e-terminated} = V_{th}^2/R_{term}$.

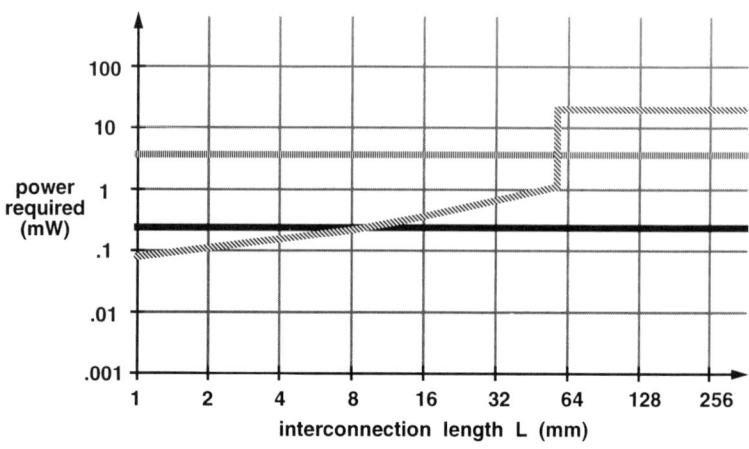

- = on-chip power dissipation for 1 optical interconnection
- = total power dissipation (on-chip + laser) for 1 optical interconnection
- = on-chip (or total) power dissipation for 1 electrical interconnection

Figure 10. Power requirements for 100-Mbps IC-to-IC interconnections based on optical modulators and metallic traces.

Assuming that the on-chip power dissipation is to be minimized, the figure indicates that the break-even interconnection trace length beyond which one would derive benefits from the use of optical interconnections occurs at $L \approx 10$ mm. Assuming that total supply power is to be minimized, the figure indicates that the break-even interconnection trace length beyond which one would derive benefits from the use of optical interconnections occurs at $L \approx 60$ mm, where terminating resistors must be added to the metallic traces. (These break-even points are slightly longer than those in many references, because different technology parameters were used and the power absorbed by the device's modulator was also included.) Thus, based on current technology parameters, free-space digital optics for IC-to-IC or MCM-to-MCM connections will probably be useful if on-chip heat management is a problem, because these interconnections typically have lengths greater than 10 mm but less than 60 mm. However, the system designer will have to pay a price for the additional power consumption within the inefficient laser power supply. On the other hand, free-space digital optics for board-to-board connections will probably be useful for both heat management problems and overall power utilization problems. (The preceding analysis compares the power required by an electronic interconnection to the power required by an optical interconnection based on modulators. A similar analysis can be performed for an optical interconnection based on laser sources within the device array, and the results based on current technology parameters would be similar, but slightly worse than the results obtained for the modulator implementation.)

3.2 Three-Dimensional Optical Interconnections

Within a system based on free-space digital optics, each of the information-bearing beams of light that emanates from a spot within an output window of the source planar device array must be routed to form a spot within an appropriate input window of the receiving planar device array. As a result, the system designs often tend to look like a pipeline of optoelectronic device arrays interconnected by beams of light. The optical hardware required to route the beams of light between consecutive device arrays must perform two basic functions: image relaying and beam steering.

The function of image relaying requires the optical hardware to gather the light emanating from a single spot in the source device array and redirect that light to form a single spot of appropriate size within the receiving device array. In an image relaying system, spots emanating from two different spatial locations in the source device array should be routed to two different spatial locations in the receiving device array.

The function of beam steering requires the optical hardware to permute the locations of the spots in the receiving device array so that their ordering is different from the spot ordering that existed in the source device array. This permutation of the spot ordering must provide the desired interconnection topology for the particular system architecture being implemented. Many different interconnection topologies have been implemented using free-space digital optics, including the perfect shuffle (Lohmann 1986; Lohmann, Stork, and Stucke 1985; Eichmann and Li 1987; Brenner and Huang 1988; Stirk, Athale, and Haney 1988; Song and Yu 1988; Stucke 1988), the crossover (Jahns and Murdocca 1988), and the banyan (Cloonan and Herron 1989).

Figure 11 illustrates these different topologies along with some optical implementations that might be used to provide the required beam-steering operations. Some of these implementations use bulk optical components (such as the beamsplitter and tilted mirrors used for the shuffle), some use micromachined components (such as the prismatic mirror arrays used for the crossover), and some use holographic elements (such as those used for the banyan), but all of them can be classified as free-space digital optical implementations.

A group of node stages connected by a set of links is typically called an *interconnection network*. Each of the interconnection networks in Fig. 11 is a two-dimensional network, because the device array pixels (or nodes, which are represented by boxes) and the optical links connecting adjacent node stages (which are represented by lines) all lie within a plane. The interconnection topologies within these networks can always be described by a set of mathematical mapping functions that defines the connectivity between nodes in adjacent node stages. For example, in the shuffle network of Fig. 11(a), there are $M = 8$ nodes in each node stage, and each node has two output links and two input links. As a result, two

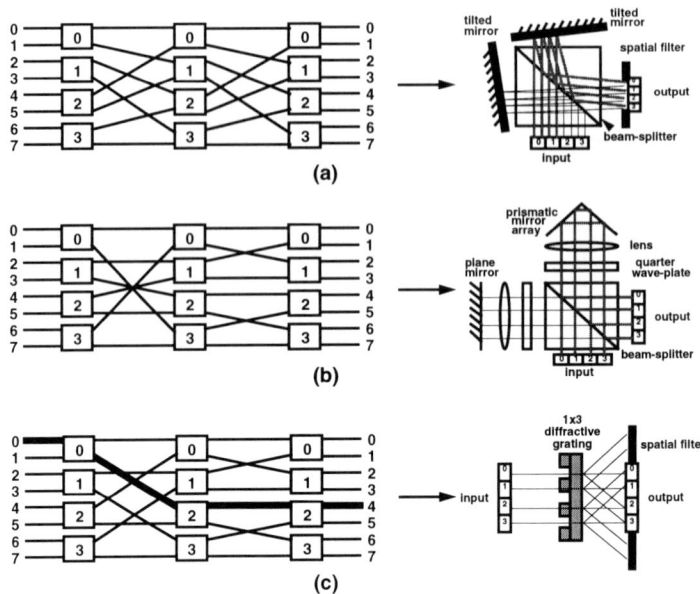

Figure 11. Interconnection topologies and their optical implementations: (a) shuffle, (b) crossover, and (c) banyan.

mapping functions (α_1 and α_2) can be used to describe the node connectivity provided by the links within the shuffle network. The first output link from node P in node stage i provides a connection to node $\alpha_1[P] = [(2P)_{\text{mod } (M-1)}]$ in stage $i + 1$, and the second output link from node P in node stage i provides a connection to node $\alpha_2[P] = [(2P + 1)_{\text{mod } (M-1)}]$ in stage $i + 1$. (Note that $X_{\text{mod } Y}$ is the integer remainder of the quotient X/Y.) Mapping functions for the other networks are described by Cloonan and Herron (1989) and Jahns and Murdocca (1988).

If a 2-D interconnection topology (such as any of those in Fig. 11) is chosen for an application that requires the use of free-space digital optics, the 2-D topology must usually be modified via a two- to three-dimensional mapping function to create a topologically equivalent 3-D interconnection topology. For example, the 2-D crossover topology of Fig. 12(a) can be converted into the 3-D crossover topology of Fig. 12(b) by folding the network about the fold line. Mathematically, the mapping of the pixels from the 2-D domain into the 3-D domain can be described by the transformation (Cloonan and McCormick 1991):

$$\beta_{\text{2-D}\to\text{3-D}} [P] \to [R,C] = \begin{cases} [\text{int}(P/J), P_{\text{mod } J}] & \text{if int}(P/J) \text{ is even} \\ [\text{int}(P/J), J - 1 - P_{\text{mod } J}] & \text{if int}(P/J) \text{ is odd,} \end{cases} \quad (6)$$

where P is the physical address of the pixel in the 2-D domain, $[R,C]$ is the row number and column number, respectively, of the same pixel in the 3-D domain, J is the number of columns in the resulting planar device array, int(P/J) is the

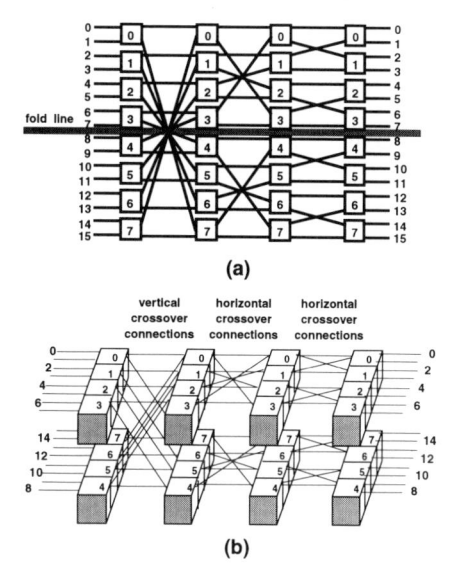

Architectural Considerations for Optical Computing and Photonic Switching 23

Figure 12. 2-D to 3-D conversions of network topologies: (a) 2-D crossover and (b) 3-D crossover.

integer part of the quotient P/J. The resulting 3-D interconnection topology is better suited for free-space digital optics, because it can capitalize on all of the pixels within a planar device array and it can also capitalize on the 2-D imaging capabilities of spherical lenses. However, the hardware implementations shown in Fig. 11 may also require some minor modifications to accommodate the 3-D interconnections. In particular, the orientation of some of the interconnection hardware must be adjusted depending on whether vertical connections or horizontal connections are being implemented in a given stage (Cloonan and McCormick 1991).

3.2.1 Image Relaying, Spot Formation, and Beam Combination

Most of the interconnection topologies that can be implemented using free-space digital optics require an image relaying function to be provided using either refractive or diffractive lenses. Thus, a fundamental formula for interconnection hardware design is the well-known lens formula, which states that $1/s_o + 1/s_i = 1/f$, where s_o is the conjugate distance from the source (object) plane to the lens' primary principal plane, s_i is the conjugate distance from the lens' secondary principal plane to the image plane, and f is the lens' focal length. Another useful formula is the lateral magnification formula, which states that $M_T = y_i/y_o = -s_i/s_o$, where y_o is the distance from a spot in the object plane to the optical axis and y_i is the distance from the image of the spot to the optical axis. These formulas are useful for many different types of imaging system implementations. Some of

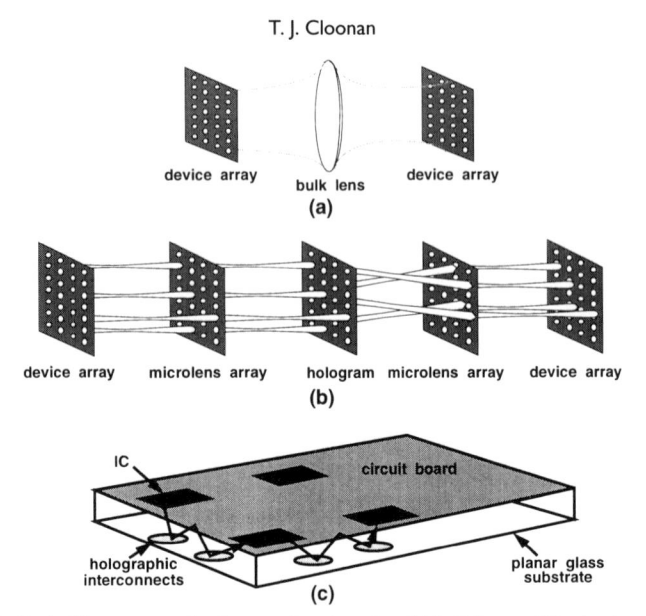

Figure 13. Optical interconnect implementations based on (a) bulk lenses, (b) microlens arrays, and (c) planar optics.

the different implementations currently being studied (Fig. 13) include systems based on bulk lenses, both refractive and diffractive (McCormick et al. 1991); systems based on microlens arrays, both refractive and diffractive (Iga et al. 1982); and planar optic systems that route the beams through a planar glass substrate with micro-optic elements etched on both sides of the glass (Jahns and Huang 1989; Jahns and Däschner 1991). [Note that the preceding formulas may not be valid in all microlens systems if the beam divergence angles are relatively small. In these cases, formulas describing Gaussian beam propagation should be used (O'Shea 1985).]

A common image relaying system that is often used to transfer a set of spots from a source device array to a similar image of spots in a receiving device array is illustrated in Fig. 14. Typically, this two-lens imaging system would transport many signal beams between the two device arrays, but to simplify the figure, only two devices in the source device array are shown to be actively creating output beams. In the image relaying system of Fig. 14, the distance between the source device array and the first lens is set equal to the focal length (f_1) of the first lens, the distance between the second lens and the receiving device array is set equal to the focal length (f_2) of the second lens, and the distance between the two lenses is set equal to the sum of the two focal lengths ($f_1 + f_2$). This arrangement is commonly referred to as an *infinite conjugate, telecentric image relay system* (or a $4f$ imaging system) because the first lens takes the light from the source device array at its front focal plane and produces an image at infinity, and the second lens takes

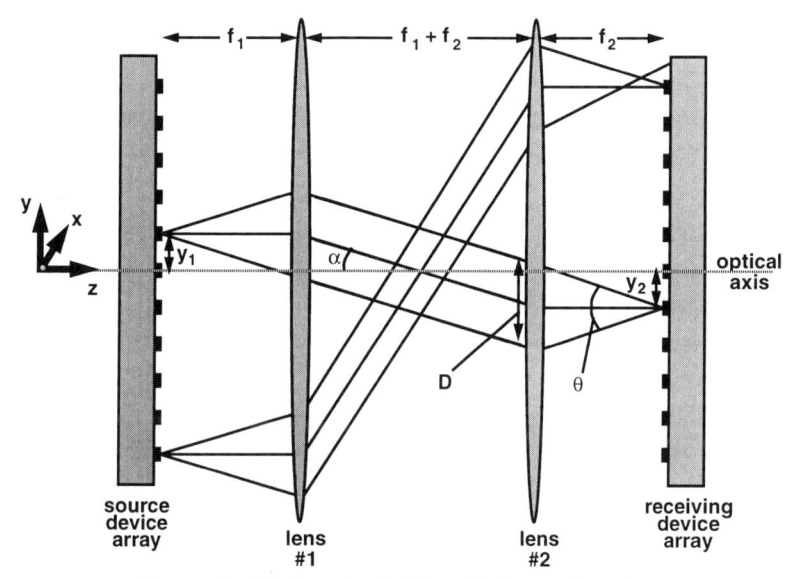

Architectural Considerations for Optical Computing and Photonic Switching 25

Figure 14. Infinite conjugate, telecentric image relay system.

that image (which would theoretically form at infinity) and produces an image at its rear focal plane. The beams emanating from spots in the source device array are diverging beams, those focusing to spots at the receiving device array are converging beams, and the beams between the lenses (which are neither diverging nor converging) are said to be collimated.

Assuming the system in Fig. 14 uses lenses with $\sin(\theta)$ distortion [instead of the more standard lenses with $\tan(\theta)$ distortion], the spot on the source device array that is a distance y_1 from the optical axis will pass through the first lens and create a collimated beam that propagates at an angle to the optical axis given by $\alpha = \sin^{-1}(y_1/f_1)$. This collimated beam will pass through the second lens and create a spot on the receiving device array that is a distance $y_2 = f_2 \sin(\alpha) = y_1(f_2/f_1)$ from the optical axis. Thus, each lens performs a spatial (spot) to angular (beam) transformation, and the overall magnification of this lens combination is given by:

$$M_T = -f_2/f_1. \tag{7}$$

Infinite conjugate, telecentric imaging systems offer several benefits within systems based on free-space digital optics, because (1) the collimated beams between the lenses will not be degraded by spherical aberration effects when optical components such as beamsplitters are placed in their path, and (2) the spot centers in the receiving device array will not be laterally displaced even if the device array is incorrectly positioned along the z axis (Prise, Streibl, and Downs 1988).

According to diffraction theory, the spots that are formed in the receiving device array by the imaging system in Fig. 14 can never have a beam waist diameter smaller than:

$$d_0 = 4\lambda/(\pi\theta) = 2\lambda/[\pi \tan^{-1}(D/2f_2)] \approx 1.27\lambda f_2/D. \tag{8}$$

This formula assumes that the light is propagating as an unclipped Gaussian beam, λ is the wavelength of the light, θ is the full convergence angle of the beam as it approaches the receiving device array plane, and D is the $1/e^2$ diameter of the beam at the second lens. Note that the approximation in Eq. (8) is only valid for small values of θ. The Gaussian beam irradiance profile $I(r)$ is symmetric about the beam axis, and it varies radially outward from the axis as a function of radius r according to the formula:

$$I(r) = I_0 \exp(-2r^2/r_0^2), \tag{9}$$

where I_0 is the irradiance at the beam axis and r_0 is the beam radius. The beam diameters d_0 and D and beam radius r_0 are defined by the points where the beam irradiance is $1/e^2$ of the value at the beam axis (O'Shea 1985).

The depth of focus (DOF) for a spot in the plane of the receiving device array can be defined somewhat arbitrarily to be twice the Rayleigh range. This is the range along the z axis near the minimum spot size over which the beam diameter remains less than $\sqrt{2}d_0$, and it is given by (O'Shea 1985):

$$\text{DOF} = \pi d_0^2/(2\lambda). \tag{10}$$

The minimum beam diameter d_0 defined by Eq. (8) is known as the *diffraction-limited spot size*. A well-designed, well-corrected imaging system (which will typically require fairly complicated multi-element or aspheric lenses that are typically very expensive) can create spots that approach this diffraction-limited spot size. Also, if the actual spots are within some small, user-defined range about the diffraction-limited spot size, the imaging system is often said to be *diffraction-limited*.

Unfortunately, most imaging systems suffer from aberrations that yield spot sizes larger than those predicted by diffraction theory and Eq. (8). Imaging systems can suffer from many different types of aberrations. Aberrations that deteriorate and blur the image by making the spot sizes larger include spherical aberration, coma, and astigmatism. Aberrations that deform the image by actually moving the spot centers to undesirable locations in the receiving device array include field curvature and distortion. Although a detailed discussion of aberration theory is beyond the scope of this text, a basic understanding of aberrations can be found by examining the three rays of light that are shown emanating from the bottom input device in Fig. 14. These three rays represent the beam axis and the two $1/e^2$ irradiance points at the edges of the Gaussian beam. Since all of these rays are emitted from a single point in the source device array, a perfect imaging system should refocus all three of these rays to a single point in the receiving device array. Unfortunately, this is not the case in Fig. 14, and the fact that the three rays do not reconverge at a single point indicates that the imaging system suffers from one or more of the aberration types listed previously.

Aberrations within an imaging system are easily identified using exact ray-trace programs that apply Snell's law ($n_1 \sin\theta_1 = n_2 \sin\theta_2$) to each of the surfaces in the imaging system. In general, the effects of aberrations are found to accumulate much more rapidly out at the edges of the receiving device array. This is one of the reasons why it is more difficult (and more expensive) to design and manufacture a well-corrected lens that images over a large FOV. The useful FOV of a diffraction-limited imaging system is therefore defined to be the area (which is a circular area for systems based on spherical lens) surrounding the center of the receiving device array where the spots are correctly positioned to within a user-defined accuracy and the spot sizes are within a user-defined range about the diffraction-limited spot size d_0. By definition, the spots in the area outside of the useful FOV are aberrated spots that are either incorrectly positioned or larger than the user-defined range of spot sizes.

In the simple imaging system shown in Fig. 14, the beams emanating from the spots in the source device array are drawn as if they were actually created by the source device array. This would indeed be the case if the output signal creation blocks within the source device array contained active sources, such as lasers or LEDs. In fact, one of the benefits of using active sources within the device arrays is that they tend to simplify the imaging optics by eliminating the need for an external light source whose beams must be routed to the source device array. If modulators are used in the output signal creation blocks of the source device array, then an external light source must be provided [Fig. 7(b)].

In addition to providing the optics to guide this light source to the source device array, the system designer must also find a way to create an array of spots from this light source to illuminate the array of modulators efficiently. If the external light source is an array of microlasers, then no further work is required. However, if the external light source is a single laser, then the single beam from the laser must be split into many beams to create the desired array of spots. One spot array generation technique that has been extensively studied is based on diffractive phase gratings (holograms) (Dammann and Gortler 1971; Killat, Rabe, and Rave 1982). Due to diffraction, the optical power within a beam that is directed at a phase grating will typically be redirected from the grating into several orders (diffracted beams) that are symmetric about the zero-order (nondiffracted) beam (Fig. 15). The grating equation describes the relationship between the angle of the incident beam θ_i and the angle of the m'th order's diffracted beam θ_d:

$$p(\sin\theta_d - \sin\theta_i) = m\lambda, \tag{11}$$

where p is the period of the grating, λ is the wavelength of the light, and m is the grating order. When the output beams from the grating are routed through a

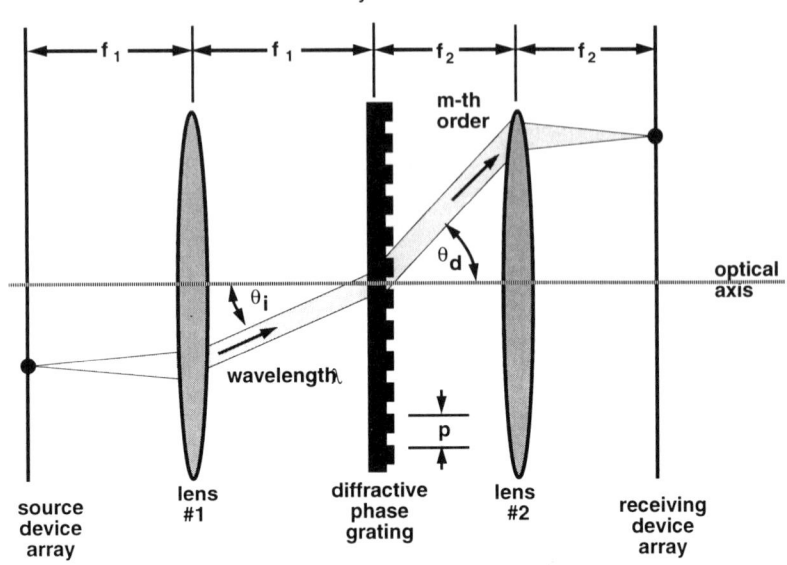

Figure 15. Beam diffraction at a grating.

lens with focal length f and $\sin(\theta)$ distortion, they will generate a set of spots that is uniformly spaced in the focal plane of the lens, and the spacing S will be given by:

$$S = \lambda f/p. \tag{12}$$

Changes in the periodic structure of the grating can force different amounts of optical power from the original beam to be routed into the different spots, and changes in the period p of the grating can force the spots to have different spacings S.

In most of the interconnection schemes used in free-space digital optical systems, some form of beam combination (and beam separation) is usually required. For example, two sets of beams originating from two different source device arrays might need to be superimposed or interleaved before being routed by shared optical hardware to a single receiving device array. In addition, most device arrays have both detectors and sources (or modulators) interleaved throughout the array. If it is a one-sided device array, the input beams being directed toward the detectors and the output beams emanating from the sources (or modulators) might have to share the same imaging optics. However, these two sets of beams must typically be separated at some point in the optical system. As a result, techniques for beam combination and beam separation have become an important research topic. There are many different ways to provide beam combination and beam separation in an imaging system, and each technique has its own limitations.

The simplest form of beam combination uses the two sides that are available on a two-sided device array [Fig. 7(a)]. However, if two sides are not available, an-

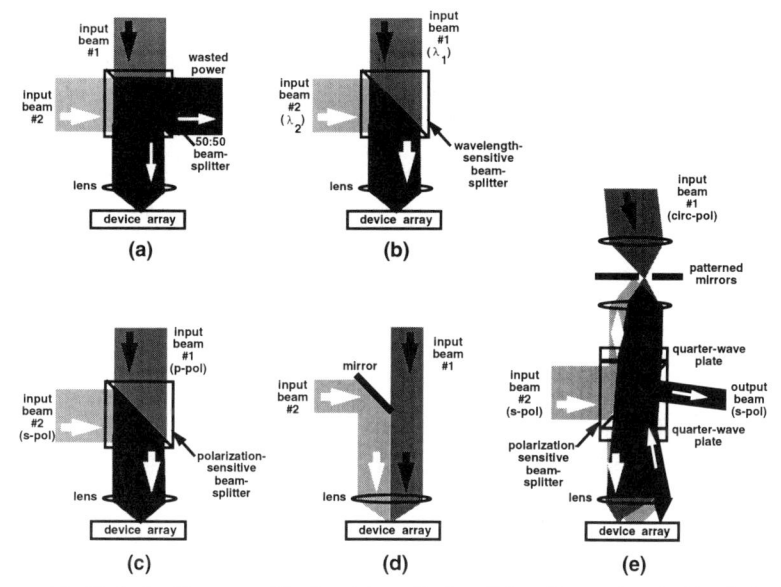

Architectural Considerations for Optical Computing and Photonic Switching 29

Figure 16. Methods of beam combination: (a) amplitude splitting, (b) wavelength, (c) polarization, (d) pupil-plane, and (e) image plane.

other simple approach to beam combination uses amplitude splitting [Fig. 16(a)]. In this approach, a 50:50 beamsplitter (which transmits half of the optical power and reflects half of the optical power) is placed in the path of two sets of incoming beams. The two input beams are then combined such that they arrive at the imaging lens with the same field angle, so they both form a spot at the same spatial location on the receiving device array. Unfortunately, half of the signal power is also wasted. If the devices within the receiving device array can be designed to operate with two different wavelengths (not always a simple task), a more efficient form of beam combination can be implemented by using a chromatic (wavelength-sensitive) beamsplitter in place of the 50:50 beamsplitter [Fig. 16(b)].

Another efficient form of beam combination (and beam separation) uses a polarization-sensitive beamsplitter [Fig. 16(c)], but this approach requires that the two sets of input beams be linearly polarized along two orthogonal axes before being directed into the beamsplitter (the *p*-polarized beam is passed by the beamsplitter, while the *s*-polarized beam is reflected by the beamsplitter). Pupil-plane beam combination (and beam separation) can use a tilted mirror across half of the lens pupil-plane to combine two sets of collimated beams without the need for special beamsplitters [Fig. 16(d)], but this approach requires that the collimated beam diameters D be decreased by a factor of 2 so the lens can accommodate the diameters from both sets of beams. Thus, assuming circular beam profiles, the resulting diffraction-limited spot sizes (d_0) must be increased by a factor of 2

[Eq. (8)], decreasing the overall system resolution. Image-plane beam combination (and beam separation) works well with polarizing optics if the two sets of spots are spatially separated in the device array, because an intermediate image plane can be created by the imaging system and an array of small patterned mirrors on a glass substrate can be positioned within that intermediate image plane to reflect one set of spots while transmitting the other set of spots [Fig. 16(e)]. The polarization-sensitive beamsplitter and the quarter waveplate retarder (which effectively rotates the polarization axis of the light) forces the light down the desired path in Fig. 16(e), allowing two sets of input beams to be combined and a single set of output beams to be separated from the shared imaging optics (McCormick and Prise 1990).

3.2.2 Interconnection Design Considerations

Each of the interconnection topologies (such as those in Fig. 11) that can be implemented using free-space digital optics carries its own unique set of advantages and disadvantages. The selection of an appropriate interconnection topology for a particular application is typically influenced by many different architectural design considerations.

Two important system characteristics that can influence the selection of an interconnection scheme are the manufacturing tolerances and alignment tolerances within the system design. As an example, the diameter of the spot in the receiving device array plane (Fig. 14) is directly related to the resolution of the imaging system, and it is apparent that this spot size must be smaller than the size of the device window into which the spot must be imaged. In fact, it is very desirable to have a spot size that is much smaller than the actual device window, because this will permit larger spot displacements without the loss of optical power, which results in larger manufacturing and alignment tolerances on the optomechanical mounts that hold the device arrays and the imaging lenses. If the spot size is too large when compared to the device window, then the $f/\#$ of the second lens (defined to be f_2/D) can be decreased to create smaller spots [Eq. (8)]. However, diffraction-limited lenses with low $f/\#$'s tend to be more difficult to design and manufacture, so they also tend to be somewhat more expensive.

The DOF of the imaging system also has an effect on the system tolerances, because a large DOF will permit the receiving device array to be positioned without high degrees of accuracy. As an example, with spots of size $d_0 = 3$ μm and a wavelength of $\lambda = 850$ nm, the resulting depth of focus is given by DOF = 16.6 μm [Eq. (10)]. With this relatively large DOF, experiments have shown that the receiving device array can actually be positioned along the z axis by hand (McCormick *et al.* 1991).

The sensitivity of the system operating speed to the optical power arriving at the receiving device array was described in Eq. (2). As a result, if high-speed operation is desired, the optical attenuation in the interconnection hardware should be minimized. There are several sources of optical attenuation in the system. One particularly troublesome source results from Fresnel reflections. Whenever an optical beam passes through an interface where there is a refractive index change, the interface will always produce some undesired Fresnel reflections. This effect can be minimized by placing thin-film antireflection (AR) coatings on all of these interfaces. Although this will increase the system cost, it will typically increase the transmittance of each interface to about 99%. However, even with 99% transmittances at each interface, a beam that passes through a large number of interfaces can still be severely attenuated, because the total transmittance through X interfaces is given by $(0.99)^X$. As an example, if an optical beam passes through 30 interfaces, the total transmittance will be $(0.99)^{30} = 0.74$, so 26% of the optical power is lost due to Fresnel reflections.

Another source of optical attenuation is found in the efficiencies of the diffractive elements and holograms (such as the spot array generators). Depending on the complexity of these elements, they typically steer only 65% to 80% of the beam's power to the desired destinations. As a result, quite a bit of the optical power is lost. In addition, the light that is incorrectly diffracted by these elements may become noise at undesired locations in the receiving device array, and this can lead to crosstalk problems that otherwise would not exist. Thus, system designers must take special precautions to avoid these crosstalk problems. One approach that helps reduce the crosstalk problems requires the receiving device array to be designed with spacer locations. The diffractive elements can then be designed to guide the undesired "noise orders" toward these spacer locations. A final source of optical attenuation can be attributed to the clipping of the optical beam edges at apertures (such as lenses) within the optical system. This type of clipping is typically referred to as *vignetting*. It must be controlled by designing the optical system with apertures that are large enough to pass the beams without substantial clipping. In prototype systems, the effects of vignetting are often confused with the effects of system aberrations, because in addition to losing some of its optical power, a vignetted beam will usually produce a blurred spot in the receiving device array as a result of diffraction effects. Because of this, vignetting problems must be avoided at a very early stage in the imaging system design.

System designers must also be concerned about the quality of the images that are passed through the system, because a greatly deteriorated image may not route the signal beams to their desired destinations in the receiving device array. As a result, the aberrations in the imaging system must be carefully controlled. One way to help minimize the effect of aberrations is to limit the FOV on the lenses, because smaller fields of view will typically have less aberration accumulation. However, the designer must weigh the benefits of this limited FOV against the architectural disadvantages. For example, fewer usable devices will be available within each device array, so the architecture's functionality will undoubtedly be affected. As a result, some form of compromise must typically be found between the FOV and the system functionality.

Another problem associated with image quality results from the fact that the overall system magnification is tightly coupled to the lens focal lengths. For example, in Fig. 14, assume a spot in the source device array is 1.0 mm out from the optical axis, assume $f_1 = 15.0$ mm, and assume $f_2 = 60.0$ mm. The spot created in the receiving device array should therefore be 4.0 mm out from the optical axis [Eq. (7)]. However, if the first lens is incorrectly manufactured with a focal length of $f_1 = 14.5$ mm and if the second lens is incorrectly manufactured with a focal length of $f_2 = 60.5$ mm, then the resulting magnification is given by $M_T = 60.5/14.5 = 4.172$, and the spot from the source device array will be imaged to a spot that is 4.172 mm away from the optical axis. It is unlikely that this spot will fall into the desired device window in the receiving device array, so it is apparent that the lens focal lengths in this system must be very tightly controlled during the manufacturing process. A final image quality problem is directly related to the sensitivity of diffractive components to laser wavelength variations. From Eq. (12), the spacing of the spots created by a diffractive component is directly proportional to the laser wavelength. Thus, if an 850.0-nm laser mode-hops to 851.0 nm, the spacing of the spots formed by the diffractive components will increase by a factor of $851/850 = 1.0012$. This will result in spot shifts on the order of 1 μm for a spot that is 1.0 mm from the optical axis, and this shift can partially move a spot out of a desired device window. As a result, the use of diffractive components within the interconnection hardware places an additional constraint on laser wavelength stability, which may have a large effect on the designer's choice of laser sources.

Other issues that system designers must address when selecting and designing an optical interconnection scheme include the overall system size requirements, the cost of the required interconnection components, the cost and complexity of component alignment, the effect that a failing component will have on the system fault tolerance and availability, the cost and complexity of repairing a failing component, the ability to observe the operating status of the components and to detect failing components, the sensitivity and susceptibility of the components to vibrations and mechanical shock, the cleanliness of the operating environment and the effect of dust on the components, the fluctuations in system operating temperature and the resulting thermal expansion of the optomechanical mounts, the sensitivity of polarization components to angular field, the logic gate utilization resulting from the selected interconnection topology (for optical computing applications), and the network blocking probability resulting from the selected interconnection topology (for telecommunication network applications).

3.2.3 Architectural Advantages Offered by Optical Interconnections

Given the general description in Section 3.2.1 of interconnections based on free-space digital optics, several interesting conclusions can be drawn.

First, these optical techniques should yield interconnections with very little crosstalk between neighboring connections. Figure 14 and Maxwell's equations indicate that the information-bearing light beams will propagate through one another without coupling any optical power. As a result, the primary sources of optical crosstalk within a free-space system will probably result from scattered light and/or a spot coupling into an undesired window within the receiving device array. However, Eq. (9) shows that the irradiance of the spot (Gaussian beam) in the receiving device array will typically be greatly suppressed in adjacent device windows, because these adjacent windows will only couple light from the tails of the Gaussian beam. For example, assume that the device windows in the receiving device array are placed on 10-μm spacings, and assume that the spot diameter d_0 within the device windows is 3 μm ($r_0 = 1.5$ μm). From Eq. (9), the irradiance of the Gaussian beam out 10 μm from its axis will be given by $2.5 \times 10^{-39} I_0$. Thus, if the optical system is well corrected (with very few aberrations) and the sources of scattered light are controlled, then crosstalk within the optical interconnections should be negligible, and the designer will be faced with the much simpler problem of controlling the minimal crosstalk that might occur in the short electrical traces on the device arrays.

Another advantage offered by free-space digital optics is the fact that the impedances along the interconnection path and the impedance of the receiver can all be very easily matched through the use of thin-film AR coatings (which were mentioned in Section 3.2.2). As a result, the undesirable reflections and ringing due to impedance mismatches (which are often encountered by high-speed circuit designers using metallic-based interconnections) are essentially eliminated. Although well-known electronic techniques (such as the addition of terminating resistors or the addition of quarter-wave transmission line sections with appropriately tuned characteristic impedances) can be used to suppress the reflections in metallic-based systems, these approaches oftentimes produce unwanted side effects. For example, the addition of terminating resistors can greatly increase the power dissipation within the interconnections, leading to more difficult thermal management problems. The addition of quarter-wave sections may require a concentrated effort to design each interconnection within the system, and may also require the use of complicated photolithographic and material deposition techniques to produce the desired characteristic impedances. As a result, this approach may lead to undesirable increases in the cost of the device-carrying MCM or circuit board. AR coating of optical components, on the other hand, can be done via batch processing, so the amortized costs should be minimal.

Signals that are routed via free-space digital optics will also encounter very little dispersion. In a free-space system, dispersion (the temporal smoothing of the edges on an optical pulse) can result from two fundamental effects: (1) different rays of light within the pulse having the same wavelength propagate along paths in the optical imaging system with different delays before being refocused by the imaging optics (which is similar to intermodal dispersion within a fiber), and (2) different wavelength components within the pulse propagate with different velocities, because the refractive indices of the materials vary with wavelength (which is similar to intramodal dispersion within a fiber) (Keiser 1983).

The inherent nature of imaging optics guarantees that the first effect will not be a problem, because according to Fermat's principle, all of the rays propagating from the source spot to the image spot must travel through the same optical path lengths with the same delay (Hecht and Zajac 1979). The varying thicknesses of the lenses in Fig. 14 guarantee that the delays along different ray paths between a given source spot and image spot will be identical.

The second dispersion-causing effect should also be minimal in most systems based on free-space digital optics, because in a typical system, the optical signals only propagate through air and glasses. Typical refractive indices of these materials vary only slightly as a function of wavelength (in particular, in the commonly used infrared region of the spectrum), so the different wavelength components within the pulse should propagate with very similar velocities (Hecht and Zajac 1979). Lower signal and clock skew is another potential benefit offered by free-space digital optics, which can help in the difficult task of synchronizing the signals in a high-speed processing system. If an infinite conjugate, telecentric imaging system is used, then because of the symmetry of the system, many of the imaging characteristics (described earlier) that lead to low dispersion will also lead to low signal and clock skew.

All of the aforementioned characteristics of free-space digital optical interconnections can help produce less signal distortion and higher interconnection bandwidths than many interconnection schemes based on metallic traces. In addition, because of the elimination of long metallic traces (which can act like transmitting and receiving antennas within the system), systems based on free-space digital optics may also help reduce the EMI problems that can plague many high-speed electronic systems.

3.3 Limitations of Free-Space Digital Optics

Although free-space digital optics may solve many of the packaging and interconnection problems that were outlined in previous sections, it should not be viewed as a panacea, because there are still some limitations that are common to both electronic implementations and optical implementations.

For example, the fundamental switching speeds of most unloaded electronic logic devices (driving no interconnection traces) and most optical logic devices will be similar. This is a direct result of the fact that the physical phenomenon of both electronic and optical device switching typically requires the transport of electrons between different regions of the device and/or the transition of electrons between the valence and conduction bands. In both electronic and optical devices, the switching speed is oftentimes limited by the internal capacitance of the device, which is directly related to the physical size of the device. The physical sizes of electronic devices and optical devices will probably not be very different in future applications, so their fundamental switching speeds will not be very different either.

Another generic problem found in both electronic and optical implementations is related to the signal propagation delay between source devices and receiver devices. Unfortunately, optical signals do not travel much faster than electronic signals, because both signals are electromagnetic waves whose propagation velocity is primarily determined by the properties of the material through which they propagate. Assuming TEM propagation of the metallic trace-guided electromagnetic signal within a homogeneous, isotropic dielectric material having dielectric constant ϵ_r and relative permeability μ_r, the wave velocity is given by:

$$v = 1/\sqrt{\mu\epsilon} = 1/\sqrt{\mu_0\mu_r\epsilon_0\epsilon_r} = (1/\sqrt{\mu_0\epsilon_1})(1/\sqrt{\mu_r\epsilon_r}) \approx c/\sqrt{\epsilon_r}, \quad (13)$$

where c is the velocity of light in a vacuum (3×10^8 m/s), and it is assumed that the material's relative permeability $\mu_r \approx 1$ (Ramo, Whinnery, and Van Duzer 1984). An electromagnetic wave guided by metallic traces is typically propagating through dielectric materials such as polyimide ($\epsilon_r = 3.5$) on the semiconductor substrate, glass-ceramic ($\epsilon_r = 4.8$) on the multichip module, and FR-4 ($\epsilon_r = 4.0$) on the circuit board or backplane (Schroen 1990). Thus, typical velocities of signals in a system based on metallic traces range from 1.3×10^8 m/s to 1.6×10^8 m/s. A similar equation is used to describe the wave velocity of electromagnetic signals whose frequency places them in the optical range of the spectrum:

$$v = c/\sqrt{\epsilon_r} = c/n, \quad (14)$$

where n is the index of refraction of the material through which the light is propagating. An electromagnetic wave guided by free-space digital optical components is typically propagating through dielectric materials such as air ($n = 1.0$) and fused silica ($n = 1.458$) (Hecht and Zajac 1979). Thus, typical velocities of signals in a system based on free-space digital optics range from 2.0×10^8 m/s to 3.0×10^8 m/s. There is very little difference between the signal velocities in the electronic implementation and those in the optical implementation, and it has been argued that a system based on free-space digital optics may actually require longer propagation distances between the source device and the receiver device due to the necessary addition of optical components such as lenses and beamsplitters (Midwinter 1988b). As a result, there will probably be very little difference between the propagation delays in systems based on metallic traces and those in systems based on free-space digital optics.

Because of the optical components that will probably be needed between adjacent device arrays, the physical size of the componentry associated with a single IC in a free-space system may appear to be quite large. In fact, working prototype systems require a volume of approximately 1 in. by 1 in. by 3 in. to support the required optical components for a single IC (McCormick *et al.* 1991). However, a fair comparison to a similar electronic system would have to consider the fact that this 3 in.[3] volume can potentially provide 2500 to 250,000 connections that are ideally terminated. If an electronic system could provided this many terminated connections, the heat dissipated in the terminating resistors would probably require advanced cooling techniques, and a fair amount of volume would be required for the cooling components. As a result, the relatively large size of the optical approach should be viewed in terms of the capabilities that it provides.

The attenuation encountered by optical signals propagating through free-space digital optics is another system limitation. In a typical imaging system, the signals propagating from one device array to another device array will pass through as many as 30 surfaces containing changes in the refractive index (McCormick *et al.* 1991). In Section 3.2.2, we saw that even with AR coatings, as much as 1% of the signal power can be lost at each of these surfaces due to Fresnel reflections. Thus, only 74% of the power leaving the first device array will arrive at the second device array.

Researchers are actively working to eliminate all of these limitations, but current prototypes must be designed and constructed even though these limitations are present.

4. A System Example

A large number of prototype systems based on free-space digital optics have been proposed within the literature, and some prototype system implementations have already been fabricated. A description of all of these proposals is beyond the scope of this text, but a detailed analysis of a simple system may prove to be instructive.

The system of interest consists of multiple stages of 2-D S-SEED arrays that are optically connected using banyan interconnections similar to those shown in Fig. 11(c) (McCormick *et al.* 1991). Each of the 1.28-mm × 1.28 mm S-SEED arrays used in the prototype contained 2048 optical windows of size 6 × 14 μm. These windows were arranged in a 64 × 32 array, where the windows were vertically spaced by 20 μm and horizontally spaced by 40 μm. Each window could accept two spatially separated input signals and one clock signal, while producing one output signal, so the entire S-SEED array actually provided 8192 optical pinouts.

The optical hardware required for two consecutive stages of these S-SEED arrays is shown schematically in Fig. 17. In this schematic, the light emitted from the 80-mW, 850-nm laser diode power supply in the first stage is partially collimated by the collimation lens. This partially collimated beam, which is typically

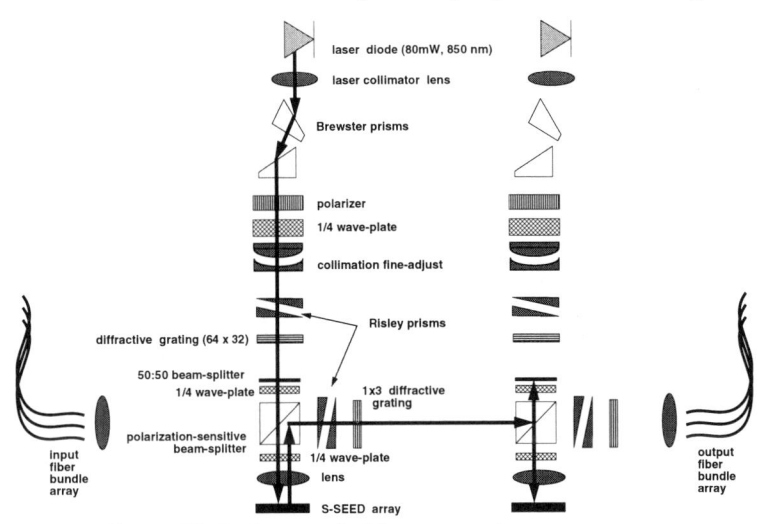

Figure 17. Hardware required for two stages in prototype system.

an elliptical beam, is then circularized by a pair of Brewster prisms. The circular beam is passed through a polarizer to guarantee linearly polarized light, and it is then routed through a quarter waveplate retarder to create circularly polarized light. This light is then passed through another set of lenses to adjust finely the collimation of the beam. The collimated beam is then routed through a pair of Risley prisms, which can be rotated to point the beam to its appropriate location on the S-SEED array. This pointed beam is then passed through a diffractive phase grating to create a 64×32 array of clock beams that can be used to interrogate the state of each of the windows in the S-SEED array.

Half of the power from this array of clock beams passes through a 50:50 beamsplitter, which is used for combining the clock beams with signal beams from the previous stage. It then passes through another quarter waveplate retarder, which converts the light back into a linear polarization state. This linear polarized light passes straight through the polarization-sensitive beamsplitter before being routed through another quarter wave-plate retarder, converting it back into circularly polarized light. The light is then imaged by the objective lens, creating 2048 clock spots in the 2048 windows of the S-SEED array. Each of these clock spots is modulated (absorbed or reflected) by the S-SEED window, and the reflected light is routed back through the objective lens, which now recollimates the light. This recollimated light is then passed through the quarter waveplate retarder, which converts it back into linear polarized light, but its plane of polarization is now oriented so that the light is reflected to the right by the polarization-sensitive beamsplitter. The light is then routed through another set of Risley prisms, which can be used to point the beams into the windows of the second S-SEED array. The pointed beams then pass through a 1×3 diffractive grating similar to the one

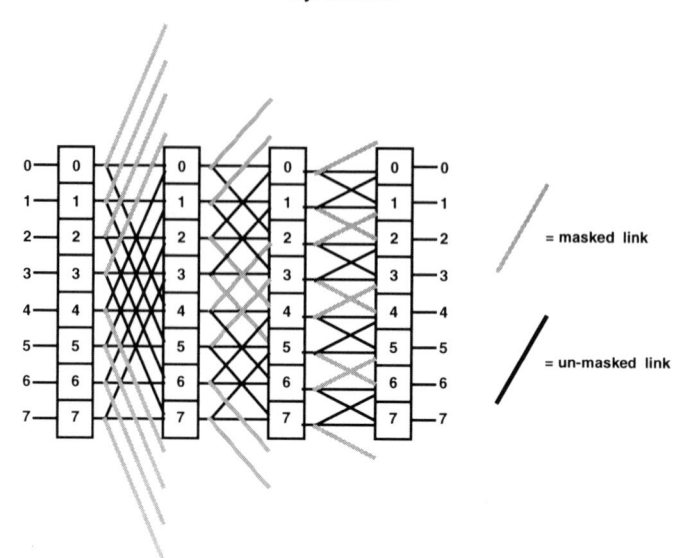

Figure 18. Banyan connections provided by a 1 × 3 diffractive grating.

shown in Fig. 15, which provides the S-SEED to S-SEED interconnection pattern illustrated in Fig. 18. By masking off the light colored links within Fig. 18, banyan connections similar to those in Fig. 11(c) can be derived from this simple space-invariant grating (Cloonan and Herron 1989).

The output beams from the diffractive grating are directed into the second polarization-sensitive beamsplitter and reflected up through a quarter waveplate retarder toward the 50:50 beamsplitter. Half of the power from this light is then reflected back down through the quarter waveplate retarder, which has modified its polarization again so that it passes through the second polarization-sensitive beamsplitter and through the quarter waveplate retarder toward the second objective lens. The modulated signal beams from the first S-SEED array are then imaged as spots within the windows of the second S-SEED array, setting the digital state of those devices for subsequent readout to be another set of clock beams that will be generated by the optics in the second stage (McCormick *et al.* 1991). Data entering and leaving the system can be carried on a fiber bundle array whose fiber matrix is imaged onto the window matrix within the device arrays (Cloonan *et al.* 1990).

A prototype of this S-SEED-based system was constructed and operated (Fig. 19). The prototype contained six stages of S-SEED arrays mounted on a 12.5-in. by 9-in. metallic base plate. Experiments showed that the system was fully functional (except for ≈5 bad device windows out of a total of 12,288 device windows in the system), but the system operating speed was limited to ≈50 kbps by the 80-mW laser diodes that were used. From Eq. (2), it can be seen that higher

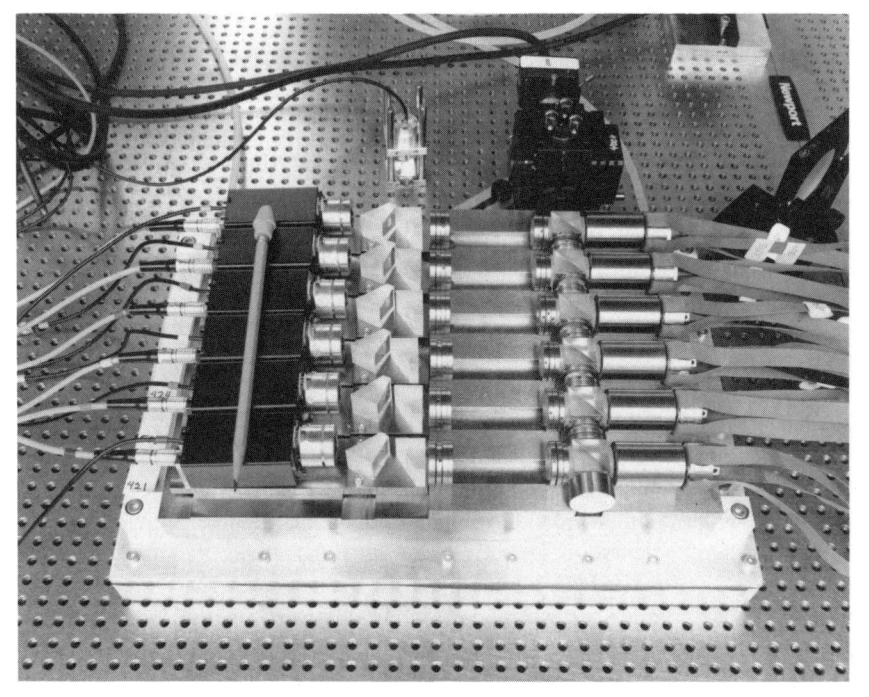

Figure 19. Six-stage prototype system.

data rates within the system can be achieved by (1) using higher power lasers (or combining several low-power lasers to produce higher power clock beams), (2) decreasing the power losses in the optical imaging system and the modulators, (3) lowering the capacitances of the devices, (4) increasing the responsivities of the devices, and (5) decreasing the switching voltages of the devices.

5. Conclusion

Systems similar to the one described earlier can be used in many different processing applications. For example, in the actual prototype of Fig. 19, ribbon cables are used to inject electronic control information into the S-SEED arrays, so these arrays use both optical and electronic pinouts. The electronic control signals are used to enable or disable the crosspoints (S-SEEDs) in the switching network, so a path (similar to the one shown by dark lines in Fig. 11(c) can be set up through all of the enabled crosspoints, providing end-to-end connectivity between the desired input port and output port (Cloonan *et al.* 1990). The blocking probability and the fault tolerance of a network based on these simple crosspoints can be improved by using larger device arrays and by adding extra stages to the network.

For example, it can be shown that a high-speed 256-input, 256-output strictly nonblocking network can be constructed with 19 S-SEED arrays, where each S-SEED array is of size 64 × 128 (Cloonan *et al.* 1991).

In addition to implementing a photonic switching network, the hardware of Fig. 19 could also be used to implement components within an optical computer. For example, if the S-SEEDs are operated as logic gates (instead of crosspoints), then they could be used to implement an optical programmable logic array (PLA) (Murdocca *et al.* 1988). The output from an optical PLA can implement any Boolean function of the binary input variables, where the output is generally implemented as a binary sum of minterms (the products of the input variables). For example, the PLA implementation shown in Fig. 20 produces the binary output S, given by $S = XY + \overline{X}\overline{Y}$. Since there are $m = 2$ input variables (and their complements) required for this Boolean function, the first $m + 1 = 3$ stages are implemented as AND gates to create the four possible minterms (XY, $\overline{X}Y$, $X\overline{Y}$, and $\overline{X}\overline{Y}$) and the last $m + 1 = 3$ stages are implemented as OR gates to combine the minterms and create the output S. The dark links within Fig. 20 are unmasked connections, while the other links require masks to block the undesired beams. Although this implementation uses only combinational logic, the use of optical feedback paths from the PLA output to the PLA input can permit the system designer to create a finite state machine, which is a fundamental building block that can be used to create many computing functions.

Another approach that uses free-space digital optics within computing and switching systems merely applies the technology to connect system modules (IC, MCMs, or circuit boards) wherever high-density, high-speed interconnections are needed within the computing environment. As an example, an ideal application of

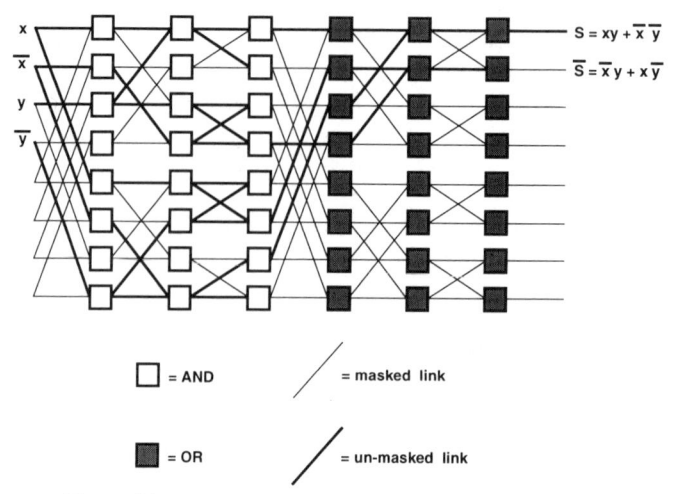

Figure 20. Optical PLA implementation of a Boolean function.

optical interconnections may be between the cache memory ICs and the processor ICs within a computer. Thus, it should be clear that both switching systems and computing systems may be able to capitalize on the potential packaging and interconnection benefits offered by free-space digital optics. Although a large amount of work is still required to turn the potential into a reality, there have already been successful research efforts in many areas that will undoubtedly help pave the way to the applications of the future. The remaining chapters in this book address several of these research areas.

REFERENCES

Bakoglu, H. B. (1990). *Circuits, Interconnections and Packaging for VLSI*. Addison-Wesley Publishing Company, Reading, MA, 112–123.
Brenner, K. H., and Huang, A. (1988). *Appl. Opt.* 27, 135–140.
Cloonan, T. J., and Herron, M. J. (1989). *Opt. Eng.* 28, 305–314.
Cloonan, T. J., and McCormick, F. B. (1991). *Appl. Opt.* 30, 2309–2323.
Cloonan, T. J., McCormick, F. B., Herron, M. J., Tooley, F. A. P., Richards, G. W., Kerbis, E., Brubaker, J. L., and Lentine, A. L. (1990). *Photonic Switching II* (K. Tada and H. S. Hinton, eds.), Springer-Verlag, Berlin, 196–199.
Cloonan, T. J., Richards, G. W., Lentine, A. L., McCormick, F. B., Hinton, H. S., and Hinterlong, S. J. (1993). *IEEE J. Quantum Electron.* 29, 619–634.
Cloonan, T. J., Richards, G. W., McCormick, F. B., and Lentine, A. L. (1991). In: *Photonic Switching 1991, Technical Digest Series*. Optical Society of America, Washington, DC, 154–157.
Dammann, H., and Gortler, K. (1971). *Opt. Comm.* 3, 312–315.
Davidson, R. P., and Muller, N. J. (1991). *The Guide to Sonet: Planning, Installing, & Maintaining Broadband Networks*. Telecom Library, Inc., New York.
Dias, A. R., Kalman, R. F., Goodman, J. W., and Sawchuk, A. A. (1988). *Opt. Eng.* 27, 955–960.
Eichmann, G., and Li, Y. (1987). *Appl. Opt.* 26, 1167–1169.
Feldman, M. R., Esener, S. C., Guest, C. C., and Lee, S. H. (1988). *Appl. Opt.* 27, 1742–1751.
Glance, B. S., Pollock, K., Burrus, C. A., Kapser, B. L., Eisenstein, G., and Stulz, L. W. (1988). WDM coherent optical star network. *J. Lightwave Technol.* 6, 67–72.
Goodman, J. W. (1989). In: *Optical Processing and Computing* (H. H. Arsenault, T. Szoplik, and B. Macukow, eds.), Academic Press, San Diego, CA, 1–32.
Goodman, J. W., Dias, A. R., and Woody, L. M. (1978). *Opt. Lett.* 2, 1–3.
Hara, K., Kojima, K., Mitunaga, K., and Kyuma, K. (1989). *IEEE Photonic Technol. Lett.* 1, 370–372.
Hartman, D. H., Lalk, G. R., Howse, J. W., and Krchnavek, R. R. (1989). *Appl. Opt.* 28, 40–47.
Hecht, E., and Zajac, A. (1979). *Optics*. Addison-Wesley Publishing Company, Reading, MA, 29–166.
Hinton, H. S. (1988). *IEEE J. Sel. Areas Commun.* 6, 1209–1226.
Hinton, H. S. (1990). *IEEE Commun.* 28, 71–89.
Iga, K., Oikawa, M., Misawa, S., Banno, J., and Kokubun, Y. (1982). *Appl. Opt.* 21, 3456–3460.
Jahns, J., and Murdocca, M. J. (1988). *Appl. Opt.* 27, 3155–3164.
Jahns, J., and Huang, A. (1989). *Appl. Opt.* 28, 1602–1605.
Jahns, J., and Däschner, W. (1991). In: *Optical Computing 1991, Technical Digest Series, Vol. 6*. Optical Society of America, Washington, DC, 29–31.
Jewell, J. L., Lee, Y. H., McCall, S. L., Scherer, A., Olsson, N. A., Harbison, J. P., and Florez, L. T.

(1990). In: *Technical Digest of 1990 International Topical Meeting on Photonic Switching.* Institute of Electronics, Information, and Communication Engineers, Tokyo, 14–19.
Jewell, J. L., Rushford, M. C., and Gibbs, H. M. (1984). *Appl. Phys. Lett.* **44,** 172–174.
Johnson, B. C. (1990). In: *Electronic Materials Handbook, Vol. 1, Packaging.* ASM International, Materials Park, OH, 398–407.
Keiser, G. (1983). *Optical Fiber Communications.* McGraw-Hill Book Company, New York, 58–73.
Kiamilev, F. E., Marchand, P., Krishnamoorthy, A. V., Esener, S. C., and Lee, S. H. (1991). *J. Lightwave Technol.* **9,** 1674–1692.
Killat, U., Rabe, G., and Rave. W. (1982). *Fiber and Integrated Optics* **4,** 159–167.
Kogelnik, H., and Schmidt, R. V. (1976). Switched directional couplers with alternating delta-beta. *IEEE J. Quantum Electron.* **QE-12,** 396–401.
Koopman, N. G., Reilery, T. C., and Totta, P. A. (1989a). In: *Microelectronics Packaging Handbook* (R. R. Tummala and E. J. Rymaszewski, eds.), Van Nostrand Reinhold, New York, 391–453.
Koopman, N. G., Reiley, T. C., and Totta, P. A. (1989b). In: *Microelectronics Packaging Handbook* (R. R. Tummala and E. J. Rymaszewski, eds.), Van Nostrand Reinhold, New York, 361–391.
Krishnamoorthy, A. V., Marchand, P. J., Kiamilev, F. E., and Esener, S. C. (1992). Grain-size considerations for optoelectronic multistage interconnection networks. To be published in *Appl. Opt.*
Lentine, A. L., Hinton, H. S., Miller, D. A. B., Henry, J. E., Cunningham, J. E., and Chirovsky, L. M. F. (1989). *IEEE J. Quantum Electron.* **25,** 1928–1936.
Lohmann, A. W., Stork, W., and Stucke, G. (1985). *Appl. Opt.* **25,** 1530–1532.
Lohmann, A. W. (1986). *Appl. Opt.* **25,** 1543–1549.
Markstein, H. W. (1991). In: *Electronic Packaging and Production.* The Cahners Publishing Company, Newton, MA, 40–45.
McCormick, F. B., and Prise, M. E. (1990). *Appl. Opt.* **29,** 2013–2018.
McCormick, F. B., Tooley, F. A. P., Brubaker, J. L., Sasian, J. M., Cloonan, T. J., Lentine, A. L., Morrison, R. L., Crisci, R. J., Walker, Hinterlong, S. J., and Herron, M. J. (1991). In: *Proceedings of the SPIE International Symposium on Optical Applied Science and Engineering.* SPIE, Bellingham, WA, paper L2.
McKnight, D. J., Vass, D. G., and Sillitto, R. M. (1989). *Appl. Opt.* **28,** 4757–4762.
Midwinter, J. E. (1988a). *Phys. Tech.* **19,** 101–108.
Midwinter, J. E. (1988b). *Phys. Tech.,* **19,** 153–157.
Midwinter, J. E., and Taylor, M. G. (May 1990). *IEEE LCS Magazine,* 40–46.
Miller, D. A. B. (1989). *Opt. Lett.* **14,** 146–148.
Murdocca, M. J., Huang, A., Jahns, J., and Streibl, N. (1988). *Appl. Opt.* **27,** 1651–1660.
Novotny, R. A., Kerbis, E., Brubaker, J. L., Basavanhally, N., and Freund, J. (1991). In: *OSA Annual Meeting Technical Digest, Vol. 17.* Optical Society of America, Washington, DC, 92.
O'Shea, D. C. (1985). *Elements of Modern Optical Design.* John Wiley & Sons, New York, 230–269.
Prise, M. E., Streibl, N., and Downs, M. M. (1988). *Opt. Quantum Electron.* **20,** 49–77.
Prucnal, P. R., Santoro, M. A., and Sehgal, S. K. (1986). *IEEE J. Sel. Areas Commun.* **SAC-4,** 1484–1493.
Ramo, S., Whinnery, J. R., and VanDuzer, T. (1984). *Fields and Waves in Communication Electronics.* John Wiley and Sons, New York, 213–216.
Rymaszewski, E. J., and Tummala, R. R. (1989). In: *Microelectronics Packaging Handbook* (R. R. Tummala and E. J. Rymaszewski, eds.), Van Nostrand Reinhold, New York, 1–64.
Sawchuk, A. A., Jenkins, B. K., Raghavendra, C. S., and Varma, A. (1987). *IEEE Comput.* **20,** 50–58.
Schroen, W. H. (1990). *Electronic Materials Handbook, Vol. 1, Packaging.* ASM International, Materials Park, OH, 436–450.
Smith, S. D. (1986). *Appl. Opt.* **25,** 1550–1564.
Song, Q. W., and Yu, F. T. S. (1988). *Appl. Opt.* **27,** 1222–1224.
Stirk, C. W., Athale, R. A., and Haney, M. W. (1988). *Appl. Opt.* **27,** 202–204.

Stirk, C. W., and Psaltis, D. (1991). In: *Optical Computing 1991, Technical Digest Series, Vol. 6.* Optical Society of America, Washington, DC, 14–17.

Stone, H. S. (1980). *Introduction to Computer Architecture.* Science Research Associates, Chicago, IL.

Stopper, H. (1990). *Electronic Materials Handbook, Vol. 1, Packaging,* ASM International, Materials Park, OH, 354–364.

Stucke, G. (1988). *Optik* **78,** 84–85.

Taylor, G. W., Simmons, J. G., Cho, A. Y., and Mand, R. S. (1989). *J. Appl. Phys.* **59,** 596–600.

Tsang, D. Z. (1991). *The Lincoln Lab. J.* **4,** 31–44.

Chapter 2
Self-Electro-Optic Effect Devices for Optical Information Processing

ANTHONY L. LENTINE

AT&T Bell Laboratories
263 Shuman Blvd.
Naperville, IL 60566

1. Introduction to Electroabsorption and SEEDs 45
2. Surface Normal Quantum Well Modulators 48
   2.1 Reflection Modulators 48
   2.2 Asymmetric Fabry-Pérot Modulators 49
   2.3 Performance of MQW Modulators 50
3. Self-Electro-Optic Effect Devices 51
   3.1 Resistor-Biased SEEDs 52
   3.2 Diode-Biased SEEDs 52
   3.3 Symmetric SEEDs 53
   3.4 Multistate SEEDs 58
   3.5 Transistor-Biased SEEDs 59
   3.6 Energy Requirements in SEEDs 60
4. Smart Pixels 64
   4.1 Logic SEEDs 64
   4.2 Integration of MQW Modulators and Electronic Circuits 67
5. Conclusion 69
   Acknowledgments 70
   References 70

1. Introduction to Electroabsorption and SEEDs

One of the more widely researched optoelectronic devices are the quantum well self-electro-optic effect devices (SEEDs) (Miller 1990). SEEDs rely on changes in the optical absorption that can be induced by changes in an electric field perpendicular to the thin semiconductor layers in quantum well material (Miller, Chemla, and Schmitt-Rink 1988). If we place the quantum well material in the intrinsic region of a reverse biased diode, then as we apply a voltage across the diode we can change its absorption. If we apply a continuous-wave optical signal to the input of the diode we can electrically control its optical output. We refer to a device operated in this manner as a *modulator*. We can also use the same device as a detector, generating photocurrent in response to an incident light beam. In a

SEED, the photocurrent generated by one or more of these detectors causes the voltage to change across one or more modulators. Thus, a SEED has optical inputs for controlling optical outputs. In this chapter, we describe the basic operation of these devices. We discuss several types of quantum well modulators and SEEDs and emphasize their application to optical signal processing.

A quantum well consists of a thin (~100-Å) material such as GaAs bounded on both sides by a material such as Al_xGa_{1-x}. As with a higher bandgap than the thin material in the center, as shown in Fig. 1. The material with the lower bandgap is called the *well* and the material with the higher bandgap is called the *barrier*. Many sections can be stacked on top of each other (i.e., barrier, well, barrier, well, barrier, etc.) to get a device consisting of multiple quantum wells (MQWs). If the barriers are thick enough and have a large enough bandgap compared to the well, then the wells act independently and the effect of having multiple wells is to multiply the absorption of a single well by the number of wells. Modern semiconductor growth methods, such as molecular beam epitaxy (MBE), enable the well and barrier thicknesses to be precisely controlled to one atomic layer.

In bulk semiconductor materials, there is a very smooth absorption spectrum starting at the bandgap energy (~870 nm for GaAs) and rising smoothly for increasing photon energy (shorter wavelength). This absorption spectrum near the bandgap changes as we apply an electric field. This effect is known as the *Franz-Keldysh effect* (Franz 1958; Keldysh 1958). In quantum well materials, the electron and hole energies are quantized and large discrete steps in the absorption spectrum are seen even at room temperature, unlike the smooth absorption spectrum observed in bulk materials. The wavelengths of these absorption steps shift with applied fields perpendicular to the wells. This behavior in quantum wells has been called the *quantum confined Franz-Keldysh effect* (Miller, Chemla, and Schmitt-Rink 1986). As the quantum wells are thickened from ~100 to

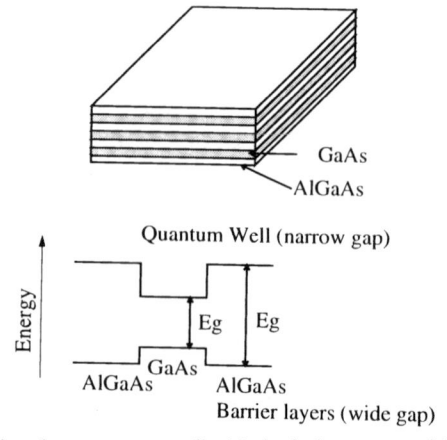

Figure 1. Semiconductor quantum wells: (a) physical structure and (b) band diagram.

~300 to 500 Å, the discrete behavior becomes almost continuous, thus the quantum confined behavior essentially becomes the Franz-Keldysh effect in bulk semiconductors.

At low temperatures in bulk materials or quantum wells, the electron-hole coulomb interaction plays a significant role. The absorption spectrum exhibits peaks, which are called *exciton peaks*. When a photon is absorbed at the wavelengths of these peaks, a bound electron-hole pair (exciton) is created that does not immediately separate into an electron and a hole but remains together like a hydrogen atom. In bulk materials, the excitons are larger (~300 Å) and are short lived, so excitonic features in the absorption spectrum are not observed at room temperature. However, in quantum wells, the exciton is confined by the wells and remains intact until the carriers escape from the wells, thus strong peaks in the absorption spectrum are seen even at room temperature.

When an electric field is applied perpendicular to the plane of the quantum wells, the electron and hole tend to move toward the opposite sides of the well. However, because of the barriers on both sides of the wells, the exciton remains intact. In bulk materials, the electron and hole would be ripped apart by the field with no barriers to keep the exciton intact. In quantum well material, applying an electric field reduces the photon energy required to create the electron and hole, thus a red shaft is seen in the absorption spectrum of quantum well material when a field is applied. This effect has been called the *quantum confined Stark effect* (QSCE) (Miller *et al.* 1984a, 1985; Miller, Chemla, and Schmitt-Rink 1988) by analogy of the Stark shift seen in the absorption spectrum of a hydrogen atom under strong applied fields. A plot of the absorption spectrum at different applied electric fields is shown in Fig. 2 (Miller, Chemla, and Schmitt-Rink 1988). The changes in absorption of the GaAs quantum wells are large; 1-μm-thick quantum

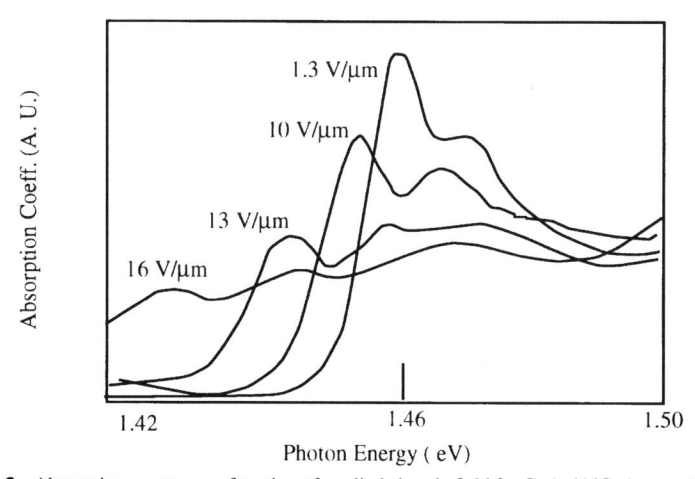

Figure 2. Absorption spectra as a function of applied electric field for GaAs/AlGaAs quantum wells (Miller, Chemla, and Schmitt-Rink 1988) ©1986 IEEE.

well material can have optical transmission changes greater than a factor of 2 with only 5 V applied. This fact enables arrays of devices to be made with acceptable performance for light propagating perpendicular to the surface of an array of such devices.

2. Surface Normal Quantum Well Modulators

In this section we discuss quantum well modulators, specifically for the case of optical signals propagating perpendicular to the surface. The basic quantum well modulator consists of a quantum well region in the intrinsic region of a reverse-biased *p-i-n* diode. When we apply a reverse-biased voltage across the diode, an electric field will be present across the intrinsic region, which in turn changes the absorption of the multiple quantum wells. As we stated earlier, in the GaAs/AlGaAs material system, changes in absorption of a factor of 2 can be obtained for 1-μm-thick quantum well regions for a voltage change of ~5 V.

Surface normal quantum well modulators can be classified into two types, transmissive mode devices and reflective mode devices, as shown in Fig. 3. For transmissive devices, the device is mounted on a piece of transparent material, such as sapphire or quartz. Light enters from one side of the device and propagates through the device and out the other side of the device [Fig. 3(a)]. For devices with GaAs wells and AlGaAs barriers made on GaAs substrates operating near ~850 nm, the GaAs substrate must be removed because it is not transparent at that wavelength. However, the GaAs substrate is transparent for devices with InGaAs wells and GaAs barriers with operating wavelengths greater than ~870 nm. InP substrates are transparent to devices with operating wavelengths longer than ~970 nm.

2.1 Reflection Modulators

A reflection modulator consists of a transverse MQW modulator with a mirror on the bottom of the device, as shown in Fig. 3(b). Light is incident on the reflection

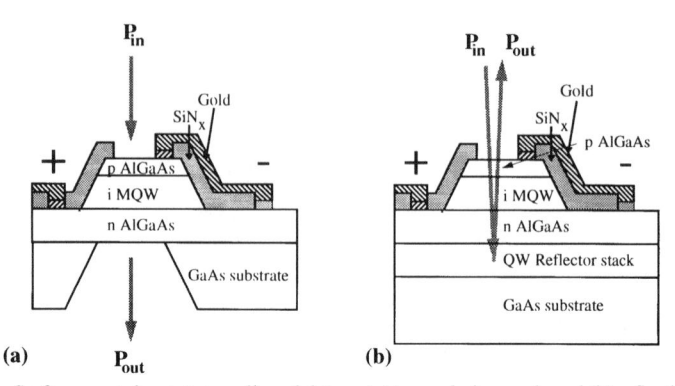

Figure 3. Surface normal quantum well modulators: (a) transmissive mode and (b) reflective mode.

modulator from the nonmirrored side. It propagates through the modulator, is reflected by the mirror, propagates back through the modulator in the other direction, and exits the modulator from the same face but in the opposite direction as the incident light beam. Polarization optics, which may not be so simple if multiple beams are incident on an array of reflection modulators of SEEDs (Prise et al. 1988), can be used to separate the input(s) from the output. The first reflective MQW modulator was made using an AlAs/AlGaAs dielectric mirror grown as part of the MBE growth between the substrate and the GaAs/AlGaAs modulator (Boyd et al. 1987). This device had the advantage that the GaAs substrate did not need to be removed, greatly simplifying fabrication. Greater contrast ratios, the ratio of the reflectivity of a device in a "high" output state to the reflectivity in a "low" output state, are possible for a given thickness of material in a reflection modulator because the optical signal passes through the quantum well region twice. Simplified mounting and improved heat sinking are possible because the device can be mounted directly onto a metallic package without the need to optically access it from both sides. The integration of optical modulators and electronic circuits may be easier using reflection modulators. Also the substrate does not need to be removed. Because of these advantages, much of the latest work on GaAs/AlGaAs SEEDs and modulators has been with reflection-mode devices.

2.2 Asymmetric Fabry-Pérot Modulators

Another type of reflection modulator uses a Fabry-Pérot cavity to improve its contrast ratio (Guy et al. 1987; Lee et al. 1988; Whitehead and Parry 1989; Whitehead, Rivers, and Parry 1989; Whitehead, Parry, and Wheatley 1989; Whitehead et al. 1990; Yan, Simes, and Coldren 1989; Pezeshki, Thomas, and Harris 1990; Boyd et al. 1991). In this devices, instead of applying an antireflection coating to the surface of the device [see Fig. 3(b)], one could epitaxially grow a dielectric mirror on the surface (similar to the one on the bottom of the modulator) or allow the reflection of the device/air interface to occur at the surface. It is possible to design a device so that this reflection will "cancel" the reflection from the back mirror. Such a device would have zero reflectivity at one applied voltage and a finite reflectivity at another applied voltage. For this to occur, the reflectivities of the front and back mirrors should be different. Because of this, these devices are often called *asymmetric Fabry-Pérot modulators* (AFPMs).

The reflectivity of a Fabry-Pérot cavity with front and back reflectivities equal to r_1 and r_2 is given by (Livescu et al. 1991):

$$R = \frac{(\sqrt{r_1} - t\sqrt{r_2})^2 + 4t\sqrt{r_1 r_2}\, sin^2\, \phi}{(1 - t\sqrt{r_1 r_2})^2 + 4t\sqrt{r_1 r_2}\, sin^2\, \phi}, \quad (1)$$

where $t = e^{-\alpha L}$ where α is the absorption coefficient of the material per unit length, L is the thickness of the quantum well region, and ϕ is equal to the phase of the total cavity length. On resonance, ϕ is equal to zero. When the numerator of Eq. (1) is equal to zero, there is no reflection and we call the cavity *matched*, in analogy to microwave matching circuits. We can subdivide AFPMs into two subclasses. Those that are matched with no applied voltage are said to be normally off and those that are matched with an applied voltage are normally on. Normally off devices will have decreasing absorption with increasing voltage and thus they are suitable for bistable SEEDs. Normally on devices are suitable as modulators or nonbistable SEEDs.

To design a device such as this, one can pick the number of quantum wells so that in the normally off condition $\sqrt{r_1} = t\sqrt{r_2}$, assuming that ϕ is an integral number of π. When an electric field is applied, αL changes and thus t changes, and the first term in the numerator is no longer zero. Also, because of the change in absorption with the electric field, there is a corresponding change in the refractive index that can be calculated using the Kramers-Kronig relations. Therefore, ϕ will no longer be an integral number times π and thus the second term in the equation is also no longer zero. This second term, the electrorefractive portion of the reflectivity change, can be as large as the electroabsorption portion of the reflectivity change (Boyd *et al.* 1991). One should be careful to include both terms when comparing different device designs.

Contrast ratios greater than 100:1 can be achieved in the laboratory on actual devices (Whitehead, Rivers, and Parry 1989). However, it will be difficult to design and fabricate many arrays of devices with that contrast ratio *at a particular wavelength*. If a 10:1 contrast ratio is required, the operating bandwidth of the device is ~3.4 nm or ±1.7 nm (Yan, Simes, and Coldren 1989). This would require material growth *accuracy* and *uniformity* to within ±0.2% (±1.7 nm/ 850 nm), which is currently beyond the capabilities of modern epitaxial growth techniques. However, if adjusting the wavelength of the laser that is being modulated is permitted, one might be able to tune the lasing wavelength to the wavelength of the Fabry-Pérot peak. Adjusting the temperature of the device might be a convenient method to align the excitonic peak wavelength with the wavelength of the Fabry-Pérot peak, because the exciton peak shifts faster as a function of temperature than the Fabry-Pérot peak (Yan and Coldren 1990). However, many applications of these devices require the devices to be designed to a specified wavelength. For example, this wavelength may be determined by the laser, as is the case with modulators designed for a Nd:YAG source at 1.064 μm.

2.3 Performance of MQW Modulators

The speed of the response of the quantum well material to an applied electric field change is estimated to be in the range of 50 to 200 fs (Schmitt-Rink *et al.* 1990). Therefore, the speed of the response of a quantum well modulator will be limited by how fast the electric field can be applied, which is limited by the circuit inductances and capacitances. Single devices in a waveguide geometry have been made that have 3-dB bandwidths equal to 40 GHz (Wakita *et al.* 1990). The fact that it was a waveguide device is a matter of choice, and a transverse device most likely could have been made at this speed. For arrays of devices, the maximum speed would be slower, because the line capacitances associated with each device would be greater. A 2×4 array of devices has been made with a 3-dB bandwidth in excess of 3 GHz (Lentine *et al.* 1990a), and a 16×8 array of devices has been made that shows rise times of ~300 ps (Chirovsky *et al.* 1991). Better performance could have been achieved in either of these two cases by further optimization of the electrical circuit. However, there is a limit to how fast one can modulate an array of devices, because of the difficulty in providing a large number of electrical interconnections. Indeed, this is the very limit that one hopes to avoid by using optical rather than electrical interconnections within large electronic systems.

One could of course use matrix addressing to get around the large number of electrical connections that needs to be input to an array of MQW modulators. For certain applications such as neural computing or electronic control of multistage interconnection networks with slow reconfiguration rates, this is an acceptable method to reduce the number of pinouts on and off of a modulator array. However, for many applications this is not acceptable. The solution to increasing the amount of information that can be brought onto or off of a chip is to have optical inputs and outputs. The remainder of this chapter addresses devices such as these.

3. Self-Electro-Optic Effect Devices

So far we have discussed the modulation of absorption of quantum well materials and some specific MQW transverse modulators. These devices are useful both for communications systems as well as some optical processing applications. However, for many optical processing applications, we desire devices that have optical inputs and optical outputs and that perform some sort of Boolean logic. Devices of this type that use the modulation of absorption in quantum wells are called *self-electro-optic effect devices* (SEEDs). The basic principle of a SEED is to use the current detected in a photodetector to change the electric field across the quantum well region of the modulators. These devices have optical inputs and optical outputs and are called *optical* logic devices, even though electrical currents flow within the devices. If the photodetector and modulator are integrated, the SEED can be quite efficient, and is one of the lowest energy devices demonstrated for optical processing.

In the rest of this chapter, we discuss various configurations of SEEDs. We begin by discussing resistor biased and photodiode-biased SEEDs. Although these devices are interesting, they are not terribly useful for optical processing because they are intrinsically *two-terminal* devices. Then we discuss the symmetric SEED, a device that has many of the characteristics of a three-terminal device. We discuss extensions of the S-SEED and discuss three-terminal transistor-biased devices.

Last, we discuss processing elements or "smart pixels" that have more functionality than standard (OR, NOR, AND, NAND) logic gates.

3.1 Resistor-Biased SEEDs

The first SEED used a single modulator in series with a resistor as shown in Fig. 4 (Miller *et al.* 1984b). In this device the *p-i-n* diode modulator also acts as the photodetector. The operation of the device can be described as follows. Suppose initially that no light is incident on the photodetector. Then, since there is no current, the power supply voltage essentially appears across the photodiode. As we increase the optical input power, the photocurrent causes a voltage drop across the resistor, and the voltage across the photodiode decreases. If we operate the device at a wavelength for which a decrease in voltage causes an increase in absorption, then this increase in absorption causes an increase in photocurrent. This increase in photocurrent causes a larger voltage drop across the resistor, further reduction in voltage across the photodiode, further increase in absorption, and further increase in photocurrent. This will continue until the quantum efficiency of the photodiode drops off as it approaches forward bias (near 0 V). The net result is that the device switches abruptly from a high- to a low-voltage state. (A similar argument can explain switching in the reverse direction.) Since we assumed increasing absorption with decreasing voltage, this switching from the high- to the low-voltage state corresponds to the optical output being switched from a high to the low optical state.

3.2 Diode-Biased SEEDs

Because it was somewhat difficult to integrate the resistors and the quantum well *p-i-n* diodes, arrays of bistable SEEDs were made that use photodiodes for the load instead of resistors (Miller *et al.* 1986; Livescu *et al.* 1988). This diode-biased SEED (D-SEED) consisted of a vertically integrated quantum well diode, ohmic connection (tunnel junction), and photodiode as shown in Fig. 5. The bias and signal beams at 850 nm passed through the load photodiode and were incident on the quantum well *p-i-n* diode, and a bias beam at 633 nm, for example, was

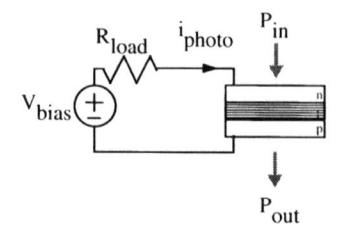

Figure 4. Resistor-biased SEED. ©1985 IEEE.

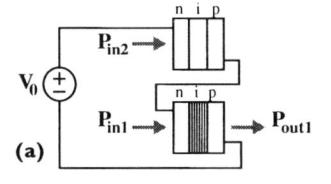

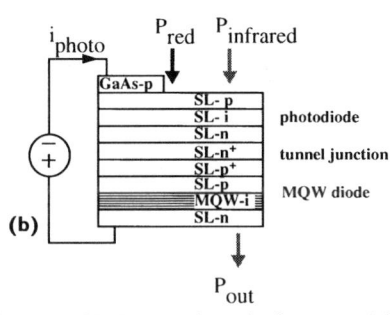

Figure 5. Diode-biased SEED (D-SEED): (a) schematic diagram and (b) layer structure (Miller *et al.* 1986).

absorbed in the load photodiode. The operating range of the devices could be scaled by adjusting this optical bias on the photodiode over a range of more than 7 decades in power. Also, the device could act as a dynamic memory, where the device could hold either of its two states for up to 30 s with both the red beam and infrared beams removed (Livescu *et al.* 1988). Simultaneously applying both beams allowed read-out of the memory state. Finally, the red beam could be used to switch the infrared beam such that an array could be thought of as visible to an infrared modulation converter or even an incoherent to coherent light modulation converter (Livescu *et al.* 1988). Both 2 × 2 arrays of 200-μm² D-SEEDs (Miller *et al.* 1986) and 6 × 6 arrays of 60-μm² D-SEEDs (Livescu *et al.* 1988) have been made.

3.3 Symmetric SEEDs

Bistable devices such as these are effectively two-terminal devices and require precise control of power supply voltages, bias beam powers, and reflections of the output back onto the system (Miller 1988). Three-terminal devices, which avoid critical biasing and provide some input/output isolation, are preferred for optical processing applications. Two devices will be described that have the characteristics of three-terminal devices. One device, the symmetric SEED (Lentine *et al.* 1989a) uses differential inputs and is bistable in the ratio of the two inputs. The second approach is to use separate photodetectors and modulators with electronic transistors for the gain mechanism (Miller 1985, 1987; Miller *et al.* 1989; Wheatley *et al.* 1987). Devices of this second type that have been made so far use single-ended inputs, which requires input contrast ratios of ~10:1 to avoid critical biasing.

The S-SEED shown in Fig. 6 has two *p-i-n* diodes, each containing quantum wells in the intrinsic region, with one diode behaving as the load for the other (and vice versa). Because the switching of the device depends on the ratio of the two optical inputs, the S-SEED is therefore insensitive to optical power supply fluctuations if both beams are derived from the same source. The device has time-sequential gain, in that the state of the device can be set with low-power beams and read out with subsequent high-power beams. The device also shows good input/output isolation, because the large output does not coincide in time with the application of the input signals. Therefore, the device does not require the critical biasing that is common to most optically bistable devices, and it has the attributes of a three-terminal device.

S-SEEDs have evolved rapidly from the first "laboratory-type" devices (Lentine *et al.* 1987) to monolithic arrays of devices made using techniques found on GaAs integrated circuit production facilities (Chirovsky *et al.* 1989). Arrays of S-SEEDs with as many as 32,768 devices have now been made (Chirovsky *et al.* 1991) and arrays with as many as 2048 devices are commercially available. A diagram of the layer structure used in these devices and a photograph of part of an array of S-SEEDs are shown in Figs. 6(b) and (c).

In operation, two sets of two beams are incident on the device as shown in Fig. 7(a). First, a set of unequal power beams (signal beams) sets the state of the device. Provided the difference in power between the signal beams is sufficiently large, we can force the device to be in one of two possible states. A contrast ratio of 2:1 is more than sufficient to ensure this, and since the signal beams will likely be derived from the output of another S-SEED, the contrast ratio will normally be greater than 2:1. Since the currents from the first diode and load diode scale with input power, it is only the ratio of the two input powers that determines the operating point. Thus, if both input signal beams are derived from the same laser, any variations of the laser power will occur in both beams, and the device will be insensitive to these fluctuations.

The second set of beams consists of equal-power clock beams that are used to read the state of the device. During the application of the signal beams, the clock beam powers must be low compared to the signal beam powers. Because the state of the device is determined by the ratio of the total power incident on each of the two quantum well *p-i-n* diodes, any clock power present when the signal beams are trying to set the state of the device will effectively degrade the contrast ratio of the input beams, possibly causing the device not to switch. After the state of the device has been set, we apply the equal power clock beams to each diode to read the state. The device will only be bistable when the optical input power levels are comparable, and will have only a single state when the power in one diode

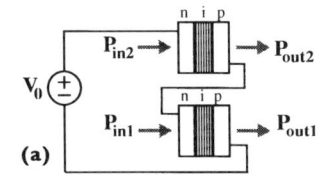

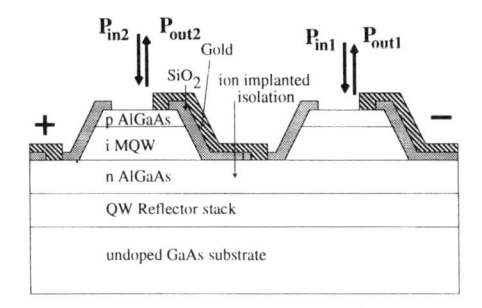

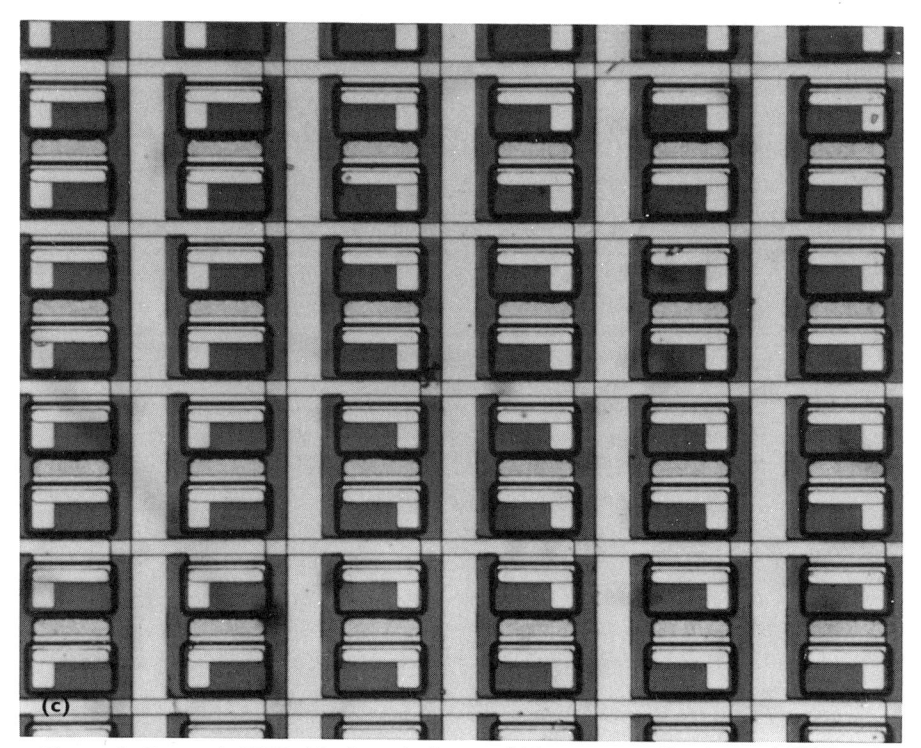

Figure 6. Symmetric SEED: (a) schematic diagram, (b) layer structure (Lentine *et al.* 1989), and (c) photograph of a section of a 32 × 32 array of devices. ©1989 IEEE.

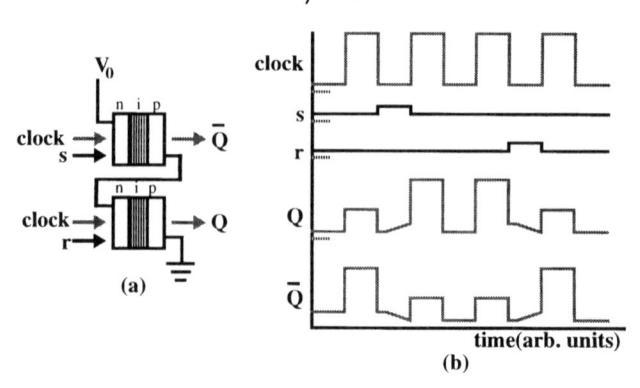

Figure 7. S-SEED operating as a clocked set-reset flip-flop: (a) schematic diagram and (b) timing diagram. ©1989 IEEE.

significantly exceeds the power in the other. Therefore, when reading the state of the device, the two clock beams must have sufficiently equal optical powers to ensure that the device remains in the bistable region, so that either state can be read out without altering it.

This device has an interesting attribute that we call *time-sequential gain*. Because the currents in both the first diode and load diode scale with input power, the operating point when read out will be independent of clock power and only dependent on the state of the device before the clocks were applied. Therefore, the input clock powers may be many times greater than the input signal powers that were used to set the state of the device, and the device has optical gain as illustrated in Fig. 7(b). It is not optical gain in the sense of an optical amplifier where the optical signal itself is amplified, but, in this device, the weaker signal beams control a set of stronger clock beams, much like in a bipolar transistor in which a weaker base current controls a stronger collector current. Because we apply the signal beams first and then the clock beams, we refer to this as time-sequential gain. In addition, because the output does not coincide in time with the application of the input, the device has effective input/output isolation in that a reflection of the output signal back onto the input will not occur at a time when the device is most sensitive to the input. Since the device can hold its state (i.e., the voltage on the two diodes) for a short period of time without any incident light, it does not matter if there is a time between the removal of the signal beams and the application of the clock beams where no light is present. Therefore, the timing of the optical inputs is not critical.

Since bistability is typically observed over several decades in optical powers (Lentine *et al.* 1990b), we can have a large effective signal gain. Of course, switching at low powers take proportionately longer, so that gain is obtained at the expense of switching speed. Thus, the device has a constant gain-bandwidth

Self-Electro-Optic Effect Devices for Optical Information Processing   57

product, just like many other amplifiers. The amount of gain in a system built entirely with S-SEEDs will be determined by the absorption losses in the devices themselves, the fan-out of the devices, and reflections, absorption, and scattering losses in the optical components used to interconnect the devices. We want to minimize these losses so that the signal beams will be as large as possible and the switching time will be small. We discuss the switching times of these devices in more detail later.

Since the S-SEED has many desirable qualities, such as insensitivity to optical power supply fluctuations and time-sequential gain, we would like to be able to perform logic functions (such as NOR, OR, NAND, and AND) in addition to memory functions (i.e., set-reset latch). We would like the inputs to be differential, thus still avoiding any critical biasing of the device. One way to achieve a logic gate operation is shown in Fig. 8(a). We will define the logic level of the inputs as being represented by the power of the signal on the set input relative to the power

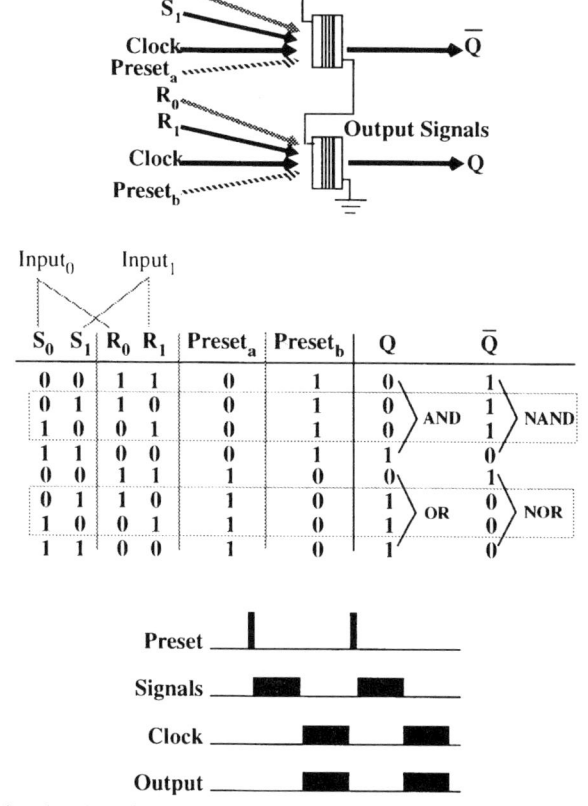

S_0	S_1	R_0	R_1	$Preset_a$	$Preset_b$	Q	$\bar{Q}$		
0	0	1	1	0	1	0	1		
0	1	1	0	0	1	0	1	AND	NAND
1	0	0	1	0	1	0	1		
1	1	0	0	0	1	1	0		
0	0	1	1	1	0	0	1		
0	1	1	0	1	0	1	0	OR	NOR
1	0	0	1	1	0	1	0		
1	1	0	0	1	0	1	0		

Figure 8. Logic using the S-SEED, showing a schematic diagram, a timing diagram, and a truth table. ©1989 IEEE.

of the signal incident on the reset input. For example, when the power of the signal incident on the set input is greater than the power of the signal on the reset input we will call this a logic "1." For the noninverting gates, OR and AND, we can represent the output logic level by the power of the signal coming from the Q output relative to the power of the signal coming from the $\bar{Q}$ output. As before, when the power of the signal incident coming from the Q output is greater than the power of the signal on the $\bar{Q}$ output, we will call this a logic "1." To achieve AND operation, the device is initially set to its off or logic "0" state (i.e., Q low and $\bar{Q}$ high) will preset pulse B incident on only one p-i-n diode as shown in Fig. 7. If both of the input signals have logic levels of 1 (i.e., set = 1, reset = 0), then the S-SEED AND gate is set to its on state. For any other input combination, there is no change of state, resulting in AND operation. After the signal beams determine the state of the device, the clock beams are then set high to read out the state of the AND gate. For NAND operation, we simply redefine the logic level as being represented by the power of the $\bar{Q}$ output signal relative to the power of the Q output signal. That is, when the power of the signal incident coming from the Q output is greater than the power of the signal on the Q output, we will now call this a logic "1." The operation of the OR and NOR gates is identical to the AND and NAND gates except that preset a is used instead of preset b. Thus, a single array of devices can perform any or all of the four logic functions and memory functions with the proper optical interconnections and preset pulse routing.

3.4 Multistate SEEDs

The S-SEED concept can be extended to any number of diodes connected in series with a voltage source (Lentine *et al.* 1989b) as shown in Fig. 9. Each diode in these multistate SEEDs (M-SEEDs) has states of high or low optical output. For a device with N diodes, only the diode with the least input power will have a high optical output and the others will have a low optical output. For three such diodes, the device acts as an enabled S-SEED, in which the light beam incident on the

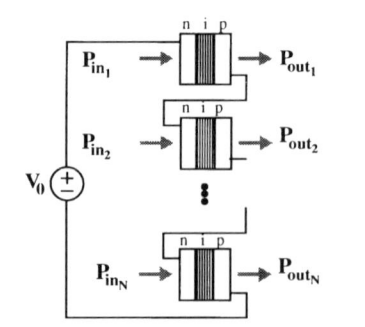

Figure 9. Voltage-biased M-SEED. ©1989 IEEE.

added third diode acts as an enable input. When the enable input is high, the remaining two diodes act as a symmetric SEED. However, when the enable input is low, all the voltage appears across the enable diode, no voltage appears across each of the two output diodes, and both outputs are low. Thus the device has three states, two active states in which the two output beams have complementary outputs, and an inactive or *high-impedance* state in which both outputs have a low output. A simple *tri-state* bus has been demonstrated using the outputs from two such devices to switch a third one (Lentine *et al.* 1990c).

3.5 Transistor-Biased SEEDs

A second class of three-terminal SEEDs has transistors that provide gain between the photodetector and modulator. To date, two classes of devices have been made. One class consists of a heterojunction phototransistor in series with a quantum well modulator (Miller 1985, 1987; Wheatley *et al.* 1987) as shown in Fig. 10. The heterojunction phototransistor may even have quantum wells in the base-collector junction (Sugimoto, Tashiro, and Hamao 1987) and may also be placed in parallel with the *p-i-n* diode in a conventional (resistively biased) SEED (Hong and Singh 1989). A second "amplified" SEED consisted of a quantum well photodiode, a GaAs MESFET, and a quantum well modulator (Miller *et al.* 1989). In this second example, the quantum well detector and modulator are identical. The top layer of the modulator was made of *n*-type GaAs and thus the MESFETs were fabricated directly on top of modulators as shown in Fig. 11. There were some compromises made in the structure; the *n*-type layer is somewhat absorbing (although it was thin) and the *p*-type layer beneath the FETs adds to an increased gate-drain capacitance, but the fabrication of the device was nearly identical to standard MESFET processing.

As optical logic devices, either the phototransistor version of the devices or the MESFET versions are similar. Both devices are single-ended devices that switch when the input(s) exceed a threshold. Such a device cannot be operated over a wide dynamic range unless the threshold is set optically. Also, these devices are not latching, so retiming of the data is not done automatically at each device stage. Last, if the expected input contrast ratio is poor, the device can be said to be *critically biased* in the sense that a small variation of the input signals can cause

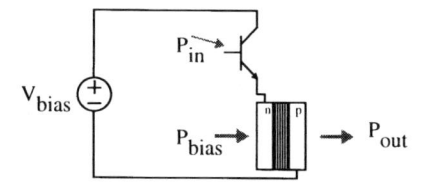

Figure 10. Transistor-biased SEED schematic diagram.

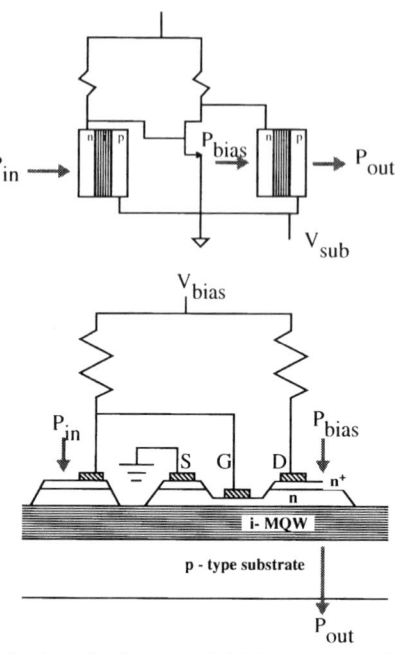

Figure 11. FET-SEED: (a) schematic diagram and (b) layer structure (Miller *et al.* 1989; ©1989 IEEE).

the device to switch. This third problem can be overcome if high-contrast quantum well modulators are available. We discussed the use of Fabry-Pérot cavities to improve the contrast ratio of reflection modulators. Of course, we can make differential devices incorporating electronic gain. These devices may be preferable since they avoid the need for "thresholding" all together. Indeed, the purpose of building these devices was more to demonstrate the capabilities to integrate monolithically electronic transistors and quantum well modulators together, rather than to demonstrate the particular logic gate they had implemented.

3.6 Energy Requirements in SEEDs

We mentioned earlier that the optical energy required in SEEDs is among the lowest of all devices proposed for switching. We show how to calculate this switching energy for S-SEEDs. For all SEEDs without electronic transistors the calculations are similar. Last, we comment on energy improvements that could be expected by using electronic transistors for gain.

The required energy can be calculated by the time it takes to charge the capacitance of the device with the photocurrent. We can model each diode in the S-

SEED by a photocurrent source in parallel with a capacitor. If we use Kirchoff's current law at the center node of the two diodes (see Fig. 6), we get:

$$P_{in_2} S(V_0 - V) - P_{in_1} S(V) = C\frac{dV}{dt} - C\frac{d(V_0 - V)}{dt}, \quad (2)$$

where C is the capacitance of a single *p-i-n* diode, P_{in_1} and P_{in_2} are the optical input powers incident on the first and second diodes, respectively, $S(V)$ and $S(V_0 - V)$ are the responsivities of the two diodes, V_0 is the power supply voltage, and V is the voltage across the bottom *p-i-n* diode. This expression is difficult to calculate directly, so we can make an approximation by assuming that the responsivity of the two diodes is constant and given by $\bar{S}$ and assuming dV/dt is equal to the voltage swing V_s divided by the switching time Δt. The voltage swing is approximately equal to the supply voltage V_0 plus twice the forward bias voltage V_f, because the device switches from one diode being slightly in forward bias to the other diode being slightly in forward bias. This forward-bias voltage is approximately equal to 1V. Substituting these quantities in Eq. (2) gives us:

$$\Delta t = \frac{C_{tot}(V_0 + 2V_f)}{\bar{S}(P_{in_2} - P_{in_1})}, \quad (3)$$

where C_{tot} is the total device capacitance across the two quantum well *p-i-n* diodes plus any additional parasitic capacitances. This method of calculating switching speeds ignores the effects of critical slowing down that are present in any bistable device. Therefore, if the input signals have rise times that are comparable to the switching time or if the ratio of the powers of the input signals only slightly exceeds the required ratio, one must solve Eq. (2) to calculate the switching speed.

We could define an optical switching energy E_{opt} that is equal to the additional optical energy that would have to be provided by a single additional beam to switch a symmetrically biased device. An approximation to E_{opt} can be found by multiplying both sides of Eq. (3) by the difference in the optical power levels incident on the two diodes. This gives,

$$E_{opt} = \Delta t \, \Delta P = \frac{C_{tot}(V_0 + 2V_f)}{\bar{S}}, \quad (4)$$

where $\Delta P = P_{in_2} - P_{in_1}$. Equation (4) shows that the speed and power scale inversely and the switching energy remains constant. [This is also evident from the exact solution to Eq. (2).]

There is also an electrical switching energy which can be defined as

$$E_{elect.} = \frac{1}{2} C_{tot}(V_0 + 2V_f)^2. \quad (5)$$

The simplest way to reduce the optical and electrical energies of the devices is to reduce the area and hence the capacitance, since both the electrical and optical switching energies are linearly related to the device capacitance. Measurements on devices with an area ranging from 100 to 10,000 μm^2 indicated an optical switching energy of ~7.5 fJ/μm^2 compared to a calculated number of ~5.9 fJ/μm^2 (Lentine et al. 1989c). The results demonstrated approximate scaling of energy with device size as expected. However, as device sizes become less than 5 μm × 5 μm, the optical system design and optomechanics design required to use the devices becomes much more difficult.

Further energy improvements without reductions in device sizes can be achieved by reducing the voltage swing in switching from one state to the other, provided the capacitance per unit area remains the same. An alternate way of stating this is that the required optical energy is proportional to the applied electric field (Miller 1990). The preceding measurements of required optical switching energies were for devices biased at 15 V with a voltage swing of 17 V. Self-biased S-SEEDs that have only a 2-V swing have been made using devices with asymmetric coupled wells (Goossen et al. 1990) and ultrashallow barriers (Goossen, Cunningham, and Jan 1990; Morgan et al. 1991). Unfortunately, none of these devices was fully integrated, so energies really could not be measured. Recently, an array of integrated S-SEEDs with ~5-μm × 10-μm optical windows has been made with an extra set of clamping diodes that allows operation with a 2-V swing by maintaining a moderate electric field across both diodes of the S-SEED at all times (Lentine et. al., 1992a). These devices had contrast ratios greater than 2:1 and measured optical switching energies as low as 340 fJ.

Another way to reduce the optical energies of S-SEEDs is to operate them as optical sense amplifiers to make them more sensitive to small signal inputs (Chirovsky, Lentine, and Miller 1989). For the S-SEED operating as a sense amplifier, a set of equal intensity beams with a wavelength (λ_1) several nanometers longer than the zero field excitonic peak wavelength (λ_0) is first applied to the device. At this wavelength, the device is *not* bistable and switches to its only stable operating point with essentially half of the supply voltage across each diode. Then the signal beams at λ_0 are applied. Recall that at λ_0, the device has two stable states consisting of approximately the supply voltage across one diode and no voltage across the other. Because, when the signal beams are initially applied, the voltage across each diode is half the supply voltage, the device is initially unstable. Therefore, any small difference in the set and reset input beams will start to switch the device toward one of its two stable states. Once, the device has been at least partially switched by the signal beams, the equal higher power clock beams (λ_0) can complete the switching. In practice, a factor of 4 improvement in the required optical signal and clock beam energies has been achieved using sense amplification in a photonic ring counter (Lentine et al. 1991).

Electronic gain has been touted as improving the required switching energy of the devices. Unfortunately, none of the devices described in the literature to date has accomplished this. For example, in the transistor-biased devices shown in Fig. 10, the base-collector capacitance needs to be charged directly with the photocurrent, not the amplified photocurrent. This is a direct result of the Miller capacitance that is present in common emitter or common source transistor amplifiers. More sophisticated circuits may be used to avoid this. For example, the first stage may provide current gain and latter stages voltage gain. However, more complex circuits require more chip area. Also, some of these circuits may reduce the required optical energies, but still require large electrical energies. In spite of these warnings, electronic gain offers perhaps the best potential for reducing the required optical energies of the devices.

The switching times of S-SEEDs have been measured as ~33 ps using mode-locked pulses (Boyd et al. 1990). The switching time of the device in that experiment was limited by the time it takes the carriers to escape from the quantum wells. The RC time constant of the devices from the ohmic contact resistances was ~5 ps (Boyd et al. 1990), the charging time of the capacitance from the photocurrent was ~2 ps (Boyd et al. 1990), and the "response time" of the quantum confined Stark effect is estimated to be a few hundred femtoseconds (Schmitt-Rink et al. 1990). We would expect the switching times of other SEEDs without transistors to be similar because the physical mechanisms that govern the operation of the devices and the device fabrication are similar. For transistor-based SEEDs, the carrier transit times through the base or channel regions is generally on the order of tens of picoseconds.

The switching times of the devices *in a system* are generally limited by the charging time of the device capacitance with the photocurrent. This photocurrent is directly proportional to the optical power of the input beams, which are derived from the outputs of one or more other devices after passing through some interconnection optics. The optical powers of these input beams are limited by saturation of the absorption of the quantum well material in the device whose state is being read and by the losses of the devices and the interconnection optics between the devices. A photonic ring counter has been made by cascading two S-SEEDs. This counter has a switching time of 40 ns when the devices are operated conventionally and 10 ns when the devices are operated as signal sense amplifiers (Lentine et al. 1991). A fundamental limit has not been reached in that experiment because the absorption losses of the devices could be reduced (perhaps new materials or new quantum well designs), the losses of the optical system could be reduced (fewer aberrations and better antireflection coatings on all of the elements), the required electric field change of the devices in going from one state to another could be reduced (self-biased SEEDs or SEEDs with electronic gain), and perhaps the devices could be made smaller. Because the physical mechanisms that limit the intrinsic speeds of the devices are fast, the key to making SEEDs operate at high bit rates in systems is to reduce the absorptive losses of the devices and of the optical system and reduce the required optical and electrical energies as much as possible.

4. Smart Pixels

While optical processing systems can be built using simple AND and OR gates alone, systems using logic gates of more complex functionality may enable more optimal systems to be built, that is, systems that require less laser power per device array, fewer device arrays, fewer optical components, or offer more tolerance to signal variations or mechanical misalignments. In this last section, we discuss two classes of devices that perform more complex functions. The first class of devices are logic SEEDs (L-SEEDs), which consist of only quantum well *p-i-n* diodes (Lentine *et al.* 1990d). L-SEEDs are fabricated using the same procedures as S-SEEDs. Various functions have been demonstrated. These include differential logic gates that do not require preset beams; devices performing the function $E = AB + CD$, which can act as an exclusive OR gate or a photonic switching node; and devices that can be optically programmed to act as switching nodes, multiplexers, demultiplexers, or optoelectronic shift registers.

We also discuss the case of quantum well modulators and detectors integrated with electronic VLSI circuitry. To date, the only demonstrated integration of this has been the single transistor demonstration of the F-SEED (Miller *et al.* 1989). However, a VLSI electronics-quantum well modulator smart pixel technology offers significant advantages over the L-SEEDs. We compare the two technologies at the end of this section.

4.1 Logic SEEDs

The basic concept of a L-SEED is illustrated in Fig. 12. The L-SEED consists of a group of input diodes with incident input signals and a pair of output diodes (i.e., an S-SEED) that modulates a pair of equal power clock beams to provide the output. The input diodes need not have quantum wells, although improved switch-

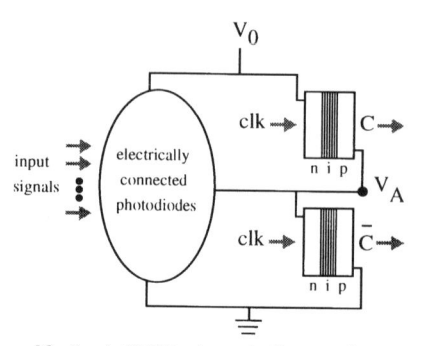

Figure 12. Logic SEED schematic diagram. ©1992 IEEE.

ing may result if they do (Lentine *et al.* 1990d). Operation starts when the input signals are applied. The photocurrents generated in these input diodes sets the output node voltage V_n. Subsequently, a pair of higher power clock beams is applied to the output S-SEED to read the state. This operation achieves the same time-sequential gain mechanism found in the S-SEED and performs retiming, logic level restoration, and wavefront quality restoration. In this chapter we will only consider the differential L-SEEDs in which a pair of beams represents the logic state of the inputs, although devices whose logic state is represented by the power levels of a single beam could also be made (Lentine *et al.* 1990d).

For differential L-SEEDs, the topology of the electrical connections between input diodes is identical to that of CMOS circuits. To obtain the required L-SEED layout, the *n*-channel devices in a CMOS circuit are replaced by diodes with incident uncomplemented signal inputs, and the *p*-channel devices in the CMOS circuit are replaced by diodes that have complemented inputs.

As an example, consider an L-SEED to implement the function $E = AB + CD$ as shown in Fig. 13. This function implements a 2 × 1 switching node if *A* and

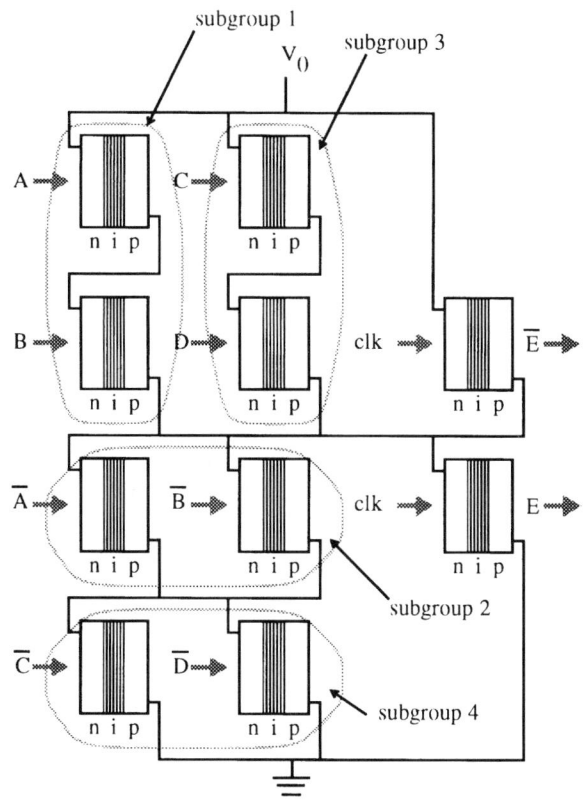

Figure 13. Logic SEED implementing the function $E = AB + CD$. ©1992 IEEE.

C are the two data input channels and B and D are the two control channels. It can also implement an exclusive OR function if $A = X$, $B = \overline{Y}$, $C = \overline{X}$, and $D = Y$. For a switching node, if control input B is a logic 1 and control input D is a logic 0, then output E is equal to data input A. Likewise, if control input B is a logic 0 and control input D is a logic 1, then output E is equal to data input C. The device arrays are differential in that the logic state of each data and control input as well the output are represented by the ratio of optical powers of two light beams. An input has a logic 1 state when the uncomplemented input is greater than the complemented input (e.g., $A > \overline{A}$).

The operation of the device can be described as follows. We can assume that, if a diode has a logic 1 incident optical signal, it will electrically go into forward bias and can be thought of as a "short circuit" across its electrical terminals. A device with a logic 0 incident on it will remain in reverse bias and can be thought of as an "open circuit." If inputs A and B are logic 1's, inputs $\overline{A}$ and $\overline{B}$ must be logic 0's because the data are complementary. Thus, subgroup 1 will be short circuited and subgroup 2 will be open circuited. Therefore, V_n will be equal to $\sim V_0$ and, when the clock beams are applied, E will be high. Similarly, if inputs C and D are logic 1's, subgroup 3 will be short circuited and subgroup 4 will be open circuited. Therefore, V_n will also be equal to $\sim V_0$ and, when the clock beams are applied, E will be high. However, if A or B is a logic 0 and C or D is a logic 0, subgroups 1 and 3 will be open circuited and subgroups 2 and 4 will be short circuited. Therefore, V_n will also be equal to ~ 0 and, when the clock beams are applied, E will be low.

The L-SEED concept can be extended to devices that contain optoelectronic transmission gates. These optoelectronic transmission gates consist of two back-to-back photodiodes and perform the function of a transmission gate in CMOS circuits. Like their electronic counterparts, these devices electrically transfer the logic state from one device to another under external control, but in these devices the control is optical.

To make a 2 × 1 photonic switching node, three S-SEEDs and two of these optoelectronic transmission gates are connected as shown in Fig. 14 (Lentine et al. 1992b). In operation, first we apply the data inputs A, $\overline{A}$, C, and $\overline{C}$ and the control inputs B and D to the switching node and subsequently apply the clock beams, clk, which are modulated by S2 to give the output data E and $\overline{E}$. Control inputs B and D are complementary. If control input B is greater than control input D (i.e., $B = 1$ and $D = 0$), then V_2 will be equal to V_1 and output E will be equal to data input A. However, if control input B is less than control input D (i.e., $B = 0$ and $D = 1$), then V_2 will be equal to V_3 and output E will be equal to data input C.

An optoelectronic shift register can be made using optoelectronic transmission gates as shown in Fig. 15. First, the input signals set the state of the first S-SEED, S1. Next, the clock beams clk1 and transfer beams Trn1 are applied simultane-

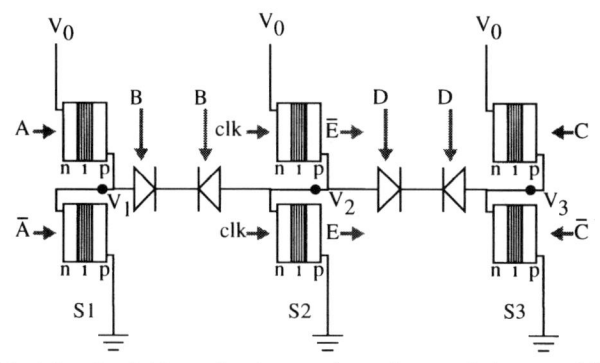

Self-Electro-Optic Effect Devices for Optical Information Processing 67

Figure 14. A 2 × 1 switching node using optoelectronic transmission gates. ©1992 IEEE.

ously. The clock beams provide an optical output signal from $S1$ and hold the state of $S2$ while transfer beams $Trn1$ transfer that state electrically to $S2$. Then, clock beams $clk2$ and transfer beams $Trn2$ are applied to S-SEED $S2$ and transmission gate $T2$ to read the state of $S2$ and transfer the voltage on $S2$ to $S3$. Simultaneously, the input signals are applied setting the new state of $S1$. Analogous to electronic shift registers, the odd-numbered S-SEEDs are called *master flip-flops* and the even-numbered S-SEEDs are called *slave flip-flops*. Because of the two-cycle nature of the clock beams, two S-SEEDs (a master-slave flip-flop) holds one bit of information. Thus, $2N$ S-SEEDs implement an N-bit shift register.

4.2 Integration of MQW Modulators and Electronic Circuits

In Section 3.5, transistors were incorporated with quantum well modulators and detectors to provide gain and input/output isolation. However, perhaps a more important application of this technology is to use the detectors and modulators to interconnect electronic circuitry. There are at least two physical configurations of this that may make sense. The first approach is to concentrate the optical inputs and outputs in a two-dimensional array surrounded by electronic circuitry, as

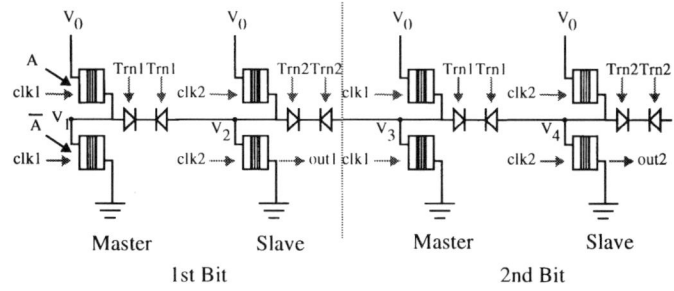

Figure 15. Optical shift register using optoelectronic transmission gates. ©1992 IEEE.

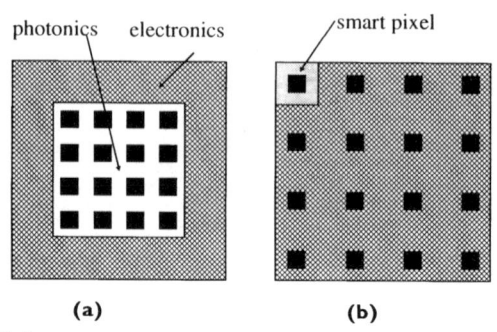

Figure 16. Optically interconnected electronic circuits: (a) physically separated electronic circuitry, detectors, and modulators, and (b) integrated electronic circuitry, detectors, and modulators (smart pixels).

shown in Fig. 16(a). This array of optical inputs and outputs may be a modulator array, a detector array, or an array of devices, such as the ones described in this chapter, that can act as both modulators and detectors. The approach in Fig. 16(a) is probably the simplest to implement today, because the electronics, the modulators, and the detectors would not need to be integrated monolithically. Another advantage of this approach is that the optical field of view is relatively small, although it will be significantly larger than a S-SEED array with the same number of inputs and outputs, because the devices will need to be spread apart to allow electrical connections to the modulators and detectors. However, the disadvantage of this approach is that the interconnections will be limited by the number of electrical paths that one can reasonably get into the modulator and detector arrays (limited most likely by crosstalk), much like today's electronic chips are limited by the number of input/output pads around the periphery of the chips.

Another approach is to integrate the electronics monolithically with the optical inputs and outputs as shown in Fig. 16(b). This approach, often referred to as *smart pixels,* solves the wiring problem because all electrical interconnections are short. However, this approach has the disadvantage of requiring a larger optical field of view and requires the monolithic integration of the electronics and the quantum well modulators, something that has been demonstrated on a small scale as was discussed with the F-SEEDs (Miller *et al.* 1989), but has not yet been done on a large scale. Although promising results have been shown growing quantum well modulators on silicon substrates (Dobbelaere *et al.* 1988, Goossen *et al.* 1989), the integration of quantum well devices with silicon VLSI has not been done. Integration of MQW modulators and detectors with silicon VLSI is advantageous over integration with GaAs electronic circuitry because higher density electronic circuits have been achieved with silicon. However, higher performance optoelectronic devices may be possible using MQW modulators integrated with GaAs electronics.

There are several advantages to monolithically integrated electronic smart pixel technologies compared to L-SEEDs. The most important of these is that the required optical energies of electronic smart pixels may be less. This is because electronic gain may be able to reduce the required input voltage swing of the detectors from the 5 to 10 V required by SEEDs to perhaps a few tenths of a volt. This translates somewhat indirectly into reduced required optical switching energies, provided intelligent circuit designs are used. Optical energies of a few tens of femtojoules should be achievable with detectors with 5-μm $\times$ 5-μm optical windows. This is not true in a hybrid electronic smart pixel technology where the detectors are not integrated with the electronics because the capacitance of a bonding pad (even with bump-bonding) would be much larger than the detector capacitance and would negate any energy advantage a reduced input voltage swing would have. A second advantage of transistor-based smart pixels is that they would not require multiple optical appearances of inputs to perform some functions, such as the L-SEED in Fig. 13 operated as an exclusive OR gate. For transistor-based smart pixels there may be only one appearance of these inputs and electronic buffer stages to isolate the detected voltages or currents generated by the optical inputs from the logic gates. Last, the complexity of the node could be greater in optically interconnected electronic smart pixels. For example, it does not seem feasible to build arrays of L-SEED microprocessors or 16-Mbit S-SEED memories.

The main advantage of L-SEEDs is their ease of fabrication. If the required optical energies could be reduced by a factor of 10 to 100 over today's devices, perhaps from improved quantum well structures and significantly reduced sizes, L-SEEDs may be viable to use in future commercial systems. If not, L-SEEDs still give a performance that is acceptable for experimental system demonstrations and can be a valuable learning tool for designing future optical processors.

5. Conclusion

In this chapter we described quantum well modulators and self-electro-optic effect devices for use in optical processing systems. SEEDs performing a variety of functions have been built and tested. These devices have many desirable characteristics compared to other devices proposed for optical processing. These include gain without critical biasing, signal logic level restoration, timing restoration, wavefront quality restoration, and operation over decades in optical powers. SEEDs have been made in large two-dimensional integrated arrays with as many as 256 $\times$ 128 elements (Chirovsky *et al.* 1991) with uniform characteristics, and the devices can operate with extremely low powers (tens of nanowatts). These important attributes of SEEDs have enabled several optical processing and photonic switching system demonstrations to be built (Prise *et al.* 1990; Cloonan *et al.* 1990; McCormick *et al.* 1991a, 1991b) with up to 2000 devices optically cascaded from one array to the next. Perhaps the most important improvement that remains to be made in the devices is to lower their required optical energies, so that these "optical processing" systems can be built at data rates that are competitive with what can be achieved in all-electronic systems.

ACKNOWLEDGMENTS

I gratefully acknowledge many employees at AT&T Bell Laboratories who contributed to the some of the work described in this chapter. In particular, I would like to thank D. A. B. Miller and L. M. F. Chirovsky for many valuable discussions on SEEDs and for designing many of the devices described in this chapter; L. A. D'Asaro, J. E. Cunningham, M. W. Focht, J. M. Freund, G. D. Guth, J. E. Henry, R. F. Kopf, J. M. Kuo, R. E. Leibenguth, G. J. Przyblyk, L. E. Smith, and C. W. Tu for material growth and fabrication of those devices; R. A. Novotny for help in characterizing these devices; T. J. Cloonan, F. B. McCormick, F. A. P. Tooley, M. E. Prise, and N. C. Craft for discussions on the applications of the devices to digital optical computing and switching; and H. S. Hinton and S. J. Hinterlong for giving overall direction and support of much of this work.

REFERENCES

Boyd, G. D., Miller, D. A. B., Chemla, D. S., McCall, S. L., Gossard, A. C., and English, J. H. (1987). *Appl. Phys. Lett.* **50,** 1119–1121.
Boyd, G. D., Fox, A. M., Miller, D. A. B., Chirovsky, L. M. F., D'Asaro, L. A., Kuo, J. M., Kopf, R. F., and Lentine, A. L. (1990). *Appl. Physl Lett.* **57,** 1843–1845.
Boyd, G. D., Livescu, G., Chirovsky, L. M. F., and Fox, A. M. (1991). *Proceedings of OSA Topical Meeting on Photonic Switching.* OSA, Washington, DC, **8,** 222–226.
Chirovsky, L. M. F., D'Asaro, L. A., Tu, C. W., Lentine, A. L., Boyd, G. D., and Miller, D. A. B. (1989). *OSA Proceedings on Photonic Switching.* OSA, Washington, DC, **3,** 2–6.
Chirovsky, L. M. F., Lentine, A. L., and Miller, D. A. B. (1989). *Conference on Lasers and Electro-Optics, 1989 Technical Digest Series.* OSA, Washington, DC, **11,** paper MJ2.
Chirovsky, L. M. F., Focht, M. W., Freund, J. M., Guth, G. D., Leibenguth, R. E., Przybylek, G. J., Smith, L. E., D'Asaro, L. A., Lentine, A. L., Novotny, R. A., and Buchholz, D. B. (1991). *Proceedings of the OSA Topical Meeting on Photonic Switching.* OSA, Washington, DC, **8,** 56–59.
Cloonan, T. J., Herron, M. J., Tooley, F. A. P., Richards, G. W., McCormick, F. B., Kerbis, E., Brubaker, J. L., and Lentine, A. L. (1990). *IEEE Photon. Technol. Lett.* **2,** 438–440.
Dobbelaere, W., Huang, D., Unlu, M. S., and Morkoc, H. (1988). *Appl. Phys. Lett.* **53,** 94–96.
Franz, W. (1958). *Naturforsch.* **13a,** 484.
Goossen, K. W., Boyd, G. D., Cunningham, J. E., Jan, W. Y., Miller, D. A. B., Chemla, D. S., and Lum, R. M. (1989). *IEEE Photon. Technol. Lett.* **1,** 304–306.
Goossen, K. W., Cunningham, J. E., Jan, W. Y. (1990). *Appl. Phys. Lett.* **57,** 2582–2584.
Goossen, K. W., Miller, D. A. B., Cunningham, J. E., Jan, W. Y., Lentine, A. L., Fox, A. M., and Ailawadi, N. K. (1990). *IEEE LEOS Annual Meeting,* 157.
Guy, D. R. P., Apsley, N., Taylor, L. L., and Bass, S. J. (1987). In: *Quantum Well and Superlattice Physics* (H. Gottfried Dohler, Joel N. Schulman, eds.), *Proc. SPIE* **792,** 189–196.
Hong, S., and Singh, J. (1989). *IEEE J. Quantum Electron.* **25,** 301–311.
Keldysh, L. V. (1958). *Sov. Phys. JTEP* **7,** 788.
Lee, Y. H., Jewell, J. L., Walker, S. J., Tu, C. W., Harbison, J. P., Florez, L. T. (1988). *Appl. Phys. Lett.* **53,** 1684–1686.

Lentine, A. L., Hinton, H. S., Miller, D. A. B., Henry, J. E., Cunningham, J. E., and Chirovsky, L. M. F. (1987). *Conference on Lasers and Electro-Optics, 1987 Technical Digest Series.* OSA, Washington, DC, **14**, 249.
Lentine, A. L., Hinton, H. S., Miller, D. A. B., Henry, J. E., Cunningham, J. E., and Chirovsky, L. M. F. (1989a). *IEEE J. Quantum Electron.* **25**, 1928–1936.
Lentine, A. L., Miller, D. A. B., Henry, J. E., Cunningham, J. E., and Chirovsky, L. M. F. (1989b). *IEEE J. Quantum Electron.* **25**, 1921–1927.
Lentine, A. L., Chirovsky, L. M. F., D'Asaro, L. A., Tu, C. W., and Miller, D. A. B. (1989c). *IEEE Photon. Technol. Lett.* **1**, 129–131.
Lentine, A. L., Chirovsky, L. M. F., D'Asaro, L. A., Kopf, R. F., and Kuo, J. M. (1990a). *IEEE Photon. Technol. Lett.* **2**, 477–480.
Lentine, A. L., McCormick, F. B., Novotny, R. A., Chirovsky, L. M. F., D'Asaro, L. A., Kopf, R. F., Kuo, J. M., and Boyd, G. D. (1990b). *IEEE Photon. Technol. Lett.* **2**, 51–53.
Lentine, A. L., Hinterlong, S. J., Cloonan, T. J., McCormick, F. B., Miller, D. A. B., Chirovsky, L. M. F., D'Asaro, L. A., Kopf, R. F., Kuo, J. M. (1990c). *Appl. Opt.* **29**, 1157–1160.
Lentine, A. L., Miller, D. A. B., Henry, J. E., Cunningham, J. E., Chirovsky, L. M. F., and D'Asaro, L. A. (1990d). *Appl. Opt.* **29**, 2153–2163.
Lentine, A. L., Chirovsky, L. M. F., and D'Asaro, L. A. (1991). *Opt. Lett.* **16**, 36–38.
Lentine, A. L., Chirovsky, L. M. F., Focht, M. W., Freund, J. M., Guth, G. D., Leibenguth, R. E., Przybylek, G. J., and Smith, L. E. (1992a). *Appl. Phys. Lett.* **60**, 1809–1811.
Lentine, A. L., Tooley, F. A. P., Walker, S. L., McCormick, F. B., Morrison, R. L., Chirovsky, L. M. F., Focht, M. W., Freund, J. M., Guth, G. D., Leibenguth, R. E., Przybylek, G. J., Smith, L. E., D'Asaro, L. A., and Miller, D. A. B. (1992b). *Proceedings of OSA Topical Meeting on Photonic Switching.* OSA, Washington, DC, **8**, 60–66.
Livescu, G., Miller, D. A. B., Henry, J. E., Gossard, A. C., and English, J. H. (1988). *Opt. Lett.* **13**, 297–299.
Livescu, G., Boyd, G. D., Chirovky, L. M. F., Fox, A. M., Morgan, R. A., Leibenguth, R. E., Asom, M. T., and Focht, M. W. (1991). *Conference on Lasers and Electro-Optics.* OSA, Washington, DC, paper CMF5, 44.
McCormick, F. B., Tooley, F. A. P., Cloonan, T. J., Brubaker, J. L., Lentine, A. L., Morrison, R. L., Hinterlong, S. J., Herron, M. J., Walker, S. L., and Sasian, J. M. (1991a). *Proceedings of OSA Topical Meeting on Photonic Switching.* OSA, Washington, DC, **8**, 48–55.
McCormick, F. B., Tooley, F. A. P., Sasian, J. M., Brubaker, J. L., Lentine, A. L., Cloonan, T. J., Morrison, R. L., Walker, S. L., and Crisci, R. J. (1991b). *Electron. Lett.* **27**, 1869.
Miller, D. A. B. (1985). U.S. Patent No. 4546244.
Miller, D. A. B. (1987). U.S. Patent No. 4716449.
Miller, D. A. B. (1988). *Optical Computing, Proceedings of the Scottish Universities Summer School on Optical Computing* Edinburgh, 1988, (F. A. P. Tolley and B. S. Wherrett, eds.), Adam Hilger, London, 55–70.
Miller, D. A. B. (1990). *Opt. Quantum Electron.* **22**, 561–598.
Miller, D. A. B., Chemla, D. S., Damen, T. C., Gossard, A. C., Wiegmann, W., Wood, T. H., and Burrus, C. A. (1984a). *Phys. Rev. Lett.* **53**, 2173–2175.
Miller, D. A. B., Chemla, D. S., Damen, T. C., Gossard, A. C., Weigmann, W., Wood, T. H., and Burrus, C. A. (1984b). *Appl. Phys. Lett.* **45**, 13–15.
Miller, D. A. B., Chemla, D. S., Damen, T. C., Gossard, A. C., Wiegmann, W., Wood, T. H., and Burrus, C. A. (1985). *Phys. Rev. B* **32**, 1043–1060.
Miller, D. A. B., Chemla, D. S., and Schmitt-Rink, S. (1986). *Phys. Rev. B* **33**, 6976–6981.
Miller, D. A. B., Henry, J. E., Gossard, A. C., and English, J. H. (1986). *Appl. Phys. Lett.* **49**, 821–823.
Miller, D. A. B., Chemla, D. S., and Schmitt-Rink, S. (1988). *Optical Nonlinearities and Instabilities in Semiconductors* (H. Haug, ed.), Academic Press, New York, 325–360.

Miller, D. A. B., Feuer, M. D., Chang, T. Y., Shunk, S. C., Henry, J. E., Burrows, D. J., and Chemla, D. S. (1989). *IEEE Photon. Technol. Lett.* **1,** 62–64.

Morgan, R. A., Asom, M. T., Chirovsky, L. M. F., Focht, M. W., Glogovsky, K. G., Guth, G. D., Smith, L. E., and Goossen, K. W. (1991). *Appl. Phys. Lett.* **59,** 1049–1052.

Pezeshki, B., Thomas, D., Harris, J. S. Jr. (1990). *Appl. Phys. Lett.* **57,** 1491–1492.

Prise, M. E., Downs, M. M., McCormick, F. B., Walker, S. J., and Streibl, N. (1988). *Physique, Colloque C2, supplement 6* **49,** 15–18.

Prise, M. E., Craft, N. C., LeMarche, R. E., Downs, M. M., Walker, S. J., D'Asaro, L. A., and Chirovsky, L. M. F. (1990). *Appl. Opt.* **29,** 2164.

Schmitt-Rink, S., Chemla, D. S., Knox, W. H., and Miller, D. A. B. (1990). *Opt. Lett.* **15,** 60–62.

Sugimoto, M., Tashiro, Y., and Hamao, N. (1987). *Conference on Lasers and Electro-Optics, 1987 Technical Digest Series.* OSA, Washington DC, 348–350.

Wakita, K., Kotaka, I., Mitomi, O., Asai, H., Kawamura, Y., and Naganuma, M. (1990). *Conference on Lasers and Electro-Optics, 1987 Technical Digest Series.* OSA, Washington, DC, **7,** paper CTUC6, 70.

Wheatley, P., Bradley, P. J., Whitehead, M., Parry, G., Midwinter, J. E., Mistry, P., Pate, M. A., and Roberts, J. S. (1987). *Electron. Lett.* **23,** 992.

Whitehead, M., and Parry, G. (1989). *Electron. Lett.* **25,** 566–567.

Whitehead, M., Parry, G., and Wheatley, P. (1989). *IEEE Proc.* **136J,** 52–58.

Whitehead, M., Rivers, A., and Parry, G. (1989). *Electron. Lett.* **25,** 52–58.

Whitehead, M., Rivers, A., Parry, G., Roberts, J. S. (1990). *Electron. Lett.* **26,** 1588–1590.

Yan, R. H., and Coldren, L. A. (1990). *Appl. Phys. Lett.* **57,** 267–269.

Yan, R. H., Simes, R. J., and Coldren, L. A. (1989). *IEEE Photon. Technol. Lett.* **1,** 273.

Yan, R. H., Simes, R. J., Coldren, L. A., and Gossard, A. C. (1990). *Appl. Phys. Lett.* **56,** 1126–1128.

Chapter 3
Vertical-to-Surface Transmission Electrophotonic Devices

KENICHI KASAHARA

Opto-Electronics Research Laboratories, NEC Corporation
34, Miyukigaoka, Tsukuba, Ibaraki 305, Japan

1. Introduction 73
2. VSTEP Concept and Motivations 74
3. LED-Mode *p-n-p-n* VSTEP 75
   3.1 Low-Power Consumption in the Electrophotonic Operational Mode 75
   3.2 Two-Dimensional Integration 77
4. Laser-Mode Vertical Cavity VSTEP 78
   4.1 Structure 78
   4.2 Optimal Design 80
   4.3 Calculation Results 80
   4.4 Device Fabrication 83
   4.5 Characteristics 84
5. Ultimate Performance Possibility 88
   5.1 Electrical-to-Optical Power Conversion Efficiency 88
   5.2 Reduction in Series Resistance 88
   5.3 Reduction in Optical Switching Energy 89
   5.4 Uniform Device Characteristics for Large-Scale Integration 90
6. VSTEP Applications 91
   6.1 Serial-to-Parallel Data Conversion 91
   6.2 Optical Self-Routing Switch 92
7. Developing Applications Technologies 93
   7.1 Assembly 93
   7.2 Advanced VSTEP Fabrication Technologies 95
8. Conclusion 96
   References 96

1. Introduction

The practical advantage of photons over electrons has been successfully demonstrated in information transmission in the form of optical fiber communications, and in information storage as optical disk recordings. Yet further expansion of optoelectronics is expected by adopting this technology for information processing.

With information processing we must consider how photonic performance and functions can markedly exceed and supplement electronic functions. This is because highly advanced information processing systems have already been developed with silicon large-scale integration (LSI) based electronics. A clue to the answer to this question will be in the fundamental differences between electron and photon properties. From the standpoint of application, the most significant differences are probably the characteristics of chargeless and small mutual interactions between photons. The small mutual interaction properties among photons and the surrounding medium have allowed the transmission of optical pulses through long optical fibers. The current success of optical disk recordings is basically a result of the noninteracting property of the optical beam, which leads to noncontact recordings.

Based on this, optical information processing should utilize this noninteracting property of the optical beam, which meets the demand for multichannel requirements in optical information processing. Elementary technological developments that support optical information processing take the form of surface-normal optical semiconductor devices. In such a system, short-distance interconnection becomes dominant. Thus, it becomes important to establish a surface-normal functional optical device that allows for a compact configuration due to an absence of electric circuits. A two-dimensionally integrable vertical-to-surface transmission electrophotonic device (VSTEP) has been developed and studied to meet such demands.

This chapter focuses on the laser-mode vertical cavity VSTEP, its design features and characteristics. The functional optical interconnection attained through the VSTEP is also shown, and developing optoelectronic technologies are discussed.

2. VSTEP Concept and Motivations

In Fig. 1, the development of optoelectronic technologies, which are leading the way from optical communication to optical computing, via photonic switch-

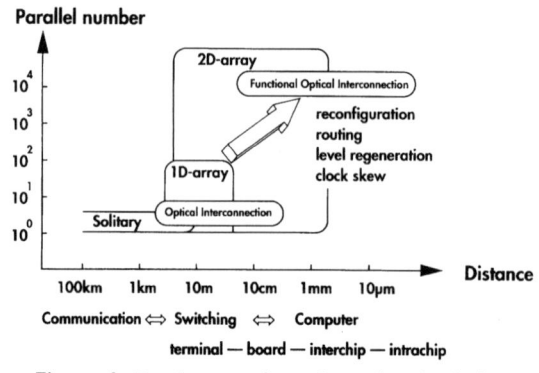

Figure 1. Development of optoelectronic technologies.

ing, are depicted as having a parallel number and distance between element devices plotted as coordinates. Optical interconnection is being thought of as a basic technology supporting such optoelectronic development. Optical interconnection is also expected to become viable for communications over short distances, for example, between terminals themselves or boards, and intrachip communications. In such future applications fields, the fundamental achievement of multichannels is needed. Thus, a two-dimensional (2-D) array device, which consists of surface-normal optical devices, is preferred to a one-dimensional (1-D) array device. Furthermore, if the surface-normal optical device is provided with such functions as switching and latching, and if it allows quick reconfiguration, routing, and level regeneration in a compact configuration, more compact systems can be made. This is because many electronic components can be eliminated. We denote optical interconnections achieved through such surface-normal functional optical devices as *functional optical interconnections*. VSTEP is a proposed concept that would allow functional optical interconnection (Tashiro *et al.* 1990; Kasahara *et al.* 1990).

The first feature of the VSTEP is a perpendicular-to-surface transmission for 2-D matrix integration. The VSTEP also features an electrophotonic configuration and allows device operation at a level that achieves low-power consumption, together with uniform and stable characteristics. With the VSTEP, the essential ideas are electrophotonic interfusion into a device level where electrons and photons mutually supplement each deficiency, resulting in performance improvements. These features are well suited to LSI.

The electrophotonic interfusion approach has been chosen over a purely photonic approach that uses, for example, a semiconductor etalon, because even though the final goal would be all-optical processing, the technology has not yet been well developed in the latter. Also we believe that the combined utilization of electrons and photons will offer far greater degrees of freedom and far more superior performance than that possible with purely photonic devices and systems. For example, the nonlinearities needed to perform memory and logic functions are generally attained much more readily and with far better control with electronic processes. Therefore, a realistic approach to photonic information processing is to explore the most efficient combination of electronics and photonics at all levels and in all aspects.

3. LED-Mode *p-n-p-n* VSTEP

3.1 Low-Power Consumption in the Electrophotonic Operational Mode

A *p-n-p-n* device is an example of a VSTEP, in which the *p-n-p-n*–doped structure exhibits thyristor-like electronic nonlinearity (Sasaki *et al.* 1982; Taylor *et al.* 1986). This device has a memory function. The switching voltage was 3.5 V and the holding voltage was 1.4 V (Fig. 2) (Kasahara *et al.* 1988). When positive-bias

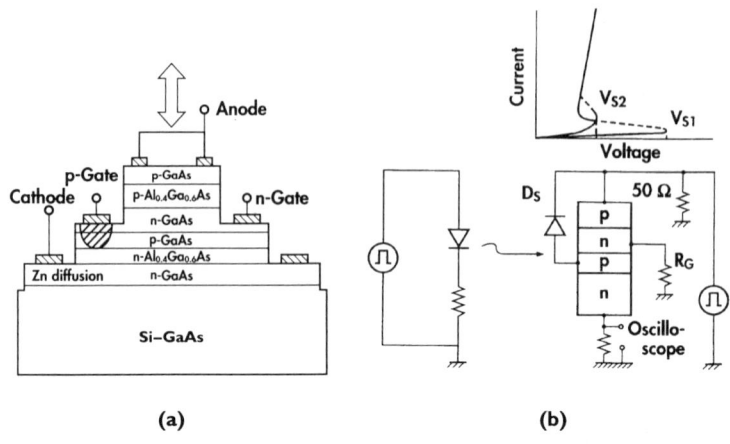

Figure 2. (a) Device structure of a *p-n-p-n* device as an example of a VSTEP and (b) circuit configuration when the *p-n-p-n* VSTEP is used.

voltage is applied to an anode and the optical pulse is incident on the *p-n-p-n* device, the device is turned on and light-emitting diode (LED) mode light emission takes place. Switching off is performed with a negative reset pulse being applied to the anode. Dual extractor-electrodes formed on *n*-GaAs and *p*-GaAs gate layers act as a bypass for the internal carriers, resulting in high-speed switch-off. The switch-off time is several nanoseconds.

During the retention period, low-power consumption of a few microwatts was attained through the electrophotonic operational mode, called *optical dynamic memory operation* (Fig. 3).

The electrophotonic concept has been extended to the task of lowering the optical switching energy by using the electronically assisted switching scheme (Fig. 4). Transient electrical precharging can be carried out by means of this scheme. Through this scheme we were able to reduce the optical switching energy P_s from 0.8 pJ to 26 fJ at 10 ns of optical write-in.

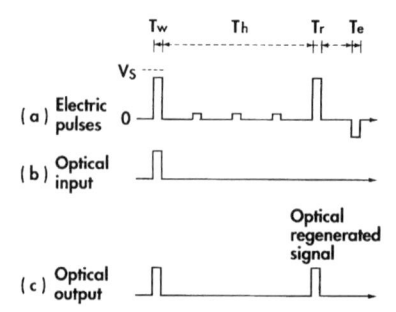

Figure 3. Timing chart of optical dynamic operation where T_w is the optical write period, T_h is the retention period, T_r is the optical read period, and T_e is the reset period: (a) electric pulses, (b) optical input, and (c) optical output.

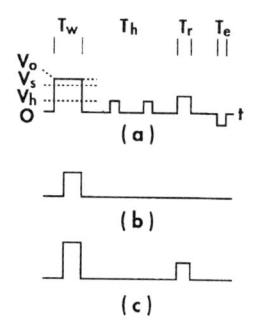

Figure 4. Timing chart of electronically assisted switching scheme.

3.2 Two-Dimensional Integration

The noticeable reduction in memory holding power and its optical switching energy, attained through the extended electrophotonic concept, is expected to permit operation of a LSI VSTEP. The feasibility of integration has been confirmed by successful fabrication of a 64-bit VSTEP.

Distribution of the switching voltage was 0.4%. In addition to the uniformity of electronic characteristics, the uniformity of light output power was also confirmed.

The feasibility of larger scale integration has also been confirmed by successful fabrication of a 1-kbit VSTEP matrix in which 32×32 *p-n-p-n* elements are integrated on a Si-GaAs substrate (Kurihara *et al.* 1991). The cell size is 30 μm $\times$ 30 μm. Anode electrodes in the same column, and cathode electrodes in the same row, are connected by their respective common anode and cathode lines (Fig. 5). An electric bias voltage is applied to each *p-n-p-n* element through the anode and cathode lines. In the application of the LSI VSTEP shown in Section 6, it is assumed that common electric bias voltage is applied to the VSTEP elements in the same row or column, or to all elements in the array. Therefore,

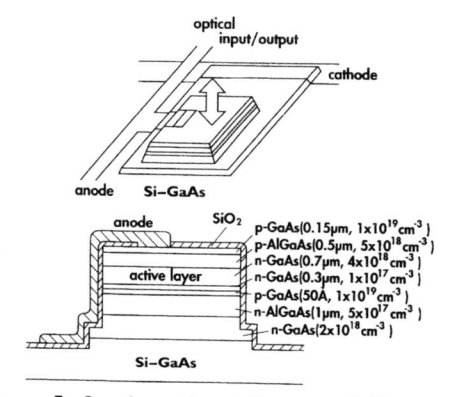

Figure 5. One element in a 1-kbit *p-n-p-n* VSTEP matrix.

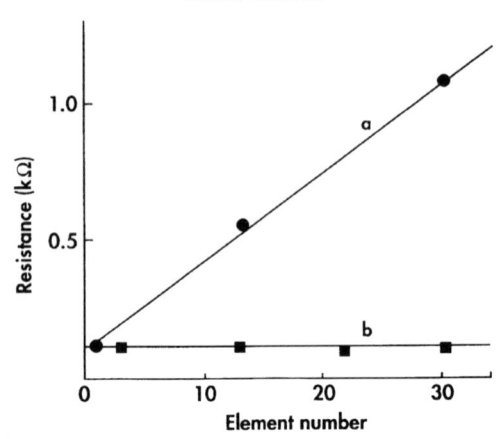

Figure 6. Element resistance during the on state for one line within a 1-kbit *p-n-p-n* VSTEP chip. Line a: lift-off process and sputtered SiO$_2$ film process. Line b: Electroplating process and P-CVD SiN film process.

the optical pulse and also the electric bias pulse being applied to the VSTEP array do not complicate the operation of the system.

The uniformity of element characteristics such as optical switching energy is critical to the parallel operation of a 1-kbit chip. The large values of the anode/cathode line resistance spoil the uniformity of the light output over the chip. Additionally, because the optical switching energy depends on the applied bias voltage, the optical switching energy is affected by resistance values of the lines.

Figure 6 shows resistance values with one element being in an on state, while the others in the same cathode line remain in an off state. The extrapolation value for a zero number indicates the resistance of one element. The line resistance between one element and an adjacent element was as high as 37 Ω when the lift-off process and the sputtered SiO$_2$ film process was used as the line formation process. In this process, the anode and cathode lines of Au/Cr with a thickness of 1500 Å were formed by the lift-off process, and the sputtered SiO$_2$ film was used for isolating the anode and cathode lines. The value noticeably decreased to 0.24 Ω when the electroplating process and the P-CVD SiN film process were introduced, allowing the formation of anode and cathode lines as thick as 1 μm. Also, the problem of Au and Cr being alloyed during the formation of the isolating film by the sputtering process could be solved by using the relatively low-temperature P-CVD process instead.

4. Laser-Mode Vertical Cavity VSTEP

4.1 Structure

In the LED-mode *p-n-p-n* VSTEP, utilized light output is limited by a Lambertian optical beam profile, which is characteristic of spontaneous emission. Low-intensity output means that the device is driven by a low optical switching speed within a cascaded connection scheme. For this reason, a vertical-cavity VSTEP (VC-VSTEP) has been fabricated (Numai et al. 1991b). This device has a *p-n-p-n* structure with an active layer and cavity mirrors at the top and bottom surfaces. Some features expected in the VC-VSTEP are vertical-cavity surface-emitting laser (VCSEL) (Iga et al. 1988) operation at an ultralow threshold current, a very small device size, high operational speed, and high-intensity light output. Also, switching and memory functions are available using this device.

The structure of a VC-VSTEP is shown in Fig. 7. The thickness and doping concentration for each layer are shown in Table 1. The active layer consists of three InGaAs layers with individual layer thicknesses being 100 Å. The active layers are sandwiched by undoped $Al_{0.25}Ga_{0.25}As$ barrier layers. They also act as photoabsorption layers in the off state. The region neighboring the active layers is undoped to avoid any influence of carrier trapping in the active layers during the off state. The upper distributed Bragg reflector (DBR) is *p*-doped (Be: $p = 3 \times 10^{18}$ cm^{-3}). The lower DBR is *n*-doped (Si: $n = 2 \times 10^{18}$ cm^{-3}). They consist of AlAs/GaAs quarter-wavelength layers. To achieve high absorption efficiency inside thin layers, an asymmetric resonator structure was used.

To utilize the reflectivity increase created by the top gold film, the thickness of the top GaAs layer in the upper DBR was determined by considering that the phase change caused by the gold film was adequately compensated.

The distance between the two DBRs is three wavelengths, where a wavelength is determined by the index of refraction of the medium. The active layers are placed one wavelength from the lower DBR and at the antinode of the standing wave in the cavity. When an active layer is placed on an antinode, the effective gain doubles, compared to a case in which the thickness of an active layer is much

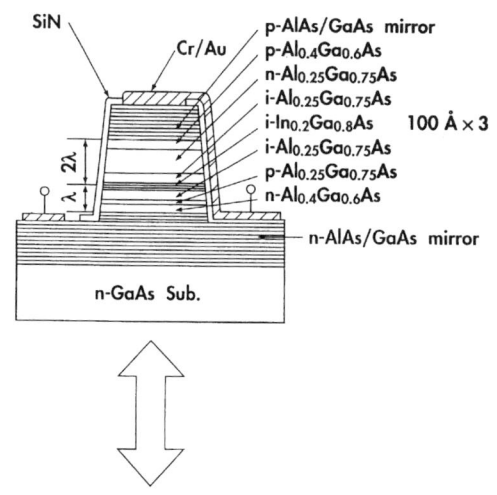

Figure 7. Structure of a VC-VSTEP.

Table I. Thickness and doping concentration for each layer. N and M indicate pair-numbers for the lower DBR and upper DBR, respectively. λ is the resonant wavelength of a DBR in the medium.

Layer	Thickness	Doping
n-AlAs/GaAs	$0.25\lambda/0.25\lambda \times N$	Si: 2×10^{18} cm^{-3}
n-Al$_{0.4}$Ga$_{0.6}$As	~1500 Å	Si: 2×10^{18} cm^{-3}
p+-Al$_{0.25}$Ga$_{0.75}$As	~50 Å	Be: 1×10^{19} cm^{-3}
i-Al$_{0.25}$Ga$_{0.75}$As	1000 Å	Undoped
i-In$_{0.2}$Ga$_{0.8}$As/Al$_{0.25}$Ga$_{0.75}$As	100 Å/100 Å × 3	Undoped
i-Al$_{0.25}$Ga$_{0.75}$As	1000 Å	Undoped
n-Al$_{0.25}$Ga$_{0.75}$As	3000 Å	Si: 2×10^{17} cm^{-3}
p-Al$_{0.4}$Ga$_{0.6}$As	~1500 Å	Be: 5×10^{18} cm^{-3}
p-AlAs/GaAs	$0.25\lambda/0.25\lambda \times M$	Be: 3×10^{18} cm^{-3}
p+-GaAs	0.16λ	Be: 1×10^{19} cm^{-3}

thicker than the period of a standing wave in a resonator. The resonant wavelength is designed to be 9500 Å. Optical beams are transmitted in and out through the GaAs substrate.

4.2 Optimal Design

Reflectivity, optical absorptivity, and threshold gain were calculated by solving the cumulative equations on the complex refractive coefficients among semiconductor layers. Parameters used in the calculation are as follows: Refractive indices at 9500 Å are 3.54 for GaAs, 3.23 for Al$_{0.5}$Ga$_{0.5}$As, and 2.96 for AlAs. Refractive index changes due to plasma effect through doping were taken into account. Free-carrier absorption α_{fc} was taken into account by using the following equation:

$$\alpha_{fc} \ (\text{cm}^{-1}) = 7 \times 10^{-18} \ p \ (\text{cm}^{-3}) + 3 \times 10^{-18} \ n \ (\text{cm}^{-3}), \quad (1)$$

where p and n are doping concentrations in n-type and p-type layers, respectively.

While the minimum size of the fabricated device is 10 μm^2, the lateral structure has not been taken into account in the calculation. The thickness of the GaAs substrate is assumed as $\lambda/4$ where λ is a resonant wavelength of a DBR. When the thickness of the substrate becomes an odd number times $\lambda/4$, threshold current is minimum. Such a case taking place, however, cannot be guaranteed in the practical sense, as is discussed in Section 5.4.

4.3 Calculation Results

Figure 8 shows reflectivity versus thickness of the top GaAs phase-compensating layer. The role of the top GaAs layer at the upper DBR is to compensate for a phase change between the semiconductor layer and the Au. The phase change is caused by a skin effect, which is characteristic of a conductor. In Fig. 8, the reflectivity is calculated when the AlAs/GaAs pair-number for the upper DBR is fixed

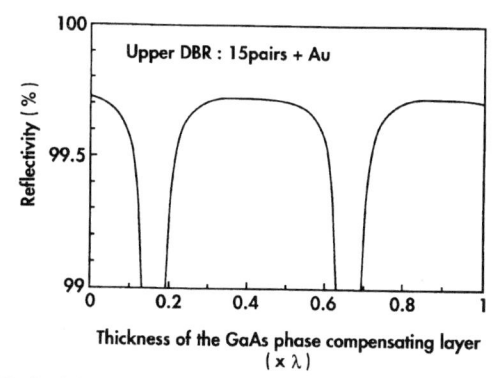

Vertical-to-Surface Transmission Electrophotonic Devices 81

Figure 8. Reflectivity versus thickness of the top GaAs phase-compensating layer.

at 15 and the thickness of the GaAs layer varies between 0 to λ. When the thickness is 0.41λ or 0.82λ, the reflectivity reaches the largest possible value of 99.7%. In a practical device, the thickness was set to 0.41λ.

Figure 9 shows reflectivity dependence on an AlAs/GaAs pair-number, where the upper DBR contains Au and a 0.41λ GaAs layer. We find that reflectivities saturate almost at 15 pairs for the upper DBR and at 24.5 pairs for the lower DBR, reaching 99.7% and 99.9%, respectively. The reflectivity of the lower DBR becomes larger than that of the upper DBR because the lower DBR has a smaller free-carrier absorption coefficient because it is n type.

Figure 10 shows threshold gain versus a pair-number for the lower DBR, where doping concentration at the lower DBR is a parameter. Threshold gain decreases by 5% by reducing carrier concentration for the lower DBR from 2×10^{18} cm^{-3} to 1×10^{18} cm^{-3}. Corresponding to the fact that reflectivity of the lower DBR saturates from almost 24.5 pairs, if a pair-number is more than that, threshold gain approaches a constant.

The total thickness of active layers in a VC-VSTEP is only 300 Å. These thin

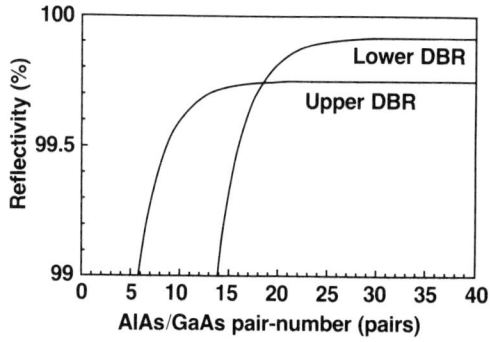

Figure 9. Reflectivity dependence on an AlAs/GaAs pair-number, where the upper DBR contains Au and has a 0.41λ GaAs layer.

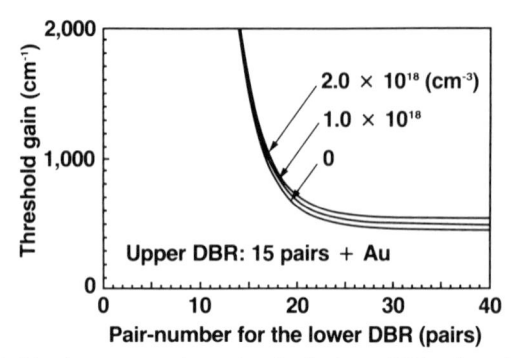

Figure 10. Threshold gain versus a pair-number for the lower DBR, where doping concentration within the lower DBR is a parameter.

active layers act as absorption layers in an off state. Maximum absorptivity per single path obtained in such thin layers is 3%, even if a higher absorption coefficient of 10,000 cm^{-1} is assumed. However, in practice, absorptivity becomes much larger through the effect of multireflection between DBRs.

The thickness of intermediate layers is set as the integer times the resonant wavelength. Accordingly, a phase between two optical beams, one reflected at a lower DBR and the other reflected at an upper DBR, is different by 180 deg. As a result, although light with a resonant wavelength is reflected most strongly using two DBRs, the reflected waves tend to cancel each other, because phases become contrary. Therefore, considering the absorption coefficient in the active layer and optimizing the reflectivities for two DBRs, high absorptivity can be attained.

Figure 11 shows total absorptivity as a function of a pair-number of the lower DBR, where absorptivity in the active layers is assumed to be 3000 cm^{-1} (Van Eck et al. 1986). As shown in Fig. 11, an optimum absorptivity of 99.2% can be obtained with 10.5 pairs. Transmittivity, reflectivity, and absorptivity in this case are shown in Figs. 12 and 13, respectively. However, since the threshold current increases, this structure for a lower DBR with 10.5 pairs is not preferable. Consid-

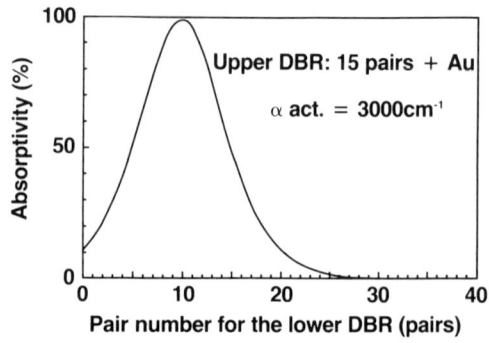

Figure 11. Total absorptivity as a function of pair-number for the lower DBR, where absorptivity in the active layers is assumed as 3000 cm^{-1}.

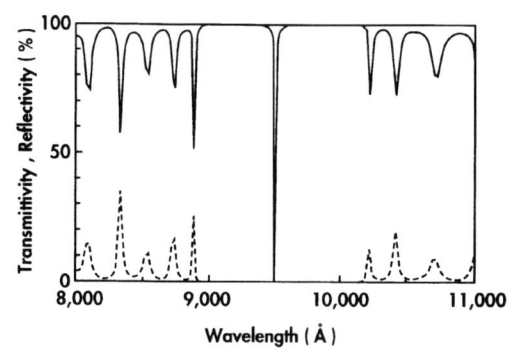

Figure 12. Transmittivity (dotted line) and reflectivity (solid line) as a function of wavelength where pair-numbers are 15 pairs for the upper DBR and 10.5 pairs for the lower DBR.

ering both threshold current and absorptivity, a structure with a lower DBR of about 14.5 pairs is preferred. In this structure, although threshold gain becomes 1500 cm^{-1}, which is three times the optimal case, absorptivity increases to 48%, which is about 30 times the case with 24.5 pairs.

4.4 Device Fabrication

The VC-VSTEP was grown on an n-GaAs substrate by molecular beam epitaxy (MBE) and fabricated in three sizes: 10, 20 and 30 μm². Mesa etching was stopped at a position a few layers down from the surface into the lower DBR. Alloyed AuGe-Ni was used as an n-side electrode formed on the surface of the GaAs layer of the lower DBR. An electrode for the p-side was formed with nonalloy AuZn. A marginal increase in resistance arising from use of the nonalloy electrode seemed to be observed. The thickness of the n-GaAs substrate was decreased to around 100 μm by polishing. Light is transmitted from the bottom side through the substrate. A pseudo-graded structure formed by nine p (or n)-doped AlAs/GaAs pairs (where total thickness was 180 Å, and the thickness of an AlAs layer was varied from 2 to 18 Å nominally by 2 Å, with the total thickness for an

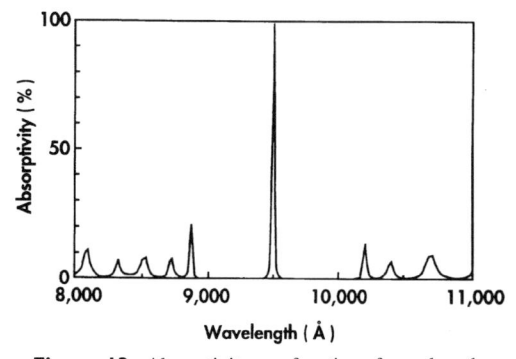

Figure 13. Absorptivity as a function of wavelength.

AlAs/GaAs pair being 20 Å) was inserted between p (or n)-AlAs/GaAs interfaces at the DBR so that the high resistance arising from the abrupt interface could be reduced.

In conventional distributed feedback (DFB) or DBR lasers, because gratings are made by the holographic method, and such processes as regrowth on the grating are utilized, the yield and uniformity of characteristics vary. However, in a vertical-cavity structure using semiconductor multilayers as the grating, because the multilayers are fabricated with high controllability by MBE, the possibility exists that very uniform device characteristics can be obtained.

4.5 Characteristics

4.5.1 Static Characteristics

The following characteristics are mainly the results of a case in which the pair-numbers for the lower and upper DBRs are 15 and 24.5, respectively.

Figure 14 shows the current-light output characteristics (duty ratio = 1/1000) in the on state for a 10-μm² device. The oscillation wavelength is 955 nm. The minimum threshold current is 1.2 mA for a 10-μm² device, 4.0 mA for a 20-μm² device, and 18 mA for a 30-μm² device. It was confirmed that all 100 VC-VSTEPs randomly extracted from a grown wafer emitted laser light. The differential quantum efficiency was about 6%. The kinks at currents around 8 and 19 mA in Fig. 14 were caused by the relatively large device size and by the influence of the external resonator mode arising from reflections off the substrate surface.

Figure 15 shows the threshold current and series resistance in an on state as a

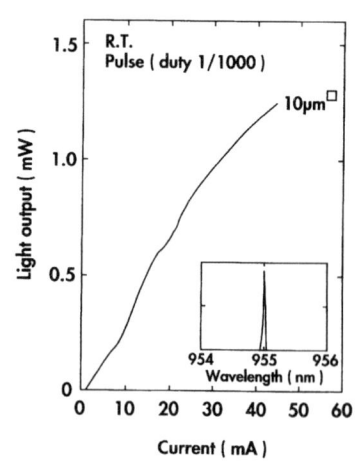

Figure 14. Current-light output characteristics in the on state for a 10-μm² device. The inset shows the oscillation wavelength at 1.1 times the threshold current.

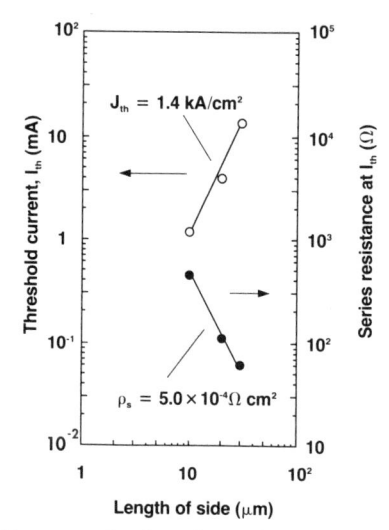

Figure 15. Threshold current and series resistance in on state as a function of side length.

function of side length. The threshold current was linearly dependent on the second power of the device size, and the threshold current density was as low as 1.4 kA/cm². The total resistivity of the device including metal-semiconductor contact resistance is reciprocally proportional to the side length, and was as low as 5×10^{-4} Ω cm². Further reductions in resistivity are expected by improving the doping profile such as doping the hetero-interfaces of p (or n)-GaAs and p (or n)-AlAs layers more heavily.

Figure 16 shows the light output characteristics for continuous-wave (cw) operation for a 10-μm² device. The inset in Fig. 16 represents the current-voltage characteristics. The switching voltage and the holding voltage were 5 and 2.5 V, respectively. This device was flip-chip bonded on solder bumps, formed on an

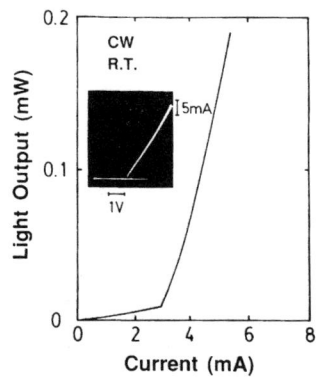

Figure 16. Light output characteristics for cw operation of a 10-μm² device.

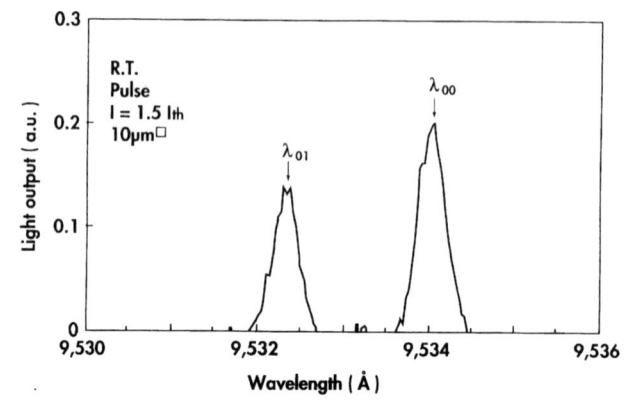

Figure 17. Oscillation spectra measured with a pulse current injection of 1.5 times the threshold current.

AlN subcarrier. In pulsed operation for a duty cycle of less than 1/10, this device shows no definite threshold due to an increase of spontaneous emissions reflected off the Au covering the mesa (Numai et al. 1991c).

Oscillation spectra are shown in Fig. 17, where measurement was accomplished by means of a pulse current injection of 1.5 times the thresholding current. Maximum resolution of the spectrometer was 0.2 Å. The reason why light emission consists of several lines with different wavelengths is because higher lateral modes simultaneously oscillate in the present device. Also, through measuring the near-field pattern, it was observed that as the oscillating wavelength shortens, the number of nodes increases. The difference between peak wavelength for each lateral mode λ_{0i} and that for a fundamental mode λ_{00} is plotted in Fig. 18. Mode separation spreads with smaller sizes. Single lateral mode oscillation is not attained even

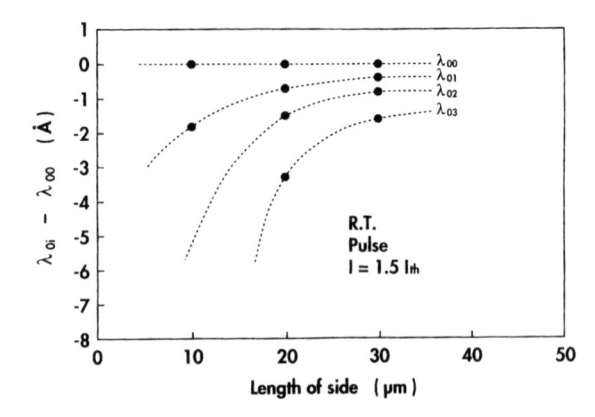

Figure 18. Difference between peak wavelengths for each lateral mode λ_{0i} and that for the fundamental mode λ_{00}.

in 10-μm² devices, but mode separation is 2 Å, which is much wider than individual linewidths of less than 0.2 Å. According to the calculation, the side length needs to be less than 5 μm in order to obtain single lateral mode operation.

4.5.2 Dynamic Characteristics

Figure 19 shows the results of an optical switching experiment using two 20-μm² VC-VSTEPs. The upper trace shows the applied voltage to the optical switch, which was set slightly lower than the switching voltage. The injected light pulse from the light source (middle trace) successfully switched the optical switch on (lower trace). After the light was removed, the optical switch remained in the on state for the period during which the voltage was applied, demonstrating the operation of the optical memory in the VC-VSTEP. Although current injection causes laser oscillation in the VC-VSTEP used as an optical switch, it can, in turn, be varied as a light source for another VC-VSTEP, when cascaded.

The minimum optical switching energy was 2.2 pJ at 10 ns of optical write-in. The 3-dB down wavelength bandwidth [full width at half maximum (FWHM)] was 8 Å. This value can be made much wider by, for example, introducing a multiple-DBR structure instead of the present two-DBR structure.

The IM modulation bandwidth of a VC-VSTEP in the on state is more than 2 GHz, because the VC-VSTEP operates as a surface-emitting laser.

Although cycle time is limited by a turn-off time of several hundreds of nanoseconds, this value can be reduced to a few nanoseconds by introducing dual-extractor gates.

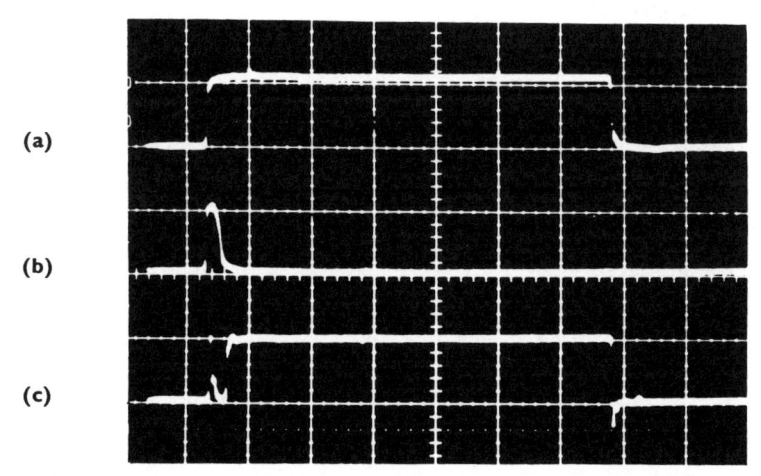

Figure 19. Optical switching experiment using VC-VSTEPs. Horizontal axis is 50 ns/div: (a) applied voltage to the VC-VSTEP used as an optical switch (5 V/div.), (b) injected optical pulse from the light source monitored with an APD, and (c) current response of the optical switch (8 mA/div.).

5. Ultimate Performance Possibility

5.1 Electrical-to-Optical Power Conversion Efficiency

Electrical-to-optical power conversion efficiency η_T is important from the application viewpoint of optical interconnections. It is defined as follows:

$$\eta_T = P_o/[I \times (V_h + IR)], \quad (2)$$

$$I = I_{th} + P_0/\eta, \quad (3)$$

$$R = R_j + R_c + R_s, \quad (4)$$

where P_o, V_h, I_{th}, η, R_j, R_c, and R_s are light output, holding voltage, threshold current, slope efficiency, equivalent resistance of the *p-n* junction, contact resistance, and series resistance, respectively. The V_h, which was measured between the anode and cathode electrodes, is 2 V. Holding current at V_h is almost negligible compared with I_{th}. Total differential resistance R is represented as a slope at a current level larger than the holding current, and is 120 Ω for a 20-μm² device. In the present device, most of the resistance is occupied by R_s, and R_s is mainly generated from the upper *p*-type DBR. The specific contact resistance per unit area (ρ_s) of the upper DBR has drastically decreased from 1.5×10^{-3} Ω cm²/period to 2.7×10^{-5} Ω cm²/period by introducing the pseudo-graded structures between *p*-AlAs and *p*-GaAs layers, which increases tunneling current.

At 1 mW of light output, η_T is 3% for a 20-μm² device. To increase η_T, we must reduce the threshold current density, J_{th}, and R. Since free-carrier absorption in the *p*-type DBR has a great influence on J_{th}, if the doping profile is optimally designed, and R decreases to less than 100 Ω, an η_T as high as 20% might be achieved.

Power consumption is also responsible for a wavelength shift. Thermal resistance obtained from an experiment was 320 K/W for a 20-μm² VC-VSTEP mounted on the AlN submount. This value almost agrees with the calculated result. The wavelength change caused by temperature was 0.6 Å/K, which is determined by the dependence on temperature of the index for semiconductor layers. If the total power consumption could be reduced to less than 5 mW, the wavelength shift could be limited to less than 1 Å.

5.2 Reduction in Series Resistance

To reduce series resistance, it is important to examine the series resistance at the DBRs, and to make an optimal design.

Figure 20 shows the temperature dependence of ρ_s for cases where the AlAs/GaAs interfaces at the DBR consist of the abrupt and pseudo-graded structures.

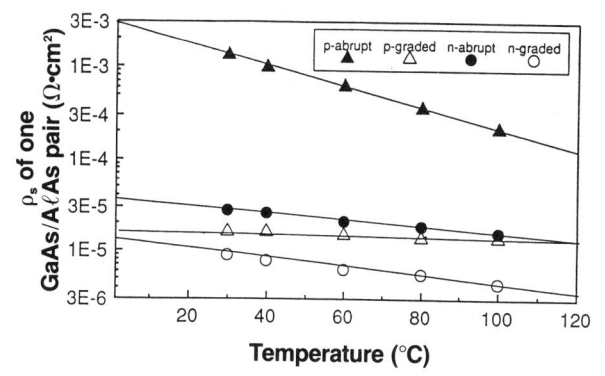

Figure 20. Temperature dependence of ρ_s of one GaAs/AlAs pair for cases where AlAs/GaAs interfaces at the DBR consist of abrupt and pseudo-graded structures.

The decrease in ρ_s at 100°C for the *p*-type pseudo-graded structure is small and 86% of that at 30°C, while ρ_s for the *p*-type abrupt structure was reduced to 16% at 30°C. With the *n*-type pseudo-graded and abrupt structures, respective ρ_s decreases for the same temperature change from 30°C to 100°C are 56% and 50%. The magnitude of thermal diffusion current flowing over a potential barrier has a large temperature dependence, while the temperature dependence of tunnel current is relatively small. In terms of the experimental results in Fig. 20, the reason why ρ_s of the *p*-type pseudo-graded structure decreased was because ρ_s of the tunnel current increased.

To optimize the parameters for the pseudo-graded structure, and to further reduce ρ_s, the magnitude of the tunnel current needs to be calculated. Here, the parameters are pair numbers, doping concentrations, and pitch.

Figure 21(a) shows the calculated results of doping concentrations. The doping concentrations for AlAs and GaAs layers outside the pseudo-graded structure are constant and 3×10^{18} cm^{-3}. The doping concentrations of AlAs and GaAs layers in the pseudo-graded structure vary from 3×10^{18} cm^{-3} to 3×10^{19} cm^{-3}. As a result, the tunnel current increases by a factor of about 5. The regions where the pseudo-graded structure is inserted correspond to the node of the internal standing wave. Therefore, high doping in those regions does not cause a threshold increase due to the increase in free-carrier absorption loss.

5.3 Reduction in Optical Switching Energy

In low optical switching energy, it is important to increase the emitter efficiency of the two transistors. For low currents, the emitter efficiency are low due to carrier recombination, which is affected by the quality of the hetero-interfaces. By means of a variation of the two-transistor model of the thyristor (Fig. 22), modified to include the effects of the photocurrent generated in the active region, a *p*-

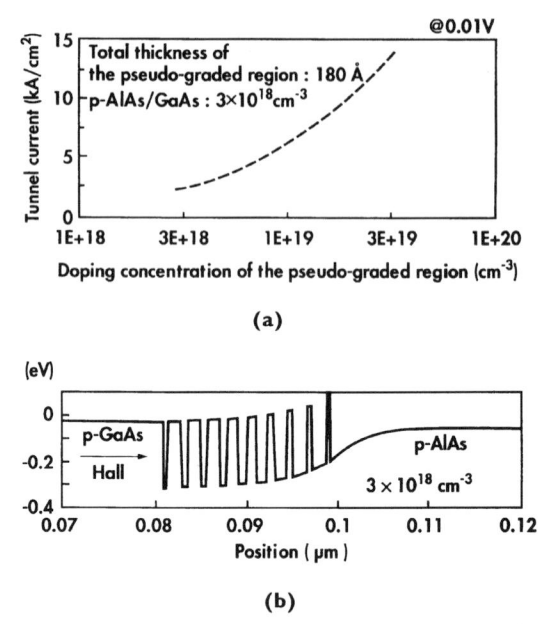

Figure 21. (a) Calculated dependence of tunnel current on doping concentrations at a *p*-type DBR. The doping concentrations outside the pseudo-graded structure are constant and 3×10^{18} cm^{-3}. The total thickness of the pseudo-graded structure is 180 Å. (b) Band structure of the valence band at 3×10^{18} cm^{-3}.

n-*p*-*n* structure was analyzed in an effort to understand the factors determining its minimum optical switching energy (Linke *et al.* 1991). Predictions for the model correlate well with measurements taken on present devices. Further reductions in optical switching energy should be possible by designing optimal doping concentrations and optimal thicknesses for gate layers.

5.4 Uniform Device Characteristics for Large-Scale Integration

To achieve high-density 2-D integrated interconnections, it is necessary to achieve uniform device characteristics. Decreasing the reflectivity of the DBR on the in-

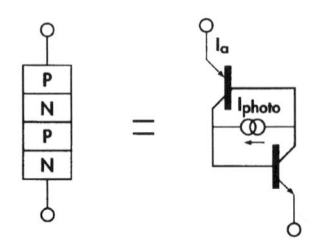

Figure 22. Equivalent circuit for the *p*-*n*-*p*-*n* VSTEP.

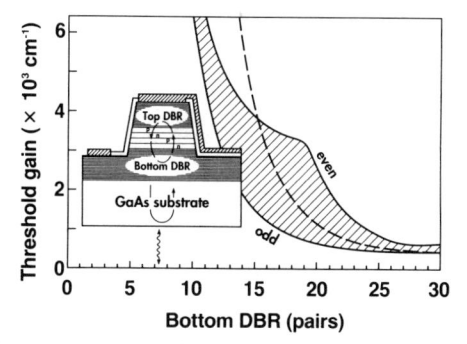

Vertical-to-Surface Transmission Electrophotonic Devices 91

Figure 23. Theoretical scatter of threshold gain before AR coating (hatched area) and after AR coating (broken line) plotted against the number of bottom DBR pairs.

put/output side enhances the influence of back surface reflection. The thickness of the substrate is difficult to control to the order of a wavelength. Thus, phase shift caused by reflection from the substrate fluctuates from device to device in the same wafer. This results in the scattering of optical characteristics. As a result, uniform device characteristics are impaired.

Even in cases using a top window structure, the influence of back surface reflection is significant because of the large differences in refractive indices between the GaAs substrate and air. Therefore, the recognition of influences created by back surface reflection is important. Moreover, the reflection phase changes dynamically within a single pulse because of a red shift in the Fabry-Pérot mode. This reflection phase change causes dynamic mode hopping within the external cavity, which is created by back surface reflection.

The effect of back surface reflection increases as the number for the bottom DBR decreases, improving the efficiency of both light emission and detection. Figure 23 shows the theoretical scatter of threshold gain before antireflection (AR) coating (hatched area) and after AR coating (broken line) plotted against the number of bottom DBR pairs. It has been confirmed that experimental threshold currents before AR coating and after AR coating agree well with the theory.

6. VSTEP Applications

6.1 Serial-to-Parallel Data Conversion

As the first stage of future parallel information processing, it is necessary to prepare a device that allows for serial-to-parallel data conversion. Also, reconfigurable optical interconnection needs to be considered, for example, when a 2-D VSTEP matrix is applied to an optical crossbar switch. However, the solution lies in how a high-speed reconfiguration scheme can be developed.

One concrete example is shown in Fig. 24 (Ogura *et al.* 1990). Electronic addressing signals are applied parallel to the anode lines of a *p-n-p-n* VSTEP matrix.

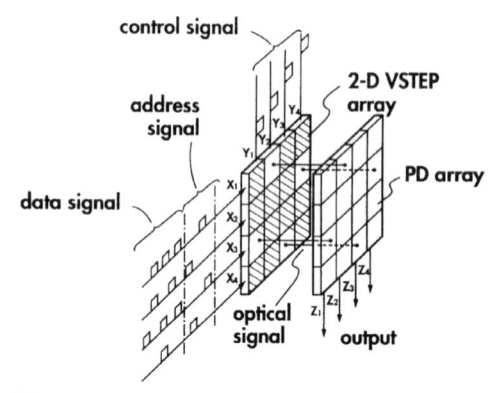

Figure 24. Reconfigurable interconnection using a *p-n-p-n* VSTEP array.

These signals are synchronized with electronic control signals, which are applied sequentially to cathode lines. The addressing signal and control signal values are set in such a way that the VSTEP switches turn on only when both signals are applied simultaneously.

Using this driving scheme, N^2 optical interconnections can be reconfigured in N time slots through $2N$ electrical control lines. This greatly alleviates the reconfiguration procedure, particularly when N increases. Actual write-in time for one row was confirmed to decrease to a few nanoseconds.

6.2 Optical Self-Routing Switch

A new optically self-routing switch has been successfully demonstrated (Numai *et al.* 1991a). If the number of optical interconnections is increased as another optical functional interconnection, it becomes difficult to provide the electric cables necessary to route optical interconnections. Asynchronous transmission mode (ATM) is a switching scheme that can handle various bit rates of services, and with its important self-routing function, is expected to play a role in future broadband networks.

VC-VSTEPs were used for the optical self-routing switch. During the on state the bias voltage for the VSTEP was set at a value where the current was below the threshold, allowing the VSTEP to act as an optical amplifier (Fig. 25).

The operating principle behind the optical self-routing switch is as follows. In this switch, an optical pilot signal is placed before the optical data signals, which are divided into VSTEPs with memory and optical amplifying functions. For each row of the VC-VSTEP array, the bias voltage signal V_1-V_3 is applied through a resistor. The VSTEP bias voltages V_1, V_2, and V_3 are raised to V_h during time slots t_1, t_2, and t_3, respectively. After that, bias signals are kept at V_1 during cell transmission time. The optical packet signal has a header bit at time slots t_1, t_2, and t_3, when an optical header bit synchronizes with a time slot having a bias signal of V_h, turning the VSTEP to the on state. When the optical header bit does not syn-

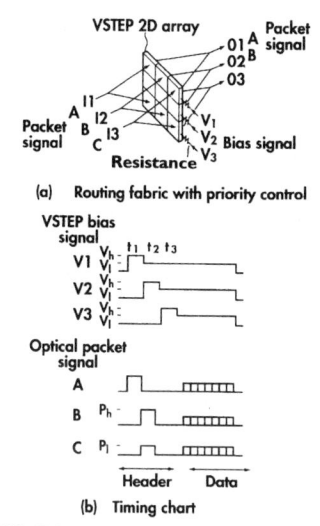

Figure 25. Principle behind optical self-routing switch.

chronize with the off state, the data bits of the optical packet signal are not transmitted, because they are absorbed in the VSTEP. The on state VSTEP functions as an optical amplifier, transmitting optical data bits during the application of the V_1 bias signal. In this way, optical packets A and B, in Fig. 25(a), can be self-routed to the specific output ports 01 and 02, respectively.

Priority control can also be achieved using the same structure, preventing optical packet signals from colliding at the output port. For example, both optical packet signals B and C, in Fig. 25(b), have header bits at time slot t_2. However, the header bit optical power of packet B is larger than that of packet C. As a result, a VSTEP, to which packet B is injected, is turned on faster than a VSTEP, to which packet C has been injected. An increase in the injection current causes a drop in VSTEP applied voltage due to resistance. Thus, the VSTEP, into which packet C has been injected, cannot be turned to the on state. In this way, priority control can be achieved by changing the optical power of the header bit.

A 4 × 4 ATM switch consisting not only of optical self-routing switches but also of optical buffer memories has been fabricated through the use of VC-VSTEPs. The optical data rate is 1.6 Gbps.

7. Developing Applications Technologies

7.1 Assembly

It is necessary to develop modules to make VSTEP applications more practical. In constituting a 2-D surface-normal module, components such as the following need to be considered: (1) optical semiconductor arrays with electrical/optical conversion functions such as VSTEPs, (2) optical passive components with lenses, branching, convergence, and permutation functions, (3) electronic components, and (4) the input/output components to a module. With optical fiber communications, input/output to a module is performed via optical fiber. However, in the application of the surface-normal module, an optical guide is not necessarily required, but the use of electronics is conceivable.

Possible structures for 2-D surface-normal modules are (1) a stacked transmission optical circuit or (2) a planar reflection optical circuit. In the former, optical signals are transmitted in the surface-normal direction one after another, stacking several components. In the latter, those components are arranged on a single surface confining optical signals on the plane.

Although the use of a stacked transmission optical circuit is attractive due to its potential for compactness, when many light emission semiconductor arrays are used, the planar reflection optical circuit is preferable due to problems of heat dissipation.

The planar reflection optical circuit has advantages of both stability and potential high-density optical interconnection. Jahns *et al.* (1992) have implemented Fourier conversion optical systems by forming lenses and beamsplitters on a quartz glass sheet.

Flip-chip bonding and optical alignment techniques are described later; they represent the fabrication technologies to produce such planar reflection optical circuits.

Figure 26 shows a process flow chart for flip-chip bonding. On the top surfaces

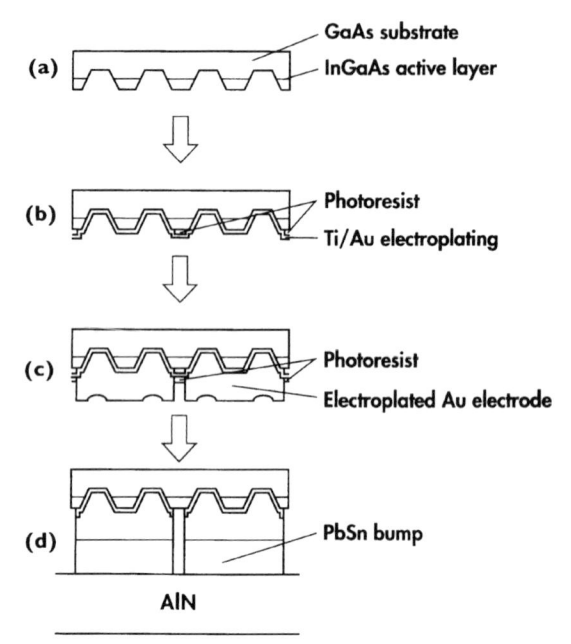

Figure 26. Process flow of flip-chip bonding.

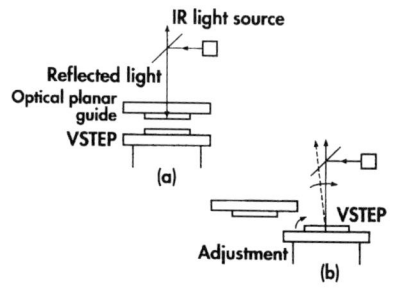

Figure 27. Optical alignment for the assembly between the VSTEP and optical planar guide: (a) Reflected light off optical planar guide is adjusted to marker. (b) Reflected light off VSTEP is adjusted to marker.

of VC-VSTEP epitaxial layers, 15-μm-thick and 150-μm² Au electrodes were formed on the anode and cathode regions by electroplating. The PbSn bumps on an AlN submount were formed with a separation of 250 μm. Flux was coated on these bumps, and the VSTEP chip was roughly positioned on it. The whole structure was on a heater, and flip-chip bonding was performed at around 150°C.

The assembly between the VSTEP and optical planar guide requires position alignment to a micrometer order of precision. Because we are assuming the focal length of the lens to be several hundreds of micrometers, the permissible tolerance for the perpendicular direction is several tens of micrometers. However, alignment in the lateral direction is more severe. Registration in the lateral direction can be adjusted using a commercially available position aligner, and by adjusting individual markers which are formed on the upper planar guide and lower substrate (Fig. 27). The important thing is to ensure that the epitaxial surface is parallel to the planar optical guide, because the thickness of the optical semiconductor wafer is reduced by polishing, and both sides of the wafer are not necessarily parallel. In our experiments, alignment precision within 2 μm was possible. After the parallel operation, a UV solidifying resin was inserted into the clearance and then hardened.

7.2 Advanced VSTEP Fabrication Technologies

Here we discuss the VSTEP fabrication technologies that need to be developed. In crystal growth technology, it becomes necessary to control the thickness of each semiconductor layer to the order of several atomic layers, and furthermore to control this thickness over large areas. Although present MBE techniques allow us to attain uniform layer thicknesses within 1% in a wafer of several square centimeters, future advanced crystal growth technology with controllability one order higher than the present technology will become necessary.

Also, the development of such crystal growth as GaAs or InP on Si, or Si/Ge strained superlattices will be necessary in order to reduce optical alignment as much as possible, to simplify assembly, and finally to allow the consideration of interfusion of Si devices. These are being studied at present. It has already been reported that dislocation density in GaAs on Si can be reduced to 7×10^4 cm^{-2}. However, considering the dislocation density of commercially available GaAs wafers, further reduction will be necessary.

In addition, it is critical to develop a process technology for forming fine, minute surface-type optical devices with ultralow power consumption and high speeds. It is theoretically predicted that when any dimension is reduced to the order of one wavelength, new physical phenomena such as cavity quantum electrodynamics start to appear. Indicators of enhancement or inhibition of spontaneous emission have been experimentally observed. As a possibility, it is thought that a surface-type optical device with ultralow power consumption will be achieved by introducing such an effect.

8. Conclusion

Functional optical interconnection attained through VSTEPs could be the first step toward the development of high-level photonic processing, including photonic switching. There is a wide variety of possible variations in the VSTEP element structure in view of the large selections offered by electrophotonic interfusion.

Depending on individual stages of optical interconnection, several different forms of optical interconnection are considered. The optical interconnections between machines is possible with correct optical fiber communication techniques. However, optical interconnection from board to board and module to module, and furthermore between interchips or intrachips, contains several technical problems that are yet to be solved. As distances shorten, problems such as interconnection density, reconfigurability, electrical-to-optical or optical-to-electrical conversion efficiency, propagation delay, compatibility with electronic device integration technologies, and assembly attain even greater significance. However, short-distance optical interconnection is currently in the spotlight not only due to expectations from the system side but also as a result of recent progress in 2-D surface-type optical semiconductor devices. Further steady research and development in cooperation with the application sector is desired.

References

Iga, K., Koyama, F., and Kinoshita, S. (1988). *IEEE J. Quantum Electron.* **24**, 1845–1855.

Jahns, J., Morgan, R. A., Nguyen, H. N., Walker, J. A., Walker, S. J., and Wong, Y. M. (1992). *IEEE Phot. Tech. Lett.* **4**, 1369–1372.

Kasahara, K., Ogura, I., Numai, T., Kosaka, H., Hamao, N., and Tashiro, Y. (July 1990). *In: Tech. Digest 3rd Optoelectronics Conf.* Chiba, Japan, 116–117.

Kasahara, K., Tashiro, Y., Hamao, N., Sugimoto, M., and Yanase, T. (1988). *Appl. Phys. Lett.* **52**, 679–681.

Kurihara, K., Tashiro, Y., Ogura, I., Sugimoto, M., and Kasahara, K. (1991). *IEE Proc. J* **138**, 161–163.

Linke, R. A., Devlin, G. E., Ogura, I., and Kasahara, K. (Nov. 1991). In: *Tech. Digest LEOS'91* San Jose, CA, 62.

Numai, T., Ogura, I., Kosaka, H., Sugimoto, M., Tashiro, Y., and Kasahara, K. (1991c). *Electron. Lett.* **27**, 605–606.

Numai, T., Sugimoto, M., Ogura, I., Kosaka, H., and Kasahara, K. (1991b). *Appl. Phys. Lett.* **58**, 1250–1252.

Numai, T., Sugimoto, M., Ogura, I., Kosaka, H., and Kasahara, K. (1991c). *Jpn. J. Appl. Phys.* **30**, L602–L604.

Ogura, I., Tashiro, Y., Kawai, S., Yamada, K., Sugimoto, M., Kubota, K., and Kasahara, K. (1990). *Appl. Phys. Lett.* **57**, 540–542.

Sasaki, A., Matsuda, K., Kimura, Y., and Fujita, S. (1982). *IEEE Trans. Electron Devices* **ED-29**, 1382–1388.

Tashiro, Y., Hamao, N., Sugimoto, M., Takado, N., Asada, S., Kasahara, K., and Yanase, T. (1990). *Appl. Phys. Lett.* **54**, 329–331.

Taylor, G. W., Simmons, J. G., Cho, A. Y., and Mand, R. S. (1986). *J. Appl. Phys.* **59**, 596–600.

Van Eck, T. E., Chu, P., Chang, W. S. C., and Wieder, H. H. (1986). *Appl. Phys. Lett.* **49**, 135–136.

Chapter 4
Microlaser Devices for Optical Computing

J. L. JEWELL AND G. R. OLBRIGHT

Photonics Research Inc.
4840 Pearl East Circle, Suite 200W
Boulder, CO 80301

1. Introduction 99
2. Optical Interconnects 100
3. Optical Logic Devices 103
4. Ultrasmall Microlasers 107
5. Conclusion 111
   References 112

1. Introduction

Vertical-cavity surface-emitting lasers (VCSELs) are gaining momentum toward becoming the key components in technologies ranging from laser scanning and printing to optical computing. Arrays of VCSELs integrated with electronic circuitry may accomplish high-bandwidth communication between computer chips, overcoming the bottleneck that presently limits the speed of computers. In the longer term, densely packed arrays of VCSEL-based logic gates may be used for photonic switching in communication networks or for digital or neural computing. In these information processing applications, minimizing the threshold is essential for maintaining acceptable power requirements and thermal dissipation. Although VCSELs represent a very young technology compared to edge-emitting diode lasers, they have shown thresholds nearly as low as the edge emitters, about 0.7 and 0.5 mA, respectively. The low VCSEL thresholds are mainly due to their extremely small active material volumes. If VCSEL technology can overcome the present limitations due to low electrical efficiency and surface recombination in extremely small devices, the resulting devices should have thresholds in the microampere range with speeds from tens of gigahertz to more than 100 GHz.

This chapter is divided into three main sections: optical interconnects, optical logic devices, and ultrasmall microlasers.

2. Optical Interconnects

The overriding limitation in the system speed of all-electronic processors is a result of the interconnects (Feldman *et al* 1988). In all-electronic processors most interconnects consist of coplanar metallic striplines. The striplines suffer from an unavoidable impedance mismatch with electronic logic; consequently, they are slow and consume large amounts of power. Also, the communication speed between elements is limited by the resistance-capacitance (RC) time constant of the interconnecting conductor. Whereas shrinking the size of the electronic components has increased their speed, the RC time constant remains constant because while the capacitance decreases with size the resistance increases (thinner wires have a higher resistance). Noise is also a problem with electronic interconnects. Loops of stripline connections, which are difficult to avoid, will generate voltage spikes whenever the signal through the loop changes. These voltage spikes add noise to the system and increase the bit-error rate and must be compensated for by error reduction schemes. Additionally, these lines must serially transmit signals from outputs of hundreds of thousands of electronic logic devices resulting in the classic Von Neumann bottleneck problem in computing (Backus 1978; Huang 1981).

A straightforward solution to the impedance mismatch and bottleneck problems of all-electrical interconnects is the implementation of optoelectronic interconnects (Goodman *et al* 1984). In Fig. 1 we compare interconnection of electronic

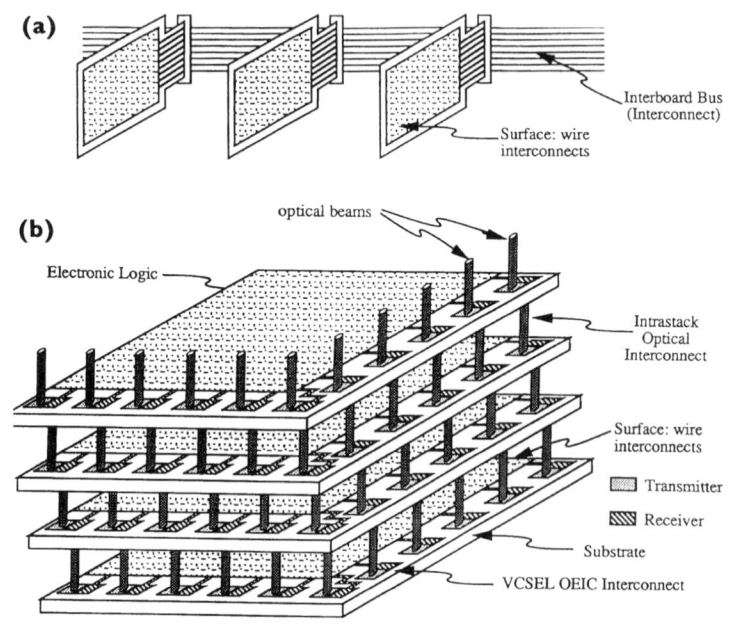

Figure 1. Comparison between (a) a processor based on all-electronic interconnects and electronic logic and (b) the ultrahigh-speed three-dimensional hybrid optoelectronic parallel processor based on electronic logic and surface-normal optical interconnects.

multichip modules (MCMs) to an optical interconnect concept. In Fig. 1(a) an impedance mismatch exists between the many electronic logic elements and the striplines over which the signals must be transmitted. Whereas in Fig. 1(b) optoelectronic interconnects act as quantum impedance matching elements (covert electrons to photons) by using optical beams for the interconnection path, thus sidestepping the problem of impedance mismatching and bottlenecking. Furthermore, the optical beams do not interfere with each other, unlike electronic signals, which strongly interact when in close proximity. Therefore, noise in the system should be substantially reduced when optical interconnects are deployed. Because striplines between chips require high power they also limit the communication bandwidth. The longer the lines, the more severely the bandwidth is limited. For the case of optical interconnects, the power requirements and supportable bandwidth do not depend on distance. The speeds of VCSELs are already more than ten times higher than mature stripline interconnect speeds and substantial improvements are foreseen in the future. Thus the optically interconnected processor depicted in Fig. 1(b) has the potential to operate at ultrahigh system speeds compared to the all-electronic processor depicted in Fig. 1(a). Clearly, for a properly designed architecture, a processor based on VCSEL optoelectronic interconnects (OEICs), utilizing parallelism, high-speed, and low-power consumption has the potential to out perform an all-electronic processor by orders of magnitude. The problems to solve en route to realizing a high-performance hybrid optoelectronic signal processing system are (1) demonstration of a high-speed, efficient, ultrasmall, OEIC transmitter/receiver; (2) design of a three-dimensional hybrid optoelectronic signal processor compatible with the transmitter/receiver OEIC interconnect technology and having the capability of multi gigabit per second operation; and (3) an optomechanical three-dimensional multistack design suitable for fabrication and capable of rigid intrastack optical interconnect alignment.

The exploded view of the optical interconnect test structure shown in Fig. 1(b) is composed of several vertically aligned stacks. Each stack consists of three parts: (1) electronic logic, (2) transmitters, and (3) receivers. An optical interconnect technology wherein all components are fabricated on a GaAs substrate could be developed using standard semiconductor growth and processing techniques. We choose GaAs substrates and electronic logic in lieu of the much more mature silicon technology because the growth and fabrication of optical semiconductors and optoelectronic devices, respectively, on silicon is impractical. Furthermore, the availability of compact, low-power consumption, wide-bandwidth optical interconnects that can be driven by small "internal-node" sized transistors forces a rethinking of the parameters of comparison of silicon and GaAs integrated circuit technology. Currently, the primary advantage of the dominant Si IC technology, complementary mixed-oxide semiconductor (CMOS) technology, over the dominant GaAs IC technology [enhancement-mode drain-coupled field effect transistor logic (DCFL)] is integration density. A typical enhancement-mode GaAs gate dissipates a large fraction of 1 mW per gate, while dense CMOS, if it could operate at the same clock rate, would dissipate ~10× lower power. A slightly higher speed GaAs technology, employing depletion-mode FETs, source-coupled FET logic is roughly 10× more power hungry—of the order of 10 mW per gate. Microprocessors with millions of transistors can be implemented in silicon, whereas GaAs is limited to roughly an order of magnitude less density because of excessive heating and power consumption. For this reason, until complementary GaAs circuit approaches are optimized, an increase in GaAs chip density appears to be stalled by the power dissipation inherent in the conventional GaAs circuit design approach. However, the advent of optical interconnects changes the foundation on which this argument is based. Because optoelectronic interconnects promise to allow interchip communication without the usual electronic current-drive penalty associated with driving high input/output capacitance (impedance mismatch) and because it also promises to avoid bottlenecking due to serial signal transmission on coplanar stripline buses, then the major driver for very large scale integration is eliminated. This is achieved by sidestepping the electrical impedance mismatch problem using quantum electrical-to-optical conversion. In face, it may be preferable to use several smaller ICs and replace long-distance on-chip interconnects with OEICs. The absence of electrical crosstalk with OEICs is clearly another advantage.

To accomplish optical interconnections, two basic classes of devices are being investigated: light emitters (e.g., lasers) and light modulators. A dramatic simplification of the optical system is gained when lasers are used rather than modulators as shown in Fig. 2. Similar simplifications and advantages are gained by the use of emitters rather than modulators in the implementation of systems performing all-optical logic.

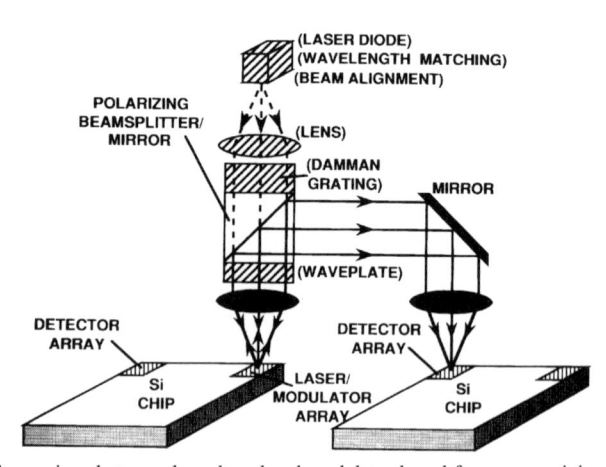

Figure 2. Comparison between laser-based and modulator-based free-space minimum-component interconnect layouts. Components marked by diagonal hatching (with labels in parentheses) are eliminated when lasers are used instead of modulators, and the polarizing beamsplitter is replaced by a simple mirror. Wavelength matching and beam alignment of the external laser diode to the modulators also become unnecessary.

3. Optical Logic Devices

Fundamental requirements for logic gates, whether electronic or optical, are high speed, low energy per operation, and tolerance to imperfection in other devices or in the overall system. Optics is considered to have greater potential than electronics for very high speed computing because of its ability to communicate the information on and off chips at speeds equal to the gate speed. To achieve the desired processing rates of the order of 10^{16} bits processed per second (e.g., 10^6 gates working at 10-GHz speed), the energy levels of demonstrated optical logic gates, about 1 to 10 pJ, imply a required power of 10 to 100 kW. These gate energies clearly need to be lowered into the low femtojoule range to make power supply and heat dissipation requirements acceptable. Two other serious but often overlooked problems are present in essentially all proposed optical computing schemes. They deal with the fact that external lasers are used to read the state of the device and provide its output, and that resonances are used (e.g., semiconductor exciton and/or cavity) to reduce the gate energy requirements. First, the external laser wavelength must precisely match the wavelength at which the gate is most sensitive. Thus all gates addressed by a given external laser must be extremely uniform in their response to wavelength. In semiconductor gates, this wavelength varies strongly with temperature and the wavelength of the external laser may also vary. Therefore, a complex arrangement of wavelength-selected devices and fine temperature controllers is needed just to make the system operational. Second, the external optics must be precisely aligned to relay the beams from the external lasers to the optical gates. These optics add a great deal of bulk and expense to the system, typically in the form of array generators, waveplates, polarizing beamsplitters, and other awkward elements. Figure 3(a) shows the minimum optics required to achieve one building block of a system that relays optical data from one array of logic gates to another. The external laser can be considered as an optical power supply for gate array 2.

A microlaser-based optical logic gate has its own light source and thus eliminates the two stated problems by its very concept. There is no external laser to be aligned or matched to the device resonance(s). The generic device comprises (1) a broadband detector, (2) a very low threshold laser, and (3) a mechanism through which the weak output of the detector can cause the laser to switch on or off. Since the detectors are broadband it is of no consequence if the lasers output different wavelengths across the arrays. Small temperature changes no longer produce any serious effect on the system performance. In short, system reliability is greatly increased. Figure 3(b) illustrates the simplification of the optical system caused by the elimination of the external laser, lens, array generator, and polarizing beamsplitter. These components tend to be very expensive and are difficult to scale down to micro-optic sizes. The comparison is directly analogous to that of Fig. 2.

The microlaser optical logic gate in its simplest configuration consists of a heterojunction phototransistor (HPT) integrated with a VCSEL (Chan *et al.* 1991;

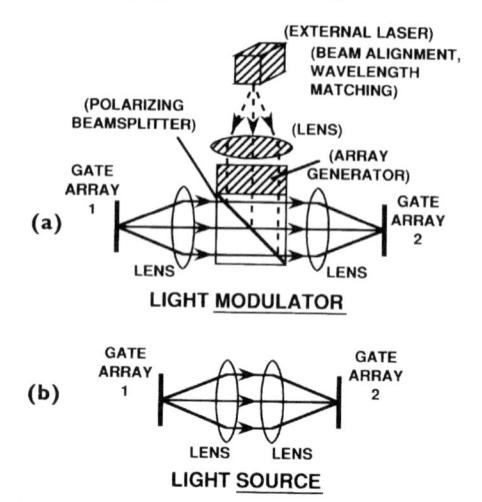

Figure 3. Comparison between (a) modulator-based and (b) laser-based free-space optical computing systems. Components marked by diagonal hatching (with labels in parentheses) are eliminated when lasers are used instead of modulators, and the polarizing beamsplitter is replaced by a simple mirror. Wavelength matching and beam alignment of the external laser diode to the modulators also become unnecessary.

Olbright et al. 1991; Bryan et al. 1991). We call the structure a surfaCe-Emitting Laser Logic (CELL) device. The CELL performs cascadable optical logic functions by absorbing a small optical input signal in the HPT, then amplifying the induced photocurrent to drive the laser above threshold. CELLs require only two electrical contacts (a single positive voltage applied across the laser anode, whereas the emitter of the HPT is grounded). The functionality of CELLs can be tuned to produce, for example, a step-function response for digital optical computing, or a smooth differentiable sigmoidal response for neural networks. Discrete cascadable CELLs and noncascadable, monolithically integrated CELLs (Chan et al. 1991) have been demonstrated. CELLs are capable of functioning as logic gates with optical inputs to the gate being to the HPT and the optical output of the gate being from the VCSEL. Boolean logic operations (i.e., AND, OR, XOR) with optical beams have been demonstrated using discretely wired CELLs (Bryan et al. 1991).

CELLs are capable of operating at speeds in the range of hundreds of megahertz (with conventional HPT designs) with optical switching energy requirements from 1 to 10 pJ for the HPT inputs. In principle, improvements can achieve much higher speeds, perhaps many tens of gigahertz with <100 fJ total energy peroperation. Figure 4 shows a cascadable CELL consisting of a VCSEL vertically integrated to an HPT. The VCSEL consists of an active quantum well region sandwiched between distributed Bragg reflectors, where the HPT consists of a wide-bandgap n-type-doped emitter, narrow-bandgap p-doped base, and narrow-bandgap n-doped collector region. The spectral response of the HPT is flat for

PHOTOTRANSISTOR ACTUATED SURFACE-EMITTING MICROLASER

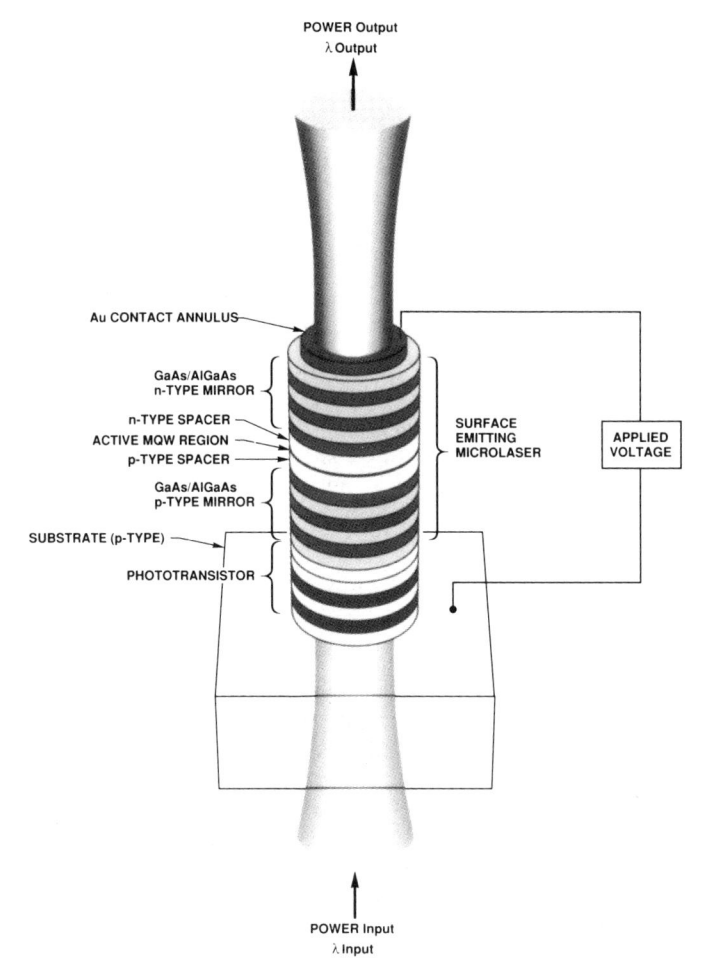

Figure 4. Structure and geometry of a GaAs-based CELL operating in the "transmissive" mode.

wavelengths above the bandgap of the collector and base regions and below that of the emitter, resulting in a wavelength-insensitive device for more than 1000 Å. Consequently, CELLs are virtually unaffected by wavelength shifts due to temperature variations on the order of tens of degrees.

Figure 5 presents the light-output versus light-input characteristic of a discrete CELL. The VCSEL consists of a four-quantum-well GaAs/AlGaAs laser described by Lee *et al.* (1990). The HPT consists of an n-AlGaAs emitter, a p-GaAs base, and an n-GaAs collector region (Olbright *et al.* 1991). The CELL has its

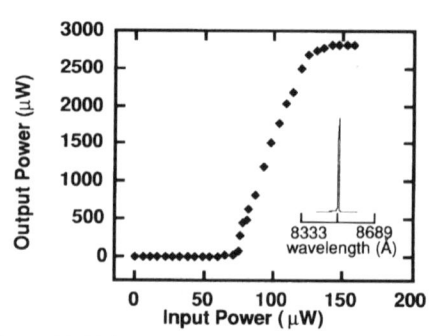

Figure 5. Light output versus light input for the CELL.

optical output wavelength at 850 nm, exhibits an overall gain factor of 20, a differential gain factor of more than 200, and a contrast ratio of 34 dB. It has a flat spectral response from 700 to 870 nm, thereby also demonstrating both wavelength-up and wavelength-down conversion.

Figure 6 shows the circuit configuration and the optical input and output signals from the CELL for AND and XOR gate operation (Bryan *et al.* 1991). For optical OR and AND, only a single CELL is required. For AND operation, the intensity of the optical inputs A and B into the HPT must be such that they can collectively, but not individually, produce enough current gain to switch on the VCSEL. For OR operation, each optical input is of sufficient power to produce enough current gain to saturate the VCSEL output power. Consequently, the OR gate can be

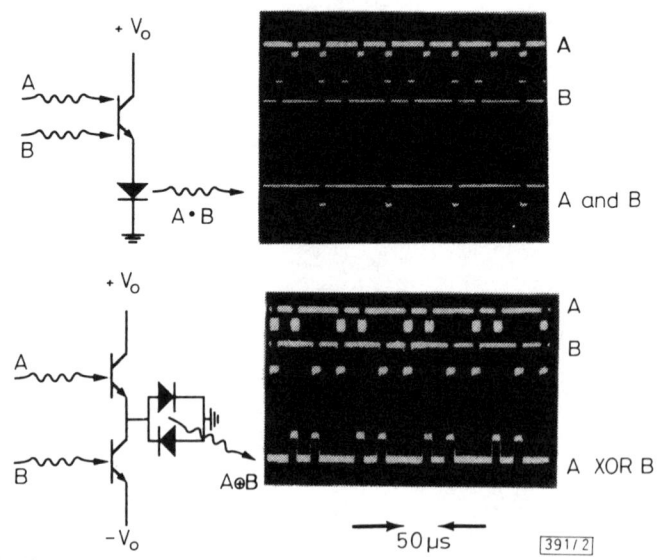

Figure 6. Digital optical circuit configurations and logical operations for optical AND/XOR gates.

achieved using the same engineered structure as the AND gate simply by adjusting the power levels of the inputs (or the electrical voltage applied to the CELLs). By configuring two HPTs and two VCSELs [Fig. 6 (lower)], optical XOR gates have been demonstrated (Bryan *et al.* 1991). Optical inverters, NOR and NAND gates using combinations of VCSELs, and phototransistors can also be realized.

4. Ultrasmall Microlasers

Microcavity lasers potentially will have ultralow thresholds in the microampere range or even lower (Yablonovitch, Gmitter, and Bhatt 1988; Yamamoto *et al.* 1989; Yokoyama and Brorson 1989; Jewell *et al.* 1989). We have observed optically pumped lasing in GaAs/AlAs microresonators as small as ~0.4 μm wide (less than half the free-space wavelength) and in various rectangular shapes. The smallest devices, ~0.4 × 0.4 μm, had the lowest threshold which was 2 pJ *incident*. This low threshold, achieved despite ~10-ps carrier lifetimes, an estimated <5% absorption efficiency in the cavity spacer, and probably low coupling efficiency of the pump beam, is encouraging for the long-range development of microcavity lasers.

The design for the structure, grown by MBE, is shown in Fig. 7. The spacer contains a single quantum well (SQW) of InGaAs designed to lase at a wavelength of ~960 nm. Small-diameter microresonators are known to exhibit size-dependent waveguide dispersion, which blue-shifts the cavity resonances. Therefore, the cavity was designed for a longer wavelength than that of the gain peak, and the thicknesses in the top and bottom mirrors were deliberately varied with the same gradient direction. This provided resonant wavelengths of about 1000 ± 50 nm, which varied with position on the wafer. Both mirrors were deigned for well over 99.9% reflectivity, resulting in a 8-μm total thickness.

Various rectangular shapes were patterned onto a bilevel resist/mask using electron-beam lithography with the dimensions indicated in Fig. 8. This provided square devices of width 1.5, 1.0, 0.7, 0.6, 0.5, 0.4, and 0.3 μm down the diagonal of the overall pattern, and rectangles of various aspect ratios and orientations in the rest. Chemically assisted ion-beam etching formed the microresonator structures (Scherer *et al.* 1989). To maximize the straightness of the sidewalls, the gas pressure and ion-beam current were varied during the etching to compensate for unavoidable rising temperature. A scanning electron micrograph (SEM) of some microresonators is shown in Fig. 9. The SEM's revealed the actual device sizes to be about 0.1 μm wider than the lithographic pattern, thus the smallest device size is ~0.4 × 0.4 μm.

Optical measurements were carried out using ~10-ps, 800-nm pump pulses and the same high-numerical-aperture focusing system we used previously [6] to investigate microresonator gates of ~0.5 μm in diameter. Figure 10 shows the setup

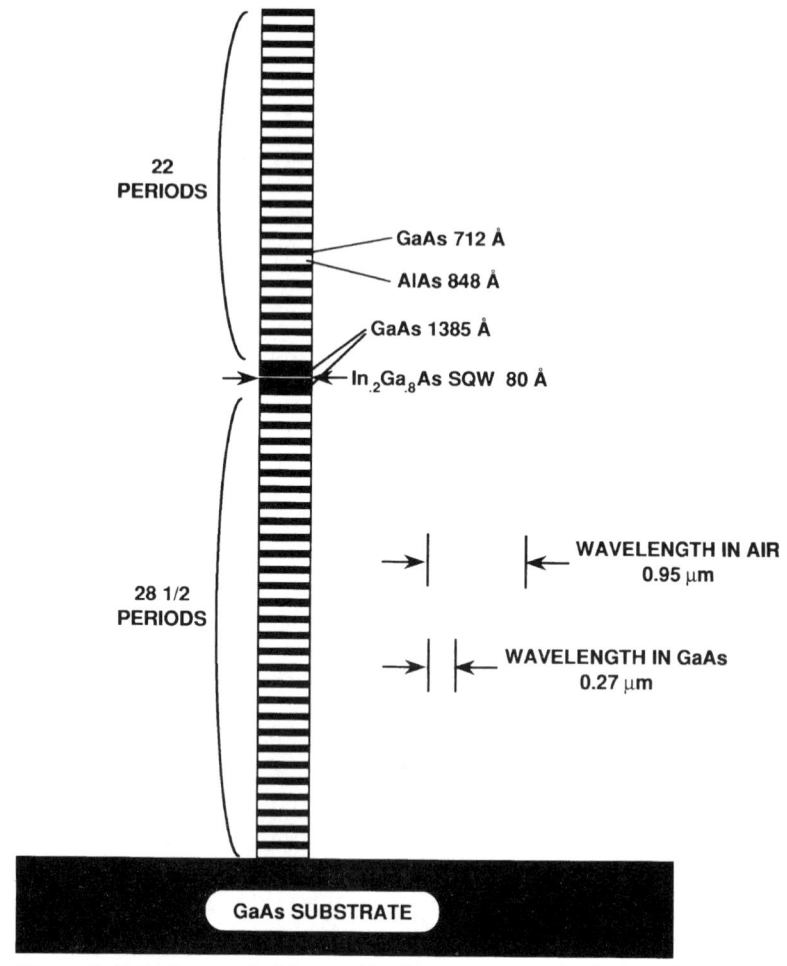

Figure 7. Scale diagram of a 0.5-μm-wide microresonator showing the MBE layer design.

with half-waveplates HW1, HW2, and HW3; polarization beamsplitters PBS1 and PBS2; and the SrTiO$_3$ hemisphere HEMI. The hemisphere has a refractive index of about 2.4, which, in conjunction with the LENS, allows us to focus the pump beam to a spot with a full width at half maximum of ~0.4 μm. Rotating HW2 revealed the polarization of the microlaser outputs. The spectrometer was an optical multichannel analyzer, which displayed the output spectrum. An acousto-optic modulator (not shown) modulated the 82-MHz mode-locked pulse train in 250-ns envelopes with a 5-μs period (5% duty cycle) to reduce heating effects.

Large unetched regions of the wafer showed lasing in the 950- to 1002-nm region, and provided calibration of the local thicknesses. The etched devices always lased at shorter wavelengths, ranging from 850 to 965 nm. If, in the etched

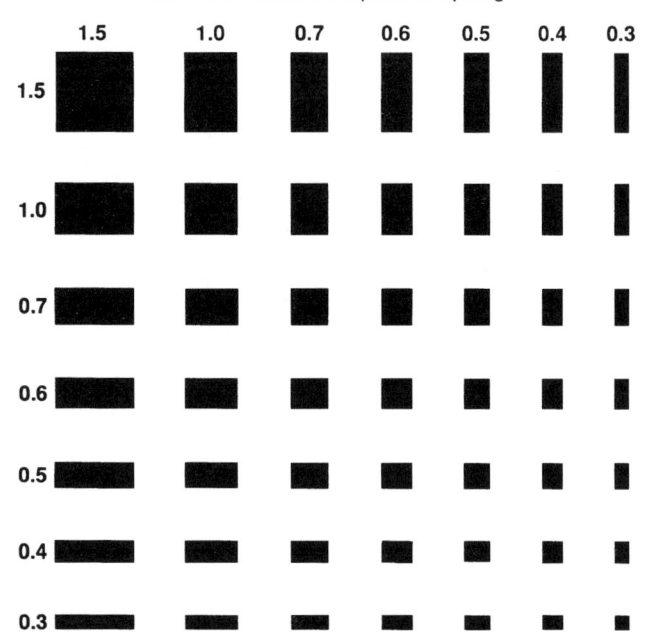

Figure 8. Lateral dimensions (in micrometers) patterned by electron-beam lithography. Actual device spacing was 3 μm center to center.

devices, only the lowest order transverse mode were lasing, there would be a clear trend of smaller widths emitting at shorter wavelengths due to the waveguide dispersion. Although this trend was sometimes observed, more often even the largest devices (1.5 μm^2) showed very large wavelength shifts, >100 nm, from the large-area laser. Since the lasing wavelength was typically in the region of 880 nm, it is clearly due to the GaAs spacer material and a higher order mode. Laser emission

**1/2 μm DIAMETER MICROLASERS
OPTICALLY PUMPED**

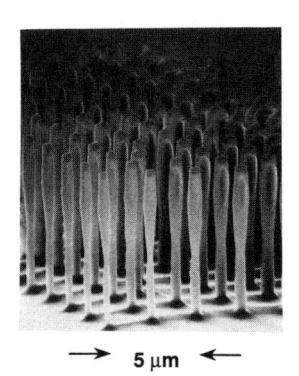

→ 5 μm ←

Figure 9. SEM of the microresonators as seen from the corner with the smallest sizes.

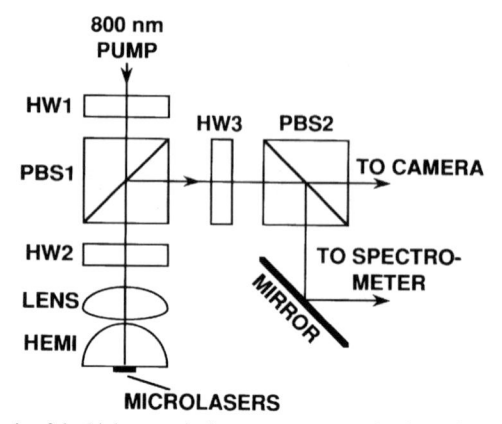

Figure 10. Schematic of the high-numerical-aperture setup used to investigate devices with dimensions smaller than the vacuum wavelength of the light.

in the 900- to 910-nm region in small devices makes it difficult to interpret either the nature of the cavity mode or the active material responsible for the lasing. At this stage of the investigation we will not attempt to do so. Polarization was often observed in the outputs, sometimes along the long axis and sometimes along the short one. It appears that selection of a cavity mode whose resonance best matches the material gain is more important than slight differences in loss for the two polarizations. A few devices showed two emission lines of opposite polarizations. For example, a ~0.6 × 0.7-μm ("real" size) device emitted at 888 nm polarized along the long axis and at 899 nm along the short one.

The lowest threshold recorded was for the smallest device of our set, ~0.4 × 0.4 μm, and Fig. 11 shows its output/input characteristic. The threshold was 2 pJ with an emitted wavelength of 865 nm. Transition of the output from unpolarized

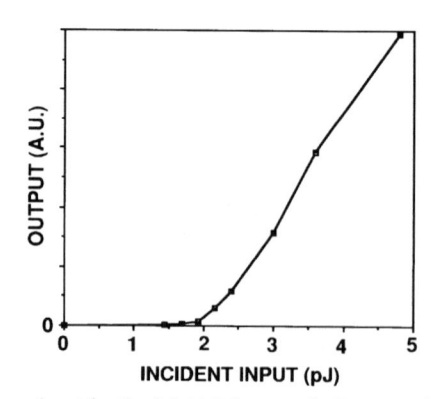

Figure 11. Output versus input for the 0.4 × 0.4-μm optically pumped microlaser. Pump wavelength was 865 nm.

below threshold to polarized above threshold verified that the device was indeed lasing. The fraction of pump light absorbed in the spacer region is estimated to be ~5% based on a constant 10^4 cm^{-1} absorption coefficient for the GaAs layers in the top mirror and the spacer. Based on more extensive determinations of the cavity absorption efficiency in a similar structure (Jewell *et al.* 1989), we feel the estimate is accurate to within a factor less than 2. This value yields an energy absorbed in the spacer of ~100 fJ, and the carrier density was ~10^{19} cm^{-3}, or about five times the density required for transparency in GaAs. Since the coupling efficiency into the microresonator should not be particularly high, the energy and carrier density should be even smaller. The expected carrier lifetime in such a small structure is ~10 ps based on our earlier gating experiments. Since the pump pulses are about 10 ps also, significant carrier reduction occurred during the pumping pulse. Considering all these photon and carrier losses, it seems clear that the carrier density was not much above that required for transparency.

To make ultrasmall microlasers a practical reality, a number of technological hurdles must be overcome. Pumping current down the mirror structures is not likely to be practical even for larger VCSELs; for submicron-diameter microlasers it is probably not worth considering. Alternate pumping geometries must be developed, perhaps transverse pumping or a hybrid transverse/vertical geometry (Jewell *et al.* 1991). Surface recombination on the sidewalls must be suppressed. So far the largest reduction in threshold after "passivating" the sidewalls is only about a factor of 3 (Clausen and Harbison 1991). Finally, these innovations must be integrated compatibly with other fabrication techniques into one complete process. Needless to say this is a formidable challenge, but the payoff would be the creation of very small, very efficient, very high speed light-emitting devices, exactly what one desires for information processing optical devices.

5. Conclusion

The geometry, scalability, and light-emitting characteristics of VCSELs make them highly desirable devices for the implementation of optical microcommunications within high-speed digital or analog information processing systems. Work has begun on integrating VCSELs with bipolar and FET-based electronic circuitry. Eventual use of extremely high-performance microlasers will rely on meeting challenging technical achievements.

ACKNOWLEDGMENTS

We would like to thank the following people for their contributions to the work presented here: T. M. Brennan, R. P. Bryan, J. Cheng, L. T. Florez, J. P. Harbison, K. Lear, Y. H. Lee, S. L. McCall, A. Scherer, L. M. Schiavone, and B. Van der Gaag.

References

Backus, J. (1978). *Comm. ACM* **21,** 613.
Bryan, R. P., Olbright, G. R., Brennan, T. M., Fu, W. S. and Tsao, J. Y. (1991). *Appl. Phys. Lett.* **59,** 1600–1602.
Bryan, R. P., Olbright, G. R., and Cheng, J. (1991). *Electron. Lett.* **27,** "Cascadable Surface Emitting Laser Logic: Demonstration of Boolean Logic," IEE.
Chan, W., Harbison, J. P., Von Lehmen, A. C., Florez, L. T., Nguyen, C. K., and Schwarz, S. A. (1991). *Appl. Phys. Lett.* **58,** 2342.
Clausen, E., and Harbison, J. P. (1991). *Electron. Lett.* 27, xx–xx.
Cheng, J., Bryan, R. P., and Olbright, G. R. (July 1991). *Appl. Opt.*
Feldman, M. R., Esener, S. C., Guest, C. C., and Lee, S. H. (1988). *Appl. Opt.* **27,** 1742.
Goodman, J. W., Leonberger, F. I., Kung, S. Y., and Athale, R. A. (1984). *Proc. IEEE* **72,** 850.
Jewell, J. L., Harbison, J. P., Scherer, A., Lee, Y. H., and Florez, L. T. (1991). *IEEE J. Quantum Electron.* **27,** 1332–1348.
Jewell, J. L., Huang, K. F., Tai, K., Lee, Y. H., Fischer, R. J., McCall, S. L., and Cho, A. Y. (1989a). *Appl. Phys. Lett.* **55,** 424.
Jewell, J. L., McCall, S. L., Scherer, A., Houh, H. H., Whitaker, N. A., Gossard, A. C., and English, J. H. (1989b). *Appl. Phys. Lett.* **55,** 22.
Jewell, J. L., Scherer, A., McCall, S. L., Walker, S., Harbison, J., and Florez, L. T. (1989c). *Electron. Lett.* **25,** 1123.
Lee, Y. H., Tell, B., Brown-Goebeler, K., Jewell, J. L., Leibenguth, R. E., Asom, M. T., Livescu, G., Luther, L., and Mattera, V. D. (1990). *Electron. Lett.* **26,** 1308.
Miller, D. A. B. (1989). *Opt. Lett.* **14,** 146–148.
Numai, T., Sugimoto, M., Ogura, I., Kosaka, H., and Kasahara, K. (1991). *Appl. Phys. Lett.* **58,** 1250.
Olbright, G. R., Bryan, R. P., Lear, K., Lee, Y. H., and Jewell, J. L. (1991). *Electron. Lett.* **27,** 216.
Scherer, A., Jewell, J. L., Harbison, J. P., Florez, L. T., Lee, Y. H., and Sandroff, C. J. (1989). *Appl. Phys. Lett.* **55,** 2724.
Wada, O., Furuya, A., and Makiuchi, M. (1989). *IEEE Photon. Techn. Lett.* **1.**
Yablonovitch, E., Gmitter, T. J., and Bhatt, R. (1988). *Phys. Rev. Lett.* **61,** 2546.
Yamamoto, Y., Machida, S., Igeto, K., and Horikoshi, Y. (1989). In: *Proc. 6th Rochester Conf. Coherence and Quantum Optics* (J. H. Eberly, L. Mandel, and E. Wolf, eds.), Plenum Press, NY, p. 1249.
Yokoyama, H., and Brorson, S. D. (1989). *J. Appl. Phys.* **66,** 4801.

Chapter 5
Physics of Planar Microlenses

MASAHIRO OIKAWA AND KENJIRO HAMANAKA

Tsukuba Research Laboratory
Nippon Sheet Glass Company, Ltd.
5-4 Tokodai, Tsukuba-city, 300-26 Japan

1. Introduction 113
2. Planar Microlenses 115
   2.1 Ion-Exchange Technology 116
   2.2 Distributed-Index Planar Microlenses 120
3. Characterization of Planar Microlenses 123
   3.1 Aberration Measurement System 123
   3.2 Aberration Properties of Planar Microlenses 125
4. Planar Microlenses with Swelled Structures 131
5. Conclusion 136
   References 136

1. Introduction

It could be said that optical processing is based on the light coupling between various optical devices. However, because light emission angles and light acceptance angles are different in the most cases, light couplings between different optical devices are not always easy to achieve. For example, a typical laser diode (LD) emits light under angle of 30 to 40°. On the other hand, a single-mode optical fiber can accept light within 5 deg. Microlenses are required to achieve effective light coupling between different optical devices. The microlens converts the numerical aperture (NA) of light rays such that effective coupling is realized.

Also important in optical computing is parallel data processing. In this scheme, optical devices may be integrated and connected in the arrayed structure. An LD array, a fiber array, and a detector array may be used. To connect these arrayed devices, one of the key components is a precisely aligned microlens array.

Monolithically integrated microlens arrays were first introduced and demonstrated in 1980. The planar microlens (PML) was the result of the introduction and demonstration of the concept of the integrated microlens array, which is based on the idea of planar technology as demonstrated by Oikawa *et al.* (1981, 1982).

Using the PML, Iga *et al.* (1982) introduced the concept of stacked planar optics. The light coupling between devices also included diffraction problems. Since the light, emitted from a light source, is spread by diffraction, it requires optical guide stems if it is to function as an optical circuit. A lens relay system is one of the practical approaches to construction of optical circuits. The stacked planar optics are the arrayed lens relay systems as shown in Fig. 1. The system is constructed with two-dimensional optical devices such as planar microlenses, filters, and mirrors. We stack these devices in tandem to realize an array of two-dimensional optical circuits such as the optical taps, branches, directional couplers, and wavelength multiplexers/demultiplexers required in optical communication systems.

Different methods are used to make microlens arrays. The two classifications of microlens are refractive and diffractive.

A microlens array fabricated by chemical etching and plasma chemical vapor deposition (CVD) was demonstrated by Khoe *et al.* (1981). They made an index distribution in an etched hole suing composite materials from Si_3N_4 and SiO_2. A microlens array using photosensitive glass was demonstrated by Borrelli *et al.* (1983). In this method, they crystallized glass substrate locally by the selective exposure of UV light and heat treatment. They demonstrated two methods of making microlenses in a glass substrate. The first method used refractive index changes in the crystallized place. The second method used shrinkage of the glass substrate by crystallization (Borrelli *et al.* 1985). They crystallized the region around the microlenses to be fabricated. The crystallization induces local shrinkage in these areas which in turn causes the other areas to swell, thereby forming a micro array lens.

Beginning in 1982, remarkable advances were made in the fabrication of the various types of diffractive lenses. Electron-beam lithography is applied in mak-

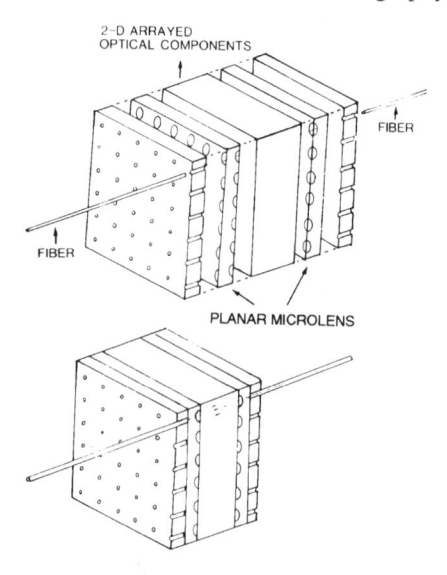

Figure 1. Stacked planar optics.

ing diffractive lenses as demonstrated by Fujita, Nishihara, and Koyma (1982). This technique enables one to make a precise diffractive pattern with a brazed grating shape. The combination of electron-beam lithography and multiple etching resulted in highly efficient diffractive lenses as demonstrated by Swanson and Veldkamp (1989).

The planar microlens is a refractive type of lens that uses index distribution and swelling induced by the ion-exchange process. In this chapter, we discuss the recent progress of PMLs and evaluate their fundamental optical characteristics. Two classes of PMLs are used to connect various optical devices: the medium-NA planar microlens and the high-NA planar microlens. The former PML (DI-PML, a distributed index planar microlens) uses a distributed index only and has a NA of around 0.2 (Oikawa et al. 1985, 1988). The latter PML (S-PML, a swelled planar microlens), with additional local swelling generated in the ion-exchange process, has an NA of greater than 0.5 (Oikawa et al. 1990a, 1990b).

2. Planar Microlenses

Planar microlenses are fabricated by planar technology, in which we diffuse a dopant selectively into a planar substrate as shown in Fig. 2. A metal mask is deposited on the glass substrate to prevent diffusion of the ion. Small windows are opened on the metal mask using a photolithographic technique, which results in a very precise arrangement of microlens arrays. The masked substrate is immersed

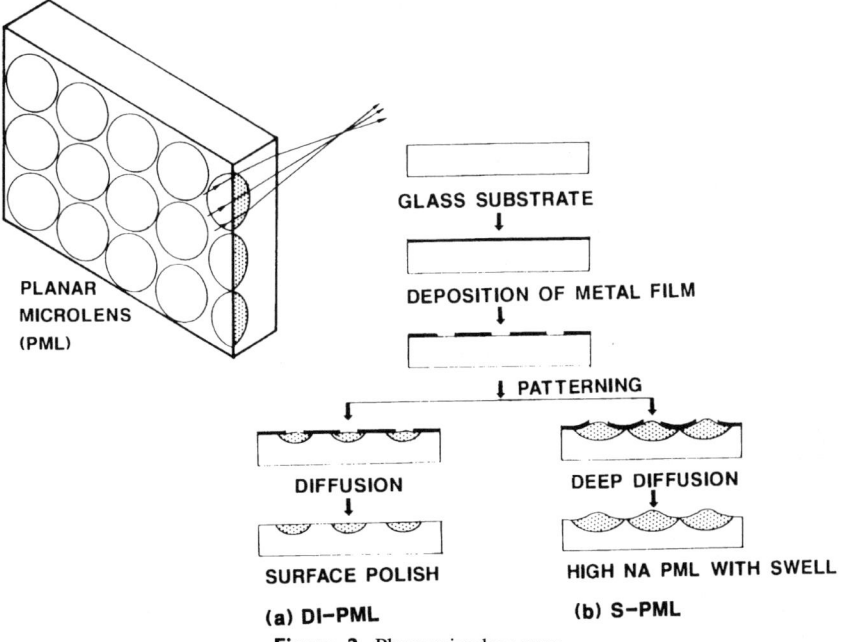

Figure 2. Planar microlens array.

in the molten salt while a suitable index distribution is formed near the window of the mask. Through the window of the mask, ions in the molten salt are diffused into the glass substrate. The diffused ions cause a higher refractive index and local swelling in the substrate, which results in the lens effect shown in Fig. 2.

2.1 Ion-Exchange Technology

The planar microlens is based on the ion-exchange technique, in which we exchange ions in a glass substrate for other ions. The glass substrate is immersed in a molten salt at high temperatures of around a few hundred degrees Celsius. Nitride salts such as $AgNO_3$, $TlNO_3$, KNO_3, etc., are widely used in the ion-exchange process. Ordinary glass is a mixture of various oxides in the amorphous phase. Among the basic network of SiO_2, glass can contain oxides of cations. The oxides of monovalent cations are ionized at a high temperature so the ions can move in the glass network and become exchangeable with other ions. Table 1 summarizes monovalent cations that can be exchanged. Each ion contributes to an increase in the refractive index of the glass. The incremental increase of this refractive index is dependent on the electron polarizability of each ion (Kitano et al. 1970).

To make PMLs, we must select ions for the exchange that have greater electron polarizability than those ions involved in the glass substrate. Since ions, which have greater electron polarizability, also have a larger ion radius, the selective ion-exchange processes causes not only index distribution but also local swelling. When we remove this swelling with polish, we obtain DI-PMLs; when we make use of the swelling, we obtain high-NA S-PMLs.

Ion exchange is a diffusion process. We found that the process has a strong concentration dependency. When we first began making PMLs, the microlenses had a smaller aberration than we expected. The fact that the ion-exchange process has this concentration dependency can be foreseen from the analysis of Doremus (1969). Doremus reveals that the concentration dependency comes from the difference of the self-diffusion constant.

If we consider the exchange of ion A and ion B, the flow of ions is:

$$\mathbf{J}_A = \mu_A E N_A - D_A grad(N_A), \tag{1}$$

$$\mathbf{J}_B = \mu_B E N_B - D_B grad(N_B), \tag{2}$$

Table 1. Refractive Index Contribution of Monovalent Cations*

Ion R	Li	Na	K	Rb	Cs	Tl
Ion radius A	0.78	0.95	1.33	1.49	1.65	1.49
Electron polarizability	0.03	0.41	1.33	1.98	3.34	5.20
Index (SiO_2 70% R_2O 30%)	1.53	1.50	1.51	1.50	1.50	1.83

*From Kitano et al. (1970).

where $\mathbf{J}_{A/B}$ are ion flows, $\mu_{A/B}$ are the mobilities, $\mathbf{E}$ is the electric field, $D_{A/B}$ are the self-diffusion coefficients, and $N_{A/B}$ are the concentrations of ions A/B, respectively. Because ions replace each other, the diffusion process is limited by the following conditions.

$$N_A + N_B = N_0 \tag{3}$$

and

$$\mathbf{J}_A + \mathbf{J}_B = 0. \tag{4}$$

Using Eqs. (3) and (4) and Einstein's relation,

$$D_{A/B} = \mu_{A/B} k_b T/q \tag{5}$$

where k_b is Boltzmann's constant, T is the absolute temperature, and q is the electric charge of the ion. The flow of ion A is described by

$$\mathbf{J}_A = -D\ grad(N_A). \tag{6}$$

Using the continuous condition, the diffusion process is described by,

$$\partial N_A/\partial t = div[D\ grad\ (N_A)], \tag{7}$$

where

$$D = D_A/(1 - \alpha\ \tilde{N}_A), \tag{8a}$$

$$\alpha = (1 - D_A/D_B), \tag{8b}$$

and

$$\tilde{N}_A = N_A/N_0. \tag{9}$$

Equation (9) describes concentration-dependent diffusion. Here, the diffusion coefficient for ion A changes from D_A to D_B corresponding to its concentration. In the limiting case,

$$\lim_{N_A \to N_0} \tilde{D} = D_B \tag{10}$$

and

$$\lim_{N_A \to 0} \tilde{D} = D_A. \tag{11}$$

Let us assume that ion A is involved in molten salt and ion B is included in a glass substrate. If the self-diffusion constant of ion A is smaller than that of ion B, diffusion proceeds faster on the glass surface where the concentration of ion A is higher. On the other hand, at the diffusion edge of ion A, where concentration of the ion is almost zero, diffusion proceeds slower. This concentration dependency has been known as the mixed alkali effect.

In the actual ion-exchange process, we use an alkali borosilicate glass, which contains two monovalent ions referred to here as ion B and ion C with relatively small electron polarizability and relatively large self-diffusion coefficients. To increase the refractive index, we exchange these ions with ion A, which has a relatively large electron polarizability. Because the self-diffusion coefficient of ion A is much smaller than that of ions B and C, concentration dependency is expected. Moreover, since we found that ion A makes glass softer, we conclude that diffusion depends strongly on the concentration during the ion-exchange process.

Figure 3(a) shows the ion concentration profiles observed with an x-ray microanalyzer (XMA). A glass block including ions B and C was immersed in the molten salt, which included ion A. Ion A diffuses into the glass substrate and ions B and C diffuse out into the molten salt. After the ion exchange, the glass plate was sliced to create one thin plate, and its cross section was observed. The ion profiles depths are measured from the surface. The same sample was also tested optically in a Mach-Zehnder interferometer to observe the refractive index profile. Figure 3(b) shows the measured profile. Assuming a uniform sample thickness, a vertical shift of the interference fringes indicates a variation in the index distribution. This index variation is almost exactly proportional to the concentration of ion A.

Figures 3(a) and (b) show the steep upward convex profiles of ion A. This ion profile denotes the strong concentration dependency of the diffusion coefficient of ion A. From the profile, the diffusion coefficient versus ion concentration is calculated using the Boltzmann-Matano method. Figure 4 shows diffusion coefficients versus the concentration of ion A. Fairly good agreement of the expo-

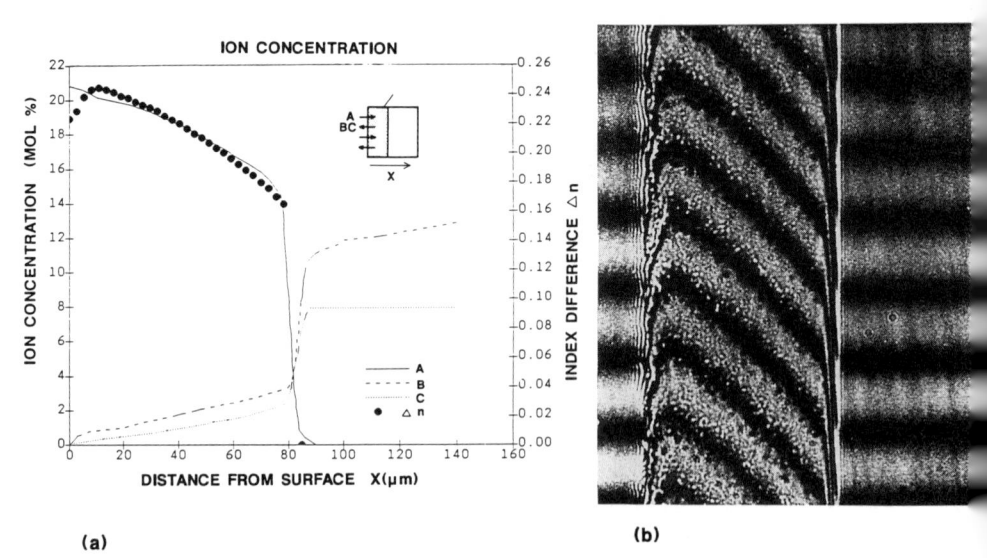

Figure 3. (a) Ion concentration profile measured by an XMA and (b) index profile measured by interference microscope.

nential approximation is obtained. The concentration dependency of ion A is expressed by

$$D(N_A) = D_0 \, exp(KN/N_0). \quad (12)$$

Here, K is estimated to be 7.3. This implies that D at $N_A = N_0$ is 340 times larger than D at $N_A = 0.2 \, N_0$.

This strong concentration dependency of the diffusion coefficient is extremely important in making a planar microlens because it reduces aberration. For a simple model, we may consider diffusion from a very small point source. If the window is small enough in comparison with the diffusion length, the window can be regarded as a small hemispherical diffusion source with radius r_m. If there is no concentration dependency, the ion concentration is given by

$$N_A = N_0 \frac{r}{r_m} \, erfc\left(\frac{r - r_m}{2\sqrt{Dt}}\right) \quad (13)$$

Here, N_0 is the saturation concentration of the ion at the diffusion source and t is diffusion time.

On the other hand, the curvature of a light ray r_k is given by

$$|r_k| = grad \, log \, n(r). \quad (14)$$

Here, $n(r)$ is the refractive index of the medium (Oikawa and Iga 1982).

Since the index increment is proportional to the ion concentration, the deriva-

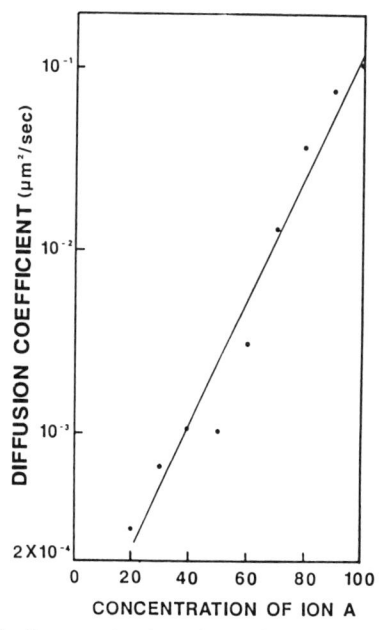

Figure 4. Concentration dependency of the diffusion coefficient.

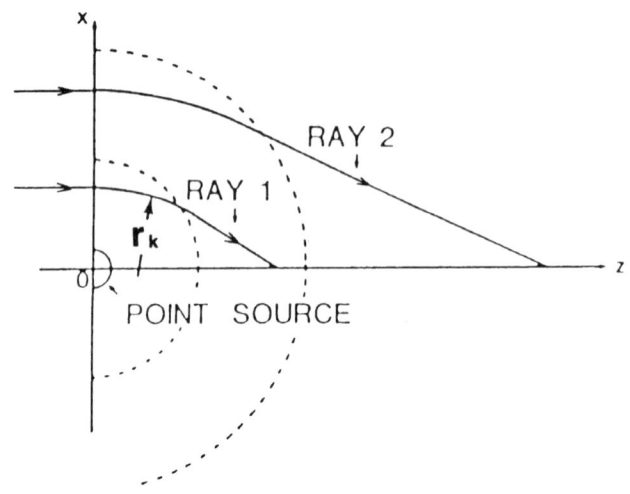

Figure 5. Ray trajectory for concentration-independent diffusion.

tive of Eq. (14) decreases monotonically and the curvature $|r_k|$ also decreases with respect to r, which causes the large aberration shown in Fig. 5. The incident ray farther from the optical axis is bent weaker than an incident ray nearer the optical axis. This analysis implies that if there were no concentration dependency, the PML would have a large aberration.

2.2 Distributed-Index Planar Microlenses

In 1980, we developed the first PML (DI-PML) to use index distribution only (Oikawa *et al.* 1981). At that time, the swelling generated by the ion-exchange process was considered an unusable structure, thus the surface was polished flat. Although this DI-PML a limited NA, it does have some advantages:

1. *Large effective diameter:* Since the refractive index profile obtained through ion exchange can be controlled almost ideally, more than 90% of the diffused diameter contributes to focusing light with small aberrations.
2. *Wide range of diameters and NAs:* By choosing suitable diffusion conditions, we can make planar microlenses with many different diameters. We have experimentally confirmed the fabrication of a planar microlens array whose diameter ranges from 10 to 1000 μm and NA ranges from 0.02 to 0.25.

Table 2. Fundamental Characteristics of Planar Microlenses

	Diameter	NA	Focal Length
DI-PML	10–1000 μm	0.02–0.25	20–4000 μm
S-PML	50–400 μm	0.4–0.6	55–500 μm

Physics of Planar Microlenses 121

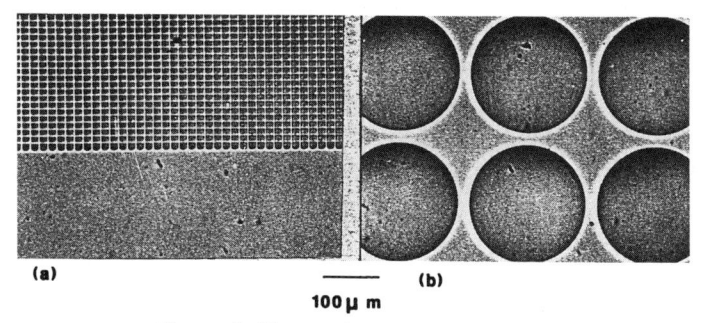

Figure 6. Photographs of planar microlenses.

3. *Flat surfaces:* Since the lens effect comes from the index distribution, the surface is flat and thus enables us to make direct contact with other optical devices on the surface.

Table 2 compares the fundamental characteristics of DI-PMLs in comparison with S-PMLs. The available maximum NA is 0.25; this NA is limited by the maximum index difference obtained through the ion-exchange process. Since long diffusion times damage the metal mask, the diameter is restricted by the diffusion time. Since the diffusion length is proportional to the square root of the diffusion time, a diffusion time four times longer than normal is required to make a lens twice as large. Figure 6 shows pictures of planar microlenses. Figure 7 shows an example of the index distribution of a planar microlens as observed with a Mach-Zehnder microscope. A thin plate is cut from the planar microlens to include the center axis. The interference pattern expresses the equi-index curves on the meridional plane. The refractive index is highest at the center on the surface

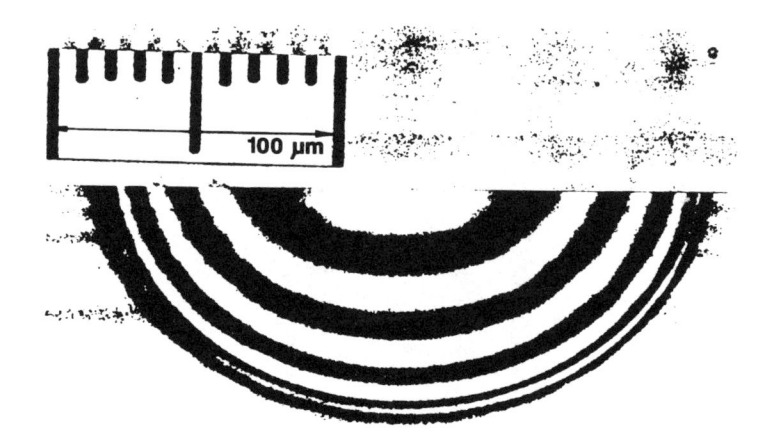

INDEX DISTRIBUTION OF PLANAR MICROLENS
Figure 7. Index distribution of PMLs.

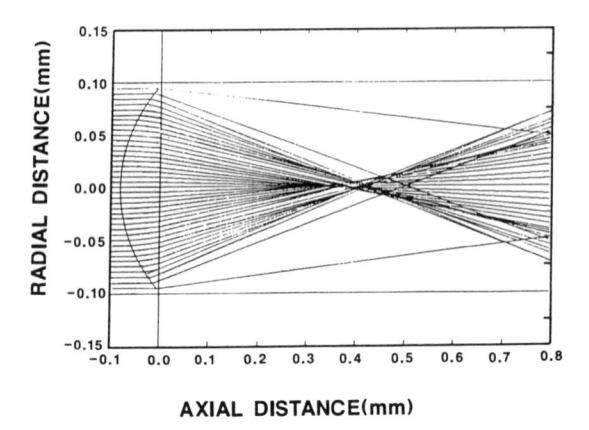

Figure 8. Ray trajectories of PMLs.

and decreases in both the radial and axial directions. In the ion-exchange process, since the diffusion of the ion has a strong concentration dependency, a steep index distribution is obtained, which results in small aberrations of the PML. The diameter of this lens is 200 μm and the depth of index distribution is 80 μm. The refractive index of the substrate is 1.542 and the maximum index difference of $\Delta n = 0.169$. The measurement of the index profile enables us to calculate the ray trajectory of the planar microlens. Figure 8 shows ray trajectories of the PML calculated from the index profile shown in Fig. 7. Almost 90% of the index distribution region contributes to focusing light with small aberrations.

Figure 9 shows the focused spot formed by the PML. The collimated light from a He-Ne Laser ($\lambda = 633$ nm) was incident in the planar microlens; this spot was drawn into focus and observed with a TV camera. The horizontal white line through the focused spot represents the cursor of the detector used to scan the intensity profile shown as the white curve under the spot. An almost diffraction-limited Airy disk with a diameter of 4.0 μm is observed.

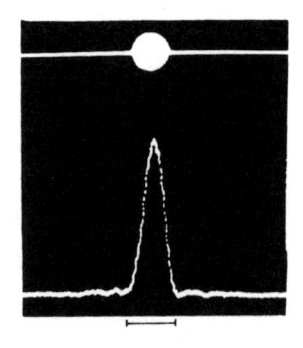

$D_s = 4$ μm ($\lambda = 0.63$ μm)

Figure 9. Focused spot of PMLs.

3. Characterization of Planar Microlenses

3.1 Aberration Measurement System

To develop the various applications of planar microlenses, it is important to evaluate their aberration properties precisely. A spherical aberration measurement technique for microlenses using a shearing interference microscope was detailed by Kokubun *et al.* (1984). We have recently developed an aberration measurement system that enables us to evaluate the detailed aberration properties, including asymmetric aberration terms. The system can apply to microlenses that are less than 100 μm in diameter.

Figure 10 shows the optical configuration of the aberration measurement system. We designed a Mach-Zehnder interferometer to make precise measurements of microlenses whose diameter range is from about 50 μm to 1 mm. A collimated He-Ne laser beam is divided into two beams. One beam, reflected by a mirror mounted on a piezoelectric transducer, acts as a reference beam. A PML is placed behind the objective lens in the other optical path. The CCD camera observes the interference pattern.

Figure 11 shows the imaging optics of the system. Because the working distance of the microscope objective is short compared to the thickness of a half prism, we placed additional imaging lenses behind the half prism to make an image of the pupil of the microlens. The microscope objective magnifies the image on the CCD plane. Generally, the aberration of the imaging optics is not a prob-

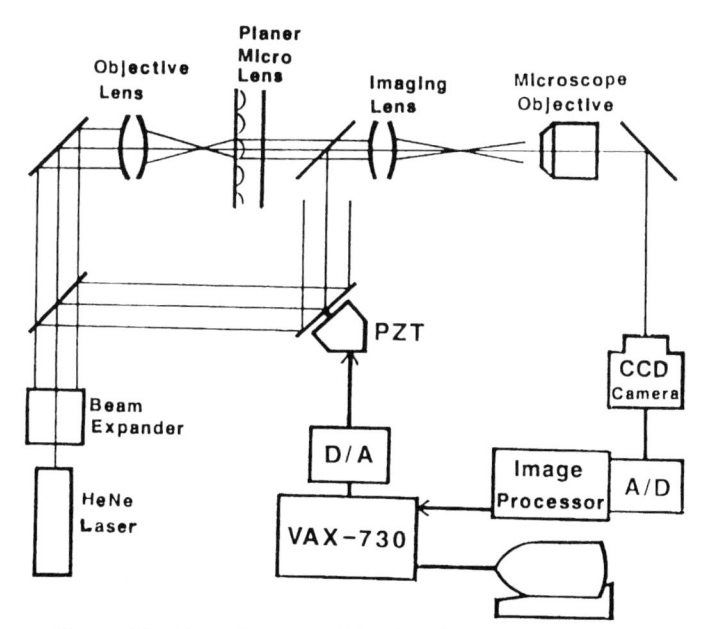

Figure 10. Schematic diagram of the aberration measurement system.

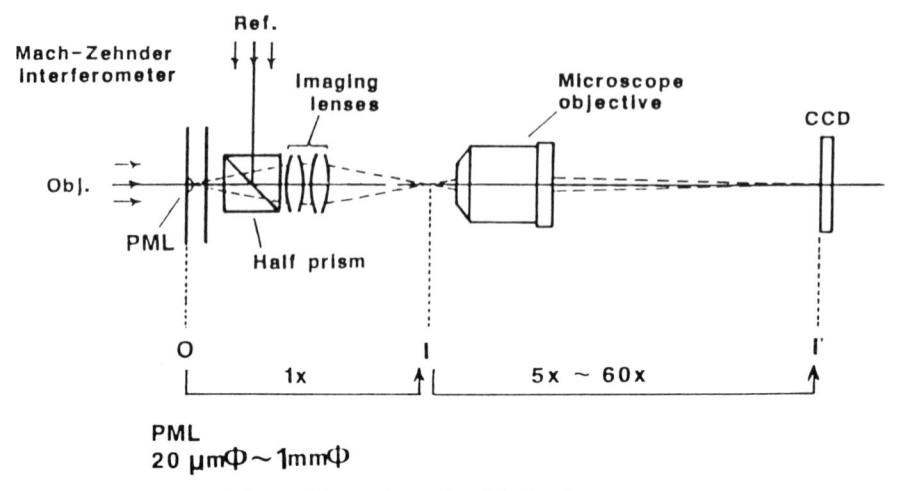

Figure 11. Imaging optics of the interferometer.

lem, because it is placed in the common path in the interferometer. However, in the case of such a small microlens, degradation of the point spread function of the imaging optics causes degradation of the interference pattern. The design of the imaging lenses must take into account the half-prism thickness to minimize the aberration.

The interference pattern is converted to an 8-bit digital image to be analyzed by a minicomputer. The piezoelectric transducer allows one to realize phase-modulated interferograms. Wavefront aberrations are automatically calculated from the digital data using the algorithm as demonstrated by Bruning et al. (1974).

$$2\pi W(r,\theta)/\lambda = \arctan \left[\frac{\sum_{j=1}^{N} I(r,\theta,l_j) \sin(2\pi l_j/\lambda)}{\sum_{j=1}^{N} I(r,\theta,l_j) \cos(2\pi l_j/\lambda)} \right]. \quad (15)$$

Here, $W(r,\theta)$ is the wavefront phase profile, $I(r,\theta,l_j)$ is the light intensity of the interferograms, l_j is the phase shift of the interferograms ($j = 1, 2, \ldots, N$), N is the number of interferograms, and λ is wavelength of the laser beam.

The estimated wavefront phase profile is fitted by Zernike polynomials (Malacara et al. 1974):

$$W(r,\theta) = \sum_{n=0}^{k} \sum_{m=0}^{n} A_{nm} R_n^{n-2m} \langle \begin{matrix} sin \\ cos \end{matrix} \rangle (n - 2m)\theta. \quad (16)$$

The rms, the third-order aberration coefficients, and so on are estimated from the Zernike coefficients after eliminating the low-order terms that depend on the mea-

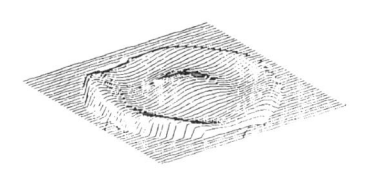

(a)　　　　　　　　　　　　　　　　**(b)**

Figure 12. Wavefront profile of planar microlens shown in Fig. 4.

surement conditions. We have also estimated the point spread function and modulation transfer function (MTF) from the Zernike coefficient.

Figure 12 shows an example of the interference pattern of a planar microlens. The diameter is 160 μm and the focal length is 420 μm. Figure 12(b) shows the wavefront aberration profile of the same lens. Table 3 summarizes the estimated aberration coefficients of the lens. The RMS value of the wavefront aberration is 0.046λ.

The repeatability of the measurements is about 0.001λ as a standard deviation of the rms values. The standard deviation of the third-order aberration terms such as W40, W31, and W22 is about 0.03λ, respectively:

W40	third-order spherical aberration	(r^4)
W31	third-order coma	($r\cos^3\theta$)
W22	third-order astigmatism	($r^2\cos^2\theta$)

The accuracy is almost constant for microlenses with diameters in the range of 50 μm to 1 mm. It degrades for lenses with decreasing diameters because of resolution limitations due to diffraction effects.

3.2 Aberration Properties of Planar Microlenses

From the many kinds of planar microlens arrays that have various specifications, we have chosen 200 samples of one specification (see Table 4). We evaluated them using the measurement system mentioned earlier. These samples have an opaque layer that has a 160-μm circular aperture on a 170-μm circular diffused region.

Figure 13 shows histograms of the rms values and third-order spherical aberration coefficients (W40). The average rms value is 0.043λ and most of the lenses have small aberrations, i.e., less than 0.07λ. Since the asymmetric aberration terms (such as coma, astigmatism, etc.) and the fifth-order spherical aberration

Table 3. Aberration Coefficients of the Lens Shown in Figs. 4 and 5

Zernike Coefficients

A00 = 2.218							
A10 = 2.926	A11 = 0.100						
A20 = 0.025	A21 = −0.088	A22 = 0.003					
A30 = 0.004	A31 = −0.039	A32 = 0.032	A33 = −0.001				
A40 = −0.015	A41 = 0.005	A42 = −0.036	A43 = −0.022	A44 = −0.012			
A50 = −0.006	A51 = −0.004	A52 = −0.015	A53 = −0.012	A54 = −0.020	A55 = 0.009		
			A63 = 0.010				

Aberration Coefficients

RMS	= 0.046	P-V = 0.27	
Spherical	3rd = −0.22		
Coma	3rd = 0.15	ANGL = 310	
Astigma.	3rd = 0.05	ANGL = 41	

Physics of Planar Microlenses   127

Table 4. Planar Microlens Samples Used for Detailed Evaluation

Diameter	Focal Length	NA	Number of Samples
160 μm	420 μm	0.19	200

term are small compared with the third-order spherical aberration term, the variations in the rms values are mainly caused by the variation of the third-order spherical aberration term.

In many cases, the planar microlens array is used as a small chip with an area of 100 mm² or less. For practical applications, we have measured the variation of the rms value over a small area of about 10 mm. The glass substrates that have many planar microlenses are divided into small regions. We have measured four to six microlenses from each small region and the variation of the third-order spherical aberration term W40 in each region is estimated. Figure 14 shows the histogram of W40*, which is defined as the difference from the local average:

$$W40^* = W40 - \langle W40^* \rangle, \quad (17)$$

where $\langle W40^* \rangle$ is the average value in each small region. The standard deviation of W40* is quite small (i.e., $\sigma = 0.038\lambda$) compared to the $\sigma = 0.278\lambda$ standard deviation of the samples overall. The result shows that the variation of aberration over small areas is negligibly small.

When we use the planar microlens as an imaging lens, aberration properties for off-axis light rays are important. Figure 15 shows the third-order coma and the third-order astigmatism. Each point represents an absolute value and direction of the aberration term measured at the off-axis angle from -5 to $+5$ deg with a step of 1 deg. The result shows that the third-order coma is the only increasing term.

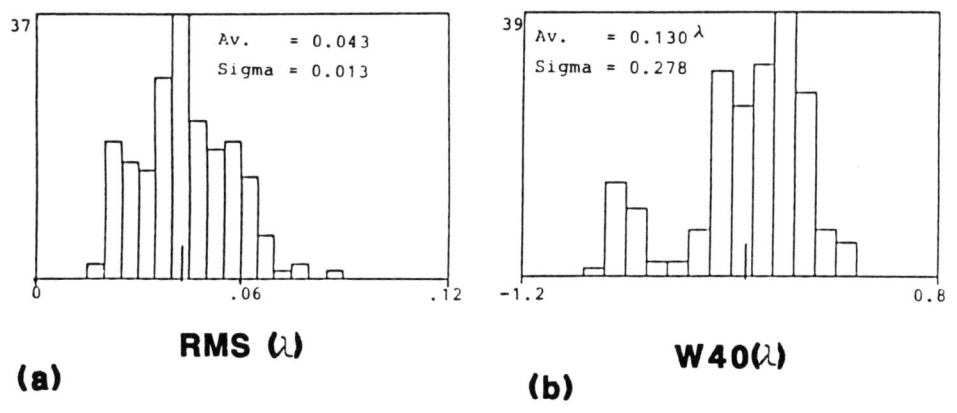

(a) Av. = 0.043, Sigma = 0.013, RMS (λ)

(b) Av. = 0.130 λ, Sigma = 0.278, W40(λ)

Figure 13. Histograms of RMS and W40.

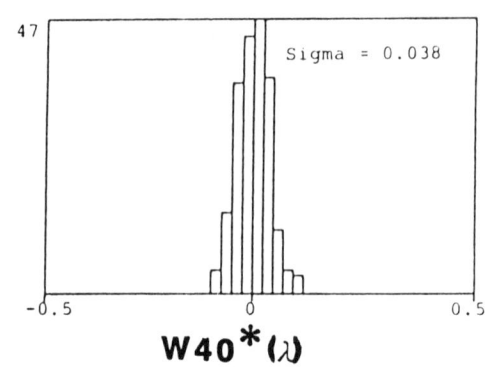

Figure 14. Histogram of W40*.

The third-order astigmatism as well as the other aberration terms are almost constant over an imaging field ±5°. Figure 16 shows that the third-order coma changes proportionally with the off-axis angle at the ratio of about 0.05λ/deg.

We also evaluated the image resolution of the PML. The image of a resolution test chart is shown in Fig. 17(a). The optical setup used in this evaluation is shown in Fig. 17(b). Figure 18 shows the modulation depth data of the PML. The MTF curve that is estimated theoretically with a diffraction-limited lens (NA = 0.19) is also shown in Fig. 18. The modulation depth is almost diffraction limited as coincident with the aberration data mentioned earlier. Additionally, Fig. 17(a) shows that the field curvature and the distortion of the microlens are small. These results show that the planar microlens can perform high-quality imaging in a wide image field.

Figures 19 and 20 show the interferograms and the aberration results of other planar microlens samples. The distributed index region corresponding to the diffused region is 80 μm and 1.08 mm, respectively. We evaluated the wavefront

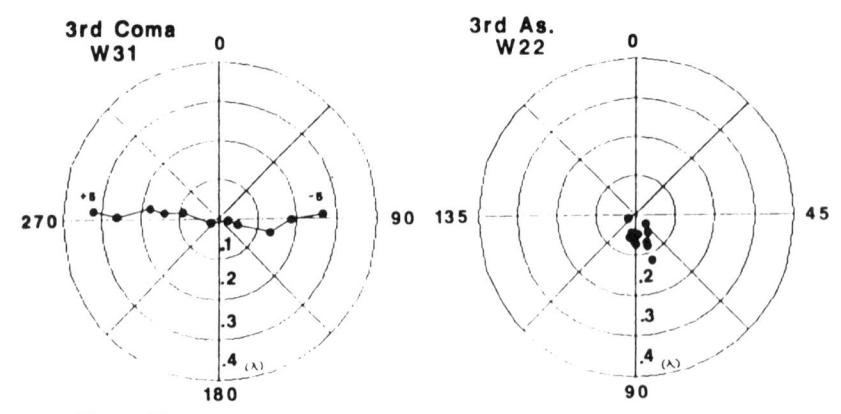

Figure 15. Coma W31 and astigmatism W22 terms measured with an inclination.

$$\triangle W31 = 0.054 \; \lambda/deg.$$

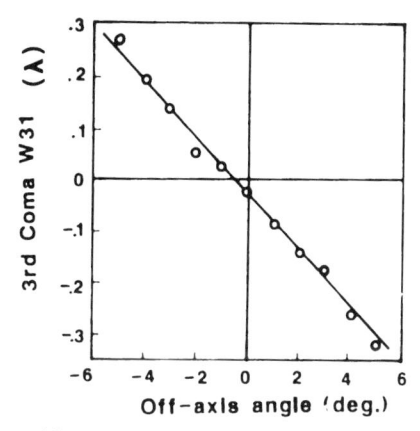

Figure 16. Variation of coma W31 versus off-axis angle.

(a)

(b)

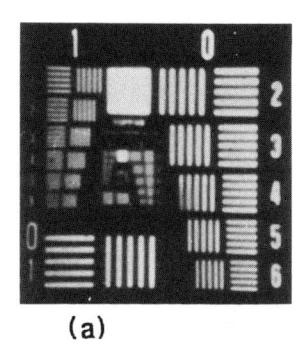

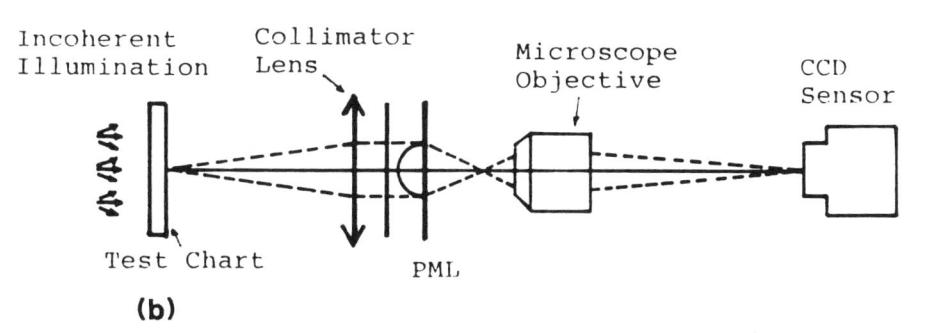

Figure 17. Imaging of a resolution chart: (a) photograph of the image and (b) the optical setup.

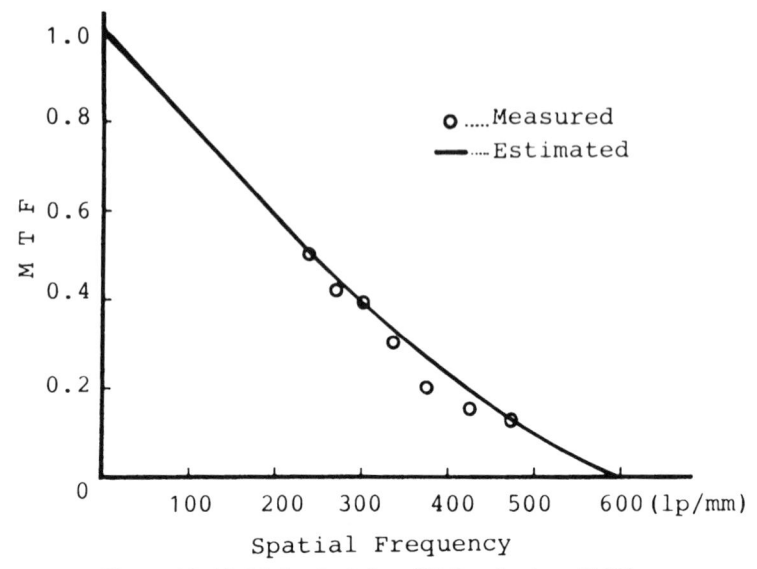

Figure 18. Modulation depth data of PML and estimated MTF.

aberration within about 90% of the gradient index region. The rms value of the 80-μm diameter microlens is 0.029λ and is almost diffraction limited. Figure 20 compares the aberration properties in the two different incident light conditions. The wavefront profiles are slightly different from each other; however, both aberration levels are not as large compared with the Marechal criterion. The results show that either setup can be used depending on the application.

Figure 19. Interferogram of a planar microlens with 80-μm diameter.

Physics of Planar Microlenses   131

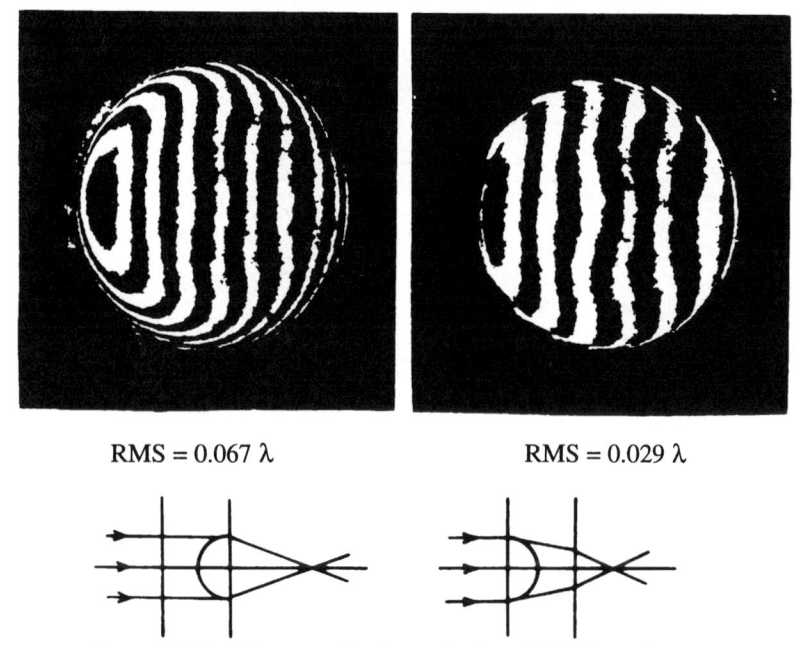

RMS = 0.067 λ   RMS = 0.029 λ

Figure 20. Interferograms of a planar microlens with 1.08-mm diameter.

4. Planar Microlenses with Swelled Structures

In this section we introduce a new class of high-NA PMLs, known as S-PMLs, which use the local swelling induced by the ion-exchange technique. Optical properties are not fully evaluated yet; however, the S-PML will provide a new possibility of array coupling between high-NA optical devices. The NA is limited when we make use of index distribution only.

In 1989, we found that the swelling induced by the ion-exchange process can be used to increase the NA of the PML. In this new class of PML, we use the difference of the ion radius during the ion-exchange process. The mechanism of swelling is shown in Fig. 21.

Figure 22 shows an array of S-PMLs and Fig. 23 shows an SEM photograph of the S-PML. The new S-PML requires a relatively large diffusion area around the window to obtain sufficient swelling height. Inside the aperture, a smooth spherical surface was obtained that contributes to the increase in NA. Here we define the aperture diameter as the lens diameter, $2a$. The swelling height of S-PML is as large as 25 μm inside the aperture.

We have fabricated the S-PMLs with diameters ranging from 80 to 200 μm. We examined two different diffusion conditions. Figure 24 shows the NA and focal length F_b versus lens diameter. The diffusion length slightly depends on its lens diameter. We measured the focal length as a distance between the focal point and

SWELLING BY ION EXCHANGE

MASK

SPHERICAL SURFACE

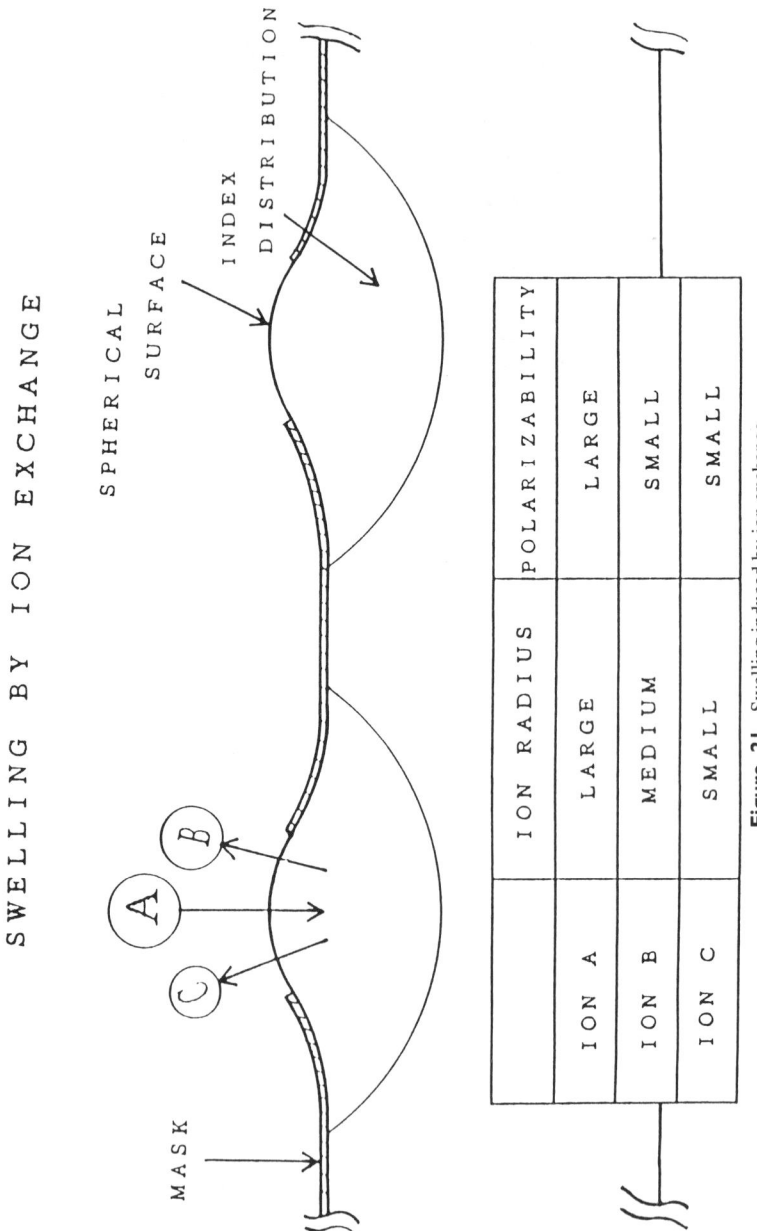

INDEX DISTRIBUTION

	ION RADIUS	POLARIZABILITY
ION A	LARGE	LARGE
ION B	MEDIUM	SMALL
ION C	SMALL	SMALL

Figure 21. Swelling induced by ion exchange.

Physics of Planar Microlenses 133

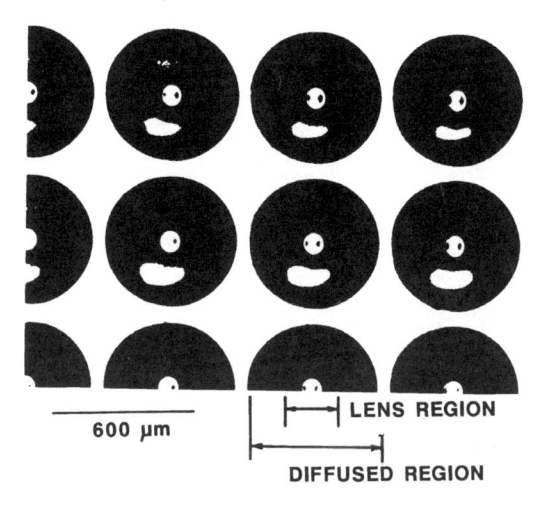

Figure 22. Array of S-PMLs.

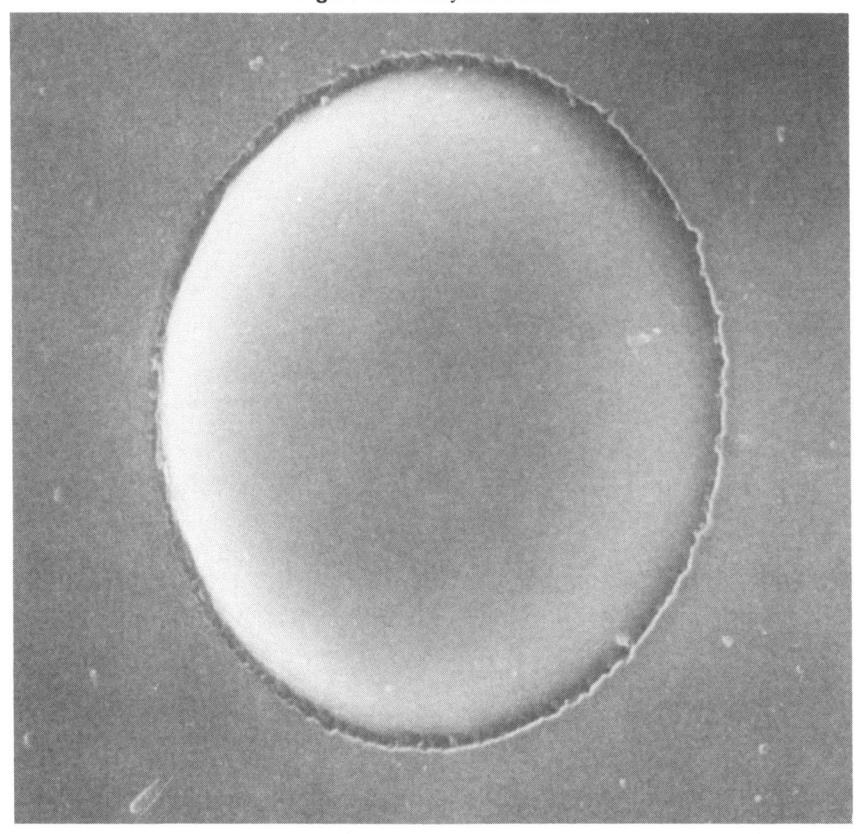

Figure 23. SEM photograph of S-PML.

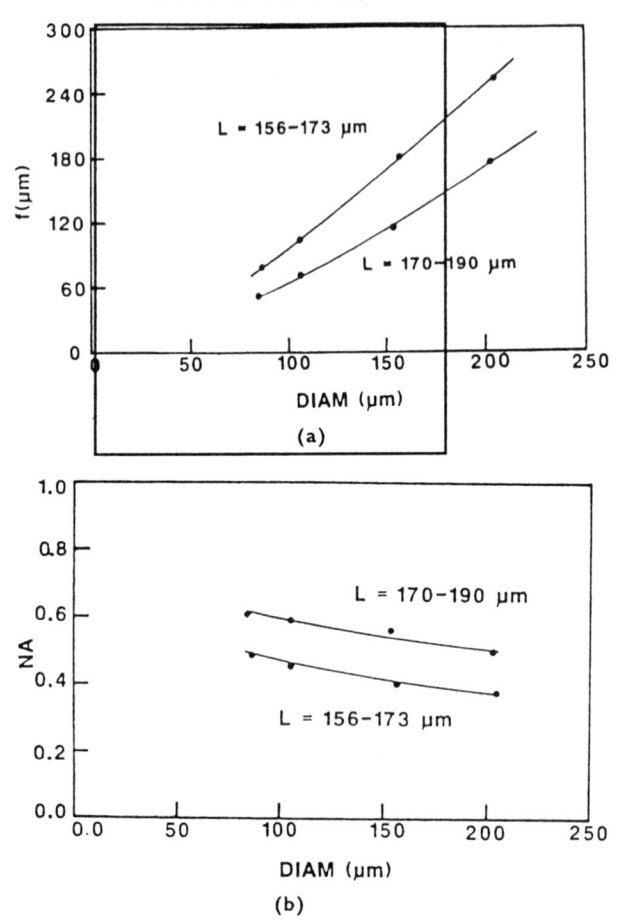

Figure 24. (a) Focal length versus PML diameter and (b) NA versus PML diameter.

the top of the surface using a collimated He-Ne laser. Since we assume that the lens effect comes mainly from the swelled surface, the principal plane is assumed to be located at the top of the swelled surface. The NA is calculated by

$$NA = \sin[\tan^{-1}(a/F_b)]. \qquad (18)$$

Figure 25 shows the focused spot of the He-Ne laser light ($\lambda = 0.63$ μm). The spot diameter is 2.5 μm, which is 1.8 times larger than the diffraction-limited Airy disk. The discrepancy is considered to be caused by the aberration of the lens. This could be improved by optimizing the fabrication process.

To examine the possibility of the S-PML as a coupling lens, we tested light coupling between an LD and an optical fiber.

In Fig. 26, we found the best coupling position of the PML by manipulating the LD in the optical axis. The Z-position of the laser diode is defined by the distance between LD and the focal point of the planar microlens. The position of an optical

Ds = 2.5 μm
λ = 0.63 μm
PML: 2a = 110 μm
Fb = 90 μm
NA = 0.52

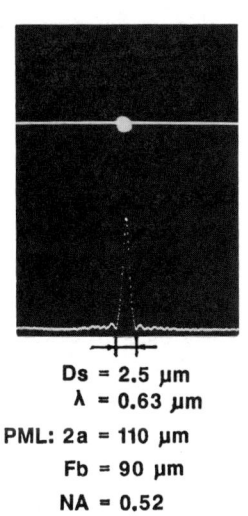

Figure 25. Focused spot of the S-PML.

fiber is optimized relative to the position of LD. The experimental coupling results for both a single-mode fiber and GI-50 fiber are also plotted. The light power accepted at the detector when it is almost making contact with the LD is defined by 0 dB. The light sensitive area of the detector is 5 mm in diameter. Each optical fiber position is optimized corresponding to the change of the LD position. The minimum coupling loss for the single-mode fiber was as small as −5.3 dB when we located the LD 45 μm away from the focal point. The minimum coupling loss was −3.1 dB for a GI-50 fiber. An InGaAsP double-heterostructure LD (Toshiba TOLD302) was used in this experiment. The LD emits light with a wavelength of 1.3 μm in the longitudinal single mode. The emitting angle is 35 deg in

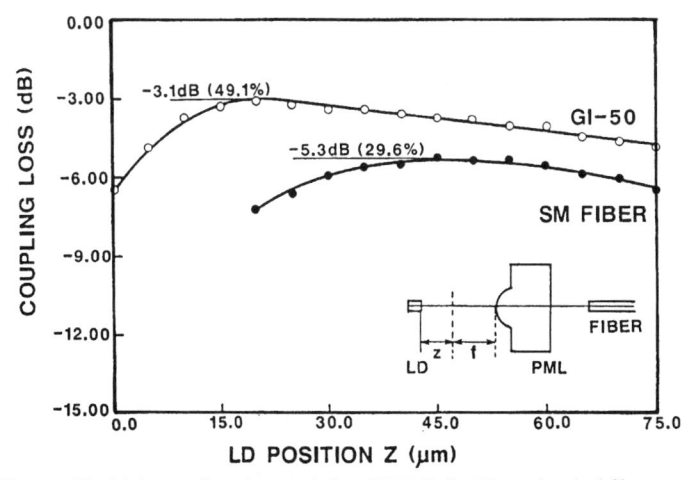

Figure 26. Light-coupling characteristics of S-PML for LDs and optical fiber.

the direction parallel to the junction and 45 deg in the direction perpendicular to the junction.

5. Conclusion

In conclusion, we have demonstrated the planar microlens and its optical characteristics. A small aberration microlens uses the concentration dependency of ion-exchange diffusion. We reiterate that the average rms value of this wavefront aberration is as small as 0.04λ. The third-order coma coefficient against the off-axis angle is $0.05\lambda/\text{deg}$. Field curvature and distortion is small. These results show that the PML is practically diffraction-limited even for wide field applications.

We have also demonstrated a new class of PMLs that features a swelled structure. The fill factor of the lens is restricted; however, the lens is able to have a large NA of more than 0.5.

Precisely integrated microlenses will provide new possibilities for optical interconnections used in optical computing and optical fiber communication systems.

ACKNOWLEDGMENTS

We would like to thank Professor Iga from the Tokyo Institute of Technology for discussions. We also appreciate the support of Mr. K. Koizumi, Dr. K. Nishizawa, and Mr. T. Kishimoto.

REFERENCES

Borelli, N. F., and Morse, D. L. (1983). *Proc. 4th Topical Meeting on Gradient Index Optical Imaging System* D1, 92–95.
Borelli, N. F., Morse, D. L., Bellman, P. H., and Morgan, W. L. (1985). *Appl. Opt.* **21**(6), 2520–2525.
Bruning, J. H., Herriott, D. R., Gallagher, J. E., Rosenfeld, D. P., White, A. D., and Brangaccio, D. J. (1974). *Appl. Opt.* **13**(11), 2693–2703.
Doremus, G. (1969). *Ion Exchange in Glass.* Marcel Dekker, New York.
Fujita, T., Nishihara, H., and Koyma, J. (1982). *Opt. Lett.* **7**, 578.
Iga, K., Oikawa, M., Banno, J., and Kokubun, Y. (1982). *Appl. Opt.* **21**, 3456–3460.
Khoe, G. D., Kock, H. G., Luijendijik, J. A., Van den Brekel, C. H. J., and Kueppers, D. (1981). *Proc. 7th ECOC,* 7.6–1–4.
Kitano, I., Koizumi, K., Matsumura, H., Uchida, T., and Furukawa, M. (1970). *J. Jpn Soc. Appl. Phys.* **39**, 63–70.
Kokubun, Y., Usui, T., Oikawa, M., and Iga, K. (1984). *Jpn. J. Appl. Phys.* **23**(1), 101–104.
Malacara, D. (1978). *Optical Shop Testing.* John Wiley and Sons, New York.
Oikawa, M., and Iga, K. (1982). *Appl. Opt.* **21**(6), 1052–1056.
Oikawa, M., Iga, K., and Sanada, T. (1981). *Jpn. J. Appl. Phys.* **20**(1), L51–L54.
Oikawa, M., Iga, K., Sanada, T., Yamamoto, N., and Nishizawa, K. (1981). *Jpn. J. Appl. Phys.* **20**(4), L296–L298.
Oikawa, M., Okuda, E., Hamanaka, K., and Nemoto, H. (1988). *Proc. SPIE* **898**, 3–11.
Oikawa, M., Nemoto, H., Hamanaka, K., and Kishimoto, T. (1990a). *Proc. SPIE* **1219**, 532–538.
Oikawa, M., Nemoto, H., Hamanaka, K., and Okuda, E. (1990b). *Appl. Opt.* **29**, 4077–4080.
Oikawa, M., Tanaka, K., and Yamasaki, T. (1985). *Proc. SPIE* **554**, 314–318.
Swanson, G. J., and Veldkamp, W. B. (1989). *Opt. Eng.* **28**, 605–608.

Chapter 6
Diffractive Optical Elements for Optical Computers

JÜRGEN JAHNS

AT&T Bell Laboratories
Room 4G-524
Crawfords Corner Road
Holmdel, NJ 07733

1. Introduction 137
2. Fabrication of Diffractive Optical Elements 139
   2.1 Fabrication Using Photolithography and Reactive Ion Etching 139
   2.2 Diffraction Efficiency and Light Efficiency 143
   2.3 Fabrication Errors 144
   2.4 Replication of Diffractive Optics 146
3. Theory of Diffractive Optical Elements 148
   3.1 Linear Blazed Gratings 148
   3.2 Diffractive Lenses 151
4. Applications of Diffractive Micro-Optics 154
   4.1 Spot Array Generation with Phase Gratings 154
   4.2 Space-Variant Interconnections 158
   4.3 Integrated Micro-Optic Packaging 158
5. Conclusion 162
   References 165

I. Introduction

In this chapter, we introduce the field of lithographically fabricated diffractive optical elements (DOEs) or more recently called *binary optical elements*. Although the use of diffractive optics has been investigated for many other applications such as lens design, sensors, components for communications systems, etc., we discuss the use of DOEs for research in digital optical computing. In that area, DOEs, for example, have been used for spot array generation, parallel interconnections, and micro-optic integration. These applications are discussed after describing the fabrication and the theory of DOEs in some detail. We begin this introduction, however, with a brief overview of the field of diffractive optics. The goals of this overview are to provide the reader with some background and, at the same time, to define the terminology we are going to use. The explanation of the terminology seems to be appropriate since, in diffractive optics, many terms exist that are not well defined or that are used inconsistently.

We will start with the simple distinction between *analog* and *digital* diffractive optical elements. Analog diffractive elements are fabricated by using the interference of two or more optical wavefronts. The interferograms are recorded in photosensitive materials such as a silver halide film or a layer of dichromated gelatin. These holographic optical elements (HOEs), as they are usually called, can be classified further according to their physical properties. For example, one can distinguish between "thin" and "thick" holograms according to whether the thickness of the recording layer is of the order of the wavelength of the light or much thicker. The physics and applications of HOEs have been described by many different authors; see, for example Caulfield (1979) and Hariharan (1984).

Digital diffractive optical elements are not fabricated by analog recording techniques but by means of computer-generated masks. The masks are written by a conventional plotter or by an electron-beam writer for obtaining very high resolution. Digital diffractive optics comprises *computer-generated holograms* (CGHs), *kinoforms,* and *binary optics.* It is difficult to find differences between the various categories because the differences are partially related to certain applications and partially blurred by the historical development.

Computer-generated holography was invented by Lohmann in the 1960s when digital computers and plotters started to become available (Brown and Lohmann 1966). A CGH is an element with binary transmission values (either amplitude or phase). Conventional Lohmann-type CGHs are based on the use of a spatial carrier, which means that the hologram is reconstructed in the first diffraction order. A cell structure is used to encode the amplitude and the phase of the wavefront. The phase is encoded indirectly by the spatial position of a pulse by means of the principle of the *detour phase.* Several overview texts are available about CGHs; the reader might consult, for example, W. H. Lee (1978) and Bryngdahl and Wyrowski (1990). Applications of CGHs in analog signal processing such as matched filtering and OTF (optical transfer function) synthesis are described in a book edited by S. H. Lee (1981).

The kinoform was introduced by Lesem, Hirsch, and Jordan (1969) as a computer-generated diffractive component that works without a spatial carrier. It is a pure phase element with a large (ideally, infinite) number of phase values. Early kinoforms were made by generating photographic plots with multiple gray levels. These were then reduced in size and the reduced pieces of film were bleached in order to obtain a phase transparency. The difficulties of this process might account for the fact that kinoforms were used less than CGHs.

In the early 1970s, *lithographic fabrication techniques,* being developed for the fabrication of integrated electronic circuits, were adapted for the fabrication of DOEs. Dammann was one of the first to suggest this approach for making beam-splitter gratings (Dammann 1970; Dammann and Görtler 1971). These gratings were implemented as binary phase gratings by etching a surface relief profile into a substrate. Arrays of diffractive lenslets were demonstrated by d'Auria et al. (1972) and Firester et al. (1973). In the 1980s, DOEs gained increasing attention for applications in the infrared where conventional optics are not readily available. This work was perpetuated by Veldkamp and coworkers who coined the term *binary optics* (Swanson 1989). Although this term is somewhat misleading as far as the physical structure of the elements is concerned, it has become widely accepted. As mentioned, another term often used to denote a "binary optics" component is *diffractive optical element,* although that term would be better used for any diffractive structure. Nonetheless, for the sake of having a short and intuitive acronym to use in the remainder of this chapter, we are going to denote DOE as a lithographically fabricated digital diffractive element.

Recently, binary optics also become one approach to implement micro-optical components such as miniature lenses or lenslet arrays. In optical computing, the already mentioned Dammann gratings are widely used to illuminate modulator arrays in digital optical computer or switching systems (Prise et al. 1990; McCormick et al. 1992). Another example of the use of DOEs in optical computing is space-variant interconnections implemented by arrays of diffractive lenslets and gratings (Sauer 1989; Jahns and Däschner 1990; Robertson et al. 1991). A second reason for the interest in DOEs results from the desire to find improved ways of packaging free-space optical systems. An example is the concept of *planar optics* (Jahns and Huang, 1989), which builds on the use of integrated circuit manufacturing technology to make miniaturized, alignment-free free-space optical systems.

Section 2 gives a brief description of the fabrication of DOEs. We also describe some of the fabrication errors and their influence on the performance of the element. A theoretical model of DOEs based on scalar diffraction theory is presented in Section 3. Several applications are described in Section 4, such as spot array generation, space-variant interconnection networks, and micro-optic integration.

2. Fabrication of Diffractive Optical Elements

2.1 Fabrication Using Photolithography and Dry Etching

Figure 1 shows pictures of a diffractive lens and a beamsplitter grating with multiple discrete phase levels. Both were fabricated by successive steps of lithography and dry etching. In this section, we describe DOE fabrication procedures. In general, both direct-write techniques and mask-based techniques can be used for the fabrication of diffractive optics. Direct electron-beam lithography has been demonstrated for the fabrication of diffractive optics by Nishihara and Suhara (1987) and Shiono et al. (1987). Here we deal with the mask-based fabrication of

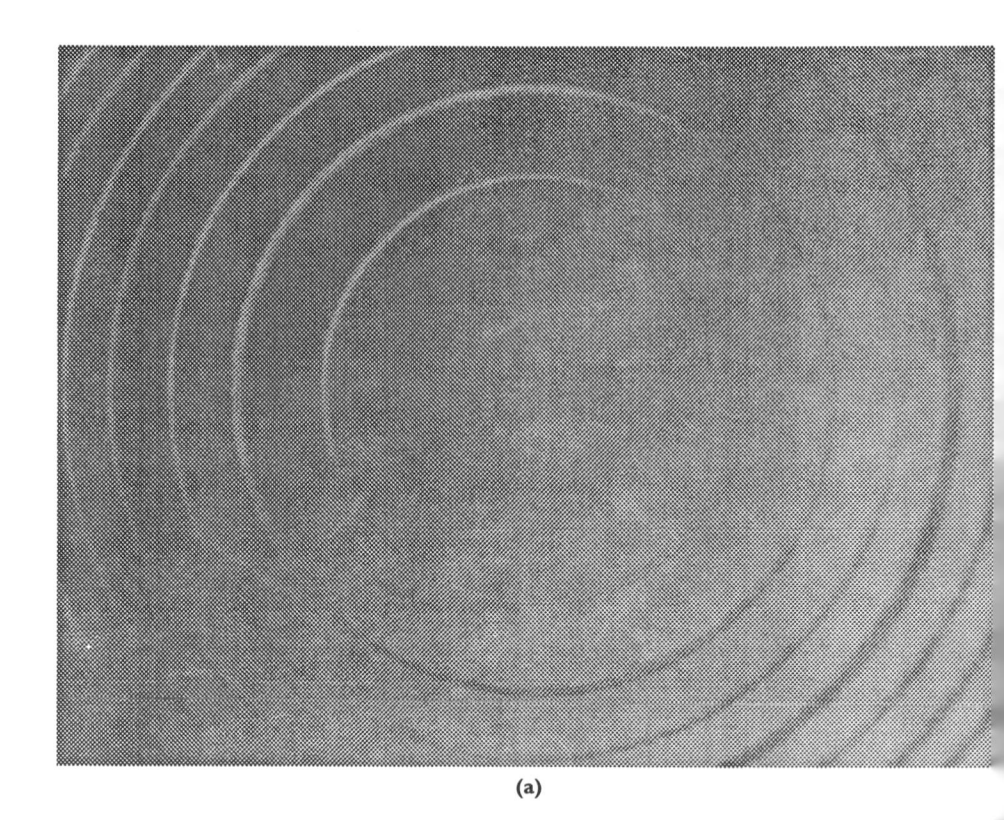

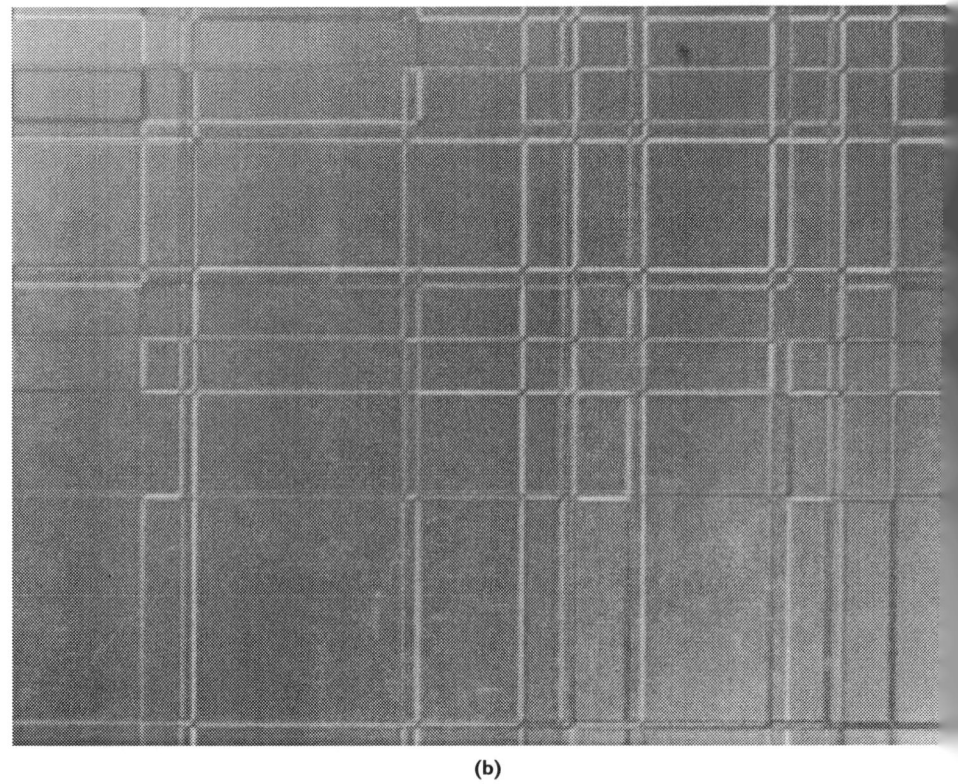

Figure 1. Examples of diffractive optical elements: (a) lens and (b) beamsplitter grating.

DOEs. It is beyond the scope of this chapter to describe the physics and technology of the various fabrication steps that are required for the production of DOEs. For more details on fabrication, the reader is referred to the literature. Several texts are available that cover practically all aspects of microfabrication (Brodie and Muray 1982; Elliott 1989; Voshchenkov 1990).

The generation of the mask data is done with the help of a computer program. This gives the user design flexibility to vary the optical parameters of a lens such as the focal length and the diameter. The design of diffractive optical elements and systems can be facilitated by the use of computer-aided design (CAD) tools (Urquhart *et al.* 1989; Downs and Jahns 1990a). Mask generation is usually accomplished with an electron-beam writer, which yields a very high spatial resolution. State-of-the-art values that can be obtained with an electron-beam writer are a positioning accuracy of 0.1 μm and a feature width of 1 μm, although much smaller values are possible. This allows one to make elements with a large space-bandwidth product, which is required for lenses with high numerical apertures and for Dammann gratings, for example. Furthermore, the precision of the electron-beam writer enables the fabrication of arrays of optical elements with exact spacings for making integrated free-space optical systems (Jahns and Huang 1989).

The fabrication of a DOE is represented schematically in Fig. 2. As an example, the figure shows the fabrication of a simple blazed grating with four phase levels, which is achieved in two fabrication steps. In general, for the fabrication of an element with $L = 2^N$ discrete phase levels, N successive fabrication cycles are required. (The fact that a discrete phase pattern with 2^N discrete phase levels can be decomposed into N binary patterns in basically the same way as an integer is decomposed into a binary number may serve as one justification for the name

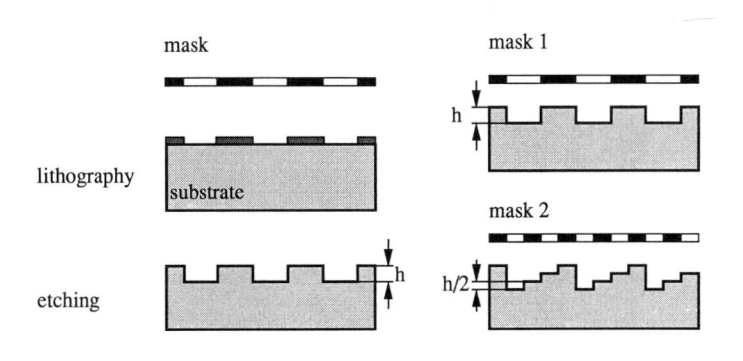

Figure 2. Fabrication of a multilevel DOE using lithography and etching. Shown on the left side is the fabrication of a binary element. A number, N of fabrication cycles yield multilevel elements with 2^N phase levels.

binary optics.) Each fabrication cycle consists of a photolithography step and an etching step as shown on the left side of Fig. 2. In the following, we explain these two steps briefly. An alternative approach is to build up structures by using thin-film deposition and lift-off techniques as described by Jahns and Walker (1990a). However, especially for DOEs with fine features of the order of 1 μm or smaller, etching usually gives better results than the lift-off technique.

The photolithography is done in a clean room with a standard mask aligner (for example, a SUSS MA 4). During this step the mask pattern is transferred into a thin film photoresist that has been spun onto the substrate. A common resist is Hoechst AZ 5214. At 4000 rpm, a spin time of 30 s results in a resist layer thickness of 1.4 μm. This is sufficiently thin for the lithography with narrow features of about 1 μm and sufficiently thick to endure the subsequent etching process. One distinguishes between positive and negative resists (Elliott 1989). Negative resists harden when being exposed; a developing solution removes unexposed resist. On the contrary, positive-tone resists loosen their molecular structure during exposure. Consequently, a developer removes exposed areas. After development, exposed areas are covered with resist when negative resist is used and the opposite occurs for positive resist. Typically, AZ 5214 is used as a positive resist. However, two additional processing steps can convert it into a negative resist (image reversal bake and a flood exposure). The exposure wavelengths are typically in the range from 300 to 400 nm, for example, at the 313-nm line of a mercury lamp. At a typical exposure intensity of 10 mW/cm^2 the exposure time is of the order of 10 s. The mask aligner can usually be operated in various modes. To obtain close contact between the substrate and the mask, it is operated in the vacuum mode. This means that the space between the mask and the chuck that holds the substrate is evacuated before exposure. This allows one to obtain high-resolution lithography with features smaller than 1 μm.

After development, the sample is etched to obtain a surface profile. This is achieved using a dry etching technique such as reactive ion etching. The physics as well as technological aspects of reactive ion-beam etching are described, for example, by Voshchenkov (1991). Here, we discuss just a few basics that are relevant for the fabrication of DOEs.

As explained earlier, several fabrication cycles are required to make multilevel DOEs. As the pattern gets finer from one fabrication cycle to the next, the etch depth also gets smaller by a factor of 2 (Fig. 2). It is important to note that this assumes the large etches are done first. For the actual fabrication, it may be advantageous to start with the smaller etches. This allows one to do the more difficult small features on an unetched planar surface.

The etch depths are chosen such that the L phase levels are spaced evenly at a phase shift of $2\pi/L$. The value for etch depth h depends on several parameters, namely, the refractive index of the substrate n_s, the index of the surrounding medium n_m, the wavelength of the light λ, and whether the element is used in transmission or in reflection. We denote h_π the etch depth that produces a phase shift of π. For a transmissive element, a phase shift of π is achieved by an etch depth

$$h_\pi^{(t)} = \lambda/2\Delta n, \tag{1}$$

where $\Delta n = |n_s - n_m|$. A reflective element requires an etch depth

$$h_\pi^{(r)} = \lambda/4n_m \tag{2a}$$

or

$$h_\pi^{(r)} = \lambda/4n_s \tag{2b}$$

For example, for $n_m = 1$ (air), $n_s = 1.458$ (quartz glass) used at a wavelength of 850 nm, a phase shift of π is achieved for $h_\pi^{(t)} = 928$ nm and $h_\pi^{(r)} = 212.5$ nm if air is the medium of propagation.

Fused silica (SiO$_2$), a commonly used substrate, is etched using a plasma of CHF$_3$ (Freon-23). The plasma is generated by an rf field in a reactive ion etcher. The etch depth is controlled using time calibration. Etch rates are typically of the order of 100 Å/min for reactive ion etching of fused silica. This value can vary depending on the various parameters that can influence the etching process.

2.2 Diffraction Efficiency and Light Efficiency

An important quantity of a DOE is its *diffraction efficiency*, η_d. Diffraction efficiency is defined as the amount of light intensity that goes into a particular diffraction order (or array of orders, as in the case of a Dammann grating) compared to the sum of intensities in all the diffraction orders. However, the diffraction efficiency is not all that matters when one considers the power budget of an optical system because other sources for loss have to be considered. For this reason, we are going to distinguish between diffraction efficiency and light efficiency. Diffraction efficiency describes only losses due to light being diffracted into unwanted orders. Light efficiency is an overall efficiency that includes diffraction losses but also losses due to reflections, absorption, and scattering from the DOE.

We define diffraction efficiency such that η_d ranges between 0 and 1. As an example, consider the case of a diffraction grating that generates only three orders, namely, the 0'th order and the ± 1'st (Fig. 3), where I_1, I_0, and I_{-1} denote the

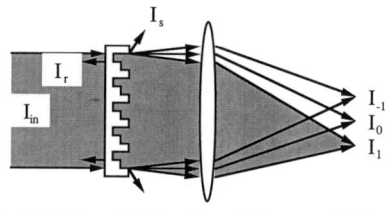

Figure 3. Definition of diffraction efficiency and light efficiency.

intensities of the $+1'$st, the zeroth, and the $-1'$st order. The diffraction efficiency for the first order can then be written as

$$\eta_d = I_1/(I_1 + I_0 + I_{-1}). \tag{3a}$$

Light is lost due to reflections from the substrate surfaces and due to scattering. The intensity of the incoming beam is denoted by I_{in}. Assuming no absorption inside the substrate, we can express the light efficiency η as $\eta = \eta_d \eta_s$ with

$$\eta_s = 1 - (I_s + I_r)/I_{\text{in}}, \tag{3b}$$

where I_s and I_r are the intensities of the scattered light and the reflected light.

The value of η_d can be calculated from the phase profile. For gratings with features that are large compared to the wavelength, analytical expressions can be written for the diffraction efficiency using scalar diffraction theory. For DOEs with smaller features that are typically of the order of a few wavelengths, the use of scalar diffraction theory may lead to wrong results. In this case, rigorous diffraction theory has to be used based on electromagnetic theory (Moharam and Gaylord 1986).

We derive analytical expressions for the diffraction efficiencies of blazed gratings and diffractive lenses in Section 3 of this chapter. Under ideal circumstances, the value of the diffraction efficiency depends only on the number of phase levels. However, various fabrication errors exist that result in a reduction of the diffraction efficiency and in losses due to scattering from the optical element. These errors can be subdivided into mask errors and processing errors. Furthermore, another effect called *shadowing* can contribute to losses.

2.3 Fabrication Errors

Mask errors are quantization errors in the generated patterns that occur because of a discrete address space and the limited resolution of the mask writer. Quantization errors result in deviations of the phase transition coordinates. They may cause a decrease in the diffraction efficiency, variations in the intensities of the diffraction orders, and can also be a source for scattered light. In the case of lenses that are formed by circular patterns, angular quantization can occur if the circles are approximated as polygons as shown in Fig. 4. The superposition of such polygon structures during the fabrication of a multilevel element can result in poorly defined borders, particularly if the number of corners in the superimposed polygons are not equal. This error may result in scattering losses.

Processing errors can be subdivided into errors introduced during the lithographic process and errors introduced during the etching process. They are, however, not independent of each other. Errors introduced during the lithographic process can be enhanced by etching. In addition, mask-to-mask alignment errors can play an important role in the fabrication of multilevel components that require several fabrication cycles.

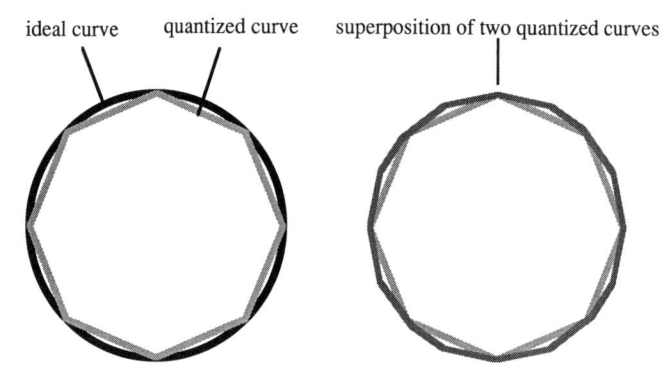

ideal curve   quantized curve   superposition of two quantized curves

Figure 4. Angular quantization in the pattern generation of diffractive lenses.

Imperfect lithography due to deviations from the ideal exposure and development time may cause linewidth errors, meaning that the feature width is either too large or too small. In particular, when one approaches the 1-μm limit where the feature widths are of the same order of magnitude as the resist thickness, the shape of the developed resist may be rounded. If the etching process is not ideally anisotropic, the angle of the sidewalls may be transferred into the glass substrate, which is not desirable. Therefore, it is important that the lithography be done with as high a contrast as possible. A specific technique to generate practically perfectly vertical sidewalls was described recently by Nagy (1992).

Etching errors include imperfect (partially isotropic) etching, etch-depth errors, surface roughness introduced by the etching process, etc. Etch-depth errors are usually not very harmful, at least as far as the overall light efficiency is concerned. They result in a uniform decrease in the amount of light coupled into all the higher orders and a simultaneous increase in the amount of light going to the zeroth order. This is usually not a serious problem for diffractive lenses although it may be a source of crosstalk in lenslet-based optical systems. The etch-depth error can, however, be bothersome for Dammann gratings where uniformity of the diffraction orders is highly desirable.

One of the most significant errors is mask-to-mask misalignment. It is intuitively clear that for a given minimum feature width w the precision of the mask-to-mask alignment has to be done with a precision of $w/10$ or better. Otherwise a significant deviation in the created phase profile will result in a rapid decline in diffraction efficiency. One of the main features, therefore, of the operation of a mask aligner is its overlay accuracy. A theoretical treatment of mask-to-mask misalignment and its influence on the performance of DOEs was given by Cox, Fritz, and Werner (1991).

Shadowing is another source of light losses (Hutley 1982) that is not due to fabrication errors but is inherent in diffractive optical elements with their discontinuous surface profiles (Fig. 5). If we assume according to Huygens's principle

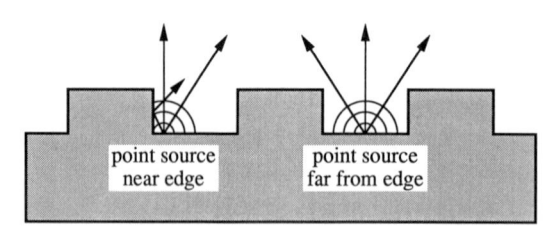

(Born and Wolf 1980) that each point on the surface of a DOE may be considered as a secondary light source that emits a spherical wave, then it is obvious from Fig. 5 that some of that light may hit the sidewalls and be scattered to arbitrary positions. It is also obvious that this effect is more severe for gratings with small periods and for transmissive elements since they have a deeper etch depth than reflective elements. This effect will, in general, be polarization-dependent, which has to be considered, especially for high-frequency gratings.

2.4 Replication of Diffractive Optics

The fact that DOEs are surface relief structures allows one to replicate them by using molding techniques. This is of interest in order to reduce the cost per optical element, particularly if the fabrication of the original (or master) is difficult and therefore expensive. The replication of diffractive optics is not new; commercially available blazed gratings, as they are often used in spectrometers, are usually replicas (Hutley 1982). The quality of the copy can, in general, be as good as the quality of the master.

An example of a replicated DOE is shown in Fig. 6 (Jahns *et al.* 1992b). In this case, a two-dimensional lenslet array with eight discrete phase levels was first fabricated on a quartz glass substrate by using optical lithography and reactive ion etching. This substrate was used as the master for the subsequent molding process. For the molding process, a 1-mm-thick PMMA (polymethylmethacrylate) folio was spun onto an optical flat. The master was then pressed onto the PMMA layer. The complete structure was put into a vacuum oven that was evacuated to a pressure of 1 Torr. For 1 h, the temperature was then slowly increased to 140°C, which is slightly above the glass temperature of the specific PMMA that we used. During this hour the molding PMMA had the chance to fill all the features of the master. After another hour the oven was turned off, the pressure was slowly increased and the temperature was reduced to room temperature. As the temperature reached lower levels, the substrate separated itself and showed a perfect imprint of the master. The finest feature in the diffractive lens was 2 μm. Much finer features can be replicated as has been demonstrated by, for example, Cowan (1990). In general, the lower limit on the size of a replicable features is determined

Figure 6. Diffractive lens with eight phase levels replicated into PMMA.

by the viscosity of the material used, which, in turn, depends on its molecular structure. PMMA, which is used as a resist for electron-beam lithography, has a demonstrated resolution of 50 nm (Smith, Spears, and Bernacki 1973).

3. Theory of Diffractive Optical Elements

In this section, we present a theoretical model of DOEs. The theory is based on scalar diffraction theory and, therefore, has a limited range, as was mentioned previously. For many situations, however, the use of the scalar model is sufficient to describe the performance of a DOE in terms of its diffraction efficiency and also in order to describe the influence of fabrication errors.

As mentioned earlier, an important parameter of a DOE is the diffraction efficiency. Diffractive optical elements are implemented with a finite number of phase levels and a discontinuous phase profile. This causes light to be diffracted into higher, unwanted orders and hence a loss of efficiency results. It is possible to calculate the theoretical diffraction efficiency of a DOE from its phase profile. In the case of blazed linear phase gratings and diffractive lenses, it is even possible to derive analytical expressions for the diffraction efficiency.

3.1 Linear Blazed Gratings

Blazed gratings are designed to optimize the amount of light going into a particular diffraction order, which is usually one of the first orders. The classical application of blazed gratings is spectrometry. For optical interconnections and optical computing, blazed phase gratings can be useful as efficient beam deflectors (Walker and Jahns 1992). Figure 7 shows the general case of a blazed linear phase grating implemented with a finite number of phase levels L and a period p. As mentioned earlier, we assume that the feature width p/L is sufficiently large so

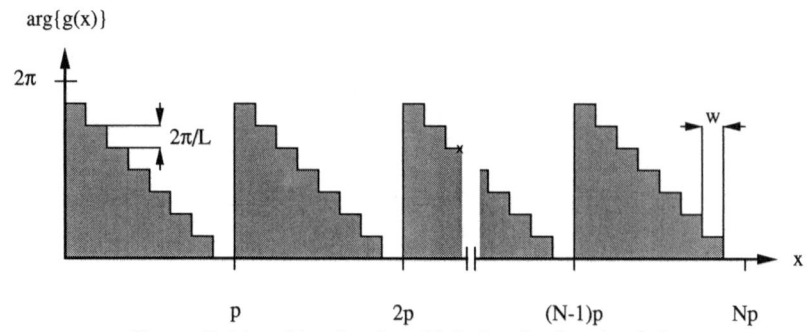

Figure 7. Linear blazed grating with L phase levels and period p.

that scalar diffraction theory applies. When illuminating the grating with a plane-wave of wavelength λ, light will be diffracted under various angles α_m that are given by the well-known equation

$$\sin(\alpha_m) = m(\lambda/n)/p. \quad (4)$$

Here, m denotes a particular diffraction order and n is the index of refraction of the material in which the light beams propagate. Unless otherwise stated, we are going to assume that $n = 1$, i.e., that the light propagates through air.

The intensities of the various orders can be computed using a simple Fourier expansion of the complex amplitude transmission of the grating. We denote the complex amplitude transmission by $g(x)$. Due to the periodicity, $g(x)$ can be expanded into a Fourier series. If we assume an infinitely extended grating, one can write

$$g(x) = \sum_{m=-\infty}^{\infty} A_m \exp(2\pi i m x/p). \quad (5)$$

The Fourier coefficients A_m give the values of the amplitudes of the various diffraction orders. They are calculated as

$$A_m = \frac{1}{p} \int_0^p g(x) \exp(-2\pi i m x/p) \, dx. \quad (6)$$

In the following, we normalize the period of the grating, i.e., $p = 1$. From this, according to Parseval's theorem (Goodman 1968), it follows that the sum of the intensities $I_m = |A_m|^2$ is equal to one:

$$\sum_{m=-\infty}^{\infty} I_m = 1. \quad (7)$$

With $p = 1$, the grating can be represented mathematically as:

$$g(x) = \sum_{k=-\infty}^{\infty} \exp(-2\pi i k/L) \, \text{rect}\left(\frac{x - k/L - 1/2L}{1/L}\right). \quad (8)$$

Using this expression and Eq. (6), the amplitude of the m'th diffraction order is calculated to be:

$$\begin{aligned} A_m &= \int_0^1 \sum_{k=0}^{L-1} \exp(-2\pi i k/L) \, \text{rect}\left[\frac{x - k/L - 1/2L}{1/L}\right] \\ &\quad \exp(-2\pi i m x) \, dx \\ &= \exp\left(\frac{i\pi m}{L}\right) \text{sinc}\left(\frac{m}{L}\right) \frac{1}{L} \sum_{k=0}^{L-1} \exp\left[2\pi i \frac{k(n+1)}{L}\right]. \end{aligned} \quad (9)$$

The sum on the right side of Eq. (9) is zero unless $n + 1$ is a multiple of L:

$$\sum_{k=0}^{L-1} \exp\left[2\pi i \frac{k(n+1)}{L}\right] = \begin{cases} L & \text{if } n = jL - 1, j \text{ integer} \\ 0 & \text{else.} \end{cases} \quad (10)$$

Figure 8(a) shows the diffraction spectra of three phase gratings with $L = 2, 4,$ and 8 phase levels. For $L = 4$ and 8, the phase profile is asymmetric as shown in Fig. 7. Note, that only every L'th diffraction order is nonzero, while with an increasing number of phase levels the intensity of the $-1'$st order increases. The diffraction efficiency η_d is given as the intensity of the $-1'$st order:

$$\eta_d = I_{-1} = \text{sinc}^2(1/L) = \left[\frac{\sin(\pi/L)}{\pi/L}\right]^2. \quad (11)$$

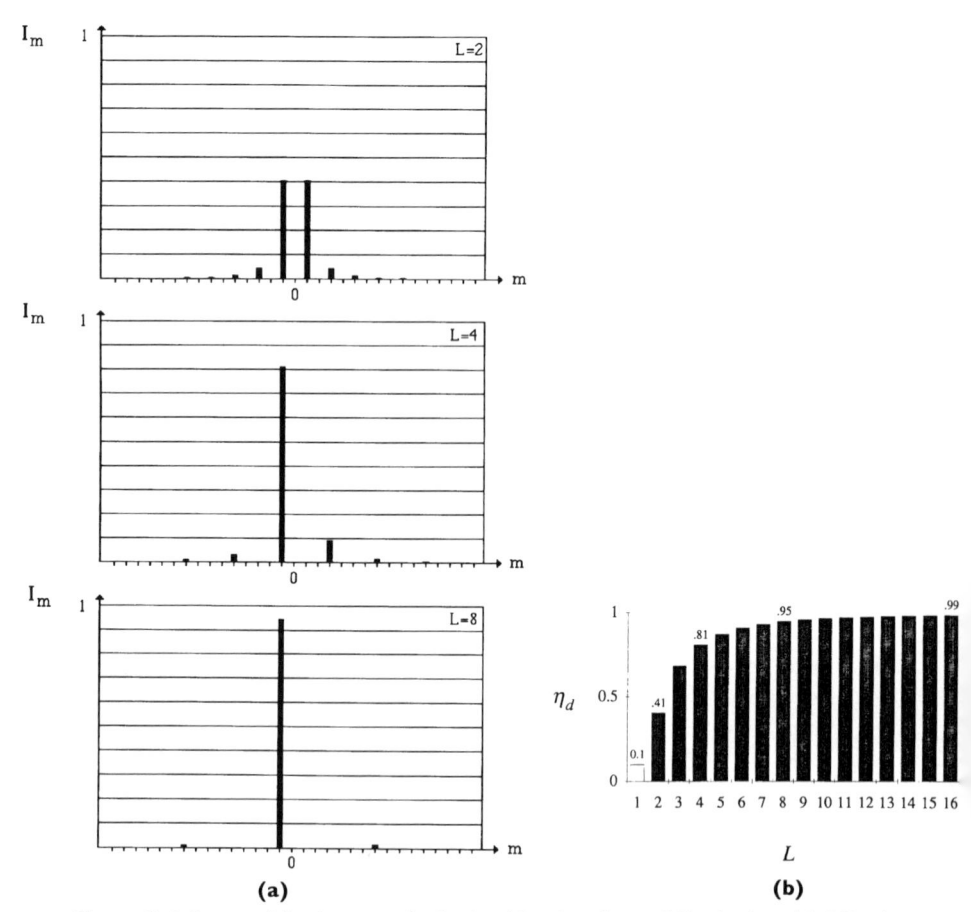

Figure 8. Influence of the phase quantization in a blazed grating or diffractive lens: (a) diffraction spectra of gratings with L phase levels and (b) diffraction efficiency as a function of L. For $L = 1$, the value for a binary amplitude grating is shown.

A graph showing η_d as a function of the number of phase levels is shown in Fig. 8(b). For small values of L, the efficiency grows very rapidly. For $L > 8$, the increase is slower as the curve approaches 1 asymptotically.

3.2 Diffractive Lenses

The action of a diffractive lens is based on near-field diffraction by a Fresnel zone pattern (FZP) as shown in Fig. 9. Like a binary linear diffraction grating, a binary FZP generates a multitude of diffraction orders. The diffraction orders are converging and diverging spherical waves. To achieve high diffraction efficiencies, the lens is implemented as a phase structure with multiple phase levels that approximate the profile of a Fresnel lens (Fig. 10). The focal length of the lens is determined by the period of the zones. The optical path length differences are multiples of the wavelength. For the j'th zone one can therefore write:

$$r_j^2 + f^2 = (f + j\lambda)^2. \tag{12}$$

From this follows:

$$r_j^2 = 2j\lambda f + (j\lambda)^2. \tag{13}$$

For the paraxial case where $f \gg j_{max}\lambda$, the radii of the rings are given as:

$$r_j^2 = 2j\lambda f. \tag{14}$$

This is the well-known case of the FZP, which is periodic in r^2. The period is r_p^2 with $r_p^2 = r_1^2$. For $j = 1$, we can derive the well-known formula for the focal length of a diffractive lens:

$$f = \frac{r_p^2}{2\lambda}. \tag{15}$$

In this case, the complex amplitude transmission of the lens can be described mathematically as:

$$g(x,y) = g(x^2 + y^2) = g(r^2) = \sum_{m=-\infty}^{\infty} A_m \exp(2\pi i m r^2 / r_p^2) \tag{16}$$

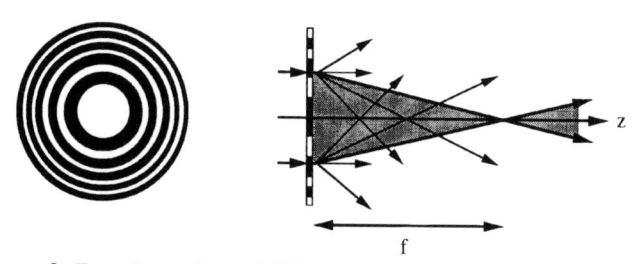

Figure 9. Fresnel zone plate and diffraction at an FZP where f is the focal length.

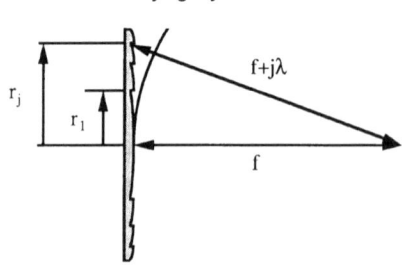

Figure 10. Construction of a diffractive lens: f—focal length; r_1—radius of the central zone; r_j—radius of the j'th zone.

As in the case of the linear grating, the Fourier coefficients A_m give the amplitudes of the diffraction orders. The diffraction efficiency of a diffractive lens as a function of the number of phase levels is therefore given by the expression of Eq. (1).

The complex wave field $u(r, \phi; z)$ at a distance z behind the lens is given as the Fresnel transformation of the complex amplitude transmission of the lens $g(r^2)$ (Goodman 1968). For an object with a radial symmetry, this can be expressed as the Bessel transform of the function $f(r) = g(r^2) \exp[(i\pi/\lambda z)r^2]$:

$$u(r, \phi; z) = \exp\left(2\pi i \frac{z^2 + r^2}{\lambda z}\right) 2\pi \int_0^R J_0(2\pi rr'/\lambda z) f(r') r' \, dr'. \quad (17)$$

Here R is the radius of the lens. By inserting Eq. (15) into this expression, one obtains for the focal plane $z_f = r_p^2/2\lambda$:

$$u(r_f, \phi; z_f) = A_{-1} \exp\left(2\pi i \frac{z_f^2 + r_f^2}{\lambda z_f}\right) 2\pi R^2 \frac{J_1[2\pi(r_f R/\lambda z_f)]}{2\pi(r_f R/\lambda z_f)} \quad (18)$$
$$+ \sum_{m \neq -1} A_m u_m(r_f).$$

The first part of the sum in Eq. (18) describes the focal spot formed by the minus first diffraction order with a constant amplitude factor $A_{-1} 2\pi R^2$. The factor A_{-1} determines the diffraction efficiency; the factor $2\pi R^2$ is the area of the lens. Aside from a quadratic phase factor, the field in the focal plane is an Airy pattern where J_1 is the Bessel function of the first order. The higher orders ($m \neq -1$) form a dilute background illumination, which, in general, is much lower in intensity than the peak intensity of the focal spot. When the lens has a rectangular shape, the spot profile is determined by a sinc(·) function. An example is shown in Fig. 11, where a lens with a square aperture was used to form a spot with a diameter of approximately 5 μm.

The description for the action of a diffractive lens given earlier may not be correct for small apertures and nonuniform (for example, Gaussian) illumination of the lens. It is well known that in this case the focus may shift with a changing Fresnel number (Kogelnik and Li 1966; Sheppard 1986). The Fresnel number is

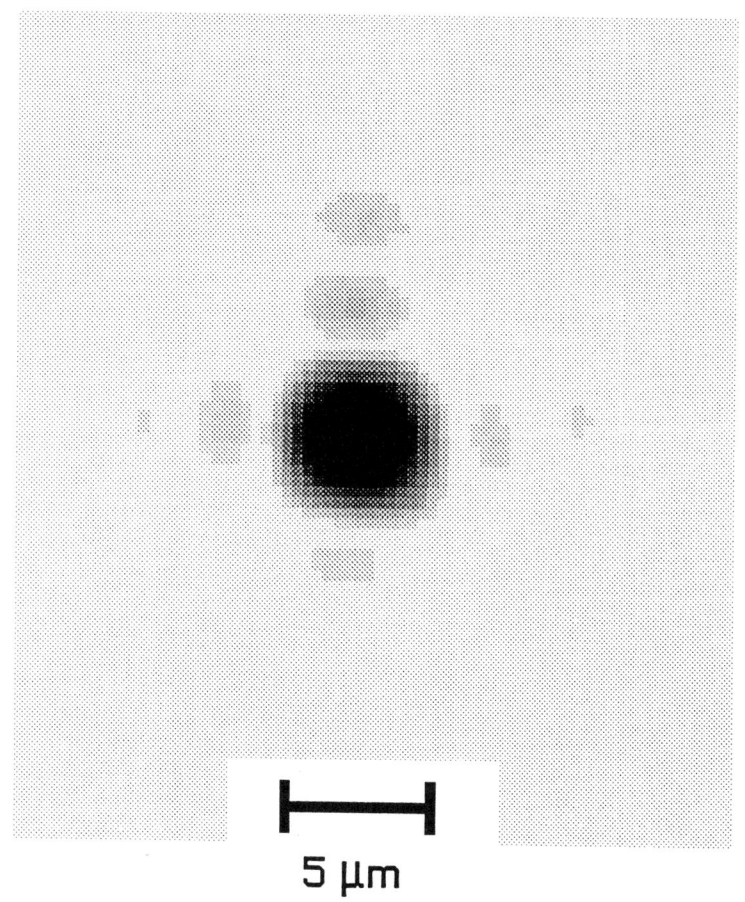

Figure 11. Magnified focal spot generated by a diffractive lens with a rectangular aperture and an f number of 3.0 (wavelength: 0.85 μm).

defined as $R^2/\lambda f$. This term is equal to twice the number of zones in a diffractive lens as can be derived from some of the earlier equations: The focal length is given as $f = r_p^2/2\lambda$ and the radius R can be written as $R = \sqrt{N} r_p$. From this it follows that the number of zones in a diffractive lens is:

$$N = R^2/2\lambda f. \tag{19}$$

We would now like to derive two more equations that are sometimes useful. First, we derive a simple equation that expresses the minimum feature size w required for the fabrication of the lens as a function of the f number ($f/\#$) and the number of phase levels L. The width of the N'th zone is $(\sqrt{N} - \sqrt{N-1})r_p$. For a structure with L phase levels, one zone is subdivided into L steps. Therefore the minimum feature size is $w = (\sqrt{N} - \sqrt{N-1})r_p/L$. By developing $\sqrt{N-1}$ into a power series and dropping the higher terms, this expression becomes: $w = r_p/(2L\sqrt{N})$. By using $f/\# = f/D = (r_p^2/2\lambda)/(2\sqrt{N}r_p) = r_p/(4\sqrt{N}\lambda)$ one can write:

$$w = 2\lambda(f/\#)/L. \qquad (20)$$

As an example, for a lens with $f/\# = 4$, made of $L = 8$ phase levels, and used at a wavelength $\lambda = 1$ μm, the minimum feature width is $w = 1$ μm. This is readily achieved with conventional optical lithography.

Finally, we discuss briefly the wavelength dependence of diffractive lenses and compare them to refractive lenses. With the expression $f_d = r_p^2/2\lambda$ for the focal length, we obtain:

$$\frac{\partial f_d}{\partial \lambda} = -\frac{f_d}{\lambda}. \qquad (21)$$

For a plano-convex refractive lens, the focal length is given as $f_r = r_c/(n-1)$ where r_c is the radius of curvature and n is the refractive index. With $n(\lambda) \approx n(\lambda_0) + (\partial n/\partial \lambda)_0(\lambda - \lambda_0)$, one can write:

$$\frac{\partial f_r}{\partial \lambda} = -\frac{(\partial n/\partial \lambda)_0}{n_0 - 1} f_r. \qquad (22)$$

To determine the ratio in the dispersion of a diffractive and a refractive lens, we assume that $\lambda_0 = 1$μm and that both lenses are made of fused silica. In this case, the values are $n = 1.45$ and $(\partial n/\partial \lambda)_0 = -0.0128$ μm^{-1} (Driscoll and Vaughan 1978). With $f_d = f_r$, one obtains for the ratio $(\partial f/\partial \lambda)_d/(\partial f/\partial \lambda)_r = -35.2$. The wavelength dispersion has opposite signs for diffractive and refractive lenses and is considerably stronger for diffractive lenses. This allows one to use diffractive optics to compensate for some of the chromatic aberrations of refractive lenses in hybrid diffractive-refractive elements (Sliusarev 1957; Stone and George 1988).

4. Applications of Diffractive Micro-Optics

Diffractive optics has been investigated for several interconnection applications in the context of optical computing and photonic switching. In this section, we review three of these applications. The first is spot array generation; the second, space-variant interconnections; and the third, integrated micro-optic packaging.

4.1 Spot Array Generation with Phase Gratings

Beamsplitting is a task that often occurs in optical systems. A specific application in optical computing is the generation of equal intensity spot arrays. This is required to illuminate arrays of light modulators; see, for example, Streibl *et al.* (1989). There are several ways to implement spot array generators using phase gratings (see Chapter 9). Here, we give a brief overview of these methods.

Dammann was the first to demonstrate the use of binary optics technology for beamsplitting applications (Dammann and Görtler, 1971). This idea has since then been pursued by many groups. Applications of Dammann gratings were suggested in the areas of fiber optic star couplers (Killat, Rabe, and Rave 1979), multiple imaging (Boivin 1972; Dammann and Klotz 1977; W. H. Lee 1979), optical beam shaping and multiplexing (Veldkamp 1981; Veldkamp, Leger, and Swanson 1986), and coherent beam summation (Leger, Swanson, and Veldkamp 1986; Leger, Swanson, and Holz 1987; Veldkamp, Leger, and Swanson 1986). For optical computing applications, Dammann gratings have been investigated for the illumination of 2-D modulator arrays (McCormick 1989; Jahns *et al.* 1989; Morrison 1992). Various aspects of Dammann gratings, such as their computation and fabrication, were published by Turunen *et al.* (1988, 1989), Taghizadeh *et al.* (1989b), Krackhardt *et al.* (1989, 1992), Mait (1989, 1990), Wang, Geng, and Kostuk (1990), and Vasara *et al.* (1991). In this section, we describe the basic idea of Dammann gratings. A more complete overview of spot array generation in general has been given by Streibl (1989) and in Chapter 9.

Dammann gratings are Fourier-type array generators that use an optical setup as shown in Fig. 12. The structure of a Dammann grating is represented in Fig. 13 for the 1-D case. To generate equal intensity beams, each period of the grating is subdivided into $N + 1$ intervals with a phase value of 0 or a phase value of ϕ. The coordinates $\{x_1, \ldots, x_N\}$ of the N transition points determine the distribution of the light energy between the various diffraction orders (Dammann and Klotz 1977). Several different designs are possible. Shown here is the design that was originally used by Dammann, where the phase profile as symmetric and where $\phi = \pi$. For this design the number of equal intensity orders that can be generated is $2N + 1$. The computation of the transition coordinates $\{x_1, \ldots, x_N\}$ is done by means of optimization techniques. The goal of the optimization is to maximize the diffraction efficiency and to minimize the nonuniformity of the diffraction

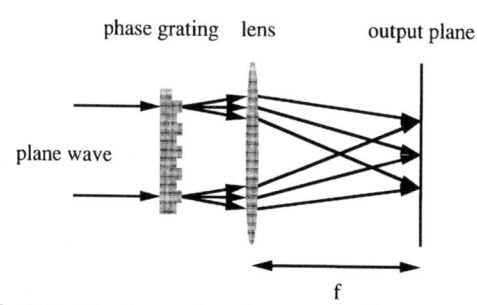

Figure 12. Optical Fourier transformation setup used for spot array generation.

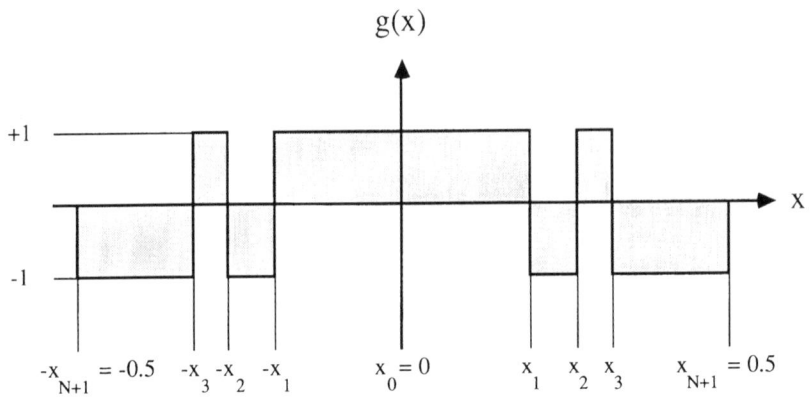

Figure 13. One period of a binary Dammann grating (1-D). The period is normalized to one. The specific case shown here uses a symmetric design around the origin and two phase values, 0 and π.

orders in the array. To generate 2-D arrays, one can simply use the approach where the grating is separable in the x and y directions, which reduces the computation to a 1-D problem. Two-dimensional, nonseparable designs have been discussed by Mait (1989).

An example of a generated spot array is shown in Fig. 14. Here a 17 × 17 array of equal intensity beams is shown. Much larger arrays have also been demonstrated, with up to 201 × 201 spots (Taghizadeh *et al.* 1989a).

Two parameters are used to classify Dammann grating designs. These are the diffraction efficiency η_d and the uniformity of the spot array, which can be expressed as $\Delta I / \langle I \rangle$. Here, $\langle I \rangle$ is the average intensity of all spots in the array, and ΔI is the maximum deviation of any diffraction order from $\langle I \rangle$. The uniformity is limited by fabrication errors as described earlier and can be of the order of a few percent. For 1-D binary gratings, the diffraction efficiency η_d is typically between 0.6 and 0.8, depending on the specific design. For a separable 2-D grating, the diffraction efficiency is given as the square of this value, which results in values between approximately 0.4 and 0.6. To improve the diffraction efficiency, multilevel designs have been investigated (Walker and Jahns 1990; Ekberg *et al.* 1992). Very high efficiencies require a large number of phase levels or, ideally, a continuous phase profile. A grating with a continuous phase profile generated by a direct laser write technique was demonstrated by Herzig, Prongué, and Dändliker (1990). The 1-D efficiency of the grating was 92%.

Designs for array generators that are different from the Dammann approach have been suggested, for example, by Feldman *et al.* (1989). In his design, Feldman uses a cell-oriented approach similar to the design of conventional computer-generated holograms (Brown and Lohmann 1966). In addition, the phase ϕ is used as a free design parameter. Other cell-based designs have been investigated recently by Bernhardt, Wyrowski and Bryngdahl (1991).

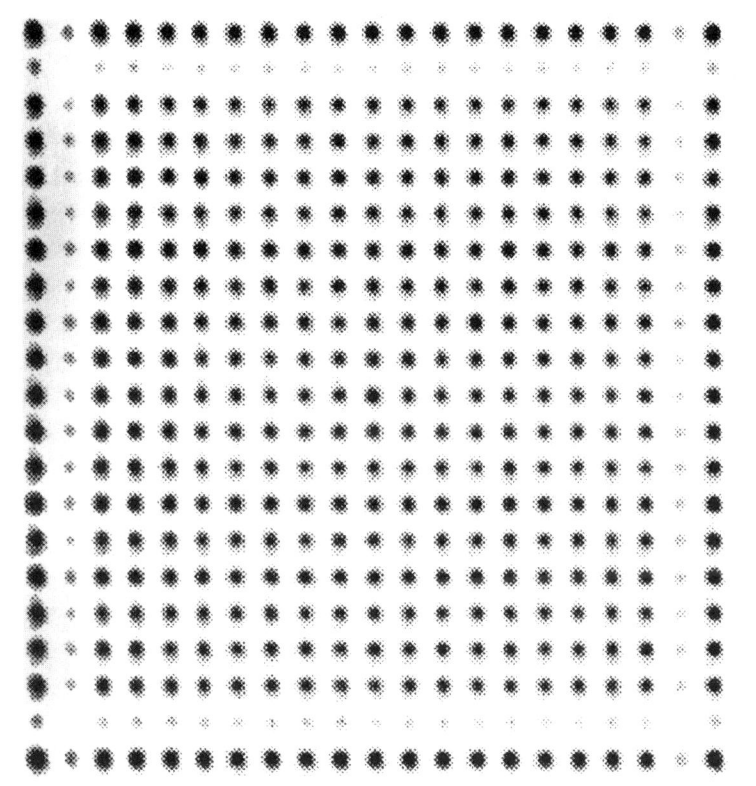

Figure 14. A 17 × 17 array of spots generated by a binary Dammann grating.

Array generation based on Fresnel propagation and imaging using binary optics elements was suggested by Lohmann *et al.* (1988) and by Leger and Swanson (1989). The advantage of these types of arrays generators is the simplicity with which the grating is designed, i.e., the grating is determined in an analytical way rather than by using time-consuming optimization algorithms. The light efficiency of the system can be very high; however, the illumination has to be done with a uniform laser beam.

Finally, we would like to mention that array generators as discussed for digital optical computing are similar to the pseudo-random diffusers used in analog optical computing. Both a diffuser and an array generator have the task of generating uniform illumination. For a diffuser this is a continuous area, whereas an array generator is supposed to generate uniform illumination in discrete spots. Pseudo-random diffusers have been implemented as binary and multilevel diffractive components (Sogawa, Hori, and Kato 1991). Phase gratings with binary or multiple discrete phase levels were also discussed for other analog optical computing applications such as optical transfer function synthesis (Jahns and Lohmann 1982).

4.2 Space-Variant Interconnections

Optical interconnection networks such as the perfect shuffle, banyan, or crossover network are of interest for optical computing and photonic switching applications. A variety of publications exists on that subject. The reader is referred to recent overview articles by Kiamilev *et al.* (1991), Kawai (1991), and Taylor and Midwinter (1991), and to Chapters 1 and 8. The use of these networks requires the implementation of space-variant interconnections for which various approaches have been demonstrated. One of them is based on the use of multifaceted diffractive elements. The element in the first array collimates and deflects the light beam (Fig. 15). An element in the second array then redirects again and focuses the light to an output position. Input and output devices may be modulator arrays such as the SEED devices (see Chapter 2) or surface-emitting devices such as the VSTEPS (see Chapter 3) and the microlasers (see Chapter 4). The optical elements can be implemented as arrays of diffractive off-axis lenslets as shown in Fig. 16. In principle, arbitrary interconnections can be implemented by means of this approach, within certain practical limits, which are determined, for example, by the fabrication. Interconnection networks for 2-D pixel arrays have been demonstrated using both analog (Kobolla, Sauer, and Völkel 1989; Restall *et al.* 1990) and digital diffractive elements (Jahns and Däschner 1990). For example, one stage of a banyan experiment is shown in Fig. 17. A system design limitation that arises when using lenslet arrays is the fact that the pixel spacing is restricted by the size of the lenses. Therefore, the approach is useful only for interconnecting *dilute arrays,* in which the pixel spacing is large. The use of multifacet optics is of interest for the concept of *smart pixels,* which is explained in Chapter 2 (see also Hinton 1988).

4.3 Integrated Micro-Optic Packaging

One of the difficulties when building complex free-space optical systems is the mechanical mounting and alignment of the components. High alignment precision

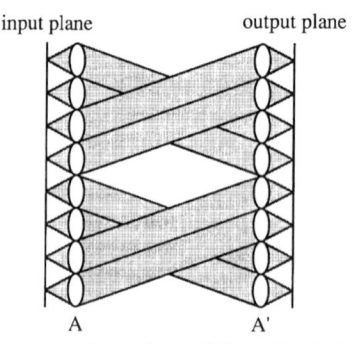

Figure 15. Space-variant interconnections using multifaceted optical elements (A and A'). In this specific example, one stage of a banyan network for a 1-D array with eight inputs is shown.

Diffractive Optical Elements for Optical Computers 159

Figure 16. Array of diffractive off-axis lenslets used to implement space-variant interconnections.

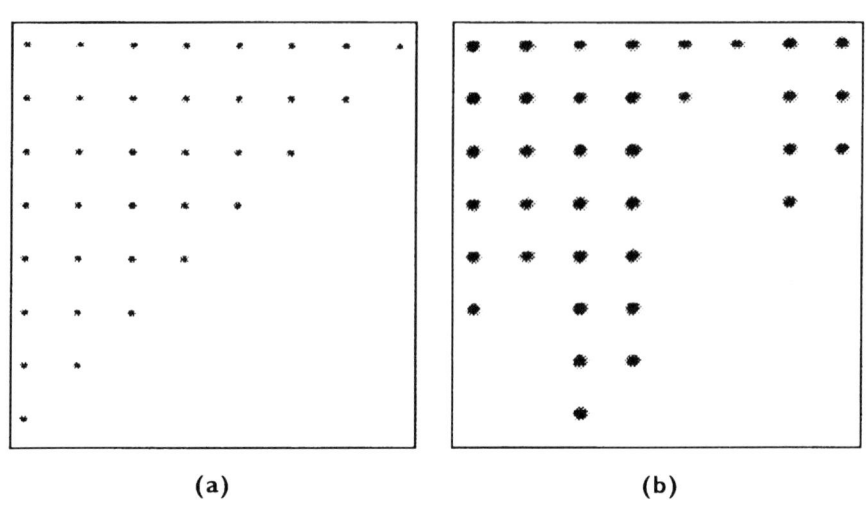

Figure 17. Experimental result of one stage of a Banyan network for an 8 × 8 array of pixels: (a) input and (b) output.

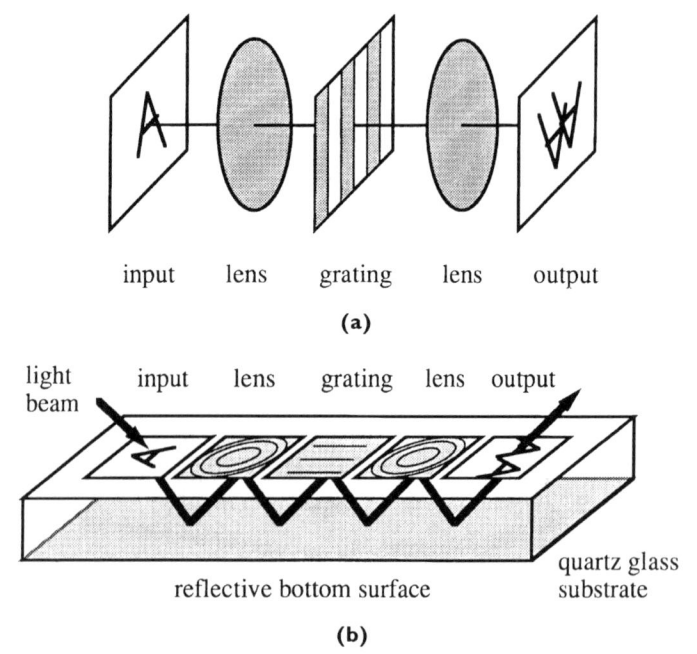

Figure 18. Concept of planar integration: (a) conventional $4f$ imaging system and (b) integrated $4f$ imaging system.

is necessary due to the dimensions of the devices (modulators, emitters, and detectors) in the input and output arrays. The dimensions are typically of the order of a few microns; consequently, the lateral alignment precision in a free-space optical system is a few tenths of a micron or about one order of magnitude smaller than the device size. While it is not impossible to achieve this precision with conventional optomechanics, it becomes difficult and costly. Because conventional optical systems are built of discrete elements such as lenses, beamsplitters, etc., they tend to be bulky and not stable with respect to mechanical and thermal influences. For this reason, it is of interest to consider packaging techniques that enable a reduction of the physical size of complex free-space optical systems and at the same time reduce cost.

It has been pointed out that in order to achieve this goal, fabrication and packaging techniques similar to those used in electronics ought to be considered (Jahns and Huang 1989). After all, electronics became cheap and reliable only after discrete elements were replaced with integrated circuits. To solve the packaging problem of free-space optics, the concept of *planar optics* was suggested (Jahns and Huang 1989). The main idea of planar optics is to build free-space optics systems on single substrates in a way that is compatible with planar fabrication techniques used in the manufacturing of integrated circuits. Therefore, *binary diffractive optics* is an interesting technology to implement planar optics.

The basic concept is visualized in Fig. 18. It shows a conventional optical $4f$ system and an integrated version. In the integrated system, the optical components are put on the surface of an optical substrate. All components are fabricated at the same time with lithographic precision. Light propagation takes place inside the substrate along a zigzag path. The substrate is several millimeters thick and of very high optical quality. To keep the light inside the substrate, the optical elements and the bottom surface of the substrate are coated with a highly reflective metallic coating, for example, silver. The use of diffractive optics and diffractive-reflective optics has been proposed for optical interconnections by several authors (Brenner and Sauer 1988; Sauer 1989; Feldman and Guest 1989; Kostuk *et al.* 1985, 1987, 1989), however, without emphasis on the packaging and manufacturing issue. An integrated array generator based on a planar optics approach was described by Kubota and Takeda (1989).

Several simple experiments have been performed to demonstrate the idea of planar optics (Jahns 1990; Downs and Jahns 1990; Walker and Jahns 1992). An experimental result obtained with an integrated $4f$ imaging system is shown in Fig. 19.

The integration of active and passive devices can be achieved by using hybrid integration techniques such as flip-chip solder bonding (Fig. 20). This technique has found many applications in electronics; its basic demonstration goes back to Miller (1969) and Goldman and Totta (1983). The use of flip-chip bonding for optoelectronic applications was demonstrated by Goodwin *et al.* (1991) and Von

(a)   **(b)**

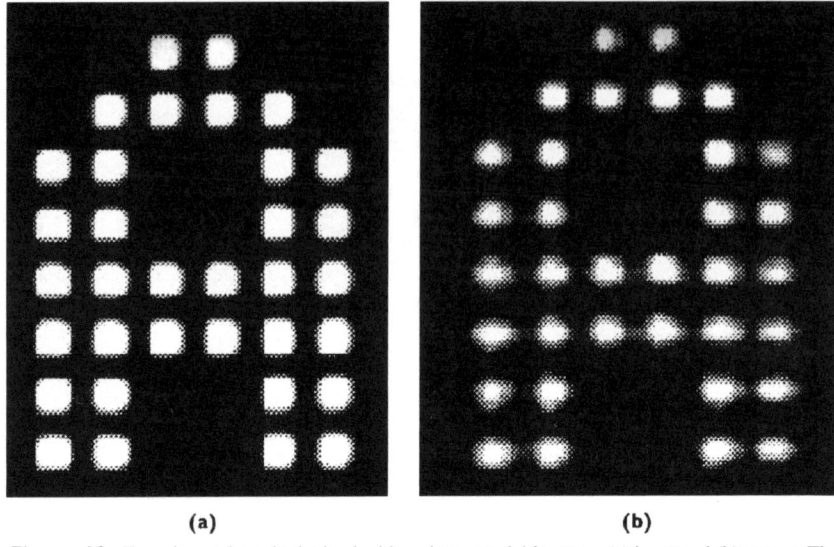

Figure 19. Experimental result obtained with an integrated 4f system: (a) input and (b) output. The pixels forming the letter "A" are 50 μm × 50 μm in size.

Lehmen *et al.* (1991). The principle of the flip-chip bonding process is shown in Fig. 20(a). Matching arrays of solder bumps on the substrate and the chip are brought in contact and pressed together. A subsequent reflow process at a temperature above the melting point of the solder can be used to achieve self-alignment of the bumps. The precision of this process is on the order of 1 μm. Metallic runners on the chip and the substrate can provide drive currents and supply voltages to the devices on the chip [Fig. 20(b)].

Flip-chip bonding as a technique to build integrated optoelectronic systems using the planar optics concept is currently being investigated (Jahns *et al.* 1992a). A microlaser chip bonded onto a planar optics glass substrate is shown in Fig. 21 (Jahns *et al.* 1992c). In combination with arrays of surface-emitting microlasers and detector arrays, one might be able to build systems that have applications in short-distance communications within computers on a board-to-board or chip-to-chip level (Sebillotte 1990; Haumann *et al.* 1990; Kim, Chen, and Lin 1991). A similar application might be optical clock distribution inside a multiprocessor system. This application has also been discussed by various authors (Zarschizky *et al.* 1990; Kostuk, Huang, and Kato 1990; Walker and Jahns 1992).

5. Conclusion

The field of diffractive optics, especially binary optics, has generated many new applications over the last couple of years due to the fact that planar lithographic

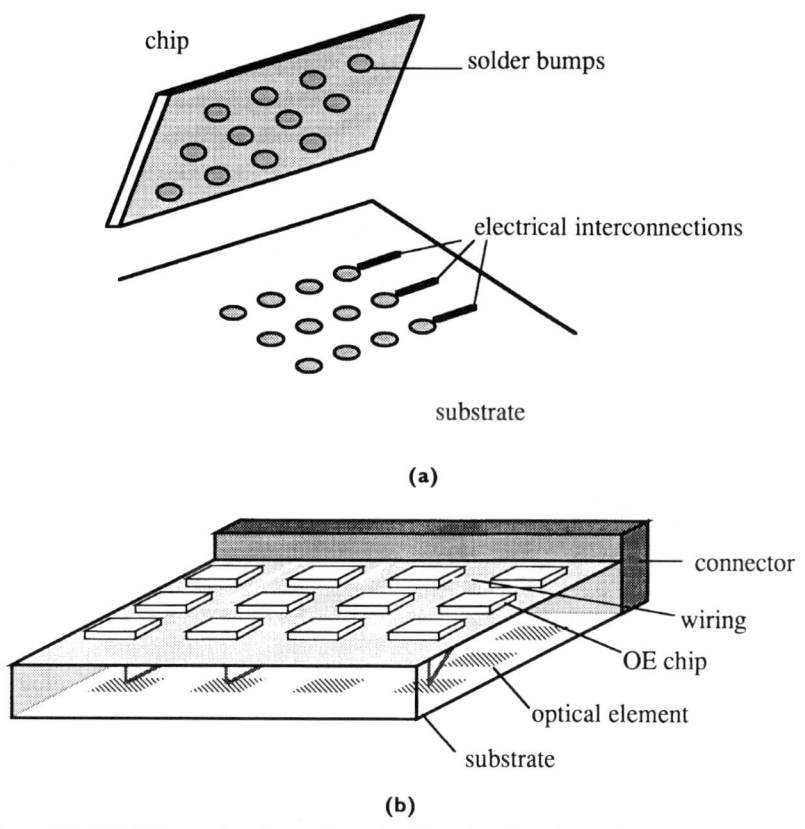

Figure 20. Hybrid integration of optoelectronic chips using flip-chip bonding: (a) bonding process [adapted from Goodwin et al. (1991) © 1991 IEEE] and (b) integrated optoelectronic system with many chips on an optical backplane. Electronic contacts and wires might be used to supply power and drive currents and a connector serving as an interface.

fabrication techniques have become more widely available for the manufacture of optical components. Besides the applications that are of interest to the optical computing community, diffractive optical elements have been used elsewhere such as in sensors, in particular, at infrared wavelengths, and lens design. It is an interesting fact that the use of lithography and dry etching techniques allows one to fabricate elements in a wide variety of different materials such as quartz glass (fused silica), silicon, gallium arsenide, zinc selenide, etc. This flexibility in the materials adds to the design flexibility of diffractive optics. A very powerful argument for binary optics is the fact that it shares the manufacturing basis of the semiconductor industry. This means that the use of this technology on an industrial scale will not require new investments in equipment, since very often the equipment already exists. It also means that the development of VLSI and ULSI

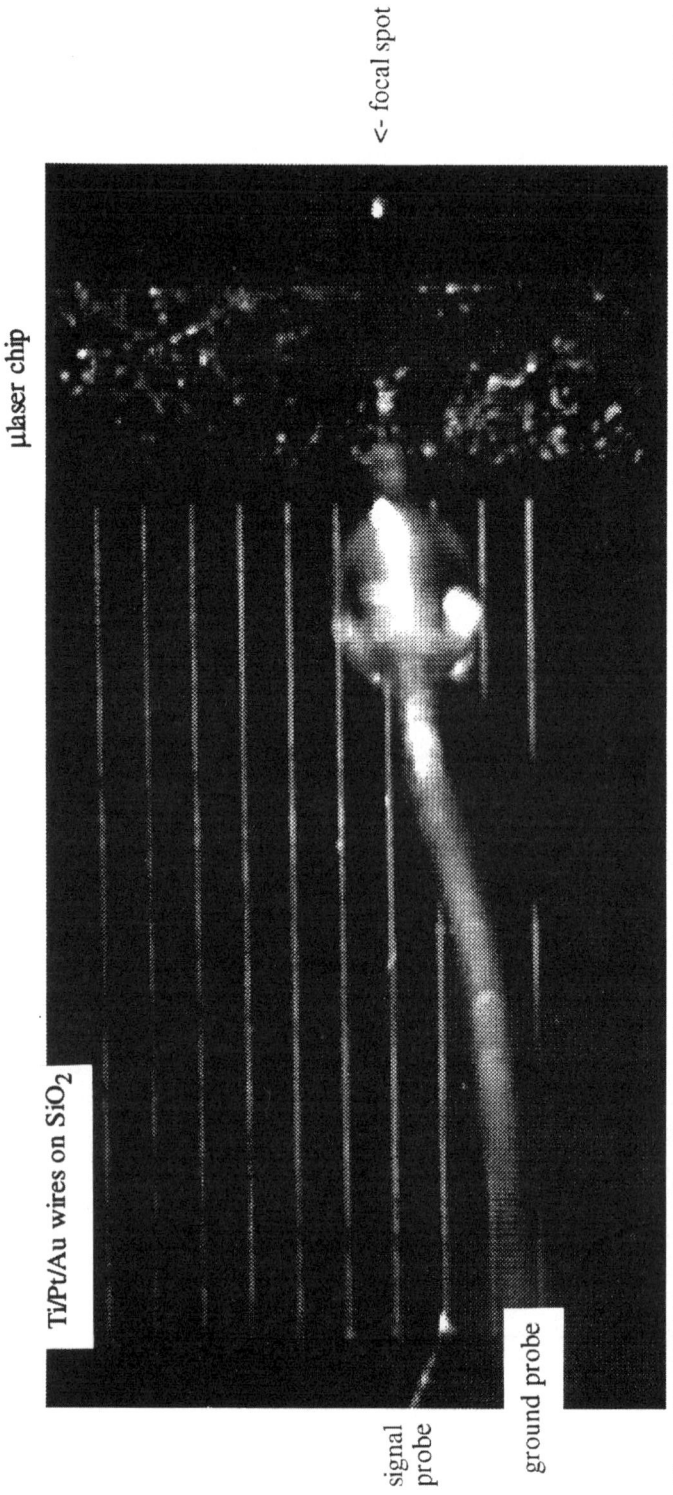

Figure 21. Hybrid integration of a gallium arsenide chip with a one-dimensional array of surface-emitting microlasers on a planar optics substrate (© 1992 IEEE). The bonding of the microlaser chip onto the glass substrate was achieved by flip-chip solder bump bonding using indium as the solder material. The lateral alignment precision is within ±2 micrometers. The optical substrate contains a matching array of microlenses and mirrors and provides a simple interconnection scheme that routes the light from each laser to well defined output positions. Each laser is addressed individually by using an electrical probe. Another probe is brought into contact with the backwide of the laser chip to provide a ground signal.

technology can also be applied to make micro-optic components and systems. Overall, one can say that diffractive binary optics is a technology that is ready for commercial applications.

ACKNOWLEDGMENT

Much of the work presented here has been a team effort to which many colleagues have contributed. I would like to acknowledge the collaboration with Walter Däschner, Avi Feldblum, Alan Huang, Bob Morgan, Rick Morrison, Hung Nguyen, Cas Nijander, Frank Sauer, Wes Townsend, Sue and Jim Walker, and Yiu Man Wong.

REFERENCES

Bernhardt, M., Wyrowski, F., and Bryngdahl, O. (1991). *Appl. Opt.* **30,** 4629–4635.
Boivin, L. P. (1972). *Appl. Opt.* **11,** 1782–1792.
Born, M., and Wolf, E. (1980). *Principles of Optics.* Pergamon Press, Oxford.
Brenner, K.-H., and Sauer, F. (1988). *Appl. Opt.* **27,** 4251–4254.
Brodie, I., and Muray, J. J. (1982). *The Physics of Microfabrication.* Plenum Press, New York.
Brown, B. R., and Lohmann, A. W. (1966). *Appl. Opt.* **5,** 967.
Bryngdahl, O., and Wyrowski, F. (1990). In: *Progress in Optics, Vol. 28* (E. Wolf, ed.), North-Holland, Amsterdam.
Caulfield, H. J., ed. (1979). *Principles of Optical Holography.* Academic Press, New York.
Cowan, J. J. (1990). *J. Opt. Soc. Am. A* **7,** 1529–1544.
Cox, J. A., Fritz, B., and Werner, T. (1991). *Proc. SPIE* **1555,** 80–88.
D'Auria, L., Huignard, J. P., Roy, A. M., and Spitz, E. (1972). *Opt. Comm.* **5,** 232–235.
Dammann, H. (1970). *Optik* **31,** 95–104.
Dammann, H., and Görtler, K. (1971). *Opt. Comm.* **3,** 312–315.
Dammann, H., and Klotz, E. (1977). *Opt. Acta* **24,** 505–515.
Downs, M. M., and Jahns, J. (1990a). OSA Annual Meeting, paper Tu-W5.
Downs, M. M., and Jahns, J. (1990b). *Opt. Lett.* **15,** 769–770.
Driscoll, W. G., and Vaughan, W., eds. (1978). *Handbook of Optics.* McGraw-Hill, New York.
Ekberg, M., Larsson, M., Hård, S., Turunen, J., Taghizadeh, M., Westerholm, J., and Vasara, A. (1992). *Opt. Comm.* **88,** 37–41.
Elliott, D. J. (1989). *Integrated Circuit Fabrication Technology.* McGraw-Hill, New York.
Feldman, M. R., and Guest, C. G. (1989). *Opt. Lett.* **14,** 479–481.
Feldman, M. R., Guest, C. C., Drabik, T. J., and Esener, S. C. (1989). *Appl. Opt.* **28,** 3820–3829.
Firester, A. H., Hoffman, D. M., James, E. A., and Heller, M. E. (1973). *Opt. Comm.* **8,** 160–162.
Goldman, L. S., and Totta, P. A. (1983). *Solid State Technol.* 91–97.
Goodman, J. W. (1968). *Introduction to Fourier Optics.* McGraw-Hill, San Francisco.
Goodwin, M. J., Moseley, A. J., Kearley, M. Q., Morris, R. C., Kirkby, C. J. G., Thompson, J., Goodfellow, R. C., and Bennion, I. (1991). *J. Lightwave Technol.* **9,** 1639–1645.
Hariharan, P. (1984). *Optical Holography.* Cambridge University Press.
Haumann, H.-J., Kobolla, H., Sauer, F., Schwider, J., Stork, W., Streibl, N., and Völkel, R. (1990). *Proc. SPIE* **1319,** 588–589.
Herzig, H. P., Prongué, D., and Dändliker, R. (1990). *Jpn. J. Appl. Phys.* **29,** L1307–L1309.
Hinton, H. S. (1988). *IEEE J. Sel. Areas Commun.* **6,** 1209–1226.
Hutley, M. C. (1982). *Diffraction Gratings.* Academic Press, New York.
Jahns, J. (1990). *Appl. Opt.* **29,** 1998.

Jahns, J., Brenner, K.-H., Däschner, W., Doubrava, C., and Merklein, T. (1992b). *Optik* **89**, 98–100.
Jahns, J., and Däschner, W. (1990). *Opt. Comm.* **79**, 407–410.
Jahns, J., Downs, M. M., Prise, M. E., Streibl, N., and Walker, S. J. (1989). *Opt. Eng.* **28**, 1267–1275.
Jahns, J., and Huang, A. (1989). *Appl. Opt.* **28**, 1602–1605.
Jahns, J., Lee, Y. H., Burrus, C. A., and Jewell, J. L. (1992a). *Appl. Opt.* **31**, 592–597.
Jahns, J., and Lohmann, A. W. (1982). *Opt. Comm.* **42**, 231.
Jahns, J., Morgan, R. A., Nguyen, H., Walker, J. A., Walker, S. J., and Wong, Y. M. (1992c). *IEEE Phot. Techn. Lett.* **4**, 1369–1372.
Jahns, J., and Walker, S. J. (1990a). *Appl. Opt.* **29**, 931–936.
Jahns, J., and Walker, S. J. (1990b). *Opt. Comm.* **76**, 313–317.
Kawai, S. (1991). *J. Lightwave Technol.* **9**, 1774–1779.
Kiamilev, F. E., Marchand, P., Krishnamoorthy, A. V., Esener, S. C., and Lee, S. H. (1991). *J. Lightwave Technol.* **9**, 1674–1692.
Killat, U., Rabe, G., and Rave, W. (1979). *Fiber and Integr. Optics* **4**, 159–167.
Kim, R. C., Chen, E., and Lin, F. (1991). *J. Lightwave Technol.* **9**, 1650–1656.
Knop, K. (1976). *Opt. Comm.* **18**, 298–303.
Knop, K. (1978). *Appl. Opt.* **17**, 3598–3603.
Kobolla, H., Sauer, F., and Völkel, R. (1989). *Proc. SPIE* **1136**.
Kogelnik, H., and Li, T. (1966). *Appl. Opt.* **5**, 1550–1567.
Kostuk, R. K., Goodman, J. W., and Hesselink, L. (1985). *Appl. Opt.* **24**, 2851–2858.
Kostuk, R. K., Goodman, J. W., and Hesselink, L. (1987). *Appl. Opt.* **26**, 3947–3953.
Kostuk, R. K., Huang, Y.-T., and Kato, M. (1990). *Proc. SPIE* **1389**, 515–522.
Kostuk, R. K., Kato, M., and Huang, Y. T. (1989). *Appl. Opt.* **28**, 4939–4944.
Krackhardt, U., Mait, J. N., and Streibl, N. (1992). *Appl. Opt.* **31**, 27–37.
Krackhardt, U., and Streibl, N. (1989). *Opt. Comm.* **74**, 31–34.
Kubota, T., and Takeda, M. (1989). *Opt. Lett.* **14**, 651–652.
Lee, S. H., Ed. (1981). *Optical Information Processing: Fundamentals*. Springer Verlag, Berlin.
Lee, W. H. (1978). In: *Progress in Optics, Vol. 16*. (E. Wolf, ed.), North Holland, Amsterdam.
Lee, W. H. (1979). *Appl. Opt.* **18**, 2152–2158.
Leger, J. R., and Swanson, G. J. (1990). *Opt. lett.* **15**, 288–290.
Leger, J. R., Swanson, G. J., and Holz, M. (1987). *Appl. Phys. Lett.* **50**, 1044–1046.
Leger, J. R., Swanson, G. J., and Veldkamp, W. B. (1986). *Appl. Phys. Lett.* **48**, 888–890.
Lesem, L. B., Hirsch, P. M., and Jordan, J. A. (1969). *IBM J. Res. Dev.* 150–155.
Lohmann, A. W., Schwider, J., Streibl, N., and Thomas, J. (1988). *Appl. Opt.* **27**, 2915–2921.
Mait, J. N. (1989). *Opt. Lett.* **14**, 196–198.
Mait, J. N. (1990). *J. Opt. Soc. Am. A* **7**, 1514–1528.
McCormick, F. B. (1989). *Opt. Eng.* **28**, 299–304.
McCormick, F. B., Tooley, F. A. P., Cloonan, T. J., Brubaker, J. L., Lentine, A. L., Morrison, R. L., Hinterlong, S. J., Herron, M. J., Walker, S. L., and Sasian, J. M. (1992) *Appl. Opt.* **31**, 5431–5446.
Miller, L. F. (1969). *IBM J. Res. Dev.* **13**, 239–250.
Moharam, M. G., and Gaylord, T. K. (1986). *J. Opt. Soc. Am. A* **3**, 1780–1787.
Morrison, R. L. (1992). *J. Opt. Soc. Am. A* **9**, 464–471.
Nagy, A. (1992). *Opt. Eng.* **31**, 335–340.
Nishihara, H., and Suhara, T. (1987). In: *Progress in Optics, Vol. 24* (E. Wolf, ed.), North Holland, Amsterdam, pp. 3–37.
Prise, M. E., Craft, N. C., LaMarche, R. E., Downs, M. M., D'Asaro, L. A., and Chirovsky, L. M. F. (1991). *Appl. Opt.* **30**, 2841–2843.
Robertson, B., Restall, E. J., Taghizadeh, M. R., and Walker, A. C. (1991). *Appl. Opt.* **30**, 2368–2375.
Sauer, F. (1989). *Appl. Opt.* **28**, 386–388.
Sebillotte, C. (1990). *Proc. SPIE* **1389**, 600–611.

Sheppard, C. J. R. (1986). *J. Opt. Soc. Am. A* **3,** 1428–1432.
Shiono, T., Setsune, K., Yamazaki, O., and Wasa, K. (1987). *Appl. Opt.* **26,** 587–591.
Sliusarev, G. G. (1957). *Sov. Phys.-Doklady* **2,** 161.
Smith, H. I., Spears, D. L., and Bernacki, S. E. (1973). *J. Vac. Sci. Technol.* **10,** 913.
Sogawa, F., Hori, Y., and Kato, M. (1991). 3rd Microoptics Conference, Yokohama, pp. 268–271.
Stone, T. and George, N. (1988). *Appl. Opt.* **27,** 2960–2971.
Streibl, N. (1989). *J. Mod. Opt.* **12,** 1559–1573.
Streibl, N., Brenner, K. H., Huang, A., Jahns, J., Jewell, J., Lohmann, A. W., Miller, D. A. B., Murdocca, M., Prise, M. E., and Sizer, T. (1989). *Proc. IEEE* **77,** 1954–1969.
Swanson, G. J. (August 1989). NTIS Publication No. AD-A213-404, MIT Lincoln Laboratory.
Taghizadeh, M. R., Turunen, J., Vasara, A., and Westerholm, J. (1989a). OSA Annual Meeting, paper TuU17.
Taghizadeh, M. R., Wilson, J. I. B., Turunen, J., Vasara, A., and Westerholm, J. (1989b). *Appl. Phys. Lett.* **54,** 1492–1494.
Taylor, M. G., and Midwinter, J. E. (1991). *J. Lightware Technol.* **9,** 791–798.
Turunen, J., Vasara, A., and Westerholm, J. (1989). *Opt. Eng.* **28,** 1162–1167.
Turunen, J., Vasara, A., Westerholm, J., Jin, G., and Salin, A. (1988). *J. Phys. D.* **21,** S102–S105.
Urquhart, K. S., Lee, S. H., Guest, C. C., Feldman, M. R., and Farhoosh, H. (1989). *Appl. Opt.* **28,** 3387–3396.
Vasara, A., Noponen, E., Turunen, J., Miller, J. M., and Taghizadeh, M. R. (1991). *Opt. Comm.* **81,** 337–342.
Veldkamp, W. B. (1981). *Opt. Comm.* **38,** 381–387.
Veldkamp, W. B., Leger, J. R., and Swanson, G. J. (1986). *Opt. Lett.* **11,** 303–306.
Von Lehmen, A., Banwell, T., Chan, W., Orenstein, M., Wullert, J., Maeda, M., Chang-Hasnain, C., Stoffel, N., Florez, L., and Harbison, J. (1991). *Proc. SPIE* **1582,** 83–91.
Voshchenkov, A. M. (1990). *Int. J. High Speed Electrons* **1,** 303–345.
Walker, S. J., and Jahns, J. (1990). *J. Opt. Soc. Am. A* **7,** 1509–1513.
Walker, S. J., and Jahns, J. (1992). *Opt. Comm.* **90,** 359–371.
Wang, L., Geng, W., and Kostuk, R. K. (1990). *Opt. Eng.* **29,** 257–262.
Zarschizky, H., Karstensen, H., Gerndt, C., Klement, E., and Schneider, H. W. (1990). *Proc. SPIE* **1389,** 484–495.

Chapter 7
Diffractive Microlenses Fabricated by Electron-Beam Lithography

TERUHIRO SHIONO

Matsushita Electric Industrial Company, Ltd.
Central Research Laboratories
Moriguchi, Osaka 570, Japan

1. Introduction 169
2. Basic Theory of Diffractive Microlenses 170
   2.1 Lens Structure and Design 170
   2.2 Theoretical Analysis of Diffraction Efficiency 176
3. Fabrication by Electron-Beam Lithography 180
   3.1 Electron-Beam Writing System 180
   3.2 Fabrication Examples 182
4. Optical Measurements 187
   4.1 Reflection and Transmission Microlenses for Normal Incidence 187
   4.2 Reflection Microlenses for Oblique Incidence 189
5. Conclusion 191
   References 191

1. Introduction

Microlenses play an important role in the field of optical computing. Microlenses are used for Fourier transformation, imaging, focusing, collimating, etc. Among the various types of microlenses, diffractive microlenses with a relief structure are of great interest, because the various diffraction-limited optical characteristics can be easily realized by forming the corresponding grating patterns. Their thin-film structure makes it possible to produce and integrate them with other optical components. In particular, a whole optical system integrated with various diffractive components on a planar substrate can be replicated simultaneously by means of an inexpensive molding process. Recent progress in microfabrication techniques, including a photoreduction method (Jordan *et al.* 1970), electron-beam lithography (Fujita, Nishihara, and Koyama 1982), ion-beam etching (Kosuge *et al.* 1984), a mechanical process (Goto *et al.* 1987), laser-beam lithography (Haruna *et al.* 1990) and thin-film deposition (Jahns and Walker 1990), has demonstrated the feasibility of a blazed relief structure. The blazed structure in the diffractive microlens can improve its focusing efficiency.

Electron-beam lithography has several advantages including a potential for submicron patterning and a flexibility in lens design and fabrication. To achieve high performance in diffractive microlenses, a different kind of electron-beam lithography technique is needed from one used in a semiconductor device process. The important requirement is the smooth scanning of an electron beam on a circle, an ellipse, or an arbitrary line, in addition to the fabrication of the blazed structure. Shiono et al. (1987a) have designed and developed a computer-controlled electron-beam writing system. Various kinds of diffractive components and their arrays can be fabricated by the computer program.

Reflection diffractive microlenses (Shiono et al. 1989) are also important, because they can be used to make the compact optical system with a folded optical path. In particular, reflection microlenses for oblique incidence (Shiono and Ogawa 1991) could be used as key devices in planar optics (Jahns and Huang 1989) and optical interconnections (Brenner and Sauer 1989) with a zigzag optical path within the substrate.

In this chapter, we discuss diffractive microlenses fabricated by electron-beam lithography. In Section 2, the basic theory of diffractive microlenses is described both for transmission and reflection microlenses. Fabrication of diffractive microlenses by electron-beam lithography is explained in Section 3. The experimental results on focusing performance and diffraction efficiency are discussed in Section 4.

2. Basic Theory of Diffractive Microlenses

2.1 Lens Structure and Design

2.1.1 *Reflection and Transmission Microlenses for Normal Incidence*

Let us consider transmission (Nishihara and Suhara 1987) and reflection (Shiono et al. 1989) diffractive microlenses, which focus a plane wave incident at the normal angle as shown in Fig. 1. Such diffractive microlenses are circular micro-Fresnel lenses. A coordinate system was chosen as shown in Fig. 1. The phase difference in the X-Y plane between the plane wave and the spherical wave converging in the substrate is given for both types of microlenses by

$$\Phi(r) = n'k[(r^2 + f^2)^{1/2} - f] \tag{1}$$

with

$$k = 2\pi/\lambda, \tag{2}$$

where λ is the wavelength in free space, n' is the refractive index of the substrate, and f is the focal length. Therefore, a device producing a phase shift of Φ in the

Diffractive Microlenses Fabricated by Electron-Beam Lithography 171

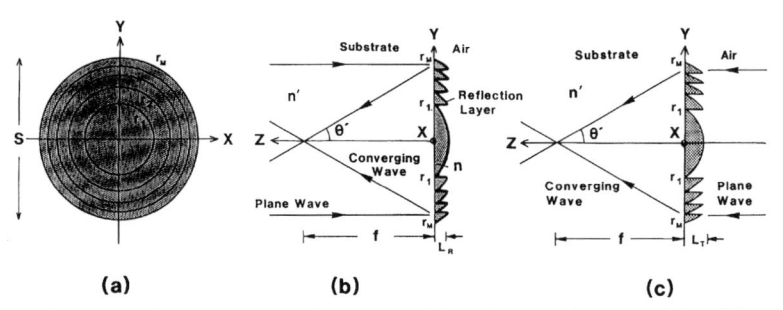

Figure 1. (a) Plane figure and cross-sectional views of (b) reflection and (c) transmission diffractive microlenses for normal incidence.

X-Y plane acts as a lens that focuses the plane wave with no aberration. Phase shift Φ_F of the diffractive lens is given by dividing Φ with a modulus 2π:

$$\Phi_F(r) = \Phi(r) - 2m\pi, \quad r_m \leq r \leq r_{m+1} \tag{3}$$

with

$$r_m = [2m\lambda f/n' + (m\lambda/n')^2]^{1/2}, \tag{4}$$

where r_m provides the zone boundaries and m is an integer satisfying $0 \leq \Phi_F \leq 2\pi$. If M is the maximum of m, the aperture size of the lens is

$$S = 2r_M = 2[2M\lambda f/n' + (M\lambda/n')^2]^{1/2}. \tag{5}$$

Maximum M also shows the total number of grating zones. The phase shift functions Φ and Φ_F are shown in Fig. 2(a). When $r \ll f$, Eqs. (3) to (5) can be approximated as follows:

$$\Phi_{Fa}(r) = n'kr^2/2f - 2m\pi, \quad r_{ma} \leq r \leq r_{(m+1)a}, \tag{6}$$
$$r_{ma} = (2m\lambda f/n')^{1/2}, \tag{7}$$
$$S_a = 2r_{Ma} = 2(2M\lambda f/n')^{1/2}. \tag{8}$$

Next, consider the thickness profile for each type of diffractive microlens. Let $L(r)$ be the thickness (groove depth) profile of the blazed layer, n be the refractive index of the blazed layer, and θ' be the focusing angle. Since the phase shift for a reflection thin lens is approximately $2nkL(r)$, the maximum thickness that optimizes the diffraction efficiency is

$$L_R = \lambda/2n, \tag{9}$$

which is derived from the condition used to make the phase difference 2π at each zone boundary. Therefore, the film thickness profile of the reflection microlens can be

$$L(r) = L_R[1 - \Phi_F(r)/2\pi]. \tag{10}$$

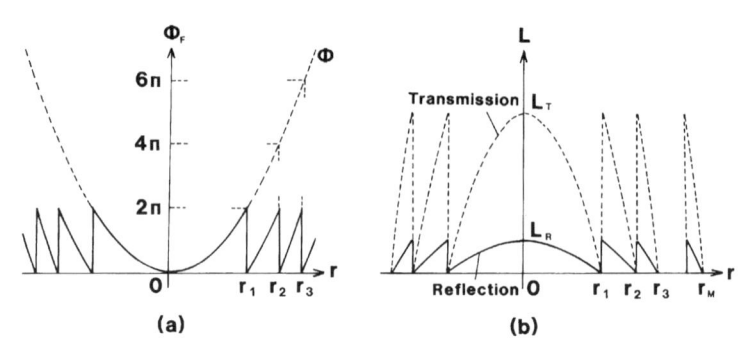

Figure 2. (a) Phase shift functions of a lens and a diffractive lens and (b) thickness profiles of reflection and transmission diffractive microlenses.

The term *thin* means that the lens has a small numerical aperture (NA), defined as

$$NA = n' \sin \theta'. \quad (11)$$

For a transmission microlens, the optimum thickness and the thickness profile are

$$L_T = \lambda/(n - 1), \quad (12)$$
$$L(r) = L_T[1 - \Phi_F(r)/2\pi], \quad (13)$$

respectively. The thickness profiles given by Eqs. (10) and (13) are shown in Fig. 2(b). Calculated from Eqs. (9) and (12), $L_R = 0.2$ μm and $L_T = 1.1$ μm for $n = 1.6$ and $\lambda = 0.6328$ μm. Note that the thickness of the reflection microlens can be remarkably reduced by the ratio:

$$L_R/L_T = (n - 1)/2n, \quad (14)$$

where $L_R/L_T = 0.19$ for $n = 1.6$, in comparison with the thickness of the transmission microlens. This reduction in thickness could provide higher resolution (Ahmed 1986) from fabrication by electron-beam lithography and improve the optical characteristics of the lens. The reflection components resist their surroundings because the reflection layer also becomes a protection layer. When using the internal reflection of the metal, they are only slightly influenced by the surface dust and surface oxidization of the metal.

2.1.2 Reflection Microlenses for Oblique Incidence

The reflection microlenses for oblique incidence (Shiono and Ogawa 1991) can be flexibly used without a beamsplitter to divide the focused wave from the incident wave. These reflection microlenses could be key devices in planar optics and optical interconnections with a zigzag optical path within the substrate.

According to aberration theory (Born and Wolf 1970), coma and astigmatism depend on the incident angle. Spherical aberration is independent of the angle; instead, it depends on the accuracy of the grating period. Coma increases with the oblique angle, while astigmatism increases with the second power of the angle. This indicates that astigmatism can be ignored for small oblique angles. But for incidence with large angles, the three types of aberration should be compensated simultaneously.

Figure 3 shows the structure of a reflection diffractive microlens for oblique incidence. The lens focuses a plane wave propagating with an oblique angle θ from the Z axis into a spherical wave converging with an optical axis symmetric to the incident wave axis. The phase shift function of the lens is derived by the ray tracing as

$$\Phi_{FO}(x, y) = n'k[(x^2 + y^2 - 2yf \sin \theta + f^2)^{1/2} - f + y \sin \theta] - 2m\pi, \quad (15)$$

where m is an integer satisfying $0 \leq \Phi_{FO} \leq 2\pi$.

Let us consider the grating patterns that provide the zone boundaries of the lens. From $\Phi_{FO} = 0$ we obtain

$$\frac{x^2}{(m\lambda/n' \cos \theta)^2 + 2m\lambda f/n'} + \frac{(y - y_{Cm})^2 \cos^2 \theta}{(m\lambda/n' \cos \theta)^2 + 2m\lambda f/n'} = 1, \quad (16)$$

with

$$y_{Cm} = -m\lambda \tan \theta/n' \cos \theta. \quad (17)$$

It is clear that this relation denotes an ellipse with a major axis of Y where the center position is $(0, y_{Cm})$, and y_{Cm} is proportional to integer m corresponding to

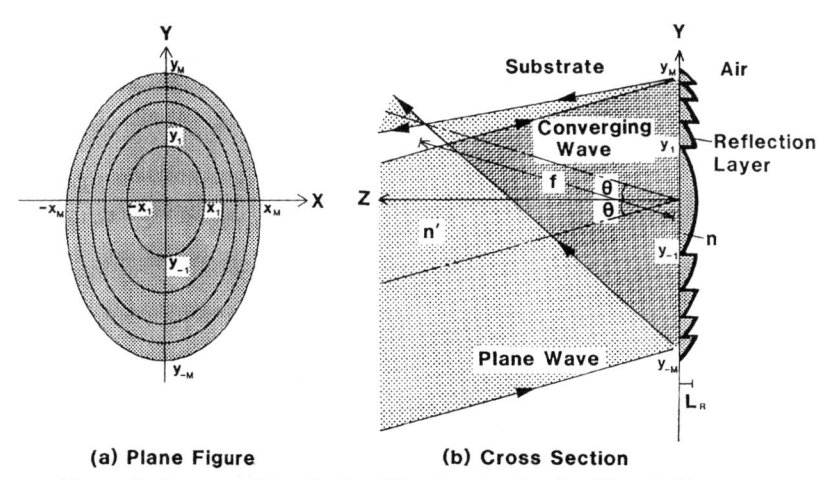

(a) Plane Figure   (b) Cross Section

Figure 3. Structure of the reflection diffractive microlens for oblique incidence.

the order of the boundary ellipse. The lengths of the major and minor axes of each ellipse are written, respectively,

$$S_{ym} = 2/\cos\theta \cdot [(m\lambda/n' \cos\theta)^2 + 2m\lambda f/n']^{1/2}, \qquad (18)$$
$$S_{xm} = 2[(m\lambda/n' \cos\theta)^2 + 2m\lambda f/n']^{1/2}. \qquad (19)$$

Lens sizes S_x and S_y are given by S_{xM} and S_{yM}, respectively. The size ratio of the major axis to the minor axis becomes

$$S_{ym}/S_{xm} = 1/\cos\theta. \qquad (20)$$

The eccentric ratio is used as a measure of an ellipse (Shiono, Setsune, and Yamazaki 1987) and is defined in terms of ellipse sizes as

$$e = [1 - (S_{xm}/S_{ym})^2]^{1/2} \qquad (21)$$
$$= \sin\theta. \qquad (22)$$

Note that the eccentric ratio is independent of order m and is determined only by incident angle θ. Therefore, it is clear that the diffractive microlens suitable for oblique incidence is composed of elliptical gratings with a constant eccentric ratio, where their center position is shifted to the $-Y$ direction in proportion to order m.

2.1.3 Rectangular-Aperture Microlens Arrays

Microlens arrays are the key devices for the 2-D parallel processing used in optical computing. Diffractive microlens arrays with a rectangular-aperture structure (Shiono et al. 1987b; Jahns and Walker 1990) have no dead space between each lens. Table 1 shows the 1-D structure and theoretical focusing characteristics for (a) a circular-aperture lens array and (b) a rectangular-aperture lens array.

Table 1. Comparison of Focusing Performance between Circular-Aperture and Rectangular-Aperture Lens Arrays

Focusing Characteristics	(a) Circular-Aperature	(b) Rectangular-Aperature
Structure	⊢S⊣	⊢S_x⊣ S_y
Collection area	$0.79 S^2$	$S_x S_y$
FWHM spot size	$1.03 \lambda f/S$	$0.89 \lambda f/S_x$ (x DIRECTION) $0.89 \lambda f/S_y$ (y DIRECTION)
Maximum intensity	$0.62(S^2/\lambda f)^2$	$(S_x S_y/\lambda f)^2$

Consider a plane wave (wavelength λ) with an amplitude of unity incident on a rectangular-aperture lens. The intensity distribution at the focal plane is given by (Born and Wolf 1970)

$$I(x, y) = (S_x S_y/\lambda f)^2 \cdot \text{sinc}^2(\pi S_x x/\lambda f) \cdot \text{sinc}^2(\pi S_y y/\lambda f), \quad (23)$$

where $\text{sinc}(\theta) = \sin(\theta)/\theta$; f is the focal length of the lens; and S_x and S_y are lens aperture sizes in the X and Y directions, respectively. The diffraction-limited FWHM (full width at half-maximum) spot size at the focal plane is calculated by

$$2W_{1/2} = 0.89\lambda f/S_x \text{ for } X \text{ direction} \quad \text{and} \quad 0.89\lambda f/S_y \text{ for } Y \text{ direction}, \quad (24)$$

and the full width of the main lobe is

$$2W_{\text{main}} = 2\lambda f/S_x \text{ for } X \text{ direction} \quad \text{and} \quad 2\lambda f/S_y \text{ for } Y \text{ direction}, \quad (25)$$

The optical power within the main lobe is calculated to be 82% of the total power. The power ratio increases to 92% when the first sidelobe is included. The maximum intensity of the first sidelobe is 4.7% of the main lobe maximum intensity.

In a similar manner, the intensity distribution in the radial direction for an ordinary circular-aperture lens is given by

$$I(r) = (\pi S^2/4\lambda f)^2 \cdot [2J_1(R)/R]^2, \quad R = \pi S r/\lambda f, \quad (26)$$

where S is a lens aperture diameter, and J_1 is a first-order Bessel function. The FWHM spot size and the full width of the main lobe are

$$2W_{1/2} = 1.03\lambda f/S, \quad (27)$$
$$2W_{\text{main}} = 2.44\lambda f/S, \quad (28)$$

respectively.

The optical power within the main lobe is 84%, and the maximum intensity of the first sidelobe is 1.8% of the main lobe maximum intensity. Note that the power contained within the main lobe shows little difference between the rectangular-aperture lens and the circular-aperture lens, but the maximum intensity ratio of the sidelobe is 2.6 times larger in the rectangular-aperture lens.

Consider the lens array with period S_x in the X direction, as shown in Table 1. The aperture size of the circular-aperture lens array must be fixed ($S = S_x$), but for the rectangular-aperture lens array, the size of S_y in the Y direction can be chosen independently of S_x. The focusing characteristics can be improved in the rectangular-aperture lens arrays. For an aspect ratio of $S_y/S_x = 1.5$, for example, the collection area that is proportional to the total focused power is improved by 1.9 times. The FWHM spot sizes are also improved by 0.58 times (Y direction) and 0.86 times (X direction). The intensity at the center of the focused spot is 2.4 times larger.

2-D lens arrays composed of rectangular-aperture lenses also have the same advantages, since their structures have no dead space between each lens. In a typical square-aperture 2-D lens array ($S_y/S_x = 1$), the collection ratio is improved by 1.3 times, the FWHM spot size by 0.86 times, and the maximum intensity by 1.6 times.

2.2 Theoretical Analysis of Diffraction Efficiency

2.2.1 Analytical Method

It is well known that the blazed thin grating with the optimum thickness given by Eq. (12) has a theoretical efficiency of 100%, neglecting the reflection loss at the grating surface (Magnusson and Gaylord 1978). The purpose of this section is to provide rigorous values for the diffraction efficiency of reflection and transmission blazed gratings and microlenses.

Diffractive microlenses are composed of curved and chirped gratings. To simplify the analysis of diffraction efficiency, we deal with linear transmission and reflection gratings with uniform period, believing that the optical tendency should be similar. By means of the differential method (Vincent 1980), Maxwell's equation was solved to satisfy the boundary conditions.

Figure 4 shows the cross-sectional views of (a) transmission and (b) reflection blazed gratings periodic along the X axis for analysis of first-order diffraction efficiency. In the transmission grating, region (I), which is above the blazed surface in vacuum, has refractive index $n_1 = 1$, and region (II), which is below the surface, is a dielectric lossless medium with refractive index $n_2 = n = 1.6$. In the reflection grating, region (I) is a metal such as Al, Au, and Ag with complex refractive index $n_1 = 1.2 - j7.0$, $0.15 - j3.2$, and $0.065 - j4.0$, respectively, and region (II) is the same medium as in the transmission grating. These complex refractive indices of the metals are typical values for $\lambda = 0.6328$ μm. A plane

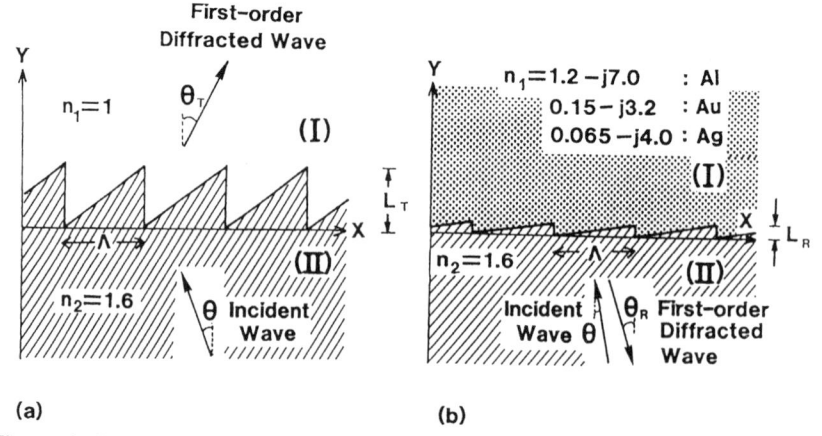

Figure 4. Cross-sectional views of (a) transmission and (b) reflection gratings with uniform period for the analysis of first-order diffraction efficiency.

wave with wavelength λ is incident at an angle θ on both gratings and the first-order diffracted wave has an angle θ_T and θ_R, respectively. Grating period is Λ, and L_T and L_R are the maximum groove depths, respectively. Assume that the incident wave is TE polarized where the electric field is parallel to the grating grooves. The electric field component satisfies Maxwell's wave equation:

$$\Delta E_Z(x, y) + k_i^2(x, y)E_Z(x, y) = 0, \quad k_i = n_i k \text{ and } i = 1, 2. \qquad (29)$$

Let us define the grating vector $K = 2\pi/\Lambda$, the propagation coefficient $\alpha_m = \alpha_0 - mK$ (m is an integer), and $\alpha_0 = k_2 \sin\theta$. With the periodicity along the X axis, the electric field is written as

$$E_Z(x, y) = \sum_{m=-\infty}^{\infty} E_m(y) \exp(-j\alpha_m x). \qquad (30)$$

The square-wave vector is defined by Fourier expansion as

$$k_i^2(x, y) = \sum_{m=-\infty}^{\infty} (k_i^2)_m \exp(-jmKx). \qquad (31)$$

By substituting Eqs. (30) and (31) into Eq. (29), a set of second-order coupled differential equations is obtained:

$$d^2 E_m(y)/dy^2 = \alpha_m^2 E_m(y) - \sum_{p=-\infty}^{\infty} (k_i^2)_{m-p} E_p(y). \qquad (32)$$

The numerical solution of Eq. (32) should satisfy the boundary conditions of the continuity of $E_m(y)$ and $dE_m(y)/dy$. The numerical integration of Eq. (32) was performed using the Numerov algorithm. The Fourier expansion number was taken as 11 from -5 to 5. The first-order diffraction efficiency was defined as the ratio of the power of the first-order diffracted wave to the power of the incident wave. Therefore, the reflection loss at the grating surface is included in the diffraction efficiency.

2.2.2 Calculated Results

Figure 5 shows the calculated first-order diffraction efficiency curves as a function of the normalized grating period when $\theta = 0$. The normalized maximum thickness of each grating was taken as $L_T/\lambda = 1/(n-1)$ and $L_R/\lambda = 1/2n$. If the period is much greater than the wavelength, the efficiency of the transmission grating is approximately 90%, but it decreases rapidly when the grating period becomes nearly comparable to the wavelength. A peak appears before the efficiency drops to zero, because the Bragg condition is satisfied at that period. For reflection grating, high diffraction efficiency can be obtained even in such a small period region ($\Lambda/\lambda \lesssim 5$), and the efficiency decreases smoothly. Among the three kinds of reflection grating, the grating with a Ag reflection layer shows the highest efficiency

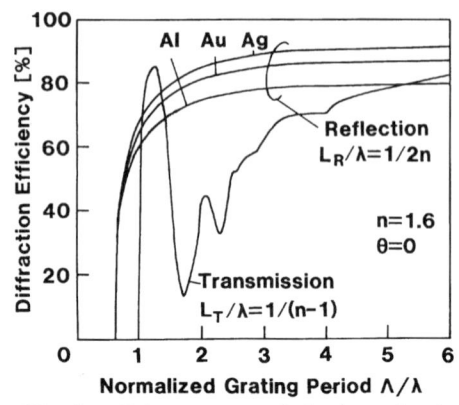

Figure 5. First-order diffraction efficiency curves calculated as a function of normalized grating period when $\theta = 0$.

as a result of the influence of the reflection loss at the metallic region. The minimum normalized grating period of a diffractive microlens with NA is given by

$$\Lambda_{min}/\lambda = 1/\text{NA}. \tag{33}$$

To obtain $\geq 80\%$ diffraction efficiency for the entire lens aperture, the NA of the transmission microlens cannot exceed 0.19 derived from $\Lambda/\lambda \geq 5.3$. But for a reflection microlens, it is found from $\Lambda/\lambda \geq 1.5$ that the NA can be increased to 0.67, which is 3.5 times that of the transmission type. These values can be approximately applied to circular and elliptical diffractive microlenses as well as cylindrical microlenses when their efficiencies show little polarization dependence.

Figure 6 shows the calculated first-order diffraction efficiency curves as a function of incident angle when $\Lambda/\lambda = 5$. At that period, the reflection grating with Al

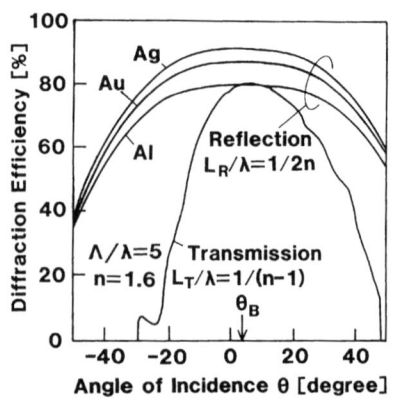

Figure 6. First-order diffraction efficiency curves calculated as a function of incident angle when $\Lambda/\lambda = 5$.

has almost the same maximum efficiency as the transmission grating. For both types of grating with such a small period, the efficiency takes its maximum value near the Bragg angle defined as

$$\theta_B = \sin^{-1}(\lambda/2n\Lambda). \tag{34}$$

Let us define the acceptance angle $\Delta\theta$ as the difference angle when the diffraction efficiency is 60%. The acceptance angle is dependent on the normalized grating period and tends to increase with the period. At $\Lambda/\lambda = 5$, the angle is 42 deg for the transmission grating, and 82 and 90 deg for the reflection grating with Al and Ag, respectively. This result indicates that use of a reflection microlens leads to both the diverging and converging spherical waves as well as the plane wave being focused with better characteristics, because the reflection microlens has a larger acceptance angle over almost all the range of period. This also means that reflection microlenses are much more suitable for oblique incidence as described in Section 2.1.2.

Figure 7 shows the calculated first-order diffraction efficiency curves as a function of normalized maximum grating thickness when $\theta = 0$ and $\Lambda/\lambda = 5$. As described in Section 2.1.1, thin reflection and transmission gratings show the maximum diffraction efficiency close to the thickness $L_R/\lambda = 1/2n$ and $L_T/\lambda = 1/(n-1)$, respectively.

For the grating period where the approximation of *thin* does not apply, the optimum thickness may differ from L_R given by Eq. (9). Figure 8 shows the calculated first-order diffraction efficiency and optimum thickness curves for a reflection grating with Ag as a function of a normalized grating period when $\theta = 0$. The dashed line in this figure shows the efficiency curve when $L_R/\lambda = 1/2n$. The optimum thickness increases as the grating period decreases. The efficiency can be improved by optimizing the thickness, especially at $\Lambda/\lambda \leq 4$. Therefore, a reflec-

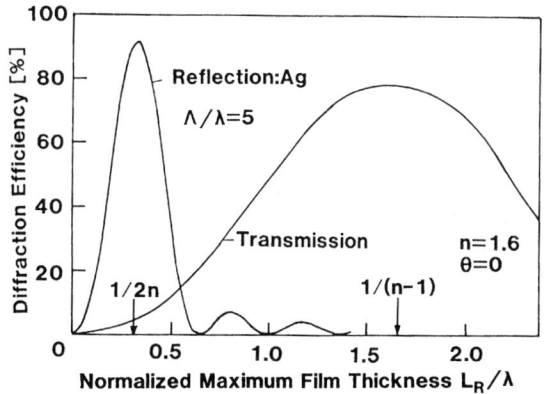

Figure 7. First-order diffraction efficiency curves calculated as a function of normalized maximum grating thickness when $\theta = 0$ and $\Lambda/\lambda = 5$.

180   Teruhiro Shiono

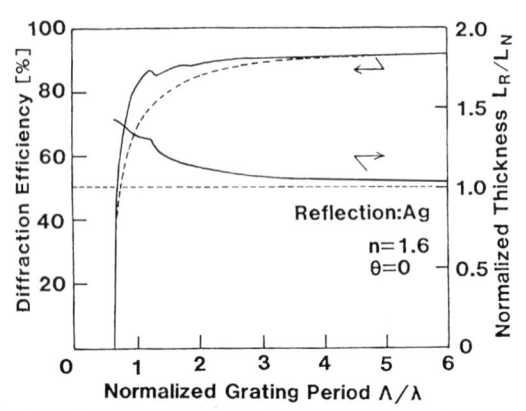

Figure 8. First-order diffraction efficiency and optimum grating thickness curves for the reflection grating with Ag calculated as a function of normalized grating period when $\theta = 0$. The dashed line shows the efficiency curve when $L_R/\lambda = 1/2n$.

tion microlens with Ag of even NA = 1.0 can give more than 80% diffraction efficiency for the entire aperture.

For the TM polarized wave where the magnetic field is parallel to the grating grooves, the numerical error increased for the reflection gratings, especially in the small grating period. Vincent (1980) describes the differential method as being more useful numerically for the TE polarized wave. One must analyze the diffraction efficiency of a reflection grating for the TM polarized wave in another way, such as by an integral method (Maystre 1980).

3. Fabrication by Electron-Beam Lithography

3.1 Electron-Beam Writing System

3.1.1 Constructions

Shiono et al. (1987a) have developed a computer-controlled electron-beam writing system for the fabrication of diffractive microlenses. A block diagram of the writing system is shown in Fig. 9. The system consists of an electron-beam irradiation unit and a control unit. The irradiation unit is a modified scanning electron microscope (SEM). The control unit includes specially designed pattern generators to reduce the amount of writing data and to make possible high-speed writing. The pattern generators, the beam blanking, and the X-Y stage are fully controlled by a minicomputer program (processing speed of three million instructions per second and writing-data transfer capability of 400 kwords/s). The accelerating voltage and the current of the electron beam can be changed from 1 to 39 kV and from 1 pA to 10 nA, respectively. The beam diameter is typically ~100 Å at 35-kV accelerating voltage and 10-pA beam current.

Diffractive Microlenses Fabricated by Electron-Beam Lithography   181

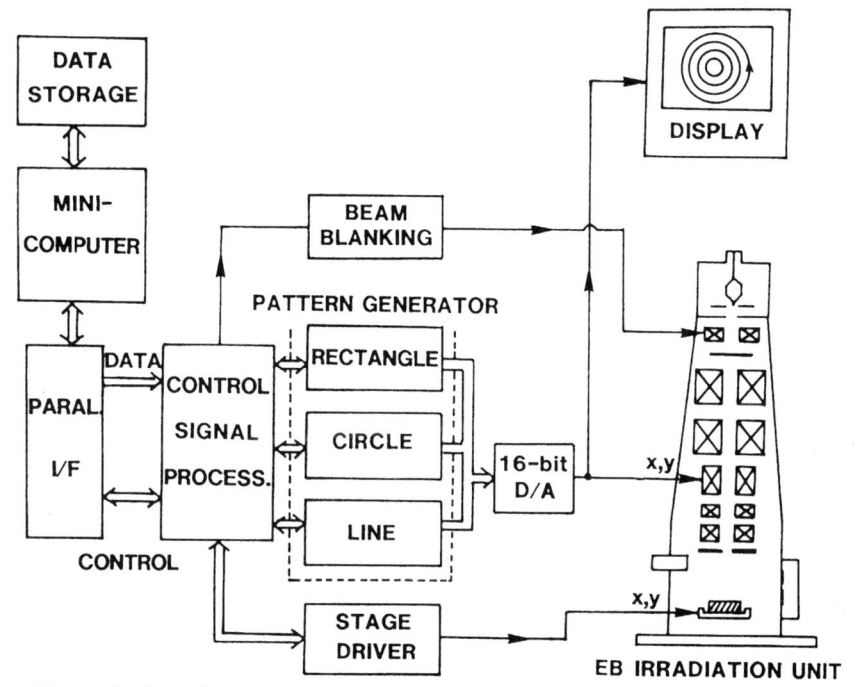

Figure 9. Block diagram of the developed computer-controlled electron-beam writing system.

For fabricating the various diffractive micro-optics components, three kinds of pattern generators were prepared. Figure 10 shows the functions of the pattern generators. The rectangle pattern generator interprets the writing data, X, Y, L, N, and H, and then the electron beam is scanned with N shots on a line within a rectangle. By means of the N function, a blazed structure can be fabricated by simple data processing.

The circle pattern generator is used to fabricate blazed circular or elliptical diffractive microlenses. This pattern generator interprets the writing data R, T, Y_C, X_B, and Y_B, and the electron beam is scanned for time T on a circle of radius R

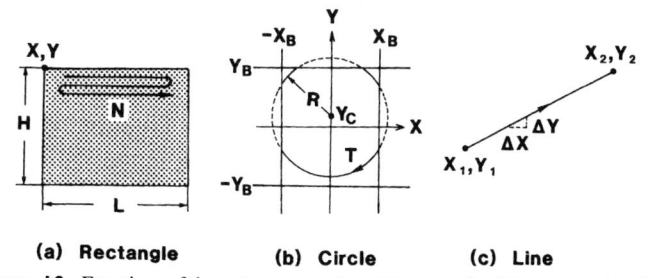

Figure 10. Functions of the pattern generators: (a) rectangle, (b) circle, and (c) line.

and center position $(0, Y_C)$. The beam is blank outside the design area $(X_B \times Y_B)$ and rectangular-aperture lenses or lens arrays (Shiono et al. 1987b) can also be made. The T datum, which modulates the scanning time, is useful for the fabrication of the blazed structure. The unit circle data are stored in EPROM microprocessors with a correction for angular distortion of the electron-beam deflection unit. The unit data from the EPROM microprocessors are multiplied to the datum R, and then the data in the Y direction are added to the datum Y_C. Such digital processing enables a circular pattern to be reproducibly written in the designed position without the drift-related phenomena observed in an analog oscillator. An ellipse can also be written either by using EPROMs with information stored on an ellipse or by changing the amplification rate of the x to y signals provided by the circle pattern generator.

The line pattern generator interprets the data X_1, Y_1, ΔX, ΔY, X_2, and Y_2, and then the line is written by adding ΔX, ΔY from the starting point (X_1, Y_1) to the ending point (X_2, Y_2), respectively. For smooth writing of a diagonal line, the decimal fraction parts of 8 bits are prepared in addition to the integer parts of 16 bits. The modulation of scanning speed, which is another method of fabricating a blazed structure, can be attained by multiplying ΔX, ΔY by the same real number.

3.1.2 Fundamental Performances

Fundamental performances of the present system were evaluated at the accelerating voltage of 35 kV. To improve generality, the patterns were fabricated on a Si substrate with a typical positive electron-beam resist, PMMA (polymethylmethacrylate), by the ordinary electron-beam direct writing technique.

Figure 11 shows a SEM photograph of a grating pattern. The resist thickness is ~0.2 μm, and the grating period and linewidth are 0.5 and 0.1 μm, respectively. This system has the ability to fabricate 0.1-μm patterns.

Figure 12 shows microphotographs of the patterns: (a) shows concentric circles and (b) concentric ellipses with a rectangular-aperture structure. It is confirmed that the system has the ability to produce smooth circular and elliptic scanning with excellent beam-blanking operation.

3.2 Fabrication Examples

3.2.1 Fabrication Process

The blazed structure can be formed because the resist thickness remaining after development depends on the electron dose (Fujita, Nishihara, and Koyama 1982). The fabrication process is almost the same for transmission and reflection microlenses. In the fabrication of the reflection microlens, the resist thickness is thinner (~1/5) and the reflection layer should be deposited last.

Figure 13 shows the fabrication process. Parts (a), (b), and (c) show the process

Diffractive Microlenses Fabricated by Electron-Beam Lithography 183

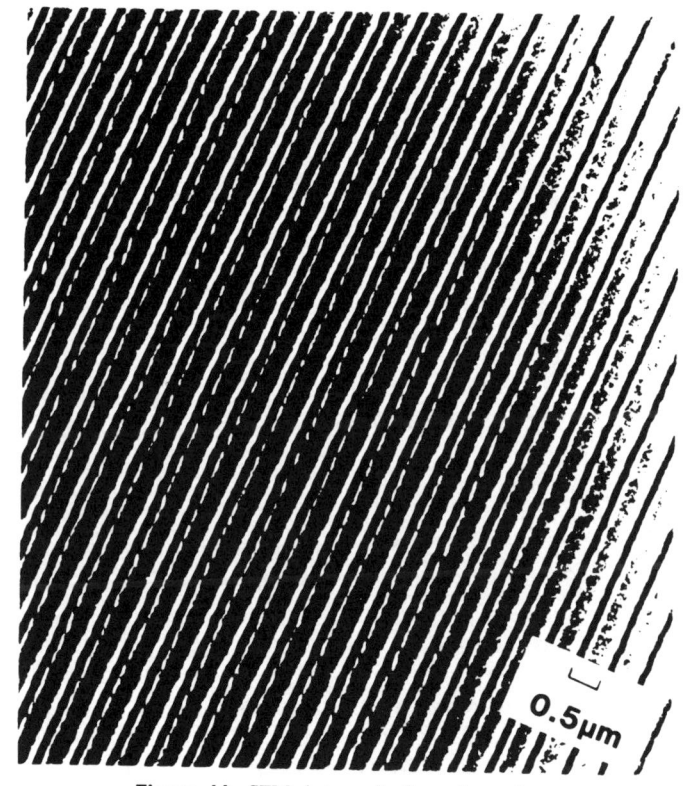

Figure 11. SEM photograph of a grating pattern.

for a transmission microlens; parts (a), (b), (c), and (d), for a reflection microlens. An electron-beam resist was spin coated on a glass substrate covered with a transparent conductive layer of indium tin oxide (ITO), which is necessary to avoid electrical charge buildup during the writing. The electron beam was circularly or elliptically scanned for a predetermined time until a specified dose was given and

(a)   (b)

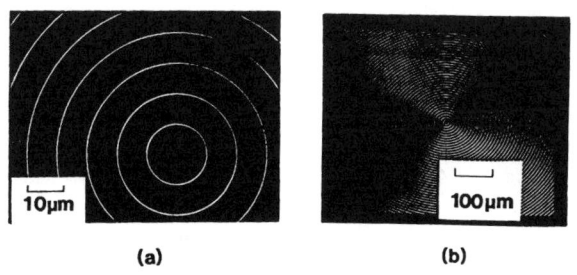

Figure 12. Microphotographs of the patterns: (a) concentric circles and (b) concentric ellipses with rectangular-aperture structure.

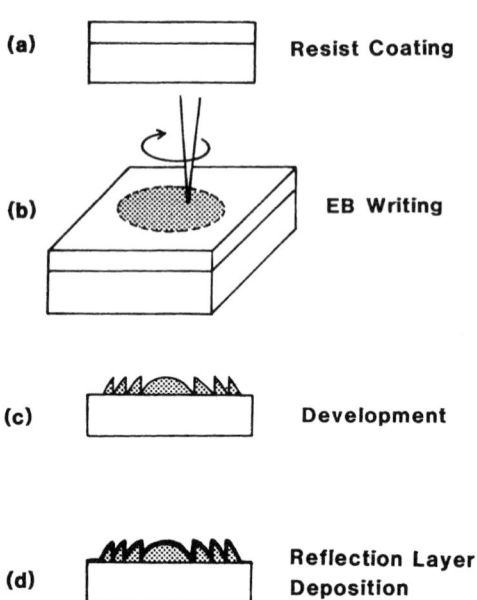

Figure 13. Fabrication process for a diffractive microlens: (a), (b), and (c) for a transmission microlens and (a), (b), (c), and (d) for a reflection microlens.

then the size of the circle or ellipse was increased by 0.1 to ~0.2 μm. The electron dose distribution was achieved by controlling the electron-beam scanning time in consideration of the resist-sensitivity curve, which depends on the groove period. Development of the resist achieved the desired relief structure. For the reflection microlens only, a metal was evaporated onto the blazed film to serve as the reflection layer. Silver with a thickness of ≥4000 Å was used to reduce reflection loss. The accelerating voltage and the current of the electron beam during the writing were 35 kV and 10 to 40 pA, respectively.

Common microlens development is of the wet type, so in this chapter we treat the microlens fabricated by wet development. But the microfabrication of blazed structures by means of a dry development process has already been demonstrated by Shiono and Setsune (1990).

3.2.2 Examples of Microlenses

For the fabrication of the blazed structure, the choice of the resist is important. When a positive resist, PMMA, for example, is used, the slope of the grating tends to be rough while the depth resolution is better. The negative resist, CMS (chloromethylated polystyrene), which Nishihara and Suhara (1987) and Shiono *et al.* (1987b) have used, exhibits high sensitivity and is barely influenced by the devel-

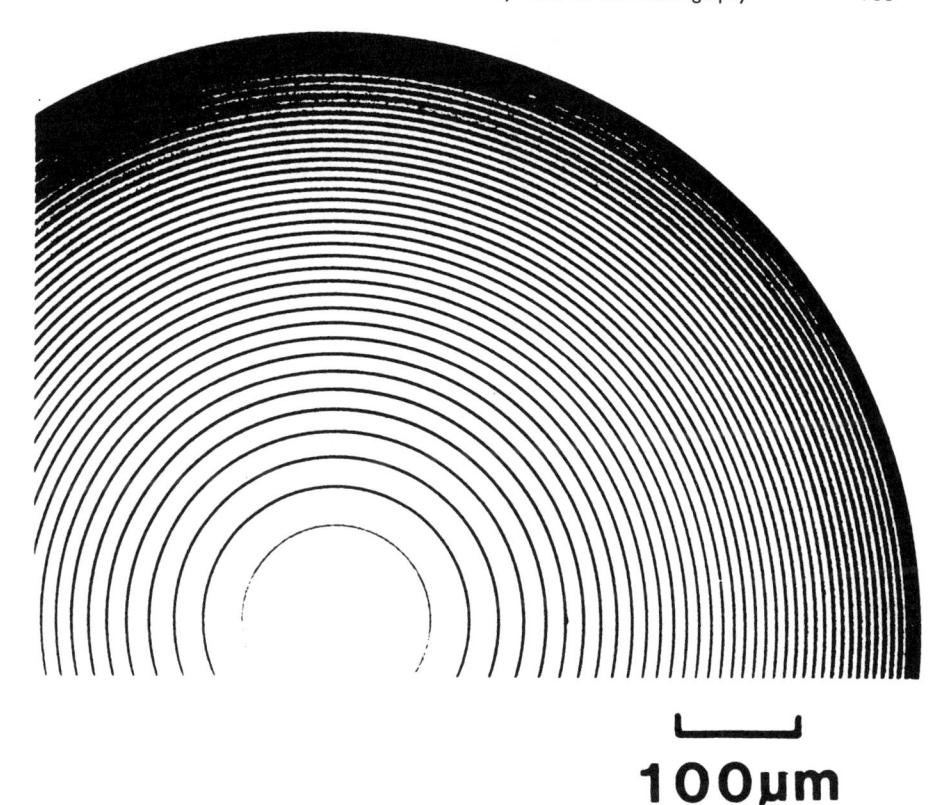

Figure 14. Microphotograph of the circular diffractive microlens.

oping conditions (the time and temperature). The grating slope made from the CMS resist can be smooth, while the depth resolution is not as good. This indicates that the CMS resist is more suitable for the fabrication of a microlens with a small NA of 0.1, which is described in this section.

Figure 14 is a microphotograph of the reflection circular microlens for normal incidence. This lens has an aperture size of 1 mm, a focal length of 5 mm in the air at a 0.6328-μm wavelength, a maximum thickness of $L_R = 0.2$ μm, a NA of 0.1, and a period modulation of 6.4 to 159 μm. The writing time was ~10 min.

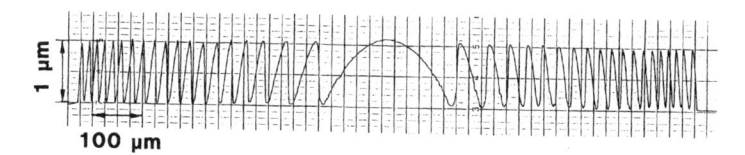

Figure 15. Measured cross-sectional profile of the transmission diffractive microlens.

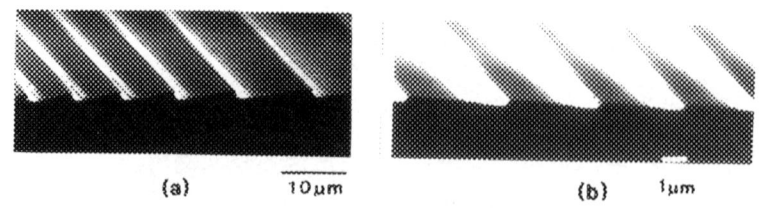

Figure 16. Cross-sectional SEM photographs of (a) a transmission diffractive microlens and (b) a reflection microlens before deposition of the reflection layer.

The measured cross-sectional profile of the transmission microlens is shown in Fig. 15. The microlens has a maximum thickness of $L_T = \sim 1.1$ μm, a focal length of 10 mm, and a period modulation of 13 to 225 μm. We can see that both the smoothly curved profile in the central part and the sawtooth relief profile in the outside parts have been realized as designed.

Figure 16 shows cross-sectional SEM photographs of (a) the transmission microlens and (b) the reflection microlens before deposition of the reflection layer. We see that a blazed structure had been made as designed for both microlenses, but in the period smaller than ~3 μm, a better profile was obtained in the reflection microlens because of the reduction of the thickness.

Figure 17 shows microphotographs of rectangular-aperture transmission microlens arrays. The lens array in Fig. 17(a) is a 2-D array with a 2 × 4 structure composed of square-aperture microlenses. Each lens has a focal length of 0.88 mm at the 0.6328-μm wavelength and an area of 125 × 125 μm². The lens array in Fig. 17(b) is a 1-D array with a 1 × 5 structure composed of vertically elongated rectangular-aperture microlenses. Each lens has a focal length of 0.75 mm and an area of 150 × 100 μm² ($S_y/S_x = 1.5$). Both lens arrays were blazed with 1.1-μm maximum thickness. The writing time was 13 min for the lens array with a 2 × 4 structure and 9 min for the 1 × 5 structure.

Figure 18 is a microphotograph of the reflection microlens for oblique incidence. This lens has an aperture size of 1 mm on the major axis, an eccentric ratio of 0.5, an incident angle of 30 deg, a focal length of 6.35 mm in $n = 1.52$ at a 0.6328-μm wavelength, a NA of 0.1, a maximum thickness of $L_R = 0.2$ μm,

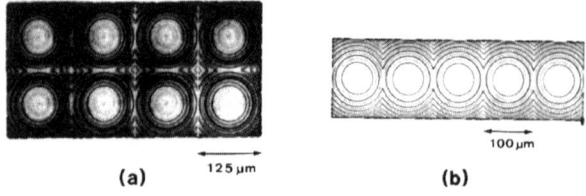

Figure 17. Microphotographs of two kinds of rectangular-aperture diffractive microlens arrays: (a) a 2-D array with a 2 × 4 structure and (b) a 1-D array with a 1 × 5 structure.

Diffractive Microlenses Fabricated by Electron-Beam Lithography   187

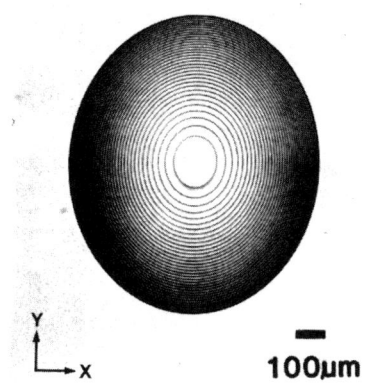

Figure 18. Microphotograph of the reflection diffractive microlens for oblique incidence.

and a maximum shift of the lens center of $y_{CM} = -9.7$ μm. The writing time was ~10 min.

4. Optical Measurements

4.1 Reflection and Transmission Microlenses for Normal Incidence

Figure 19 shows the experimental arrangement for measuring the focusing performance of (a) transmission and (b) reflection microlenses for normal incidence. The microlens was illuminated at normal angle by an expanded He-Ne laser beam ($\lambda = 0.6328$ μm), and the focused spot was projected by a microscope objective lens on a charge-coupled device (CCD) image sensor. For the reflection microlens,

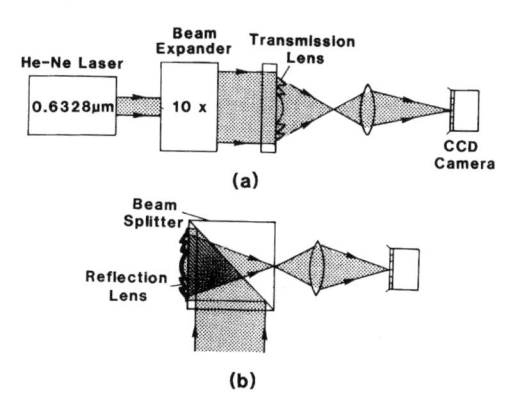

Figure 19. Experimental arrangement for measuring the focusing performance of (a) transmission and (b) reflection microlenses for normal incidence.

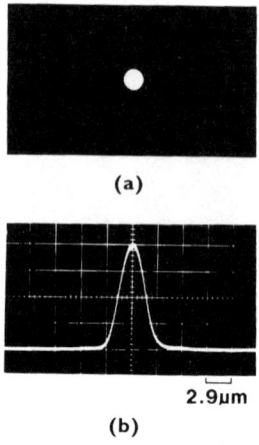

Figure 20. Light spot and intensity profile observed at the focal plane in the circular diffractive microlens shown in Fig. 14.

the beamsplitter (cubic half-mirror) was used and the focused spot was observed near the side opposite to the lens as shown in Fig. 19(b).

Figure 20 shows the light spot and the intensity profile observed at the focal plane in the reflection microlens shown in Fig. 14. The spot exhibited an excellent circular pattern where the sidelobe was scarcely detected. The FWHM of the profile was 3.3 μm. This value agrees with the diffraction-limited spot size calculated by Eq. (27). For the transmission microlens, the diffraction-limited focusing performance was also obtained. The focusing efficiency was found to be higher than 70% both for reflection and transmission microlenses with NA = 0.1. It is estimated from the theoretical analysis in Section 2.2. and the fabrication results that the efficiency of the reflection microlens with NA $\gtrsim$ 0.2 becomes much higher than that of the transmission microlens. Further improvement should be possible by optimization of the resist materials and the processing conditions.

Figure 21(a) shows photographs of the light spots and the intensity profile measured with a microscope objective lens (10×) in the 2-D microlens array shown in Fig. 17(a). Note that the incident beam was focused into as many light spots as the number of lenses. The focused spots showed little difference among the lenses. One of the focused spots was evaluated in detail using a microscope objective lens (40×). The photographs of the light spot and the intensity distribution are shown in Fig. 21(b). The sidelobes were observed on a crossed pattern, but their maximum intensity was at most a few percent of the main lobe. The measured FWHM spot size (4.0 μm) agrees with the theoretical one calculated by Eq. (24). For the 1-D microlens array shown in Fig. 17(b), excellent focusing performance was also obtained.

Diffractive Microlenses Fabricated by Electron-Beam Lithography   189

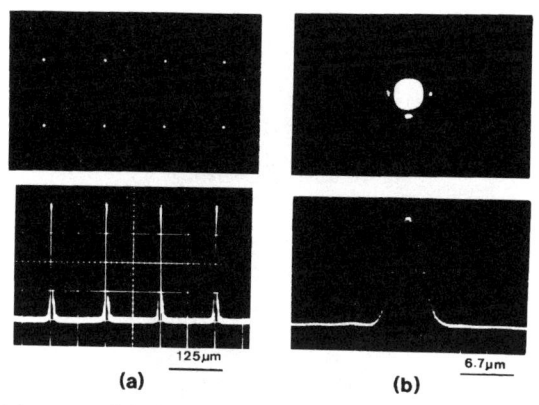

Figure 21. (a) Light spots and the intensity profile in the 2-D microlens arrays shown in Fig. 17(a), and (b) an expanded light spot of one of those shown in (a) and the intensity profile.

4.2 Reflection Microlenses for Oblique Incidence

Figure 22 shows the experimental arrangement for measuring the focusing performance of the reflection microlens for oblique incidence. The reflection microlens fabricated on the glass substrate was attached to the prism so that both optical axes can be vertical to the prism surface, and it was illuminated by an expanded He-Ne laser beam, where the incident angle was 30 deg. The focused spot near the prism surface was projected on a CCD image sensor by a microscope objective lens (60×).

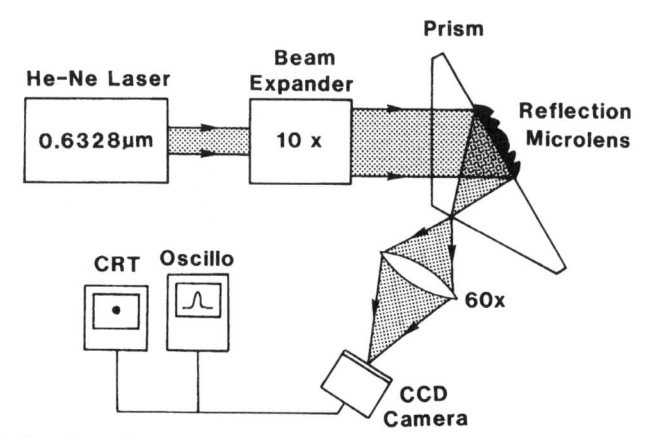

Figure 22. Experimental arrangement for measuring the focusing performance of the reflection diffractive microlens for oblique incidence.

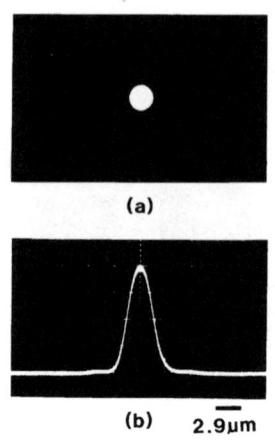

Figure 23. (a) Light spot and (b) intensity profile observed at the focal plane in the diffractive microlens shown in Fig. 18, which is fabricated by optimal design where θ = 30 deg.

Figure 23 shows (a) the light spot and (b) the intensity profile observed in the microlens fabricated using the optimal design described in Section 2.1.2. The spot exhibited an excellent circular pattern. The measured FWHM spot size (3.2 μm) also agrees with the diffraction-limited value calculated by the diffraction formula (Born and Wolf 1970). The focusing efficiency was measured to be as high as 78% including the reflection loss at the metallic region.

The aberrations of the focused spot were evaluated in microlenses fabricated differently from the optimal design. Figure 24(a) shows the focused spot observed in a microlens fabricated without shifting the center position of the ellipses [y_{Cm}

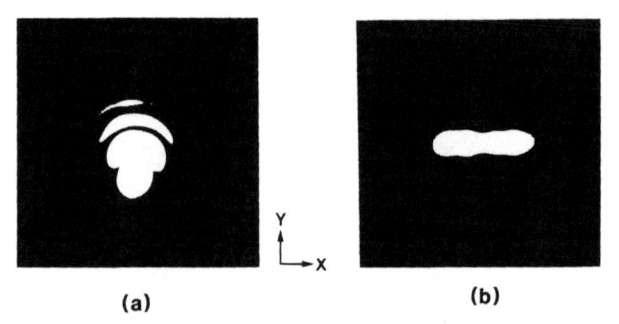

Figure 24. (a) Light spot observed at the focal plane in a diffractive microlens fabricated without shifting the center position of the ellipses ($y_{Cm} = 0$) where θ = 30 deg. Typical coma occurred. (b) Light spot observed at the focal plane in the Y direction in a diffractive microlens fabricated by changing the size from S_x from the designed value where $e = 0.47$ and θ = 30 deg. Typical astigmatism appeared.

= 0; elliptical micro-Fresnel lens (Shiono, Setsune, and Yamazaki 1987)]. Typical coma occurred. Figure 24(b) shows the focused spot observed in a microlens fabricated by changing the size of S_x from the designed value, where $e = 0.47$. The spot was elongated in the X direction. A typical astigmatism appeared. These results demonstrate that shifting the center position of the ellipses and making the elliptical patterns can compensate the coma and astigmatism, respectively.

5. Conclusion

In this chapter, the design, characteristics, and electron-beam fabrication of diffractive microlenses were described. The flexibility of electron-beam lithography can result in various kinds of high-performance diffractive optical components. Both transmission and reflection microlenses including their arrays fabricated by this method exhibited diffraction-limited focusing performance with efficiencies of greater than 70%. It is stressed that the reflection diffractive microlenses are very promising because their fabrication accuracy and optical characteristics can be greatly improved. It has also been demonstrated that reflection microlenses for oblique incidence showed diffraction-limited focusing performance at a large oblique angle of 30 deg. These diffractive microlenses could be used as key devices in the field of optical computing.

ACKNOWLEDGMENTS

I thank Prof. H. Nishihara, Prof. Y. Ichioka, Dr. M. Haruna, Dr. T. Suhara, and Dr. S. Ura, Osaka University, for their helpful discussions. I also thank Dr. T. Nitta, Dr. K. Kanai, Dr. K. Wasa, and Dr. H. Ogawa for their continuous encouragement and Dr. O. Yamazaki, Dr. K. Setsune, Dr. T. Mitsuyu, and H. Higashino, Matsushita Electric, for their useful suggestions.

REFERENCES

Ahmed, H. (1986). *Sci. Prog.* **70**, 473–487.
Born, M., and Wolf, E. (1970). *Principles of Optics*. Pergamon, Oxford.
Brenner, K.-H., and Sauer, F. (1989). *Appl. Opt.* **27**, 4251–4254.
Fujita, T., Nishihara, H., and Koyama, J. (1982). *Opt. Lett.* **7**, 578–580.
Goto, K., Mori, K., Hatakoshi, G., and Takahashi, S. (1987). *Jpn. J. Appl. Phys.* Suppl. **26-4**, 135–140.
Haruna, M., Takahashi, M., Wakahayashi, K., and Nishihara, H. (1990). *Appl. Opt.* **29**, 5120–5126.
Jahns, J., and Huang, A. (1989). *Appl. Opt.* **28**, 1602–1605.
Jahns, J., and Walker, S. J. (1990). *Appl. Opt.* **29**, 931–936.
Jordan, J. A., Hirsch, Jr., P. M., Lesem, L. B., and Rooy, D. L. Van (1970). *Appl. Opt.* **9**, 1883–1887.
Kosuge, K., Sugama, S., Ono, Y., and Nishida, N. (1984). *Conference Digest of the 13th Congress of the International Commission for Optics,* Science Council of Japan and Japan Society of Applied Physics, Sapporo, pp. 526–527.
Magnusson, R., and Gaylord, T. K. (1978). *J. Opt. Soc. Am.* **68**, 806–809.

Maystre, D. (1980). Chap. 3 in: *Electromagnetic Theory of Gratings* (R. Petit, ed.), Springer-Verlag, Berlin.
Nishihara, H., and Suhara, T. (1987). *Prog. Opt.* **24,** 1–37.
Shiono, T., Kitagawa, M., Setsune, K., and Mitsuyu, T. (1989). *Appl. Opt.* **28,** 3434–3442.
Shiono, T., and Ogawa, K. (1991). *Appl. Opt.* **30,** 3643–3649.
Shiono, T., and Setsune, K. (1990). *Opt. Lett.* **15,** 84–86.
Shiono, T., Setsune, K., and Yamazaki, O. (1987). *Trans. Inst. Electron. Inf. Commun. Eng. Jpn.* **J70-C,** 1044–1051.
Shiono, T., Setsune, K., Yamazaki, O., and Wasa, K. (1987a). *J. Vac. Sci. Technol. B* **5,** 33–36.
Shiono, T., Setsune, K., Yamazaki, O., and Wasa, K. (1987b). *Appl. Opt.* **26,** 587–591.
Vincent, P. (1980). Chap. 4 in: *Electromagnetic Theory of Gratings* (R. Petit, ed.), Springer-Verlag, Berlin.

Chapter 8
Parallel Optical Interconnections

D. E. SMITH, M. J. MURDOCCA, and T. W. STONE

Rutgers University
Department of Computer Science
New Brunswick, NJ 008903

1. Optical Considerations in Free-Space Parallel Interconnects 193
   1.1 Introduction 193
   1.2 Macro-Optics 194
   1.3 Micro-Optics 196
   1.4 Summary 201
2. Interconnects 201
   2.1 Introduction 201
   2.2 Perfect Shuffle MINs 204
   2.3 Banyan MINs 206
   2.4 Crossover 209
   2.5 Irregular Interconnects 212
3. Architectural Considerations 213
   3.1 Low-Level Optical Interconnection 214
   3.2 Improvement to Low-Level Interconnection 216
   3.3 Architectural Implications of Reconfigurable Interconnects . . . 217
4. Designing with Imperfect Arrays 220
   4.1 Utilizing Imperfect Arrays 221
       References 224

1. Optical Considerations in Free-Space Parallel Interconnects

1.1 Introduction

Parallel optical interconnections are a central facet of many optical computing architectures. In this chapter some of the basic and practical principles of optics, interconnects, and computer architecture are discussed on an introductory level, in the context of optical interconnects. Many schemes are available for connecting the outputs of one array of logic gates or emitters with a subsequent array of gates or detectors. When free-space imaging is used for this purpose, trade-offs exist among the options encountered in the optical system design. For example, a single lens (or system) may be used to image simultaneously an entire array of optical gates, as was done in the AT&T S-SEED-based digital optical processor (Prise *et al.* 1991). At the other extreme, each optical gate can be imaged with its own lens or optical system. While there is a continuum of cases between these two extremes, this section contains a discussion of some of the primary trade-offs in the limiting cases of such *macro-optics* and *micro-optics* approaches, respectively. In this section an approximate geometrical model is presented for the purpose of building intuition about the trade-offs imposed by beam spreading due to diffraction and the resultant crosstalk. In actual system design one should more carefully evaluate the magnitude of this type of crosstalk using diffraction theory, some results from which are used later in this chapter. The details of such a diffraction analysis are beyond the scope of this chapter, and the basic principles are readily obtained in texts including Goodman (1968), Reynolds *et al.* (1989), and Born and Wolf (1964). The discussion here is based on uniform amplitude waves and square apertures in order to illustrate *first-order* dependencies. These conditions are appropriate for many applications, but other complicating factors are often encountered. For example, if waves with a Gaussian amplitude profile are used, additional effects resulting from truncation must be considered. A detailed discussion of this case is given in the literature (Siegman 1986; McCormick *et al.* 1991).

1.2 Macro-Optics

Consider the geometry of Fig. 1, in which a single lens is used to image an array of optical gates. It is assumed that the lens is in air and has focal length f, aperture stop diameter D, field extent W, and corresponding field angle β, as shown. In this configuration the lens images the array to infinity, and may be thought of as the first half of an imaging system that is symmetric about the stop. The smallest spot size obtainable from an ideal lens with no "aberrations" is limited by diffraction. These aberrations are errors in imaging rays from points in the object plane to ideally conjugate points in the image plane. The size of a diffraction-limited spot

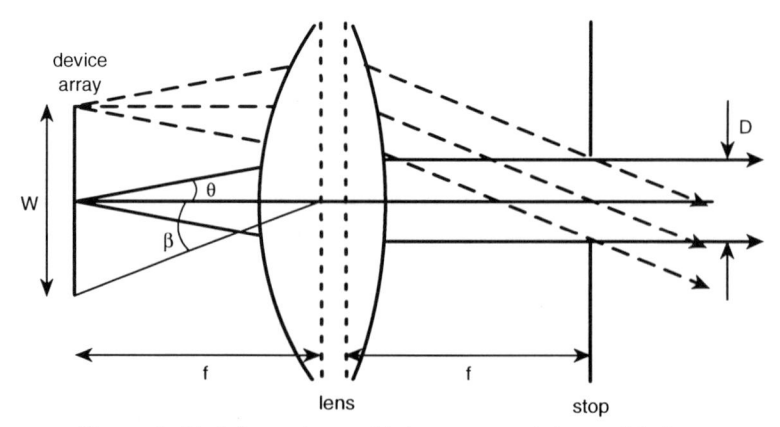

Figure 1. Single lens system used to image an extended array of devices.

is related to the numerical aperture (NA) of the lens. For a lens in air, the NA is sinθ, where θ is the half-angle of illumination of the lens, as shown in Fig. 1. In practice, some aberrations are always present, and if they are not kept small, the aberrations can increase the imaged spot size beyond that of the diffraction limit. A practical trade-off involving the field extent W and aberrations of the lens is immediately encountered.

From diffraction theory we find that diffraction effects, such as a limit to the smallest obtainable focused spot size from a lens, become more pronounced as the lens aperture size D decreases. For example, an ideal aberration-free lens that is truncated (by a slit stop) to numerical aperture NA will image a point input object into a diffraction-limited spot of width equal to λ/NA, where λ is the wavelength of light used in the imaging (Smith 1966). Given a focused spot diameter d required on the subsequent plane of devices, the NA of the imaging lens is therefore constrained by diffraction according to the relation:

$$\mathrm{NA} = \sin\theta \geq \frac{\lambda}{d}. \qquad (1)$$

From this equation and Fig. 1, we can see that to reduce the diffraction-limited spot size d from a lens the focusing beam half-angle θ must be increased; or equivalently, the focal length f must be decreased and/or the aperture diameter D must be increased. For example, with $\lambda = 0.8$ μm and $d = 4$ μm the NA of the lens must be 0.2 or greater, which corresponds to a full-angle of convergence of 23 deg at the focus. As long as the aberrations of the lens are kept small enough that the spot sizes are essentially limited by diffraction, maintaining the NA above this value will provide the desired (or smaller) spot sizes in the focal plane. However as the field extent W is increased, the field angle β over which the lens must provide such extremely low aberrations is increased, and so too is the required complexity of the lens (as measured by the number of elements, use of aspheric surfaces, tighter tolerances, etc.). Diffraction-limited performance at one wavelength can be achieved at these large NAs by a single lens element for the case of on-axis imaging (β = 0 deg), while many elements are usually required to provide comparable imaging over even a moderately extended field (β = 10, 20 deg, etc.).

To provide for a large number of spots with the required size (i.e., large space-bandwidth product), it is desirable to increase the field extent W over which acceptable imaging is obtained. A trade-off between the magnitude of aberrations and an increase in the field width W can be seen by considering the scaling of an acceptable lens with a goal of increasing W and hence the number of devices that can be simultaneously imaged. When a lens is scaled uniformly, e.g., by increasing all linear dimensions by a factor of γ, the surface radii, diameters, separations, field extent, and focal length are all increased by the same factor. Thus angles including θ and β are preserved, the NA of the lens is left unchanged, and the diffraction-limited spot size (in the absence of aberrations) is also unchanged. The larger field extent seems to be exactly what is desired in order to increase the space-bandwidth product. However, in a practical lens of this complexity, many types of aberrations are present and must be balanced to keep their overall magnitudes acceptable.

Consider a real "diffraction-limited" lens designed to produce imaging of the device outputs to a required spot size over an input field extent W. In the design of such a lens the aberrations are massaged by varying the lens parameters (curvatures, thicknesses, glasses, etc.) so that the net errors caused by the aberrations are of the order of the spot size of the same lens limited only by diffraction. When this lens is scaled up by γ as discussed earlier, the forms of these aberrations remain the same, but the errors resulting from the aberrations scale by γ. After scaling, although the diffraction-limited spot size remains the same, the aberrations (which were balanced to within tolerance before scaling) are now γ times larger. As a result of the larger actual spot size, the larger field extent of the scaled-up lens may not provide for a net increase in number of devices that can be simultaneously imaged. Of course, a new lens design may be sought to reduce the magnitude of aberrations in the scaled lens to those the lens had prior to scaling, but usually at a cost of increased complexity (if even achievable). Further discussion of these scaling properties and motivations for micro-optics are given in the literature (Lohmann 1989; Jewell and McCall 1989; Jewell et al. 1990). This trade-off in lens complexity for field size (and thus number of gates) is an important reason for considering the use of many simpler lenses, each operating over a greatly restricted field, as considered in the next section.

1.3 Micro-Optics

The situation is very different for the case in which a separate microlens is used for each optical device in the array. This configuration is illustrated in Fig. 2,

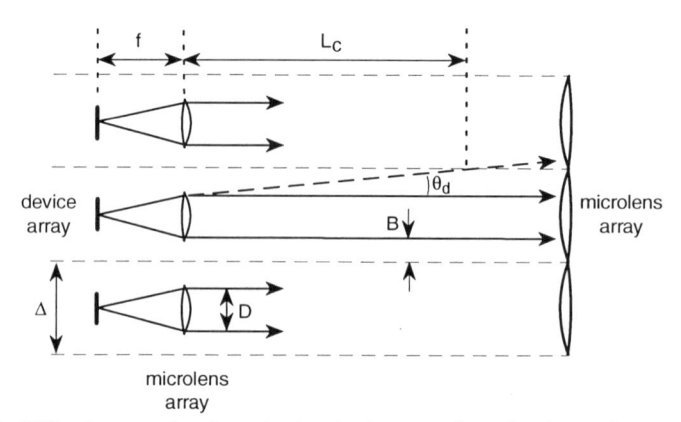

Figure 2. Diffraction spreading from simple microlenses, each used to image the output from a single on-axis device to infinity.

where the center-to-center device spacing is given by Δ. In this section we assume that spatially coherent beams and diffraction-limited lenses and spot sizes are used. Since the output or input portion (window, microlaser, detector, etc.) of the device may be located on the axis of the associated microlens, the performance of the lens does not need to be maintained over an extended field. This *zero-field* condition and scaled-down size greatly reduce the required complexity of the lens design. However, since the centers of the microlenses are separated by Δ, the microlens diameters must be smaller than or equal to Δ so that they do not overlap. The resulting small lens diameters give rise to a major trade-off between device spacing and propagation distance limits. The latter is caused by diffraction and the need to limit crosstalk between neighboring channels. These issues are discussed in this section.

The minimum NA of each microlens is constrained by the required spot size d at the device or optical gate, according to the same relation given in Eq. (1). Although these NAs are still usually large, the zero-field operation and small size reduce the complexity so that diffraction-limited performance can be obtained using simple refractive or diffractive elements, often with only a single surface containing optical power. For example, to obtain a spot size of 4 μm at the device with $\lambda = 0.8$ μm, each microlens would require a minimum NA of 0.2, exactly as in the macro-optics case discussed previously. However, in this case the diameter of the elements is limited by the device spacing Δ, which is typically only tens or hundreds of microns. For a gate spacing and lens diameter of 80 μm, the focal length of each microlens would thus be less than 196 μm.

Diffraction spreading caused by these small lens diameters forms the basis of a major trade-off in the micro-optic imaging approach. The detrimental effect of this diffraction is illustrated next by two examples: the *collimated array* (Figs. 2 and 3), and the *focused array* (Figs. 4 and 5). In the following examples, we assume that the microlenses are maintained at a NA that matches the required focal plane spot size, as discussed previously. This restriction still leaves a free parameter among the choice of either the microlens focal length or diameter. The following trade-offs will be illustrated with microlens diameter D as a variable, but subject to the *nonoverlapping* constraint that $0 \leq D/\Delta \leq 1$. Thus, the microlens focal length will be constrained in the following examples as D varies in order to meet the required NA.

1.3.1 Collimated Array

In the collimated array example, which is shown in Fig. 2, the output or input portion of each of the devices resides on the axis of and in the back focal plane of a dedicated microlens. Light emanating from each device is therefore collimated by the lens and propagates toward the next stage. This next stage may consist, for example, of another microlens array used to focus the beams onto a detector array, or a microlens array used as a relay stage for the channels, or it could consist of a single large lens as in the hybrid micro/macro system of Lohmann (1989, 1991). The trade-offs involved in these many options are beyond the scope of this chapter. The aperture of each microlens is truncated at a diameter D, and due to this finite extent the output beam suffers diffraction spreading. Although as a consequence of this truncation some light is scattered through very large angles and into distant channels (contributing to crosstalk), in this simplified geometrical model we assume that most of the light is contained within the region bounded by a diffraction angle $\theta_d = \sin^{-1}\lambda/D$, as illustrated. This diffraction angle is related to the angular spread of light far from a slit of width D; see, for example, Hecht (1987) and Guenther (1990). Complicating diffraction effects, particularly near the lens, are ignored in this model. A *critical distance* L_c is defined as the propagation distance over which the beam augmented by the diffraction angle θ_d does not cross over into the neighboring channel, and is illustrated in Fig. 2.

This critical distance is a function of the microlens diameter, and contours of constant L_c are shown in Fig. 3 as a function of varied fill factor D/Δ and device spacing Δ. For example, consider an array with a device spacing of $\Delta = 200$ μm and light of wavelength 0.85 μm. If the lens is only 10 μm in diameter ($D/\Delta = 0.05$), there will be a *buffer zone* of width $B = 95$ μm (see Fig. 2) on each side of the microlens over which the light may spread before crossing into the neighboring channel. However the diffraction spread angle of the beam from such a small lens is large (4.9 deg), and after only $L_c = 1.1$ mm the beam would begin to spread beyond the 95-μm buffer and mix with the neighboring signal. Similarly, as the microlens diameter approaches the gate (device) spacing, the critical distance L_c is also very small. Near this other extreme, if $D/\Delta = 0.95$ ($D = 190$ μm) the diffraction angle is a much smaller 0.26 deg, but the buffer zone width is now reduced to $B = 5$ μm, and L_c is again only 1.1 mm. However, for less extreme values of D/Δ (e.g., near 0.5), L_c is much larger (nearly 6 mm). Since the diffraction angle decreases with increasing lens diameter, one might suspect that low

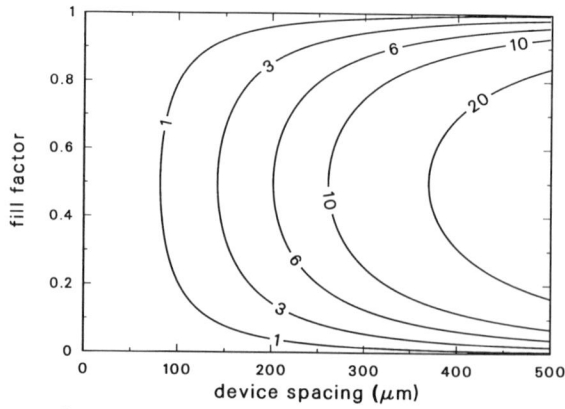

Figure 3. Contours of constant critical distance (mm) for the collimated array example as a function of fill factor D/Δ and device spacing Δ, with $\lambda = 0.85$ μm.

crosstalk could be maintained over longer distances if the full width Δ could be utilized for the microlens apertures. Effective use of these larger apertures can be accomplished by slightly focusing the beam emerging from the microlens, thus avoiding the condition mentioned earlier in which any spreading of the collimated beam from a lens with $D = \Delta$ results in crosstalk. This focused array configuration is discussed in the following section.

1.3.2 Focused Array

A second example of the diffraction-based trade-offs in device spacing and propagation distance is given in the focused array, which is illustrated in Fig. 4. A similar method of slightly focusing a beam to extend its unexpanded range is discussed for Gaussian beams in Siegman (1986). In Fig. 4 the microlenses are located at a distance slightly larger than their focal length from the source array, causing the emerging beam to be converging or focused, rather than collimated as in the previous example. The amount of focusing is chosen to be just enough that the outwardly diffracted rays from the microlenses emerge parallel to the microlens axis, as illustrated by the collimated dashed ray. It is seen from Fig. 4 that this amount of focusing corresponds to a back focal distance l' for the microlenses given by:

$$l' = \frac{D}{2 \tan\theta_d}, \qquad (2)$$

where as before $\theta_d = \sin^{-1} \lambda/D$. In this geometrical approximation, these rays will not cross into neighboring channels. But the focusing rays (solid lines and inwardly diffracted dashed lines) will pass through focus and eventually, after criti-

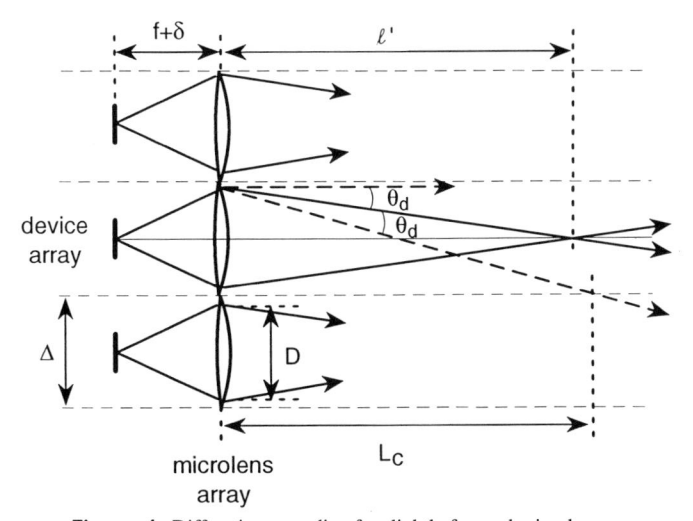

Figure 4. Diffraction spreading for slightly focused microlenses.

cal distance L_c as shown, expand into neighboring channels and produce crosstalk. The trade-offs between device spacing and fill factor for this case are illustrated in Fig. 5. The critical distance for this focused array example is significantly larger than that for the previous example, and the largest critical distances occur for fill factors of unity, i.e., where the microlens diameter D is equal to the device separation Δ.

In the preceding discussions, several simple geometrical models have been presented so that a few of the basic trade-offs involved with free-space optical interconnection can be understood. Below a connection is made between the latter focused array model and elementary diffraction theory, which enables a quantitative estimate of the crosstalk found at the distance L_c for the focused array. With the assumption of small angles it can be readily shown that the critical distance for the focused array case with $D = \Delta$ (fill factor = unity) is approximately given by:

$$L_c \approx \frac{D^2}{2\lambda}. \tag{3}$$

From elementary diffraction theory, we know that the image of a point input created by an ideal lens of finite aperture is not a point but rather a diffraction pattern consisting of a bright central lobe surrounded by oscillating bands or rings of light with rapidly diminishing intensity. Typically about 84% of the energy in such a diffraction pattern lies within the central lobe (Smith 1966). For a fixed microlens

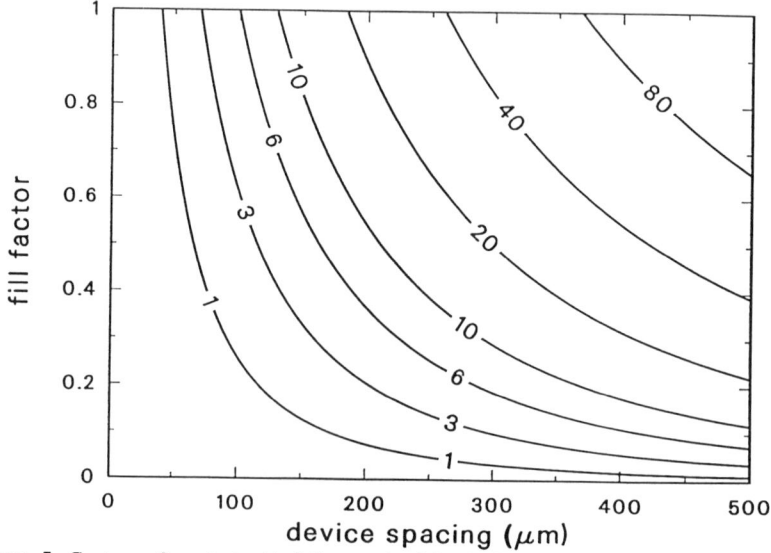

Figure 5. Contours of constant critical distance (mm) for the focused microlens array as a function of fill factor D/Δ and device spacing Δ, with $\lambda = 0.85$ μm.

diameter D, the width w of this diffraction-limited central lobe increases as the image distance l' increases (i.e., as the NA decreases). It can also be shown (again assuming small angles) that as l' approaches L_c, the width w of the central lobe of this focused spot diffraction pattern becomes approximately equal to the diameter D of the microlens. Thus considering the case where $D = \Delta$ and $l' = L_c$, this central lobe fills the channel width Δ, and the remaining light that is contained in the surrounding diffraction rings is distributed over neighboring channels as crosstalk.

1.4 Summary

Optical interconnection using free-space propagation is a broad topic that contains a plethora of approaches and configurations. Each of these is characterized by its set of trade-offs in complexity, fabrication, device number and density, crosstalk, etc., with diffraction often occupying a central role in these considerations. In Section 1 simple geometrical models were considered as a vehicle with which to illustrate the role of diffraction as a basic consideration in this topic. In one extreme, a single imaging system may be used to image a large array of devices, and trade-offs between lens complexity and the size of the array are immediately encountered. At the other extreme, arrays of microlenses may be used to image individual devices, where trade-offs in limiting diffraction-based crosstalk are conspicuous. There is much area in between these extremes and, of course, many trade-offs are found in any specific optical system. For example, the macro-optics approach lends itself to systems in which all the inputs are treated similarly. This property is central to systems described as *space invariant,* as opposed to systems where neighboring inputs may be treated very differently (*space-variant* systems). The micro-optics extreme, with its separate lenses for each input device, can readily be applied to the latter system types. An excellent discussion of these concepts is found in Goodman (1968, 1981).

2. Interconnects

2.1 Introduction

Interconnects, whether optical or electronic, are conduits for data transmission between processors. They are used in a wide variety of applications and consequently come in many different types. Interconnects provide connections between computers, between circuit boards in a computer, between chips on a circuit board, or even between gates on a chip. These networks can be implemented optically by splitting an input image in two, suitably fragmenting, magnifying, and rearranging these, and then recombining them. Classic optical interferometers provide convenient hardware configurations for many of these operations, and are therefore the basis of many optical interconnect approaches. Of the many basic types of interferometers suitable for these applications (Hariharan 1985) only configurations based on the Michelson interferometer are presented here.

The interconnects presented can be used as the communication component of a fine-grain parallel computer or as the fundamental building block of a permutation network. These uses employ a multistage approach in which interconnections and processor stages are interleaved. Such networks are known by the acronym MIN (multistage interconnection network). The interconnection stages in a MIN are typically fixed at the time of design (see Section 3.3 for a deviation from this approach) with each stage specified independently. In general, MINs can handle any number of inputs; however, they are most effective when the number of inputs is a power of 2 (i.e., $n = 2^i$). Figure 6 shows a 16-input MIN with four processor stages of eight processors each and three interconnection stages that each employ a different interconnection pattern.

2.1.1 Permutation Networks

A permutation network accepts a vector of inputs and produces an output that is a permutation of those inputs. Such networks can be constructed using 2 × 2 crossbar switches as the processor stages. [For example, the 32 processors in Fig. 6 would each be a 2 × 2 crossbar. An $n \times k$ crossbar has n inputs and k outputs

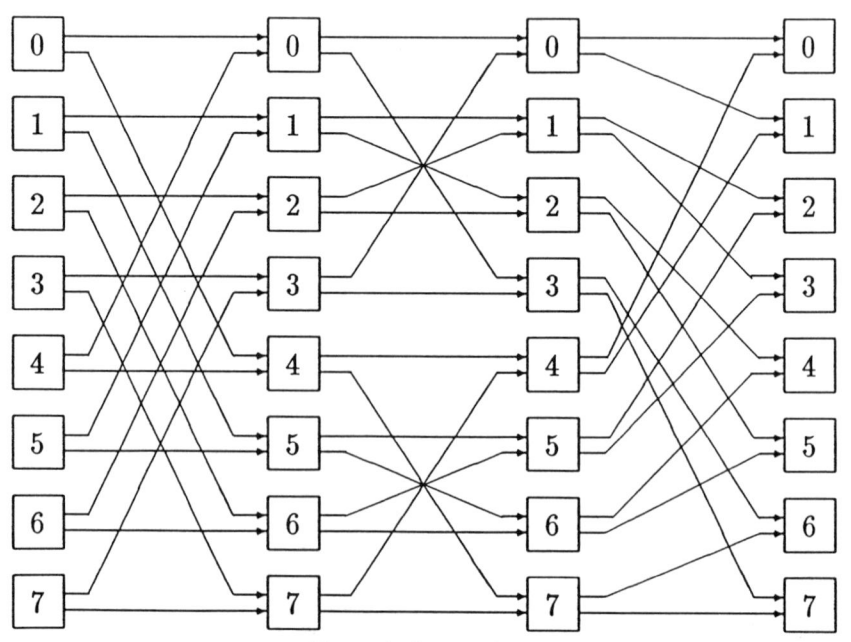

Figure 6. A sample MIN.

and is capable of routing each of the n inputs to any (or all) of the k outputs thus providing n^k unique routes.] The permutation produced is determined by the setting of these crossbars and is independent of the data being permuted. The effectiveness of a permutation network is determined by its cost and communication latency. The ideal network would have minimum cost and minimum latency; however, since cost is inversely related to latency, the ideal is unattainable and acceptable nonoptimal alternatives must be considered.

One of these alternatives, an $n \times n$ crossbar, is a minimum latency network that does not use a MIN. This network not only performs all permutations but supports all n^n possible interconnections including broadcast interconnections that route a single input to more than one output. It has n^2 connection points and, since any path from input to output passes through exactly one processor, a network diameter (i.e., the length of the longest communication path between any two processors) of 1. Since every communication path is of length 1, the network latency is minimal; however, the cost, as measured by the number of connection points, is prohibitive even for modest values of n.

Permutation networks based on MINs typically have $O[n\lg(n)]$ connection points [the notation $\lg(n)$ is used to denote $\log_2 n$] and achieve a network diameter of $O[\lg(n)]$. As such, MINs are significantly less expensive than crossbars but have larger latencies. MINs provide less capability than crossbars supporting all $n!$ interconnections corresponding to permutations but only some, and not all, of the broadcast connections.

Crossbars are clearly superior to MINs when latency and capability are considered; however, as noted previously, their cost is prohibitive for even modest values of n. Consequently, most permutation networks have been implemented as MINs.

2.1.2 Point-to-Point Interconnection Network

MINs can also be used in fine-grain massively parallel applications. In these applications, the processors are not 2×2 crossbars but rather small processing elements (PEs) such as used in the POEM approach (Kiamilev *et al* 1989), or at the extreme two input gates with a fan-out of 2. In the example of Fig. 6, each box would be a processor that computes a binary function of its inputs, which is then routed to the two connected processors on its right.

The interconnection capability for networks used in this manner is determined by the application of the machine. If the machine is application specific, the MIN would be customized to provide only the connections required of that application. Conversely, if the machine is used for many applications, it would need to support every connection required of any applications. Thus as the applications become more general the need to support all possible connections increases.

MINs that provide such a general connection capability are termed *point-to-point networks*. Such networks are specified by the input/output pairs that require a connection path and the type of interconnections used. When every input/output pair requires a connection path, the network is termed a *complete point-to-point network*. For general applications that require most, if not all, interconnections a complete network is desirable. A complete point-to-point network has a cost of $O[n\lg(n)]$, as measured by the number of processors, and achieves a network diameter of $O[\lg(n)]$; however, the cost and diameter of these networks is about 50% less than a permutation network with the same number of inputs.

2.2 Perfect Shuffle MINs

The perfect shuffle interconnect gets its name from a technique for shuffling cards in which the deck is cut into two parts, which are then interleaved with one another. If the cut divides the deck into equal parts and the interleaving combines the cards in an alternating fashion the result is a *perfect* shuffle. For a more detailed discussion of perfect shuffle interconnects refer to Akl (1985), Stone (1987, 1971), and Wu and Feng (1981).

When a sequence of perfect shuffles are placed one after the other, a MIN with identical interconnects is formed. If $\lg(n/2)$ perfect shuffle interconnects are interleaved with $\lg(n)$ processor stages, a complete point-to-point network, called a *complete perfect shuffle MIN* (C-psMIN), is obtained. This C-psMIN has a processor cost (i.e., the number of processors contained in the MIN) of $(n/2)\lg(n)$ and diameter $\lg(n)$. Figure 7 shows a C-psMIN with $n = 16$.

A similar approach can be used to build a permutation network based on the perfect shuffle interconnect and is called a *permuting perfect shuffle MIN* (P-psMIN). P-psMINs are composed of two or more C-psMINs and as such have higher costs and diameters. One such network is formed by overlapping the output crossbar stage of a C-psMIN with the input crossbar stage of a complete reverse perfect shuffle MIN (ie., a network obtained by exchanging inputs and outputs and reversing the flow of the data; pictorially it is obtained by horizontally flipping the network and reversing the interconnection arrows). This network is symmetric about its central crossbar stage and has connection-point costs (see following paragraph) $2n[2\lg(n) - 1]$ and diameter $2\lg(n) - 1$. It employs two interconnection patterns, the perfect shuffle and reverse perfect shuffle interconnection.

The connection-point cost of a permutation network is defined as the number of connection points within the network. This measure is used to allow direct comparison with other crossbar networks. For other comparisons, a different measure, such as the number of processors, might be preferred. In this section each processor in a permutation network is a 2×2 crossbar that contributes four connection points. Consequently, the connection-point cost is a factor of 4 larger than the *equivalent* processor cost.

An equivalent network can be built by connecting the output of a C-psMIN to the input of a C-psMIN through a single bit-reversal interconnection (Parker 1980). This network requires one special bit-reversal interconnect tailored to the

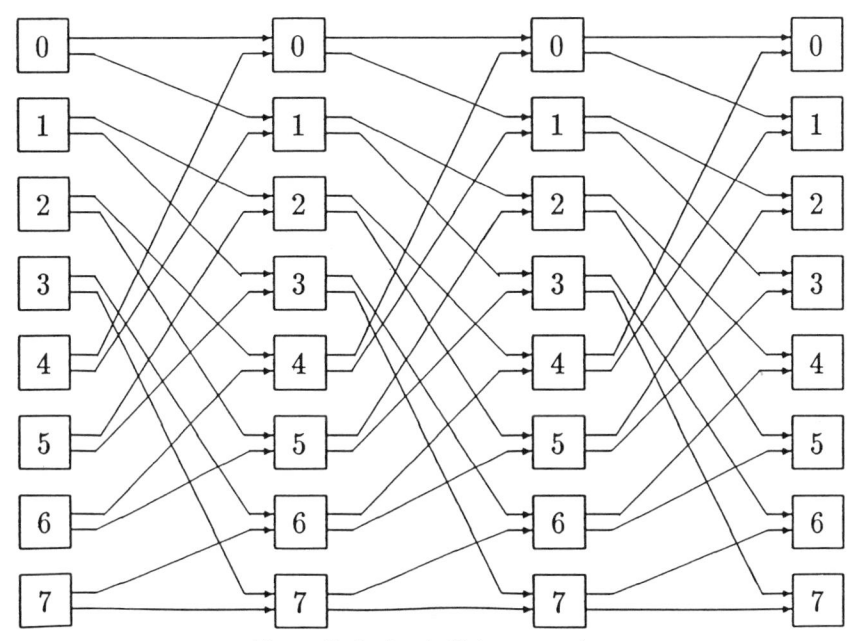

Figure 7. Perfect shuffle interconnection.

number of inputs, but does not require the reverse shuffle interconnections. It has a slightly larger cost [$4n\lg(n)$] and diameter [$2\lg(n)$] than the P-psMIN described previously.

A true P-psMIN (i.e., one that uses only perfect shuffle interconnects) can be formed using a sequence of $3\lg(n) - 3$ perfect shuffle interconnects (Huang 1986). Although this network requires only the prefect shuffle interconnect, its cost and diameter are roughly 50% larger than either of the P-psMINs described earlier.

2.2.1 Optical Implementation

Figure 8 shows a Michelson arrangement that provides the perfect shuffle interconnection. The input passes $P1$ and enters the beamsplitter where the image is split with one image sent upward and the other to the left. These images are reflected by mirrors $P3$ and $P2$, respectively. The mirrors are oriented at an angle to the beamsplitter causing the reflected images to be offset from the incoming image. The offsets are chosen so that combining the reflected images produces, in the central portion of the image, the perfect shuffle pattern. This central portion of the combined image is then magnified and transmitted to the output. Figure 9 shows the optical images as they would appear at various points in the Michelson

206 D.E. Smith, M.J. Murdocca, and T.W. Stone

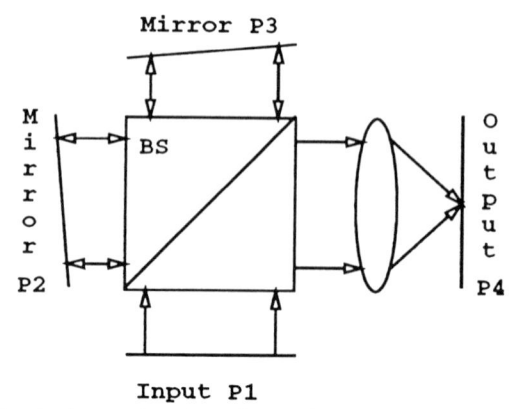

Figure 8. Michelson implementation of a perfect shuffle (adapted from Brenner and Huang 1988).

arrangement for an eight-input perfect shuffle interconnect. A more detailed description of this and alternative implementations can be found in Brenner and Huang (1988).

2.3 Banyan MINs

The banyan interconnect can also be adapted to produce a MIN for either a complete point-to-point banyan MIN (C-bynMIN) or a permuting MIN based on the banyan interconnect (P-bynMIN). In contrast to the perfect shuffle, the banyan interconnects differ from stage to stage; however, the connection graph for the C-bynMIN is isomorphic to the C-psMIN presented in Section 2.2. When $\lg(n/2)$ banyan interconnects are interleaved with $\lg(n)$ processor stages, a C-bynMIN is produced.

Figure 10 shows a 16-input banyan network with three interconnection stages interleaved with four processor stages. Although each interconnection stage differs from the rest, within a stage the interconnection is composed of several smaller identical patterns. The leftmost interconnection stage is a single 16-input pattern, the center is two 8-input patterns, and the rightmost is four 4-input patterns. For a more detailed discussion of banyan interconnects refer to Goke and Lipovski (1973).

A P-bynMIN can be formed by overlapping the output crossbar stage of a C-bynMIN network with the input crossbar stage of a complete point-to-point re-

Input Image:					0	1		2		3		4		5		6		7
Left Offset Image (P2):	0		1		2		3		4		5		6		7			
Right Offset Image (P3):							0		1		2		3		4		5	6	7
Full Combined Image:	0		1		2		3	0	4	1	5	2	6	3	7	4		5	6	7
Center Combined Image:								0	4	1	5	2	6	3	7			
Magnified Center Image:							0		4		1		5		2		6	3	7

Figure 9. Images passing through the perfect shuffle apparatus.

[Figure: Banyan interconnection diagram with 8 nodes (0-7) across 4 stages]

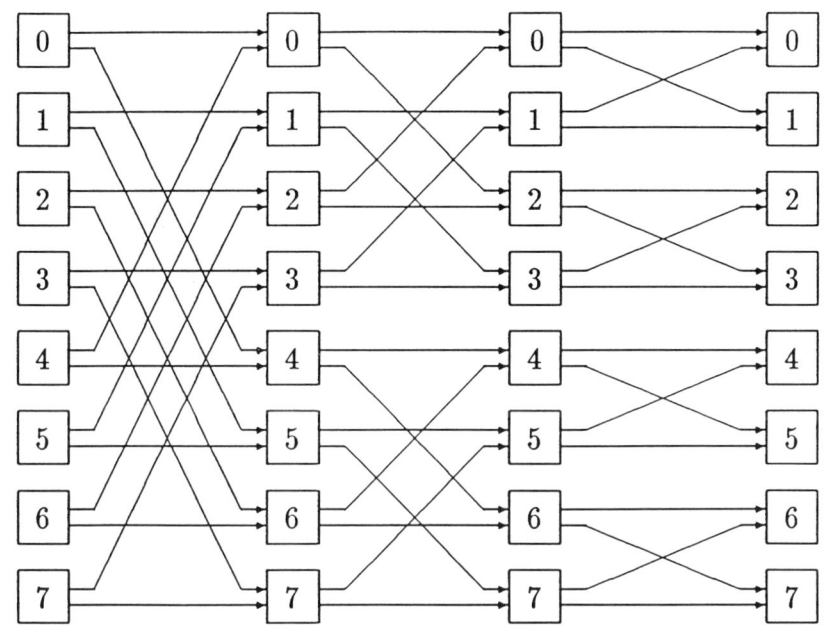

Figure 10. Banyan interconnection.

verse banyan MIN. This network is symmetric about its central crossbar stage and has a connection-point cost of $2n[2\lg(n) - 1]$ and diameter $2\lg(n) - 1$. Because of the similarity between the banyan and reverse banyan, the P-bynMIN network uses exactly the same interconnection patterns, but twice as many of them, as the C-byn MIN.

2.3.1 Optical Implementation

Figure 11 shows a Michelson arrangement employing polarization techniques to provide the banyan interconnection. The polarized input image passes $P1$ and enters the polarizing beamsplitter $BS1$ where it is split based on its polarization. The p polarized light is transmitted downward to plane $P2$ while the s polarized light is reflected to plane $P4$. These two paths are processed independently and implement the straight and crossed connections of the banyan interconnect, respectively.

The apparatus that implements the straight connection accepts the p polarized light arriving at $P2$. This light passes through a quarter-waveplate, is reflected back from mirror $P3$, and again passes the quarter-waveplate. After passing through the quarter-waveplate twice, the plane of polarization is rotated 90 deg and the light returned to $BS1$ is s polarized. This light enters $BS1$ and due to its s polarization is reflected left to output plane $P7$.

The apparatus that implements crossed connections accepts the s polarized light

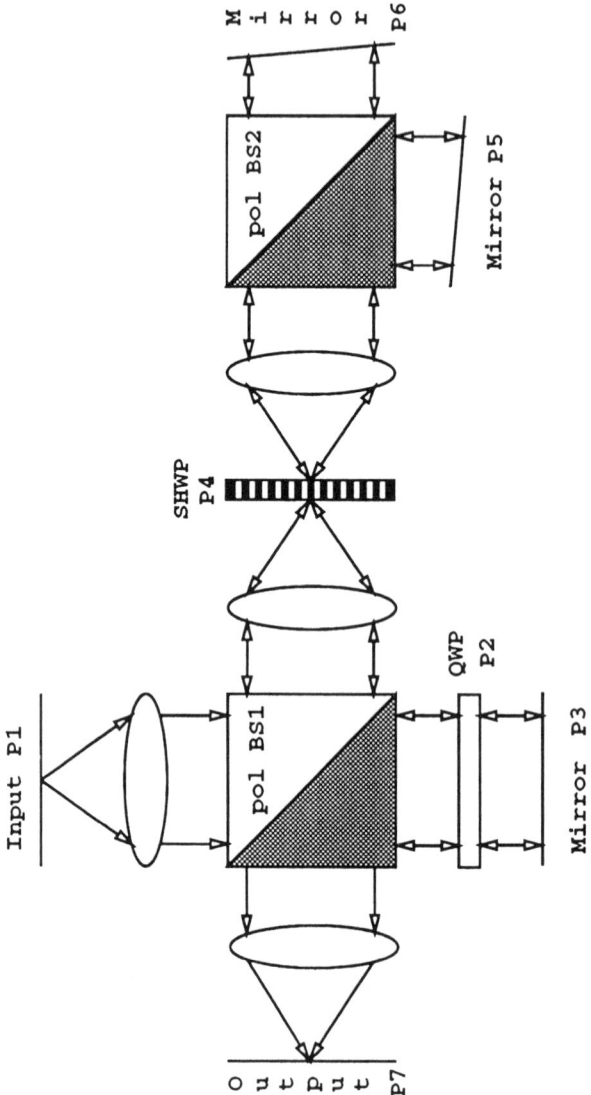

Figure 11. Michelson implementation of a banyan network (adapted from Jahns 1990).

arriving at *P*4. Conceptually, this image is composed of two classes, which must undergo different offsets, one corresponding to the downward offset shown in Fig. 10 and the other to the upward offset. To split these two classes, the individually addressable half-waveplate at *P*4 is designed to change the *s* polarization of all images belonging to one of these classes to *p* polarization while leaving images in the other class with *s* polarization. These polarized images enter the polarizing beamsplitter *BS*2, where they are split sending the *s* polarized light down and the *p* polarized light to the right.

Mirrors *P*5 and *P*6 reflect the *s* and *p* polarized images back to *BS*2. The reflected images are offset from the incoming images based on the orientation of mirrors *P*5 and *P*6. Since *P*5 and *P*6 do not change the polarization, the images are combined at *BS*2 and returned to the addressable half-waveplate *P*4. The images once again undergo selective polarization rotation based on the design of *P*4 and are all returned to *BS*1 with *p* polarization. These images will be transmitted straight through *BS*1 and arrive at the output with *p* polarization. Not all interconnects can be implemented using this approach; however, the buddy property of the banyan interconnect guarantees that any image entering *P*4 from *BS*1 will have its polarization changed exactly once before returning to *BS*1. A more detailed description of this implementation as well as alternatives can be found in Jahns (1990).

2.3.2 Split and Shift

The AT&T optical processor (Prise *et al.* 1991) is based on a split and shift interconnect that is a restricted form of the banyan. While the banyan interconnect shown in Fig. 10 routes one-half of its paths straight through, one-quarter of its paths down at a fixed angle, and one-fourth of its paths up at the same angle, an analogous split and shift would route one-half of its paths up and the other one-half of its paths down. One possible optical implementation of the split and shift can be realized by a subcomponent of the banyan apparatus consisting of beamsplitter *BS*2 and mirrors *P*5 and *P*6 of Fig. 11.

2.4 Crossover

The crossover interconnect is topologically equivalent to the banyan and can also be adapted to produce either a complete point-to-point MIN (C-coMIN) or a permuting MIN (P-coMIN). As with the banyan, the crossover interconnects differ from stage to stage.

Figure 12 shows a 16-input half-crossover network with three interconnection stages interleaved with four processor stages. As with the banyan, each interconnection stage differs from the rest; however, within a stage the interconnection is composed of several smaller identical crossovers. The leftmost interconnection

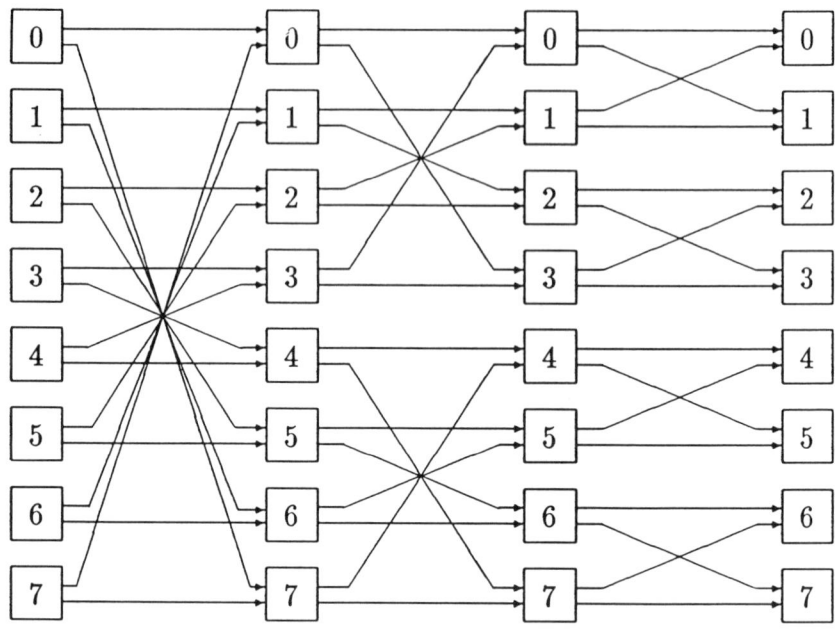

Figure 12. Half-crossover interconnection.

stage is a single 16-input half-crossover, the center is two 8-input half-crossovers, and the rightmost is four 4-input crossovers. Notice that the half-crossover can be formed from the banyan by reversing the last $n/2$ processors of the banyan while keeping the connections attached. For a more detailed discussion refer to Jahns and Murdocca (1988).

When $\lg(n/2)$ crossover stages are interleaved with $\lg(n)$ processor stages, a C-coMIN is produced. This network is topologically equivalent to the perfect shuffle and banyan network presented in Sections 2.2 and 2.3.

A P-coMIN can also be constructed. This network is identical to the banyan network except for the replacement of the banyan interconnect by the crossover interconnect. Its costs and diameter are $2n[2\lg(n) - 1]$ and $2\lg(n) - 1$, respectively.

2.4.1 Optical Implementation

Figure 13 shows a Michelson implementation of a crossover interconnect. The input image passes $P1$ and enters the beamsplitter BS where it is split and transmitted along two paths. The straight-through connections shown in Fig. 12 are implemented in the rightmost portion of the apparatus. The light following this

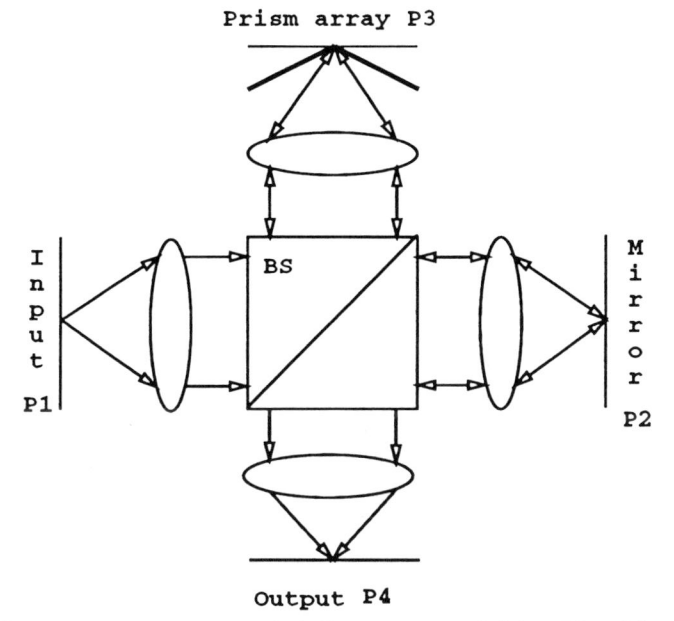

Figure 13. Michelson implementation of a half-crossover network (adapted from Jahns and Murdocca 1988).

path is transmitted to mirror $P2$ where it is reflected back into the beamsplitter, finally arriving at output plane $P4$.

The crossover connections are implemented by the upper portion of the apparatus. This path routes the images upward toward the prism in plane $P3$ where they are crossed and reflected back. The crossing is accomplished by a partitioned reflecting 90-deg prism containing 2^s partitions, where s is the stage number of the crossover MIN. Figure 14 shows an example of the crossover prism used in the second (i.e., $s = 1$) stage of an 8-input MIN. A more detailed description of this implementation as well as alternatives can be found in Jahns and Murdocca (1988).

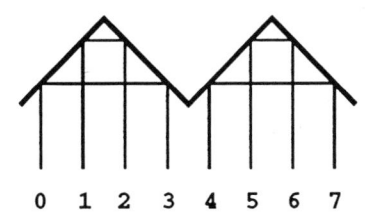

Figure 14. Second stage partitioned reflecting prism (adapted from Jahns and Murdocca, 1988).

2.5 Irregular Interconnects

Regular interconnects are sometimes preferred to irregular interconnects in order to simplify the optical setups. For example, regular interconnects are typically produced by space-invariant methods, which may support greater propagation distances as discussed in Section 1.1. However, from an architectural perspective, a regular interconnect poses limitations on connection complexity since it is just a special case of the more general class of irregular interconnects. Irregular interconnects are preferred when they can be supported by the optics, and one such method is discussed here.

With irregular (or arbitrary space-variant) interconnects, light from elements in an input array may be coupled to elements in an output array according to any desired scheme and without regard for where light from neighboring elements is directed. This type of interconnect may be achieved optically, for example, by means of multiplexed holographic elements (e.g., Goodman *et al.* 1984; Kostuk, Goodman, and Hesselink 1987; Feldman and Guest 1989; Lee, Gu, and Psaltis 1989) or micro-optics (e.g., Jahns and Däschner 1990; Schwider *et al.* 1990; Robertson *et al.* 1991; Kawai 1991). As discussed in Section 1.1 the micro-optics approach involves many trade-offs in balancing diffraction effects and crosstalk. These and other trade-offs including efficiency and manufacturability are strongly related to the nature of the particular elements used. For example, the lenses may be fabricated by means of contoured refractive surfaces and/or gradient-index materials (e.g., Sugiyama *et al.* 1986; Popovic, Sprague, and Neville Connell 1988; Liau *et al.* 1989; Oikawa *et al.* 1990); surface relief diffractive structures (e.g., Miyamoto 1961; Jordan *et al.* 1970; Fujita, Nishihara, and Koyama 1981; Shiono *et al.* 1987; Buralli, Morris, and Rogers 1989; Swanson and Veldkamp 1989; Jahns and Walker 1990; Hosokawa and Yamashita 1990); or volume diffractive elements (e.g. Kostuk, Goodman, and Hesselink 1985, 1987; Ambs *et al.* 1988; Ford, Lee, and Fainman 1990; Haumann *et al.* 1990; Robertson *et al.* 1991).

One method of achieving an arbitrary interconnection scheme is through the use of spatially variant holographic optical elements (HOEs) in dichromated gelatin (Haumann *et al.* 1990; Robertson *et al.* 1991). The basic idea is to use a matched pair of space-variant HOEs, in which each pair consists of two arrays of individual holographic elements. The subholograms in each array redirect individual light beams, so that each beam has a separate imaging system.

Figure 15 shows a schematic of an HOE-based interconnect. For this example, the space-variant interconnect implements an irregular interconnection pattern, although regular interconnection patterns can be implemented equally well. The input beams are permuted according to the reconstruction angles of the lenses in $H1$. The use of a second hologram $H2$ allows for all of the beams to emerge along parallel axes.

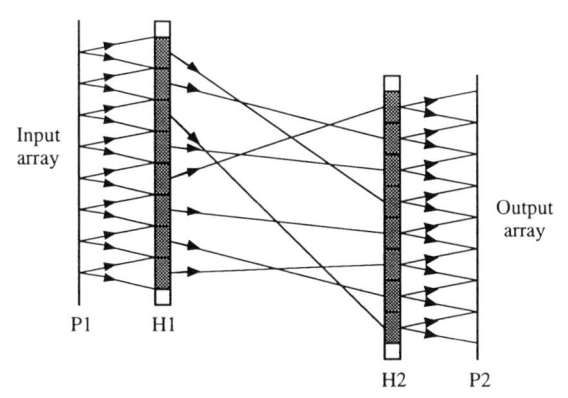

Figure 15. Schematic showing a holographic implementation of an arbitrary interconnect, where $P1$ is the input array, $P2$ is the output array, and $H1$ and $H2$ are interconnection HOEs (adapted from Robertson *et al.* 1991).

3. Architectural Considerations

Optical interconnects have been proposed and demonstrated for various levels in the computer hierarchy. System-to-system interconnects using fibers are currently in use over great distances in long-distance telecommunication networks. Free-space propagation of light through the atmosphere has also been considered for shorter distances, of the order of a few kilometers, as a backup for microwave repeaters in telecommunication applications. One problem with this scheme is that atmospheric conditions such as rain and fog, and even flocks of geese, can block the backup link.

System-to-system fiber interconnects within a campus or building are in common use, and offer the advantages of low weight and high-bandwidth communication when compared with conductors such as copper. At these distances, communication is typically handled with fibers, although free-space infrared (IR) links are also used in office environments. An advantage of IR links over the fiber links is that devices connected to a network can be moved without disturbing network cables.

Board-to-board interconnects over just a few tens of centimeters are used in AT&T's 5ESS private branch exchange (PBX) switch. Fibers carry information between boards and account for a small fraction of the volume of the switch, although optoelectronic conversion circuitry and drive circuitry for the fibers fill approximately one-third of each board. There is some controversy over whether board-to-board interconnects with fibers at this small scale are cost effective. Currently, it appears that the use of fibers for board-to-board interconnects may be near the break-even point for cost versus performance, although this may not necessarily be true for free-space interconnects, which are discussed later.

A significant cost of creating conventional electronic computers results from the complexity of the wiring topology. At one extreme, two integrated circuits (ICs) may need to cross as many as 100 or more connections on a circuit board, which results in 100 × 100 = 10,000 vias (vertical connections between two levels of a board). This forces a greater separation between ICs than if some other interconnection scheme is used. An example of a free-space optical approach that connects one board to another has been proposed by Dickinson and Prise (1990) in which each chip with outgoing lines is electrically connected to modulator chips, which mate with detector chips on the same board or on another board, so that communication between ICs is handled optically. This allows for greater density on boards, although arbitrary interconnection patterns can be difficult to accommodate optically due to short focal lengths as discussed in Section 1. This property is typical when introducing optics into successively lower levels in the computer hierarchy with linear imaging systems: The more primitive the level, the more regular the optical interconnects. Note that, in general, metal interconnects scale in the opposite manner: irregular at the low level, and regular at the high level. This property does not necessarily apply when short focal lengths can be accommodated, for example, as in the POEMs (Kiamilev *et al.* 1989) chip-to-chip approach for interconnecting fine-grain processing elements (PEs), which is discussed later, or in the planar optics approach of Jahns and Huang (1989), which is intended to make electronics and optics more compatible.

For rise times of the order of 2.5 ns or less, an argument can be made that speed and power payoffs for optical interconnections occur when distances are longer than a few millimeters. However, optical interconnects have been applied at the logic gate level, and systems have been demonstrated for fibers (Benner *et al.* 1991) and for free-space optics (Prise *et al.* 1991; Cloonan *et al.* 1991). The actual distance depends on the technology under consideration (3-μm CMOS, for the example cited here) but is typically on a large enough scale (several millimeters) to preclude the use of optical interconnects at the gate level unless switching speeds are pushed beyond 5 GHz. A few advantages of using free-space optics at the gate level, even at suboptimal switching speeds, are simplicity in system fabrication, and gate-level reconfiguration, which is discussed later.

3.1 Low-Level Optical Interconnection

A model of a digital optical computer that has been demonstrated at AT&T (Prise *et al.* 1991) uses gate-level optical interconnection as shown in Fig. 16. The model consists of alternating arrays of optical logic gates and free-space regular interconnects. Masks in the image planes block light at selected locations so that the interconnects are customized to perform specific logic functions such as addition or sorting. The system is fed back onto itself, and an input channel and an output

Parallel Optical Interconnections 215

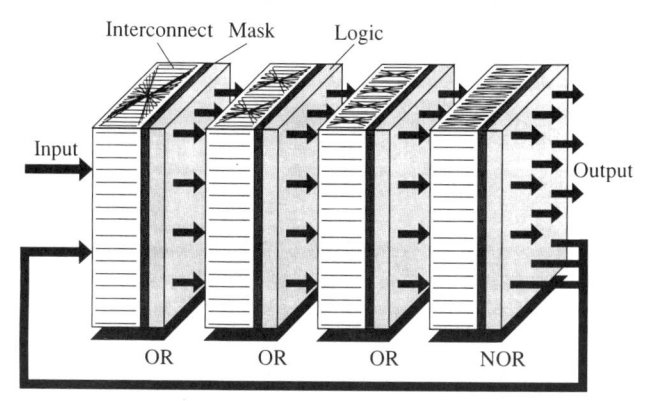

Figure 16. Arrays of optical logic gates are interconnected with optical crossovers (Jahns and Murdocca 1988). Masks in the image planes block light at selected locations customizing the system for specific functions.

channel are provided. Feedback is imaged with a single-row vertical shift so that data spiral through the system, allowing different sections of the masks to be used on each pass. Optical signals travel orthogonally to the device substrates.

Unlike conventional digital design for electronic circuits in which the placement of wires is abstracted away during the design phase, the object of digital design for the model shown in Fig. 16 is to map arbitrarily complex digital circuits onto the regular structure. The positions of the logic gates are fixed, all gates have fan-in and fan-out of two, all devices on the same array perform the same function such as OR or NOR, and the interconnects between arrays have a regular structure such as in those discussed in Section 2. The only choices available to the circuit designer are the positions of the inputs, the positions of the outputs, and the configurations of the masks that block unwanted connections. The general approach to digital design that supports this model is to first generate all minterms, and then to select and combine the minterms that are needed to implement specific functions (Murdocca 1990). A dual-rail logic system is adopted since the strict regularity does not support a relative inversion, because every signal travels through the same number of logic gates of the same type. Various optical schemes can eliminate the need for this added cost, such as exchanging pairs of output beams for complementary optical logic devices.

An example of a dual-rail 3-to-8 decoder is shown in Fig. 17. The three input variables x, y, and s appear at the top as well as their complements. Eight outputs are produced at the bottom. Heavily shaded connections indicate where light is allowed to pass, and lightly shaded connections are disabled by configuring fixed masks in the output planes of the crossover interconnects.

The circuit is implemented in one pass through the model shown in Fig. 16.

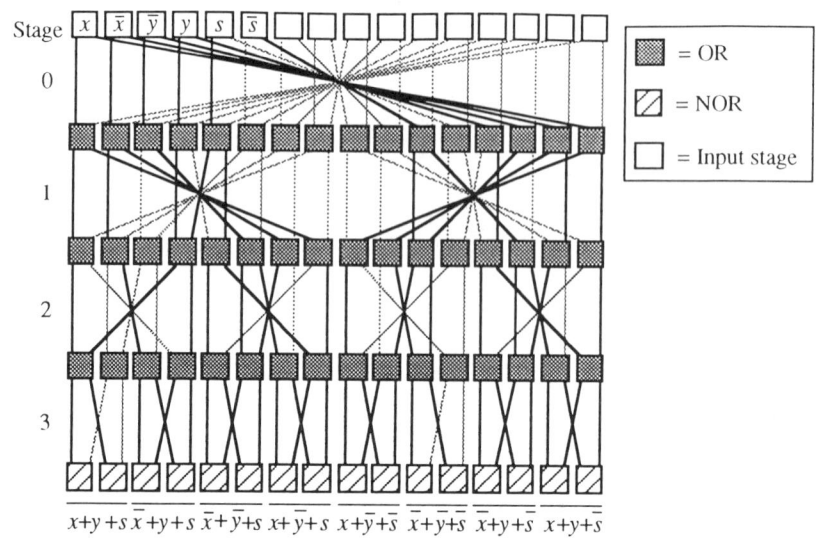

[Figure: A dual-rail 3-to-8 decoder diagram with stages labeled 0, 1, 2, 3 and outputs $x+y+s$, $\overline{x}+y+s$, $x+\overline{y}+s$, $\overline{x}+\overline{y}+s$, $x+y+\overline{s}$, $\overline{x}+y+\overline{s}$, $x+\overline{y}+\overline{s}$, $\overline{x}+\overline{y}+\overline{s}$. Inputs at top: x, $\overline{x}$, $\overline{y}$, y, s, $\overline{s}$. Legend: filled = OR, hatched = NOR, empty = Input stage.]

Figure 17. A dual-rail 3-to-8 decoder is implemented with crossover interconnects in an OR-NOR network. Lightly shaded connections are blocked by fixed masks in the output planes of the crossover interconnects. Total gate count is $16 \times 4 = 64$. The bottom stage is not included in the count since it is the top stage of the succeeding circuit.

Circuit breadth and depth are relatively small when compared with more complex interconnection schemes using a fan-in/fan-out of two as argued by Murdocca (1990), so that although gate count is somewhat high, it is not so high that it offsets the practical gains in simplifying the optical interconnects. For some situations, however, the gate count can be very high when compared with an alternative approach as described next.

3.2 Improvement to Low-Level Interconnection

A small amount of flexibility in the optical system can have a significant effect on the size and performance of the target optical processor. Consider again the 3-to-8 decoder circuit shown in Fig. 17, which is 16 logic gates wide and four levels deep (the bottom row is not counted since it is the top row of the succeeding circuit), making a total of $16 \times 4 = 64$ logic gates. If fan-in and fan-out are increased from two to four, and irregularity is allowed in the interconnects, then the same function can be achieved in an $8 \times 1 = 8$ gate circuit as shown in Fig. 18. A savings of a factor of 8 in gate count is achieved, and latency (circuit depth) is reduced from four to one. Thus an irregular interconnection scheme and a fan-in/fan-out of greater than two offer significant improvements to circuit breadth and depth. This observation is made without considering the increased

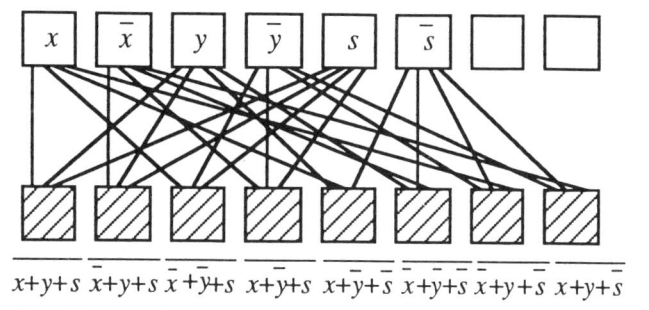

$$x+y+s \quad \overline{x+y+s} \quad \overline{x}+\overline{y}+s \quad x+\overline{y}+s \quad x+\overline{y}+\overline{s} \quad \overline{x}+\overline{y}+\overline{s} \quad x+y+\overline{s} \quad \overline{x}+y+\overline{s}$$

Figure 18. The AND stage of a three-variable programmable logic array (PLA). Total gate count is $8 \times 1 = 8$. The bottom stage is not included in the count since it is the top stage of the succeeding circuit.

complexity of the underlying optics, and it is this additional complexity that has traditionally driven gate-level interconnection to conform to regular topologies such as in the AT&T systems (Prise *et al.* 1990; McCormick *et al.* 1990).

3.3 Architectural Implications of Reconfigurable Interconnects

Some portion of a digital circuit is nearly always underutilized because only one of a number of available functions is used at a time. If some information is known in advance about a computation regarding the complexity of logic that is needed, then greater efficiency can be realized through a mechanism that reconfigures the circuit during operation. Consider the simple four-function arithmetic unit shown in Fig. 19. Only one of the four available units for addition, subtraction, multiplication, and division will be used at any one time, but the physical hardware must be continuously present when a static interconnection network is used. A reconfigurable approach may exploit this property by eliminating the decoder circuitry and the hardware for the unused three functions (indicated by the highlighted region). The elimination of underutilized logic reduces the depth and width of the circuit, which results in a faster, more compact circuit.

The programmable optoelectronic multiprocessor (POEM) model (Kiamilev *et al.* 1989) is based on wafer-scale integration of optoelectronic PEs and reconfigurable free-space optical interconnects as illustrated in Fig. 20. Electrical interconnects are used for local interconnection within PEs, and HOEs are used for interconnection among PEs. The POEMs approach is potentially more energy efficient, faster, and denser than its all-electronic and all-optical counterparts because it balances electronics and optics for inter-connection at the break-even point, which is argued to be typically in the range of a few millimeters for current very large scale integration (VLSI) technology. An analysis by Miller (1989) arrives at a similar result—that all but the shortest connections within chips should

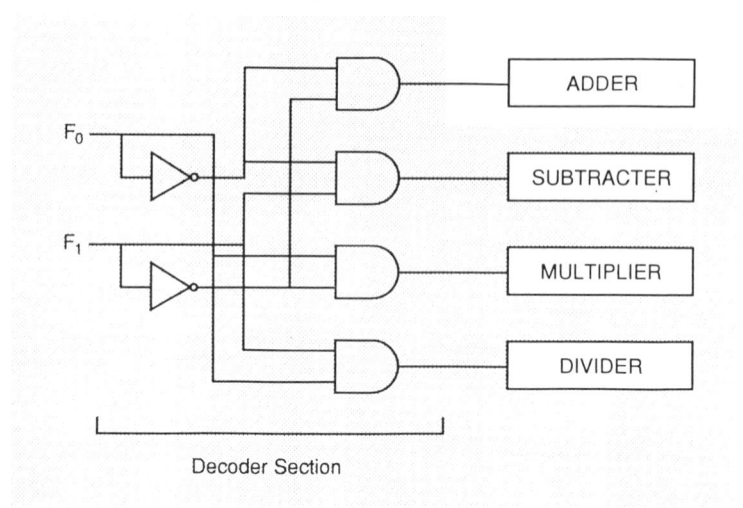

Figure 19. Block diagram of a four-function arithmetic unit. The decoder translates a logical encoding ($F0$) and $F1$) into a spatial location. That is, for each binary pattern applied at $F0$, $F1$, exactly one arithmetic unit is enabled. The shaded region indicates the underutilized portion of the circuit when the adder is being used.

be handled optically. An advantage of using reconfigurable interconnects among PEs is that the effective diameter of an interconnection network can be reduced when compared with a multistage interconnection network.

In one configuration that makes use of reconfigurable interconnects, a fixed number of control sequences are stored externally, such as in a photorefractive material (Ford, Lee, and Fainman 1990) or with reprogrammable masks, and are

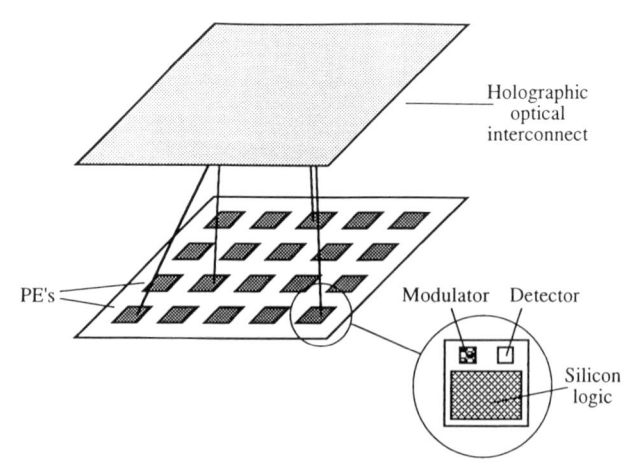

Figure 20. Model of the UCSD POEM approach. Arrays of electronic PEs are interconnected holographically (Kiamilev *et al.* 1989).

imaged into the system on demand. The order of execution is not determined until the time of execution, since the ordering depends on data and intermediate results.

A potential opportunity for reconfigurable interconnects is the application of Gaussian elimination to the solution of linear equations. The process is data-independent if the problem of pivoting, which involves rearranging rows so that the top left element of the coefficient matrix is relatively large, is ignored. However, in the real world, zeros or very small numbers do in fact appear in the position of the top left element, so that the pivoting problem must be addressed.

A reconfigurable interconnection technology can offer a solution by simply reconfiguring the decoder section of the memory that stores the rows of the matrix. For example, consider the augmented coefficient matrix shown in Fig. 21 for three linear equations in three unknowns. The indices in the upper left corners of the 12 cells indicate the addresses of the memory locations that store the corresponding coefficients.

Figure 22 shows two decoder circuits for the memory that map 4-bit addresses into spatial locations. The circuit on the left is a conventional decoder that maps addresses into locations according to the matrix layout shown in Fig. 21. This circuit might be implemented optically using the form for a 3-to-8 decoder shown in Fig. 17. The circuit on the right shows the configuration of a decoder that swaps the top and bottom rows of the matrix by changing the crosspoint settings through some reconfigurable interconnection approach. Notice that the actual data have not moved. Only one-sixth of the crosspoints are changed between the two forms, even though three-quarters of the elements are interchanged. Further, for a modest word size of 32 bits, the total number of bits that are effectively interchanged is $0.75 \times 12 \times 32 = 288$ bits, even though only 16 crosspoints are changed in the decoder. An important property of this approach is that the modified decoder is simply projected into the system without regard for the actual data being interchanged, so that explicit data paths between all possible pairs of rows that might be interchanged do not need to be provided. This effect is more greatly pronounced for complex interchange operations such as a transpose, in which every element is affected. A single pattern that is imaged into the decoder in a single step is all that is required to implement the transpose.

$$a_{00} x_0 + a_{01} x_1 + a_{02} x_2 = b_0$$
$$a_{10} x_0 + a_{11} x_1 + a_{12} x_2 = b_1$$
$$a_{20} x_0 + a_{21} x_1 + a_{22} x_2 = b_2$$

0 a_{00}	1 a_{01}	2 a_{02}	3 b_0
4 a_{10}	5 a_{11}	6 a_{12}	7 b_1
8 a_{20}	9 a_{21}	10 a_{22}	11 b_2

Figure 21. An augmented matrix is shown for a system of linear equations in three unknowns. Indices in the upper left corners of cells indicate the storage locations in a random access memory.

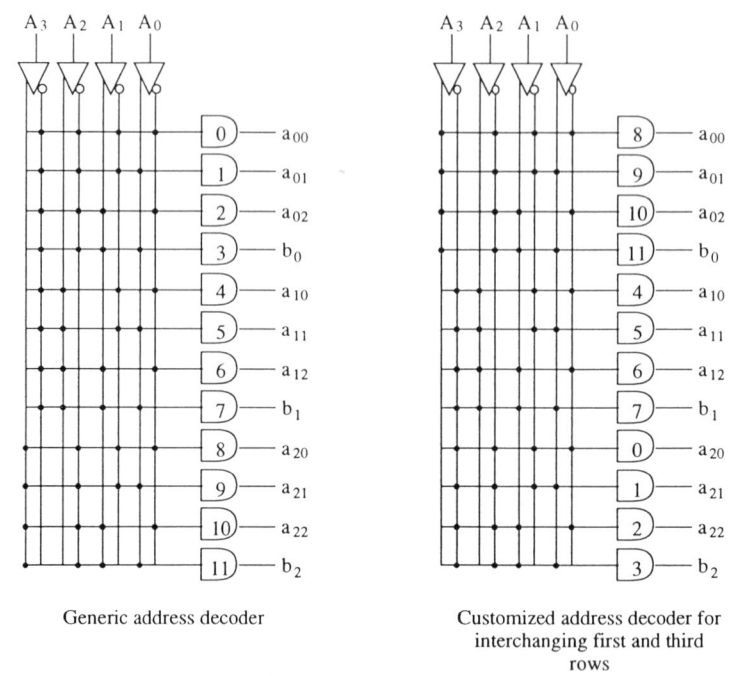

Figure 22. Two forms are shown for a four-variable address decoder. The configuration on the left corresponds to the cell numbering shown in Fig. 21. The configuration on the right corresponds to a cell numbering in which the top and bottom rows are interchanged. Only one-sixth of the crosspoints are changed between the two forms, even though three-quarters of the elements are interchanged.

4. Designing with Imperfect Arrays

The model of a fine-grain digital optical computer presented in Section 3.1 results in a design strategy that is extremely sensitive to the fabrication yield associated with the optical arrays. The model is insensitive to the technology used to fabricate arrays and works equally well with many device technologies such as S-SEEDs (Lentine *et al.* 1987) or Si/PLZT modulators (Lee *et al.* 1986). It is also insensitive to the details of the interconnect, accepting either free-space or fiber-based interconnects, perfect shuffles, banyan, or crossover networks (see Section 2), and space-invariant interconnects employing bulk optical components or space-variant interconnects employing diffractive optical elements such as holograms. The model lends itself to a practical optical implementation (Prise *et al.* 1990) by keeping the design and fabrication tasks largely independent of one another.

A computer design under this model is composed of one mask for each processor component and can be completed without detailed knowledge of fabrication technologies. The array fabrication task can likewise be completed independent of the design task. The result of the design and fabrication tasks are then brought together in a final assembly phase that *assigns* optical arrays to stages of a design, thereby assembling an optical computer meeting the design specifications. This approach is extremely effective when the fabricated optical arrays have no imperfections (Murdocca 1990; Murdocca *et al.* 1988). However, when imperfect arrays are fabricated (and discarded) the effectiveness of the model is brought into question. The problems of lower fabrication yield can be overcome in the assembly phase, which makes use of imperfect arrays rather than discarding them.

4.1 Utilizing Imperfect Arrays

Imperfect arrays can be used during the assembly phase due to the interaction between two key aspects of this model: (1) a design uses only a portion of the gates on an array and therefore partitions the gate locations within a processor component into two classes, *extraneous* and *vital;* and (2) arrays can be tested in a postfabrication phase to locate and record faulted gates, thus partitioning the gates on an array into two classes, *faulted* and *working*. The assembly phase uses this information to assign arrays to stages such that only *vital* locations of a processor component are guaranteed to be assigned *working* gates of an array (i.e., *extraneous* locations of a processor component may be assigned *faulted* gates on the array). Under these conditions it is possible and, in fact, likely that the assembly phase will use imperfect arrays in design stages.

The ability of the assembly phase to make use of imperfect arrays creates a situation in which the *effective* yield of a fabrication process is no longer a direct trade-off between the number of *perfect* arrays produced and the cost of producing them. It is rather dependent on several other factors. For a fixed-interconnect design, the relevant parameter is the likelihood that a typical array will be usable in a typical stage. This likelihood is dependent on many factors including the algorithm for assigning arrays to stages, the fraction of *vital* locations in a design (i.e., design density), the fraction of *faulted* gates on an array (i.e., fault density), the stage and array sizes, and the possible orientations of arrays within a stage.

4.1.1 Array Assignment by Means of Bipartite Matching

Array assignment based on a bipartite matching algorithm (Aho, Hopcroft, and Ullman 1983; Tarjan 1983; Smith 1992) increases array utilization by considering all fabricated arrays and designed stages and assigning arrays so that a maximum number of systems are assembled. This method introduces no additional costs in design or fabrication and can be used with all existing technologies. Rather, it increases the assembly cost by the addition of a computation component into the assembly process. For optimal assignments this cost can be large; however, near-optimal approximate solutions increase effective yield by between 50% and 100%.

4.1.2 Increasing Yield by Means of Oversized Arrays and Translation

The effective yield can be further increased by fabricating arrays that are oversized with respect to design stages and then positioning these arrays using translation, either horizontal or vertical, into the stages. Because the oversized array can be positioned in many ways in a stage, the likelihood that faulted gates on an array can be aligned with the *extraneous* locations in a stage is increased.

As an example consider Fig. 23, which depicts the task of orienting a 3 × 4 array within a 3 × 3 stage so that no *faulted* gate collocates with a *vital* stage location. Note that, by means of only translation, the array can be oriented two ways in each slot (i.e., with the lower left corners aligned and with the upper right corners aligned). With the lower left corners aligned, the array is consistent only with S_1 and with the upper right corners aligned the array is consistent only with S_2. Use of either one of the orientation choices exclusively prevents the array from being consistent with one of the stages; however, allowing both orientations permits the array to be consistent with both slots.

As with bipartite matching techniques, oversized arrays can be used with all existing technologies; however, it does introduce additional costs in both the fabrication and assembly tasks. Fabrication cost is increased by two effects: (1) oversized arrays are guaranteed to waste fabricated gates (e.g., the example of Fig. 23 uses only 9 of the 12 fabricated gates and therefore wastes at least 25% of the fabricated gates), and (2) assembly cost is increased since placement of arrays in stages requires greater precision. Any decision to use oversized arrays must balance the trade-off between the additional fabrication cost and the resulting increase in effective yield.

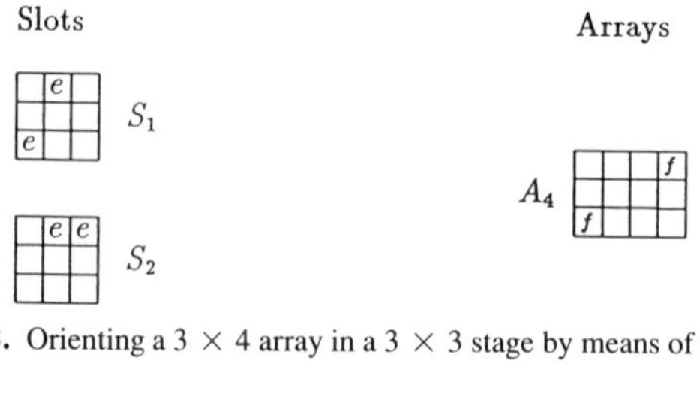

Figure 23. Orienting a 3 × 4 array in a 3 × 3 stage by means of translation.

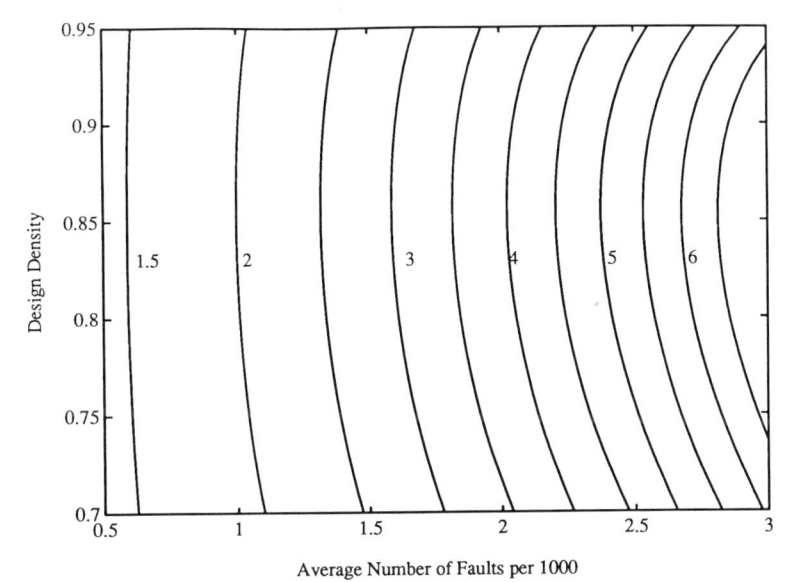

Figure 24. Improvement using bipartite matching, oversized arrays, and 180-deg. rotation.

4.1.3 Rotation

The likelihood that imperfect arrays will be used can also be increased by rotating arrays. Rotations do not require oversized arrays and therefore introduce no additional fabrication cost; however, they do introduce additional assembly costs in determining the orientation. In addition, rotations are further limited in applicability since many technologies cannot support this scheme.

4.1.4 Effect of Optimal Assembly on Effective Yield

Figure 24 shows the increase in array utilization possible when a bipartite match is employed with oversized arrays and 180-deg rotations. The increase shown is the ratio of array utilization for this technique to a technique that relies on perfect arrays. Notice that it varies from a low of about 1.4 to a high of 7.0 and that for fault densities greater than 1 per 1000 these methods provide an *effective* yield that is at least two times better than an approach that uses only perfect arrays.

Acknowledgements

This work has been jointly supported by the Air Force Office of Scientific Research and the Office of Naval Research under grant N00014-90-J-4018. The reconfigurable interconnect work has been supported by the Strategic Defense Initiative Office under contract F49620-91-C-0055, which is administered through the Air Force Office of Scientific Research. Partial support was also provided by DARPA under grant 97100400.1320-7604 through NASA NAG 2-668.

REFERENCES

Aho, A. V., Hopcroft, J. E., and Ullman, J. E. (1983). *Data Structures and Algorithms.* Computer Science and Information Processing. Addison-Wesley Publishing Company, Reading, MA.

Akl, S. G. (1985). *Parallel Sorting Algorithms.* Academic Press, Orlando, FL.

Ambs, P., Fainman, Y., Esener, S., and Lee, S. H. (1988). Computerized design and generation of space-variant holographic filters: 2 : Applications of space-variant filters to optical computing. *Appl. Opt.* **27**(22), 4761–4765.

Benner, A. F., Bowman, J., Erkilla, T., Feurstein, R. J., Heuring, V. P., Jordan, H. F., Sauer, J., and Soukup, T. (1991). Digital optical counter using directional coupler switches. *Appl. Opt.* **30**(29), 4179–4289.

Born, M., and Wolf, E. (1964). *Principles of Optics.* Macmillan, New York.

Brenner, K. H., and Huang, A. (1988). Optical implementation of the perfect shuffle interconnection. *Appl. Opt.* **27**(1), 135–137.

Buralli, D. A., Morris, G. M., and Rogers, J. R. (1989). Optical performance of holographic kinoforms. *Appl. Opt.* **28**(5), 976–983.

Cloonan, T. J., Lentine, A. L., McCormick, F. B., Paker, M. F., Sasian, J. M., Tooley, F. A. P., Morrison, R. L., and Hinterlong, S. J. (1991). Optical free space switching network using S-SEED-based 2-modules and computer-generated holographic banyan interconnections. In: *Technical Digest of the 1991 OSA Annual Meeting.* Optical Society of America, p. 83.

Dickinson, A., and Prise, M. E. (1990). Free-space optical interconnection scheme. *Appl. Opt.* **29**(14), 2001–2005.

Feldman, M. R., and Guest, C. C. (1989). Interconnect density capabilities of computer generated holograms for optical interconnection of very large scale integrated circuits. *Appl. Opt.* **28**(15), 3134–3137.

Ford, J. E., Lee, S. H., and Fainman, Y. (1990). Application of photorefractive crystals to optical interconnection. In: *Digital Optical Computing II, Proc. SPIE* **1215,** 155–165.

Fujita, T., Nishihara, H., and Koyama, J. (1981). Fabrication of micro lenses using electron-beam lithography. *Opt. Lett.* **6**(12), 613–615.

Goke, L., and Lipovski, G. (1973). Banyan networks for partitioning multiprocessor systems. In: *Proc. First Annual Symposium on Computer Architecture,* ACM/IEEE, New York, pp. 21–28.

Goodman, J. W. (1968). *Introduction to Fourier Optics.* Physical and Quantum Electronics Series. McGraw-Hill Book Company, San Francisco, CA.

Goodman, J. W. (1981). Linear space-variant optical data processing. In: *Optical Information Processing Fundamentals* (S. H. Lee, ed.), Springer-Verlag, Berlin, pp. 235–260.

Goodman, J. W., Leonberger, F. J., Kung, S. Y., and Athale, R. A. (1984). Optical interconnections for VLSI systems. *Proc. IEEE,* **72**(7), 850–866.

Guenther, R. D. (1990). *Modern Optics.* John Wiley and Sons, New York.

Hariharan, P. (1985). *Optical Interferometry.* Academic Press, Sydney, Australia.

Haumann, H. J., Kobolla, H., Sauer, F., Schwider, J., Stork, W., Streibl, N., and Völkel, R. (1990). Holographic coupling elements for optical bus systems based on a light-guiding optical backplane. In: *Optics in Complex Systems, Proc. SPIE* **1319,** 588–589.

Hecht, E. (1987). *Optics*. Addison-Wesley Publishing Company, Reading, MA.
Hosokawa, H., and Yamashita, T. (1990). ZnS micro-Fresnel lens and its uses. *Appl. Opt.* 29(34), 5106–5110.
Huang, S. T. (1986). Finite state model and compatibility theory: New analysis tools for premutation networks. *IEEE Trans. Computers* C-35(7), 591–601.
Jahns, J. (1990). Optical implementation of the banyan network. *Opt. Commun.* 76(5,6), 321–324.
Jahns, J., and Däschner, W. (1990). Optical cyclic shifter using diffractive lenslet arrays. *Opt. Commun.* 79(6), 407–410.
Jahns, J., and Huang, A. (1989). Planar integration of free-space optical components. *Appl. Opt.* 28(9), 1602–1605.
Jahns, J., and Murdocca, M. J. (1988). Crossover networks and their optical implementation. *Appl. Opt.* 27(15), 3155–3160.
Jahns, J., and Walker, S. J. (1990). Two-dimensional array of diffractive microlenses fabricated by thin film deposition. *Appl. Opt.* 29(7), 931–936.
Jewell, J. L., and McCall, S. L. (1989). Microoptic systems: Essential for optical computing. In: *Optical Computing, 1989 Technical Digest Series*, Optical Society of America, 9, 136–139.
Jewell, J. L., McCall, S. L., Lee, Y. H., Scherer, A., Gossard, A. C., and English, J. H. (1990). Optical computing and related microoptic devices. *Appl. Opt.* 29(34), 5050–5053.
Jordan, Jr., J. A., Hirsch, P. M., Lesem, L. B., and Van Rooy, D. L. (1970). Kinoform lenses. *Appl. Opt.* 9(8), 1883–1887.
Kawai, S. (1991). Free-space multistage optical interconnection networks using micro lens arrays. *IEEE J. Lightwave Technol.* 9(12), 1774–1779.
Kiamilev, F., Esener, S., Paturi, R., Fainman, Y., Mercier, P., Guest, C. C., and Lee, S. H. (1989). Programmable optoelectronic multiprocessors and their comparison with symbolic substitution for digital optical computing. *Opt. Eng.* 28(4), 396–409.
Kostuk, R. K., Goodman, J. W., and Hesselink, L. (1985). Optical imaging applied to microelectronic chip-to-chip interconnections. *Appl. Opt.* 24(17), 2851–2858.
Kostuk, R. K., Goodman, J. W., and Hesselink, L. (1987). Design considerations for holographic optical interconnects. *Appl. Opt.* 26(18), 3947–3953.
Lee, H., Gu, X.-G., and Psaltis, D. (1989). Volume holographic interconnections with maximal capacity and minimal cross talk. *J. Appl. Phys.* 65(6), 2191–2194.
Lee, S. H., Esener, S. C., Title, M. A., and Drabik, T. J. (1986). Two-dimensional silicon/PLZT spatial light modulators: Design considerations and technology. *Opt. Eng.* 25(2), 250–260.
Lentine, A. L., Hinton, H. S., Miller, D. A. B., Henry, J. E., Cunningham, J., and Chirovsky, L. M. F. (1987). The symmetric self electro-optic effect device. In: *Conference on Laser and Electro-optics Technical Digest Series*, Optical Society of America, 14, postdeadline paper.
Liau, Z. L., Diadiuk, V., Walpole, J. N., and Mull, D. E. (1989). Gallium phosphide microlenses by mass transport. *Appl. Phys. Lett.* 55(2), 97–99.
Lohmann, A. W. (1989). Scaling laws for lens systems. *Appl. Opt.* 28(23), 4996–4998.
Lohmann, A. W. (1991). Image formation of dilute arrays for optical information processing. In: *Technical Digest of the 1991 Annual Meeting*, Optical Society of America, p. 211.
McCormick, F. B., Tooley, F. A. P., Cloonan, T. J., Brubaker, J. L., Lentine, A. L., Hinterlong, S. J., and Herron, M. J. (1990). A digital free space photonic switching network demonstration using s-seeds. In: *CLEO 1990 Technical Digest Series*, Optical Society of America, 7, postdeadline paper.
McCormick, F. B., Tooley, F. A. P., Cloonan, T. J., Sasian, J. M., and Hinton, H. S. (1991). Microbeam optical interconnections using microlens arrays. In: *Proceedings on Photonic Switching*, Optical Society of America, pp. 90–96.

Miller, D. A. B. (1989). Optics for low-energy communication inside digital processors: quantum detectors, sources, and modulators as efficient impedance converters. *Opt. Lett.* **14**(2), 146–148.

Miyamoto, K. (1961). The phase Fresnel lens. *J. Opt. Soc. Am.* **51**(1), 17–20.

Murdocca, M. J. (1990). *A Digital Design Methodology for Optical Computing.* The MIT Press, Cambridge, MA.

Murdocca, M. J., Huang, A., Jahns, J., and Streibl, N. (1988). Optical design of programmable logic arrays. *Appl. Opt.* **27**(9), 1651–1660.

Oikawa, M., Nemoto, H., Hamanaka, K., and Okuda, E. (1990). High numerical aperture planar microlens with swelled structure. *Appl. Opt.* **29**(28), 4077–4080.

Parker, Jr., D. S. (1980). Notes on shuffle exchange type switching networks. *IEEE Trans. Computers* **C-29**(3), 213–222.

Popovic, Z. D., Sprague, R. A., and Neville Connell, G. A. (1988). Technique for monolithic fabrication of microlens arrays. *Appl. Opt.* **27**(7), 1281–1284.

Prise, M. E., Craft, N. C., Downs, M. M., LaMarche, R. E., D'Asaro, L. A., Chirovsky, L. M. F., and Murdocca, M. J. (1991). Optical digital processor using arrays of symmetric self-electro-optic effect devices. *Appl. Opt.* **30**(17), 2287–2296.

Prise, M. E., Craft, N. C., LaMarche, R. E., Downs, M. M., Walker, S. J., D'Asaro, L. A., and Chirovsky, L. M. F. (1990). Module for optical logic circuits using symmetric self electro-optic effect devices. *Appl. Opt.* **29**(14), 2164–2170.

Reynolds, G. O., DeVelis, J. B., Parrent, Jr., G. B., and Thompson, B. J. (1989). *The New Physical Optics Notebook: Tutorials in Fourier Optics.* Society of Photo-Optical Instrumentation Engineers and American Institute of Physics, Bellingham, WA.

Robertson, B., Restall, E. J., Taghizadeh, M. R., and Walker, A. C. (1991). Space-variant holographic optical elements in dichromated gelatin. *Appl. Opt.* **30**(17), 2368–2375.

Schwider, J., Stork, W., Streibl, N., and Völkel, R. (1990). Possibilities and limitations of space-variant holographic optical elements for switching networks and general interconnects. In: *Optics in Complex Systems, Proc. SPIE* **1319,** 130–131.

Shiono, T., Setsune, K., Yamazaki, O., and Wasa, K. (1987). Rectangular-apertured micro-Fresnel lens arrays fabricated by electron-beam lithography. *Appl. Opt.* **26**(3), 587–591.

Siegman, A. E. (1986). *Lasers.* University Science Books, Mill Valley, CA.

Smith, D. E. (1992). Fault avoidance for fixed-interconnect optical computers. *Appl. Opt.* **31**(2), 0167–0177.

Smith, W. J. (1966). *Modern Optical Engineering.* McGraw-Hill Book Company, New York.

Stone, H. S. (1971). Parallel processing with the perfect shuffle. *IEEE Trans. Computers* **C-20**(2), 153–161.

Stone, H. S. (1987). *High-Performance Computer Architecture.* Electrical and Computer Engineering. Addison-Wesley Publishing Company, Reading, MA.

Sugiyama, H., Kato, M., Misawa, S., and Iga, K. (1986). Fabrication of planar microlens by transverse electromigration method. *Jpn. J. Appl. Phys.* **25**(12), 1959–1960.

Swanson, G. J., and Veldkamp, W. B. (1989). Diffractive optical elements for use in infrared systems. *Opt. Eng.* **28**(6), 605–608.

Tarjan, R. E. (1983). *Data Structures and Network Algorithms.* SIAM, Philadelphia, PA.

Wu, C. L., and Feng, T. Y. (1981). The universality of the shuffle exchange network. *IEEE Trans. Computers* **C-30**(5), 324–332.

Chapter 9
Multiple Beamsplitters

NORBERT STREIBL

Physikalisches Institut der Universität Erlangen-Nürnberg
Staudtstr. 7, 8520 Erlangen, Germany

1. Introduction 227
2. Applications 228
3. Panopticon 228
4. Performance Parameters 229
5. Image Plane Beamsplitters 231
6. Fresnel Plane Beamsplitters 234
7. Fourier Plane Beamsplitters 237
8. Beam Shaping 243
9. Noise 244
10. Chromatic Errors 244
11. Irregular Geometries 245
12. Conclusion 246
    References 247

I. Introduction

A multiple beamsplitter or star coupler is an optical component that splits one incoming beam of light into a multitude of partial *beamlets*. If the partial beams are arranged in a regular array, we call it an *array generator*. Such an array generator is necessary in optoelectronic and optical data processing, in which two-dimensional arrays of optical modulators, optical logic devices, or optically bistable devices have to be illuminated by read-out or bias beams. Apart from illumination applications in information processing, the need often arises to split or join optical information propagating in different channels, that is fan-out and fan-in. The number of beams in a multiple beamsplitter should be adapted to the number of optical channels. The modal shape of each single beam should be adapted to the modes acceptable for the individual channels. In this chapter, different physical principles for multiple beamsplitting and array generation are introduced and the practically relevant performance parameters are identified (see also the review by Streibl 1989).

2. Applications

Recently, optically bistable elements, optical logic gates, and optoelectronic devices, which modulate the transmission or the reflection of an incoming light beam, have been demonstrated. They might be applied to short-range parallel optoelectronic interconnections within data processing systems, such as a multiprocessor or a telephone switch, for communication between electronic modules, boards, hybrid circuits or chips (Goodman *et al.* 1984). Additionally, fundamental research is carried out on all-optical data processing whereby these devices are employed as optical logic gates (see, for example, Streibl *et al.* 1989). In both applications multiple beamsplitters are required (1) for illuminating modulator-type devices, that is, for the distribution of optical energy, and (2) for fan-out (splitting) and fan-in (joining) of optically transmitted information. The required number of partial beams of such beamsplitters ranges from two to two-dimensional arrays of 128 × 128 and more beamlets. Often regular arrays of beams are needed and we call the corresponding optical component an *array generator*. Hence, arrays of light modulators usually require an array generator for light-efficient illumination.

Apart from more conventional beamsplitters, special devices for multiple beamsplitting have been investigated previously for other applications, including multiple imaging (see, for example, Newman and Rible 1966; Groh 1968; Dammann and Görtler 1971; Lee 1979), space-variant image processing (for example, Asthana *et al.* 1988; Gregory and Liu 1984), and optical data storage (Hill *et al.* 1975).

3. Panopticon

A confusing variety of multiple beamsplitters has been proposed in the past. Probably the oldest multiple imaging device is a children's toy, the kaleidoscope, in which the aperture is filled with several beam deflectors (usually mirrors) so that different parts of the aperture project different images side by side. Thus, one simple picture is multiplied to a beautiful mosaic.

Other approaches are based on arrays of pinholes (Newman and Rible 1966; Kalestynski 1975), fly's eye lenses, i.e., arrays of microlenses or *lenslets* (Walker *et al.*, 1988), arrays of microtelescopes or *telescopelets* (Lohmann and Sauer 1988; Lohmann, Sinzinger, and Stork 1989) on Fraunhofer-diffraction at specially designed gratings (Boivin 1972; Matthijsse 1978; Lee 1979), such as Dammann-gratings (Dammann and Görtler 1971; Veldkamp, Leger, and Swanson 1986; McCormick 1988; Turunen *et al.* 1988; Mait 1989, 1990; Jahns *et al.* 1989; Krackhardt and Streibl 1989), number theoretical gratings (this somewhat surprising application of seemingly "pure" mathematics is treated in Schröder 1985), lenslet gratings (Machida *et al.* 1984; Streibl *et al.* 1991), conventional interferometrically recorded point holograms (Groh 1968; Groh and Velzel 1969; Aebischer and Agbani 1975; Seyd-Darwish *et al.* 1991), or computer-generated holograms and kinoforms (see, for example, Dammann 1969, 1970; Feldman and Guest 1989; Turunen, Vasara, and Westerholm 1989; Herzig, Prongue, and Dändliker 1990; Walker and Jahns 1990; Wyrowski 1990, 1991), on Fresnel-diffraction at specially designed gratings exhibiting the fractional Talbot effect (Lohmann 1988; Leger, Scott, and Veldkamp 1988), on optical coordinate transformations (Hossak, McOwan, and Burge 1988), on leaky waveguides (Kubota and Takeda 1989), on phase contrast imaging (Lohmann *et al.* 1988a, 1988b), or on cascades of beamsplitting devices (Hill *et al.* 1975; McCormick 1988). There may be even more basic physical principles for beamsplitting. The decision of which method for array generation is to be used in any practical application depends on the acceptable trade-offs. Our aim is to find a baseline for such comparisons.

All approaches to array generation have in common that somewhere in the optical system a special component is used to split or redirect the incoming light into the partial beams. In most cases a nonabsorptive phase component is employed here in order to conserve light. Multiple beamsplitters can be classified according to the location within the optical system where this special component is situated:

1. *Image plane beamsplitters* use a special component located in an image plane conjugated to the array of devices, which divides the field geometrically.
2. *Fresnel plane beamsplitters* are characterized by a Fresnel-diffraction step between the special component and the device-array.
3. *Fourier plane beamsplitters* are usually based on division of the wavefront by diffraction at a specially designed grating or on division of the aperture. Usually, an optical Fourier transformation of the special component is involved.
4. *Cascade-type beamsplitters* comprise a stack of simple elements, which perform beam splitting *recursively*. The branching of the incoming light into the partial beam occurs in a tree fashion.

These four general approaches are discussed in detail in the following sections.

4. Performance Parameters

Beamsplitters can be compared with respect to different performance parameters as follows.

The *splitting ratio* is the number of beams generated out of one incoming beam.

Splitting ratios ranging from two to two-dimensional arrays up to 128×128 and more are of interest.

The *splitting geometry* describes the splitting angles and the geometrical arrangement of the partial beams. In many practical situations array generators, i.e., beamsplitters with regular geometry (partial beams on a Cartesian or hexagonal raster) are required.

Often the partial beams emerging from a beamsplitter are focused down to an array of spots. The *compression ratio* is the quotient of the bright area of a spot and the whole area of the elementary cell of the spot pattern. It measures how well the partial beams are separated from each other. Compression ratios between two and several hundred are desirable in different applications.

In general, the intensities of the partial beams of a multiple beamsplitter can be all different from each other; in array illuminators, they are all equal. The *inhomogeneity* is the maximum deviation of the actual intensity of a partial beam from its design value.

A related parameter is the *background suppression ratio,* which describes the ratio between the spot intensity and the background of stray light present in any optical system. The inhomogeneity and background suppression ratio measure the *noise* of the array generator in the bright and dark areas of the array.

The *light efficiency* specifies how much energy of the incoming laser beam is converted into the partial beams and how much is lost. Efficiencies of more than 50% are desirable. Inefficiency may result from the use of absorptive components, stray light, and/or diffraction into unwanted diffraction orders.

The *modal shape* of the beamlets of a beamsplitter is an important aspect in many applications. First, for the illumination of arrays of identical devices, all the individual beamlets should have identical modes across the array. Neither the direction of the beam nor the size or the shape of the spot should change across the array. This isoplanatic requirement includes as a necessary condition the fact that the array generation system should be telecentric, i.e., its exit pupil should be located at infinity. Second, if arrays of very small devices or single-mode fibres have to be provided with light, the shape of the individual beamlets itself becomes crucial: Small devices have a mode structure of their own. Consequently, light can be coupled into a device only if there is a sufficiently large overlap between the mode of the beamlet and the device. Hence, the telecentric property of the array generator and, in some cases, a customized mode structure for each beamlet are desirable.

The *spatial and temporal coherence properties* of the generated spots are important parameters. Unless required by the application, incoherent methods may be preferable because of their higher signal-to-noise ratio (SNR), i.e., a lack of coherent noise and speckles.

Obviously, the *manufacturability* and *cost* are important issues. Lithographic techniques, for example, are favorable because they provide ease of manufacturing of special components.

In the following sections we present some sample systems that are characteristic for the different approaches.

5. Image Plane Beamsplitters

The principle of an *image plane beamsplitter* is that an extended bundle of light is subdivided *geometrically* in many adjacent partial bundles. The most obvious and most naive approach is to use a pinhole array to define bright spots on a dark background. This is not discussed further because the incurred light loss is unacceptable in most cases. In a much more efficient approach, a fly's eye lens, a lenslet array, an array of Fresnel zone plates, or holographic lenses are illuminated by an expanded beam such that different parts of this input beam focus directly down onto different locations [Fig. 1(a)]. Splitting ratios of $100 \times 100 = 10^4$ and more are feasible and depend only on the availability of lenslet arrays (see, as an example, Walker *et al.* 1988).

A second, similar idea [Fig. 1(b)] is the use of an array of telescopes to compress the incoming beam into a small area. The telescopes can be of the Newton or Galilei type, composed of conventional lenses or holographic lenses (Lohmann and Sauer 1988), or of the Brewster type, composed of prisms (Lohmann, Sinzinger, and Stork 1989). The light efficiency of all methods based on lenslet arrays has as an upper bound of the efficiency of the lenslet arrays themselves. If the aperture of the lens is round, as usual, a densely packed Cartesian lenslet array contains an area of maximally $\pi/4 \approx 78\%$ covered with lenses, a hexagonal array has a maximum fill factor of $\sqrt{3} \cdot \pi/6 \approx 90\%$. Therefore, holographic or other special lenses with rectangular (hexagonal) apertures, leading to 100% fill factors, are required for light-efficient beamsplitting.

A third image plane approach is the phase-contrast array illuminator (Lohmann *et al.* 1988a, 1988b) schematically illustrated in Fig. 1(c), in which the spot array is first fabricated in the form of a phase mask. By phase-contrast imaging, that is, by spatial filtering, this phase transparency is converted into an intensity distribution. In principle, this conversion is free from light loss. Splitting ratios of 32 $\times$ 32 have been demonstrated; again larger arrays pose no major technological problems. Figure 2 shows an experimental result. Conventional phase-contrast imaging renders weak microscopic phase structures visible. In our case it is a very stringent requirement, however, that the background be completely dark. With phase contrast there is a direct trade-off between compression ratio and background suppression: Only at low compression ratios (less than 16) can the background remain completely dark; for compressions 16 to 81 in two-dimensional arrays the background becomes gray.

A fourth image plane approach [Fig. 1(d)] is based on a waveguide, which has grating couplers on its surface. These taps couple light out of the waveguide at those locations, where partial beams are wanted (Kubota and Takeda 1989). A

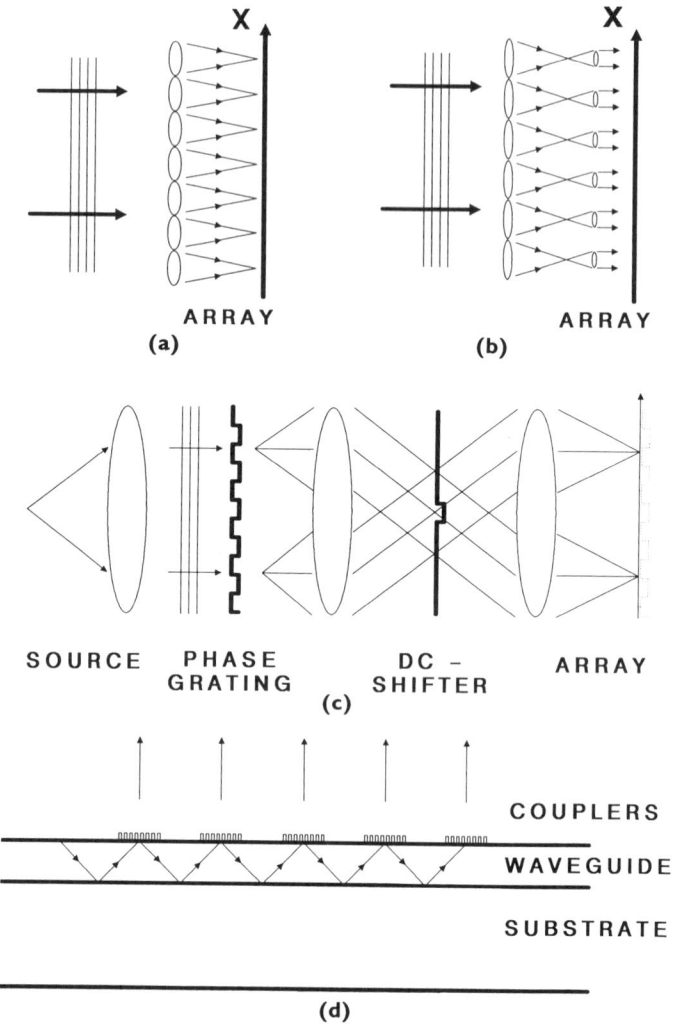

Figure 1. Sample image plane array generators: (a) lenslet array, (b) telescopelet array, (c) phase-contrast system, and (d) tapped waveguide system.

splitting ratio of 16 × 16 = 256 was demonstrated, albeit with large inhomogeneity, due to exponential decay of the light intensity within the waveguide. In principle, by designing couplers with the right efficiency this inhomogeneity is avoidable.

In general, all image plane beamsplitters suffer from the fact that an inhomogeneous profile of the input beam is directly inherited by the partial beams, thus causing inhomogeneity. For example, a Gaussian laser beam leads to very unequal

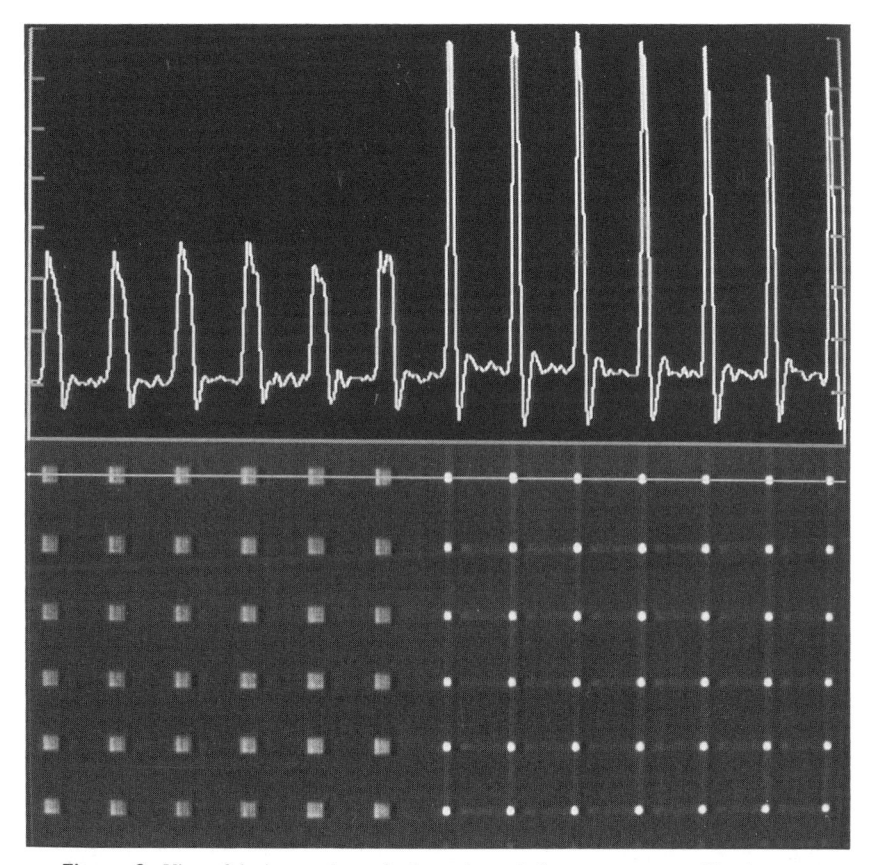

Figure 2. View of the image plane of an experimental phase-contrast array illuminator.

partial beams. Hence, where inhomogeneity is an important issue, additional measures have to be taken to equalize the beam. Such methods for *de-Gaussing* are available: Absorbing plates are used, which have a spatial absorption profile that is *anti-Gaussian*. Unfortunately, such a plate causes considerable light loss. Or, alternatively, a tandem of specially designed phase plates was proposed for beam shaping (Kreuzer 1969), which, in principle, is a lossless method.

The splitting ratio of an image plane array generator can be large compared to the Fourier-type approach to be discussed later. It depends only on the size of the splitting components, for example, the number of lenses contained in the lenslet array. In practice, the limit is given by the space-bandwidth product, that is, the number of pixels that can be handled by the overall optical system. The compression ratio can also be very large for lenslets and telescopelets, where it is basically given by the Fresnel number of the lens, that is, the number of its Fresnel zones: A lens with focal length f and diameter d produces at a wavelength λ a focus with a diameter of $\lambda f/d$; the compression c_{1D} in one dimension is the ratio of this diameter to the pitch of the lenses, which can be their diameter d, thus leading to $c_{1D} = d^2/(\lambda f)$ and a two-dimensional compression of $c_{2D} = c_{1D}^2$. For the phase-contrast array illuminator, however, the compression is limited to values between 16 to about 81, with reduced background suppression in the latter case.

All approaches mentioned are light efficient, since they involve phase components only. The modal shape of the partial beams is different in all approaches mentioned. Lenslets ideally produce Airy disks as focal patterns, from which approximately spherical waves emerge. The telescopelets yield—as long as the geometrical optics is considered valid—little patches of planewaves, which propagate without broadening except from diffraction. The phase-contrast method also produces little patches of light, whose form can be further influenced by design of the phase mask and the spatial filter. By proper design of the grating coupler, a wide variety of modal shapes can be achieved in the waveguide method. Ultimately, in the limit of very small spots, the modal shape produced in all approaches becomes similar to a diffraction-limited beam. It is worth mentioning that in some image plane array generators adjacent beams can be mutually incoherent given an incoherent illumination. The merits of incoherence will become clear in the section on coherent noise. Since image plane beamsplitters geometrically split the field, they are unsuitable for multiple imaging, where Fourier-type beamsplitters are employed instead.

6. Fresnel Plane Beamsplitters

The second basic method is *Fresnel plane beamsplitters,* in which Fresnel diffraction, that is, the light propagation from the splitting component to the receivers, plays a role. The distinction of these methods from image plane methods, such as the lenslet and the telescopelet, is sometimes fuzzy. For example, one approach is based on coordinate transformations (Hossak, McOwan, and Burge 1988), whereby a phase plate—or equivalently a hologram of it—is used to redirect the incoming light beams. Due to this redirection, in the receiver plane the density of beams and therefore the local intensity distribution can be changed arbitrarily; thus an optical coordinate transformer (Kreuzer 1969; Bryngdahl 1974) can be used to redistribute and concentrate the input beam into partial beams.

Figure 3 shows an array generator based on the fractional Talbot effect (Lohmann 1988), which has a working principle completely different from lenslets or telescopelets. It is based on multiple-beam interference of the diffraction orders of a grating in the region of Fresnel diffraction: A phase grating is designed in such a way that at a certain distance from the grating the diffracted light is concentrated

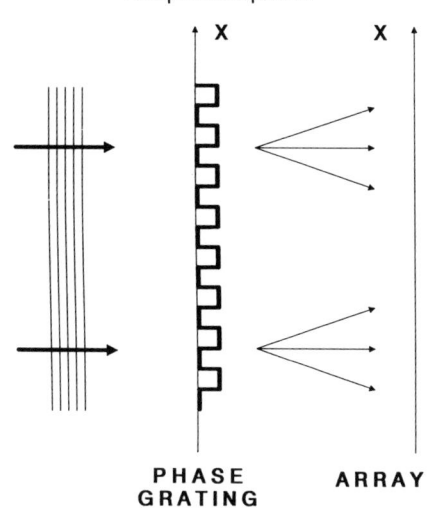

Figure 3. Schematic of a Fresnel plane array illuminator based on the fractional Talbot effect.

in bright spots on a dark background. The splitting ratio is given by the number of grating periods and may be very large (100 × 100 was demonstrated experimentally). Designs exist for binary phase gratings yielding a compression ratio of up to 16 (Lohmann 1988; Thomas 1989).

Figures 4 and 5 from Thomas (1989) show experimental demonstrations of light concentration by using the fractional Talbot effect. In the plane $z = 0$, where it is physically located, the binary phase grating (with rectangular grooves, a duty cycle of one-third, and a phase shift of $2\pi/3$) shows a homogeneous intensity distribution. With increasing distance z from the grating, the light is redistributed in complicated patterns, as is shown for several depths in Fig. 4. In one special plane at $z = z_T/3$ the light is concentrated into homogeneous bright bars on a completely dark background, whereby $z_T = 2p^2/\lambda$ denotes the Talbot distance for a grating with period p and wavelength λ. Figure 5 shows a view of the output plane for such a two-dimensional grating, which yields a two-dimensional array of bright spots.

Compared with image plane array generators, the inhomogeneity due to the input laser beam profile can be somewhat alleviated although not eliminated: By choosing several Talbot lengths as working distances, some averaging of the input beam occurs over several grating periods. Also laser beam de-Gaussing may again precede the beamsplitting. With binary phase gratings the compression of a Talbot system is severally limited (to a value of 16), not unlike phase-contrast imaging. On the other hand, with continuous phase grating profiles, arbitrary compression may be achieved: A lenslet array, where the lenses are *coherent,* which means that they all have the same phase profile, will also exhibit the Talbot effect and has unlimited compression. As a caveat, however, we should add that only lenslet

$z = 0$

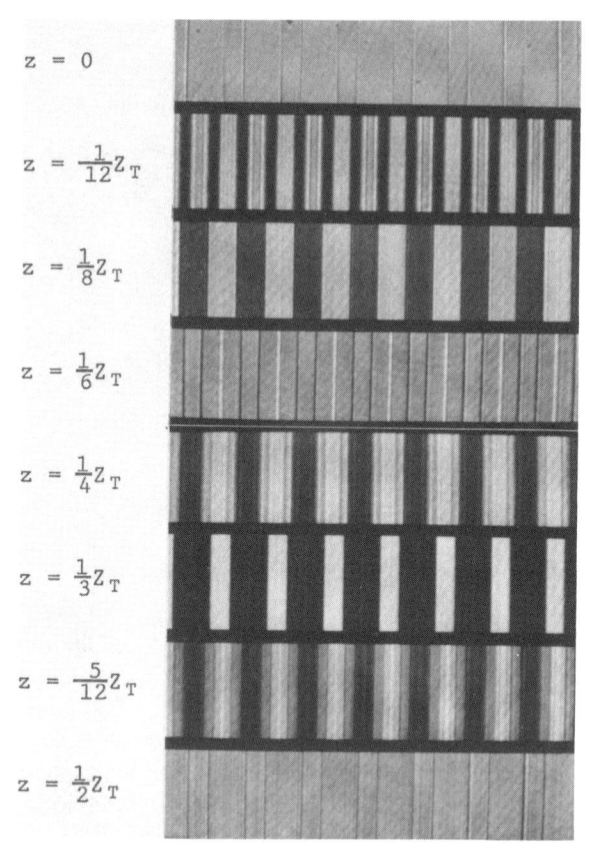

$z = \frac{1}{12}z_T$

$z = \frac{1}{8}z_T$

$z = \frac{1}{6}z_T$

$z = \frac{1}{4}z_T$

$z = \frac{1}{3}z_T$

$z = \frac{5}{12}z_T$

$z = \frac{1}{2}z_T$

Figure 4. Light distribution behind a phase grating exhibiting the fractional Talbot effect in different depths z behind the grating (from Thomas 1989).

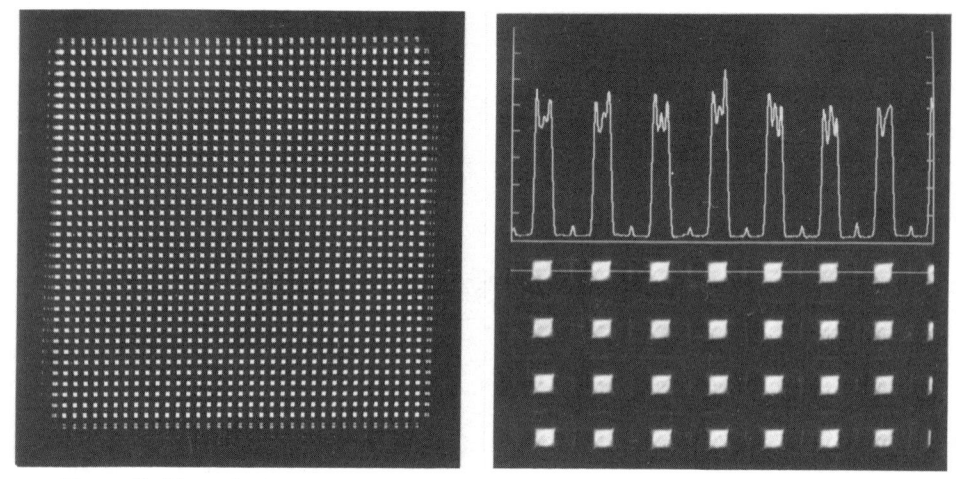

Figure 5. Direct photograph of the output of a two-dimensional Talbot array illuminator (from Thomas 1989).

arrays manufactured by photolithographic techniques or other technologies with similar precision have the required accuracy and reproducibility in phase to be used in such multiple-beam interference experiments.

Like image plane beamsplitters Fresnel plane beamsplitters cannot be used for multiple imaging of objects except from the self-imaging effects of the Talbot gratings themselves.

7. Fourier Plane Beamsplitters

The third basic approach is that of *Fourier plane beamsplitters*, in which the beamsplitting occurs at infinity. Usually (the kaleidoscope is a counterexample), the wavefront is physically divided by a diffraction phenomenon, as is shown in principle in Fig. 6. Fourier plane array generators have been widely studied in contexts ranging from multiple imaging over beam diffusors to concert hall acoustics (Schröder 1985).

Fourier-type beamsplitters often involve the combination of a special diffractive component and an optical Fourier transform. In the case of a Fourier plane array generator, the overall profile across the array—that is, the intensity distribution between the partial beams—is practically independent from the incoming laser profile. Let $g(x, y)$ be the amplitude distribution of the laser beam, for example, approximately a wide Gaussian beam. Let $f(x, y)$ be a period of a diffraction grating with period p, which is used to generate the array. For simplicity we assume here that the period is the same in x and y direction, although this is no necessary condition. The laser beam is required to illuminate several periods of the grating. Then, after the optical Fourier transformation with focal length f we

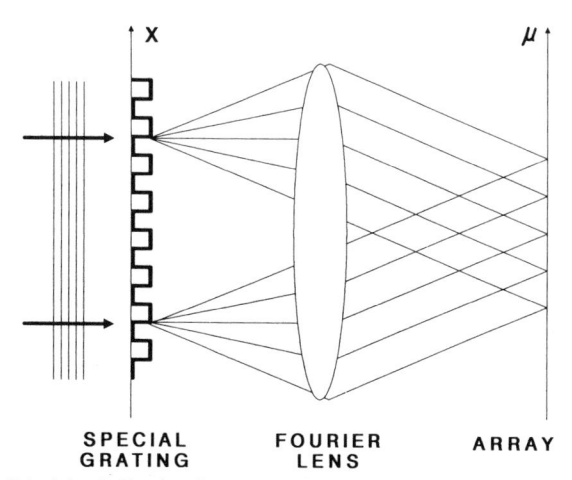

Figure 6. Principle of a Fourier plane beamsplitter based on diffraction at a special grating.

observe in the Fourier plane the intensity distribution (the Fourier transform is denoted by capital letters):

$$I(\mu, \nu) = \left| \sum_{m,n=-\infty}^{+\infty} F(m/p, n/p) \cdot G(\mu - m/p, \nu - n/p) \right|^2 \quad (1)$$

$$\approx |F(\mu, \nu)|^2 \cdot \left| \sum_{m,n=-\infty}^{+\infty} G(\mu - m/p, \nu - n/p) \right|^2,$$

where $\mu = x/(\lambda f)$ and $\nu = y/(\lambda f)$ denote the spatial frequencies. The approximation that decouples the envelope function $|F(\mu, \nu)|^2$ and spot profile $|G(\mu, \nu)|^2$ holds as soon as a sufficient number of periods of the grating—say, ten periods—are illuminated by the laser. The envelope $F(\mu, \nu)$ of the generated array depends solely on the accurate design and manufacturing of the diffraction grating $f(x, y)$, whose Fourier transform it is. On the other hand, the modal shape of the individual beamlets $G(\mu, \nu)$ is completely determined by the shape of the incoming laser beam $g(x, y)$. The modal shape can be modified by shaping the incoming beam.

The earliest examples of Fourier-type array generators were pinhole gratings (Newman and Rible 1966) for multiple imaging and holograms of pinhole gratings, so-called *point holograms* Groh 1968; Groh and Velzel 1969; Aebischer and Agbani 1975). Pinhole gratings make use of the fact that the Fourier transform of a comb function is another comb function (the reciprocal grating in crystallography):

$$f(x) = \sum_n \delta(x - np) \xleftrightarrow{\text{Fourier transform}} F(\mu) = \sum_m \delta(\mu - m/p). \quad (2)$$

Pinhole gratings make very inefficient use of light, however, since they work well only with very small pinholes and throw out most of the incoming light.

Point holograms can be manufactured by recording the interference pattern of N partial beams and the reference beam. Intermodulation between the partial beams causes parasitic gratings that result in stray light or light loss. On the other hand, a hologram can easily be manufactured to be more light efficient than a pinhole mask. Alternatively, one may record multiplex holograms sequentially into a thick holographic emulsion. As long as sufficiently thick emulsions, large angles, and few partial beams are involved, excellent results can be obtained as can be seen from the experimental results in Fig. 7 (Kobolla *et al.* 1991).

Alternatively the grating can be generated by a computer and be manufactured by lithographic techniques. This procedure gives maximum design flexibility. Not only the intensity but also the phase of the partial beams can be chosen arbitrarily. If the phase is free, then the light efficiency can be optimized by varying the phases suitably. Or one can adapt to certain design constraints, such as a binary phase profile in the grating. The Dammann grating (Dammann and Görtler 1971; Veldkamp, Leger, and Swanson 1986; McCormick 1988; Turunen *et al.* 1988;

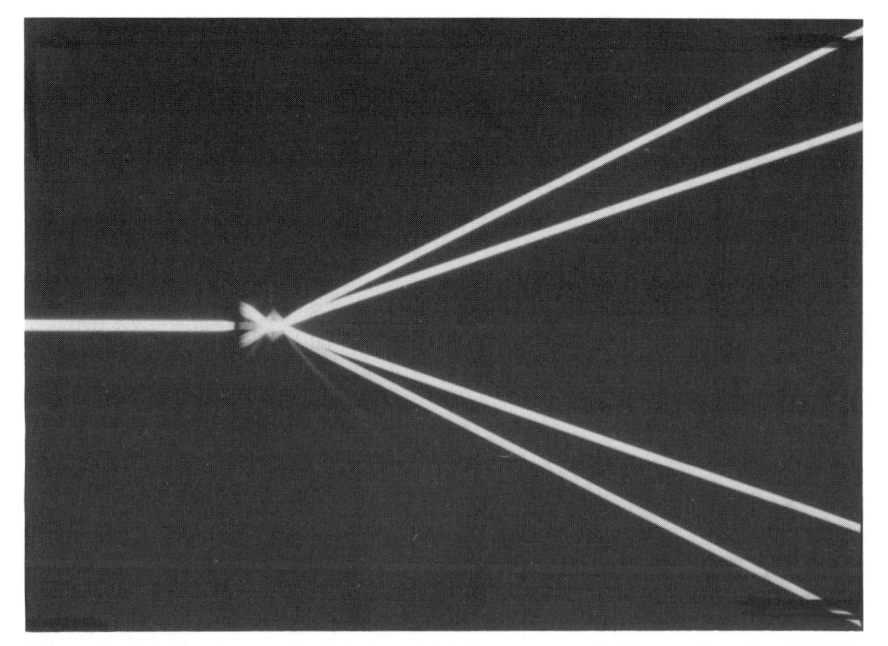

Figure 7. Multiplex hologram in dichromated gelatine acting as a 1:4 beamsplitter (from Kobolla *et al.* 1991). The propagation of light is visualized by immersion of the hologram in fluorescent dye. Note the missing of the zero diffraction order, indicating the high overall diffraction efficiency.

Mait 1989; Jahns *et al.* 1989; Krackhardt and Streibl 1989) is a specially designed binary phase grating, which exhibits a number of diffraction orders of equal intensity. Binary gratings are especially attractive, since lithographic techniques can be employed for their fabrication. Dammann gratings with splitting ratios ranging from three up to several thousand were demonstrated. No unique solution exists for the problem of designing Dammann gratings that are light efficient and easy to manufacture (Krackhardt and Streibl 1989). Hence, nonlinear numerical optimization procedures are used. For large splitting ratios the design of a highly efficient grating as well as its fabrication pose formidable problems (Jahns *et al.* 1989). Figures 8 and 9 show, respectively, the mask structure and diffraction orders of a Dammann grating. The location of the transitions between the two phase levels (indicated by black and white in Fig. 8) are the only degrees of freedom available for the design of the grating with N diffraction orders with equal intensity. Their location is therefore very critical for high splitting ratios N.

It is therefore advantageous to use phase structures with a number of phase levels or continuous phase distributions. Number theoretical phase gratings (Schröder 1985), which have many equal diffraction orders, have been employed for optimizing concert hall acoustics or in radar technology to design broadband

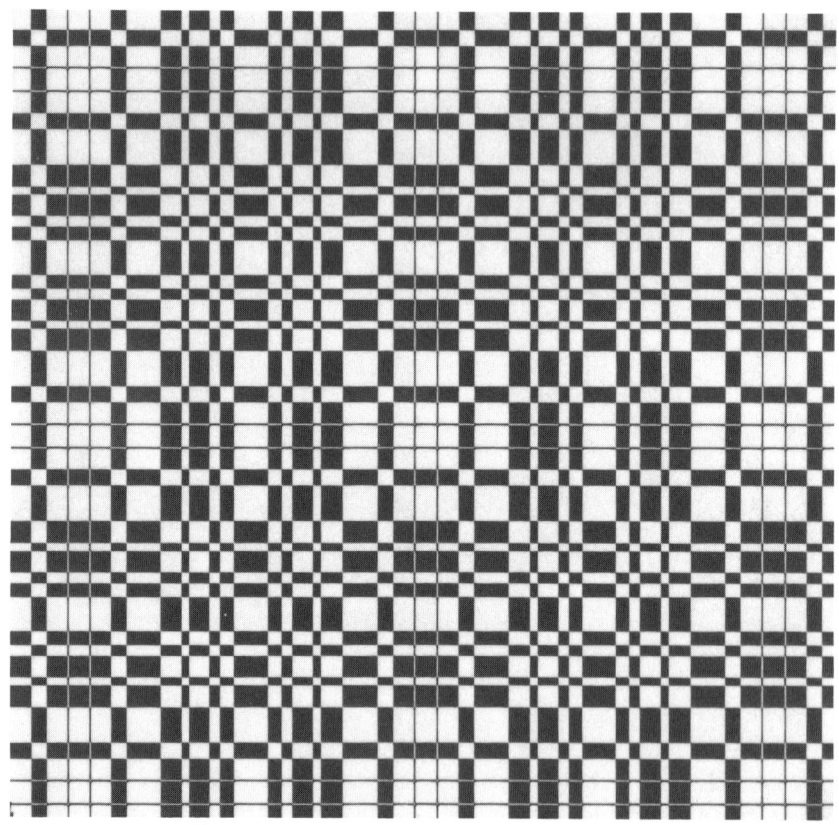

Figure 8. Binary mask structure of a Dammann grating.

signals with a low peak factor. The optical counterpart is computer-generated holograms and kinoforms, which have been extensively investigated in the past (Dammann 1969, 1970; Feldman and Guest 1989; Turunen, Vasara, and Westerholm 1989; Herzig, Prongue, and Dändliker 1990; Mait 1990; Walker and Jahns 1990; Wyrowski 1990, 1991).

A special diffraction grating with continuous phase distribution and remarkable behavior is once again a fly's eye lens—a lenslet array (Machida *et al.* 1984; Streibl *et al.* 1991). Note that lenslet arrays have been employed for a long time in incoherent illumination systems for homogeneous light distribution and aperture matching within the so-called *honeycomb-condensor* systems. A coherent lenslet array consisting of lenses with focal length s on a pitch p with exactly identical phase profiles has in each single period the complex transmission function

$$f(x) = \text{rect}(x/p) \cdot \exp(-i\pi x^2/\lambda s) \tag{3}$$

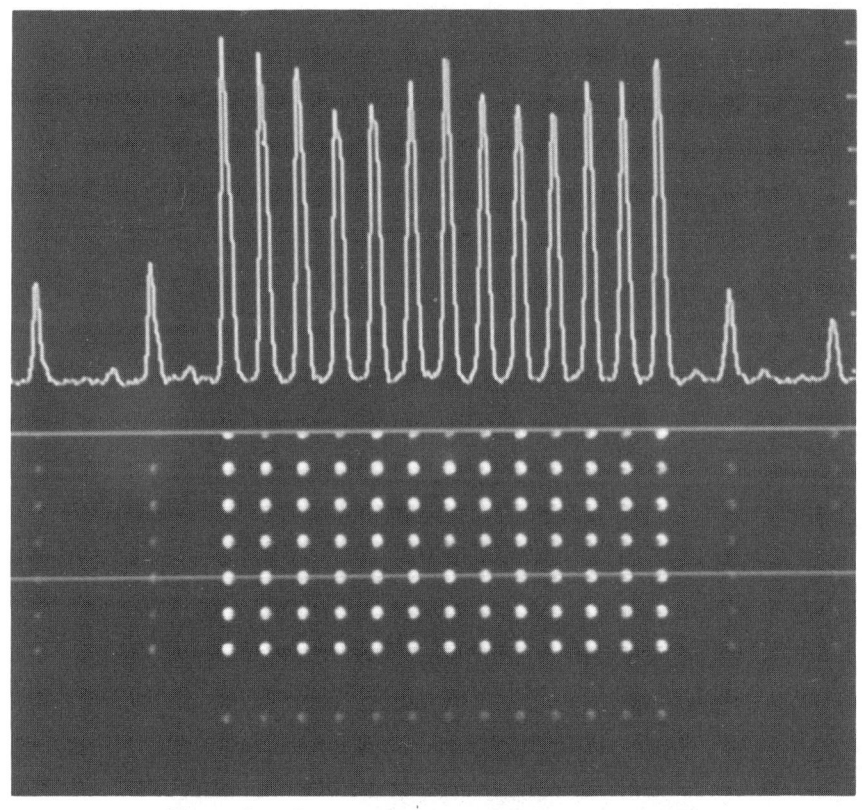

Figure 9. Diffraction pattern obtained at a Dammann grating.

and approximately (within the stationary phase approximation) the Fourier coefficients

$$F(m/p) \approx \begin{cases} \text{constant} \cdot \exp(+i\pi\lambda s m^2/p^2) & \text{if } |m| \leq p^2/(2\lambda s) \\ 0 & \text{otherwise} \end{cases}, \quad (4)$$

which means that an array of spots of equal intensity and a quadratic phase relationship is generated. The number of spots happens to be the Fresnel number of the lenslet $p^2/(\lambda s)$. Diffraction at the aperture of the lenses causes deviation from the stationary phase approximation, which results in edge ringing of the array. This effect can be alleviated by an array of field lenses or by spatial filtering (Streibl *et al.* 1991). Figure 10 shows an experimental result of the Fourier transform of a lenslet array: The spot array is fairly homogeneous. The experiment was

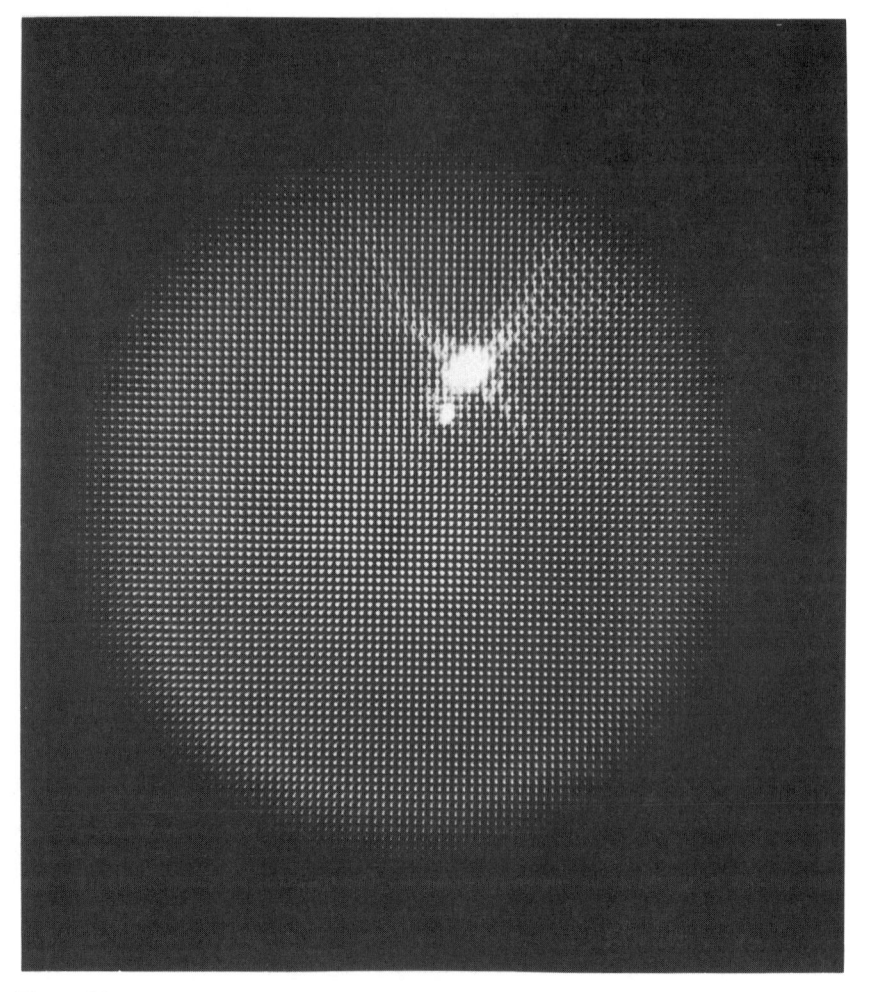

Figure 10. Array generated by Fourier transformation of a lenslet array with field lenslet (after Streibl *et al.* 1991).

performed in a reflection geometry; thus the bright first-order reflex becomes very pronounced. By employing two arrays in transmission, this reflex can be avoided.

In general, the larger the required splitting ratio, the more difficult it is to produce homogeneous arrays by Fourier methods. The reasons are the accuracy requirements in the design and the manufacturing of special phase objects $f(x, y)$ (Jahns *et al.* 1989). High compression ratios are feasible; the compression ratio is given simply by the number of periods of the grating $f(x, y)$. A grating consisting of 10 × 10 periods comprises a compression of 100. The product of compression and the splitting ratio is the space-bandwidth product that is required from the optical elements following the multiple beamsplitter, for example, the Fourier lens.

8. Beam Shaping

The shape of the partial beams of a multiple beamsplitter is sometimes important to control, especially if the beams are to be coupled into small devices, single-mode fibers, etc. The first item to discuss about beam shaping is, of course, *spatial filtering*. This is simplest for the Fourier plane array generators, where the Fourier plane is directly accessible and where one may include an additional spatial filter in the grating. However, for any other approach to array generation an additional spatial filtering setup can be cascaded behind the array generator. The basic problem with spatial filtering is that it is a subtractive method. A spatial filter can only attenuate or phase shift the light of a given spatial frequency. It cannot, however, amplify or create any new spatial frequency component. Methods for mode shaping without light loss can work along the lines of the beam shaper consisting of two phase components that was invented by Kreuzer (1969).

An important special case of mode adaptation occurs if *dilute arrays* of very tiny devices with a large separation between them have to be illuminated. In the direct approach, an array generator would be needed with a very large aperture (to focus down on very small devices) and with a very high compression ratio (to concentrate the light on the devices and not into *dead space* between them). To obey both restrictions, systems with an extremely large space-bandwidth product are necessary. A lenslet array situated above the devices may serve to trade space for the compression ratio: Above each device there is a lenslet, one focal length away, with a large aperture. Hence, a low-aperture external beam can be used to illuminate the lenslet, which then provides the large apertures locally to couple into the device. Effectively, the requirements on the space-bandwidth product of the external bulk optical system are alleviated by a factor given by the ratio of the diameter of the lenslets and the devices.

Another special case of beam shaping is cascading of beamsplitters, that is, to use the output of the preceding beamsplitter as input for the next. In this way, the splitting ratios multiply and large arrays may be generated *recursively* or in the fashion of a tree. The simplest example of this type of array generator is binary trees of 1:2 beamsplitters. For biasing arrays of nonlinear Fabry-Pérot interferometers, cascades of (polarizing) beamsplitting devices (Wollaston prisms) have already been employed (Jewell *et al.* 1985). Cascades of polarizing beamsplitters have also been employed in the past for digital deflectors (Hill *et al.* 1975). Meanwhile, other array generators, namely, Dammann gratings (McCormick 1988), have also been cascaded to increase the splitting ratio. The main disadvantage of cascading is the fact that errors accumulate. Any inaccuracy in one stage of the system will show up later at many places. The important asset of cascading is the huge splitting ratio that can be achieved.

9. Noise

Diffraction-limited performance over a large field and with a good SNR is difficult to achieve with any optical system, but it is especially hard if we are working with coherent light. If incoherent beams are sufficient, multiple light sources are therefore preferable to coherent beamsplitting systems.

This is illustrated by the estimation derived by Jahns *et al.* (1989), which applies to any optical system used to generate or transmit coherent arrays. It is assumed that, due to surface roughness or aberrations, phase errors are distributed across the aperture, which are described by a wave aberration $W(x, y)$. The mean square phase error is then given by $\Delta\Phi = 2\pi \cdot \Delta W/\lambda$ with the mean square wave aberration ΔW across the aperture and the wavelength λ. For a multiple beamsplitter with splitting ratio M and light efficiency η, the inhomogeneity (relative errors of intensities of the partial beams) is estimated by

$$\Delta I/I \sim M \cdot \Delta\Phi/\eta. \tag{5}$$

There is a direct trade-off between stray light and phase errors and—maybe surprisingly—the more partial beams we attempt to generate, the more critical the phase errors become. For example, for an efficiency of $n = 50\%$, $M = 100$, and $\Delta I/I \sim 10\%$, one must require $\Delta\Phi \leq 10^{-3}$. From a physics point of view these tight tolerance requirements can be understood by comparison with the optical precision of a Fabry-Pérot interferometer. In both cases a discrete and very sharp transmission characteristic is achieved by multiple-beam interference; in the case of the Fabry-Pérot interferometer, in wavelength; in the case of the multiple beamsplitter, in space or in angles. Hence, tolerancing is similarly critical in both cases.

10. Chromatic Errors

Some array generators work with a range of wavelengths, for example, most image plane array generators, which are based on geometrical optics. However, multiple beamsplitters based on diffraction, namely, Fourier plane array generators, exhibit chromatic errors (Groh and Velzel 1969). Let $\Delta\lambda/\lambda$ denote the relative spectral width of the light source with wavelength λ. The m'th diffraction order of a grating displays a spectrum of the light source with a spatial width of $\Delta x = m \cdot \Delta\lambda f/p$, where f denotes the focal distance of the Fourier lens and p the grating period. For an array generator with compression ratio β we will have to require this width Δx to be less than the distance between two adjacent diffraction orders $\lambda f/p$ divided by the compression ratio β. This leads to a boundary for the allowable spectral bandwidth of the light source:

$$\lambda/\Delta\lambda \sim \beta \cdot m. \tag{6}$$

In other words, the spectral purity must be better than the compression times the number of partial beams (in one direction), that is, the space-bandwidth product. A challenging but interesting way to overcome this grating dispersion would be to design Fourier lenses for *white light* that compensate the grating dispersion within some given wavelength range.

In the case of the array illuminator based on the Talbot effect, the physics is somewhat different. The arrays generated by different wavelengths do not have different pitch, as in the Fourier-type array generator, but they are displaced in depth due to the wavelength dependence of the Talbot length $z_T = 2p^2/\lambda$. This poses a problem if this displacement is larger than the depth of focus of the Talbot pattern, which in turn depends quadratically on the aperture of the wavefield behind the grating, which is basically determined by the number σ of significantly contributing diffraction orders:

$$\lambda/\Delta\lambda \sim 4\sigma^2. \tag{7}$$

This means that "simple" Talbot-effect array generators, which rely only on $\sigma = 1$ to 5 diffraction orders, such as the one shown in Figs. 4 and 5, do not need high spectral purity.

11. Irregular Geometries

In many applications the beamlets generated by a multiple beamsplitter are arranged in a two-dimensional Cartesian grid. Sometimes, however, optical devices are packed in a non-Cartesian grid, for example, in a hexagonal geometry. The development of array generators adapted to hexagonal geometries is a straightforward generalization of Cartesian systems. A Cartesian array generator can usually be decomposed into two crossed one-dimensional array generators. Consider, for example, a Dammann grating $U(\mu, \nu) = V(\mu) \cdot V(\nu)$, which is separable in the x and y directions. Hexagonal grids are separable in nonorthogonal directions; therefore, by "crossing" appropriately scaled and rotated versions of one-dimensional gratings, hexagonal or other arbitrary regular grids can be constructed: $U(\mu\nu) = V(a\mu + b\nu) \cdot V(c\mu + d\nu)$, whereby the constants a, b, c, and d determine the geometry.

Nonseparable array generators are more challenging, but they can also be constructed by two-dimensional design methods (Mait 1989). Such components are very useful in optical computing as spatial filters, for example, in systems where several shifted versions of an image-plane have to be superimposed. Also they are useful where irregular arrays have to be generated, for example, for selective powering in PLAs (Streibl *et al.* 1989). In general, all computer holograms and kinoforms can be considered to be irregular array generators and the major design problem today is to achieve the maximum diffraction efficiency of these structures (Wyrowski 1991).

Conclusion

Many methods exist for multiple beamsplitting. They can be classified into systems relying on Fourier transformation, Fresnel diffraction, imaging, and cascaded beamsplitters. These systems can be compared with respect to their splitting ratio, compression ratio, background suppression ratio, homogeneity, light efficiency, modal shape, geometry, and manufacturability. Different approaches have to be judged by the system designer in terms of these parameters with respect to their application. Fortunately for the designer, there are big differences between the different types of array generators. Table 1 attempts to summarize some of these issues. Where available, numerical values for experimental results are given (in parentheses). The values, however, do not represent the technological limit, since in most cases only feasibility experiments have been performed.

Table 1. Comparison Between Different Systems for Array Generation

System	Splitting Ratio	Compression	Homogeneity	Efficiency
Pinhole grid (image plane)	= number of pinholes	= fill factor of pinhole grid	similar to input beam	≈ 0%
Lenslet (image plane)	= number of lenses (100 × 100)	= Fresnel number (≥100)	similar to input beam	= fill factor of lenslet (50–100%)
Telescopelet (image plane)	= number of telescopes (5 × 5)	= magnification factor (4)	similar to input beam	= fill factor of lenslet (50–100%)
Waveguide (image plane)	= number of couplets (16 × 16)	design dependent (≈4)	exponential decay	potentially large (?)
Phasecontrast (image plane)	= number of periods (32 × 32)	4–9 (one-dim.) 16–81 (two-dim.) (16 and 81)	similar to input beam	→ 100%
Talbot effect (Fresnel plane)	= number of periods (100 × 100)	9 (for binary gratings) (9)	similar to input beam	→ 100%
Pinhole grid (Fourier plane)	≈ fill factor of pinhole grid	= number of pinholes	sinc-function envelope	≈ 0%
Dammann (Fourier plane)	~ 3–30 more by cascading (81 × 81)	= number of periods (e.g., 100)	depends on splitting ratio and fabrication	40–80%
Lenslet (Fourier plane)	= Fresnel number of lenslet (≥50 × 50)	= number of periods (e.g., 100)	depends on edge diffraction and fabrication	→ 100%
Konoform (Fourier plane)	design dependent	design dependent	fabrication dependent	→ 100%

ACKNOWLEDGEMENTS

The author is grateful to numerous people for technical discussions, for building some of the systems, and for contributing various ideas, big and small: Maralene Downs, Jürgen Jahns, Uli Krackhardt, Adolf Lohmann, Rick McCormick, Joe Mait, Uwe Nölscher, Mike Prise, Frank Sauer, Johannes Schwider, Willi Stork, Jim Thomas, and Sue Walker.

Some aspects of this work were supported by the Deutsche Forschungsgemeinschaft under grant SFB 182 and by the Bundesministerium für Forschung und Technologie under grant TK 0435. The author, however, is solely responsible for the contents.

REFERENCES

Aebischer, N., and Agbani, A. B. (1975). *Nouvelle Revue d'Optique* **6,** 37.
Asthana, P., Akiba, A., Yamaki, T., Nishizawa, K., and Oikawa, M. (1988). *Opt. Lett.* **13,** 84.
Boivin, L. P. (1972). *Appl. Opt.* **11,** 1782.
Bryngdahl, O. (1974). *J. Opt. Soc. Am.* **64,** 1092.
Dammann, H. (1969). *Phys. Lett.* **29A,** 301–302.
Dammann, H. (1970). *Optik* **31,** 95–104.
Dammann, H., and Görtler, K. (1971). *Opt. Commun.* **3,** 312.
Feldman, M. R., Guest, C. C. (1989). *Opt. Lett.* **14,** 479–481.
Goodman, J. W., Leonberger, F. J., Kung, S.-Y., and Athale, R. A. (1984). *Proc. IEEE* **73,** 850.
Gregory, D. A., and Liu, H. K. (1984). *Appl. Opt.* **23,** 4560.
Groh, G. (1968). *Appl. Opt.* **7,** 1643.
Groh, G., and Velzel, C. H. F. (1969). *Optik* **30,** 257.
Herzig, H. P., Prongue, D., and Dändliker, R. (1990). *Jpn. J. Appl. Phys.* **29,** L1307–L1309.
Hill, B., Krumme, J.-P., Much, G., Pepperl, R., Schmidt, J., Schmidt, K. P., Witter, K., and Heitmann, H. (1975). *Appl. Opt.* **14,** 2607.
Hossak, W. J., McOwan, P., and Burge, R. E. (1988). *Opt. Commun.* **68,** 97.
Jahns, J., Downs, M. M., Prise, M. E., Streibl, N., and Walker, S. J. (1989). *Opt. Eng.* **28,** 1267.
Jewell, J. L., Lee, Y. H., Duffy, J. F., Gossard, A. G., Wiegmann, W., and English, J. H. (1985). *Optical Bistability III, Proc. Topical Meeting* (H. M. Gibbs, P. Mandel, N. Peyghambarian, and S. D. Smith, eds.), Springer, New York, 32–34.
Kalestynski, A. (1975). *J. Opt. Soc. Am.* **65,** 1443.
Krackhardt, U., and Streibl, N. (1989). *Opt. Commun.* **74,** 31.
Kobolla, H., Schmidt, J., Sheridan, J., Streibl, N., and Völkel, R. (1992). Holographic optical beamsplitters in dichromated gelatine. *J. Mod. Optics* **39,** 881.
Kreuzer, J. L. (1969). Coherent optical system yielding an output beam of desired intensity distribution at a desired equiphase surface. U.S. Patent 3476463.
Kubota, T., and Takeda, M. (1989). *Opt. Lett.* **14,** 651.
Lee, W. H. (1979). *Appl. Opt.* **18,** 2152.
Leger, J. R., Scott, M. L., and Veldkamp, W. B. (1988). *Appl. Phys. Lett.* **52,** 1771.
Lohmann, A. W. (1988). *Optik* **79,** 41.
Lohmann, A. W., Lukosz, W., Schwider, J., Streibl, N., and Thomas, J. (1988b). *Proc. SPIE* **963.**
Lohmann, A. W., and Sauer, F. (1988). *Appl. Opt.* **27,** 3003.
Lohmann, A. W., Schwider, J., Streibl, N., and Thomas, J. A. (1988a). *Appl. Opt.* **27,** 2915.
Lohmann, A. W., Sinzinger, S., and Stork, W. (1989). *Appl. Opt.* **28,** 3835.
Machida, H., Nitta, J., Seko, A., and Kobayashi, H. (1984). *Appl. Opt.* **23,** 330.
Mait, J. N. (1989). *Opt. Lett.* **14,** 196–198.
Mait, J. N. (1990). *J. Opt. Soc. Am. A* **7,** 1514–1528.
Matthijsse, P. (1978). *J. Opt. Soc. Am.* **68,** 733.
McCormick, F. B. (1988). *Opt. Eng.* **28,** 299

Newman, P. A., and Rible, V. E. (1966). *Appl. Opt.* **5,** 1225.
Schröder, M. R. (1985). *Number Theory in Science and Communications,* 2nd Ed. Springer Berlin, 296 ff.
Seyd-Darwish, I., Legendre, Ph., Chavel, P., and Taboury, J. (1991). *Annales de Physique* **16,** 103–110.
Streibl, N. (1989). *J. Mod. Optics* **36,** 1559–1573.
Streibl, N., Brenner, K.-H., Huang, A., Jahns, J., Jewell, J., Lohmann, A. W., Miller, D., Murdocca, M., Prise, M., and Sizer, T. (1989). *Proc. IEEE* **77,** 1954.
Streibl, N., Jahns, J., Nölscher, U., and Walker, S. J. (1991). *Appl. Opt.* **30,** 2739–2742.
Thomas, J. A. (1989). Binary phase elements in photoresist, thesis, Physikalisches Institut der University of Erlanger-Nürnberg, Germany.
Turunen, J., Vasara, A., and Westerholm, J. (1989). *Opt. Eng.* **28,** 1162–1167.
Turunen, J., Vasara, A., Westerholm, J., Jin, G., and Salin, A. (1988). *J. Phys. D,* **21,** 102.
Veldkamp, W. B., Leger, J. R., and Swanson, G. J. (1986). *Opt. Lett.* **11,** 303.
Walker, S. J., and Jahns, J. (1990). *J. Opt. Soc. Am. A* **7,** 1509–1513.
Walker, A. C., Taghizadeh, M. R., Mathew, J. G. H., Redmond, I., Campbell, R. J., Smith, S. D., Dempsey, J., and Lebreton, G. (1988). *Opt. Eng.* **27,** 38.
Wyrowski, F. (1990). *Proc. SPIE* **1211,** 2–10.
Wyrowski, F. (1992). *Diffraction Optics: Design, Fabrication and Applications,* Technical Digest (Optical Society of America, Washington D.C. 1992) vol. 9, pp. 147–150.

Chapter 10
Photorefractive Optical Interconnects

ARTHUR E. CHIOU

Rockwell International Science Center
1049 Camino Dos Rios
Thousand Oaks, CA 91360

1. Introduction 249
2. Classification of Optical Interconnections 251
3. Photorefractive Effect 256
   3.1 Passive Holographic Storage: 257
   3.2 Photorefractive Two-Wave Mixing 266
   3.3 Optical Phase Conjugation in Photorefractive Materials 268
4. Interconnections Based on Passive Holographic Storage in Photorefractive Media . . . 270
   4.1 Photorefractive Beam Steering 271
   4.2 Programmable Optical Interconnections by Means of Multiplexed Holograms . . . 272
   4.3 Parallel N^4 Weighted Optical Interconnections 273
5. Interconnections Based on Photorefractive Energy Coupling 273
   5.1 Energy Efficient $N \times N$ Crossbar Network 274
6. Interconnections Based on Photorefractive Phase Conjugation 279
   6.1 Matrix-Tensor Multiplication Based on Four-Wave Mixing 279
   6.2 Interconnections Based on Self-Pumped Phase Conjugation 279
   6.3 Interconnections Based on Mutually Pumped Phase Conjugation 280
7. Conclusion 282
   References 282

1. Introduction

Optics is playing an increasing role in information science and technology from storage and transmission of information to switching and processing (Berra *et al.* 1989; Flannery and Horner 1989; Neff 1987). Optical interconnection (Goodman 1989; Goodman *et al.* 1984; Sawchuk and Jenkins 1986) deals with the use of optics (photons) instead of conventional electronics (electrons) for communication in a wide range of applications in computers, especially the high-end machine, massively parallel computer (Guha *et al.* 1990) and neural networks (Caulfield, Kinser, and Rogers 1989; Psaltis *et al.* 1990), in broadband switching in telecommunication (Hinton 1990), and in local area network.

Regardless of the specific application, a generic optical interconnection system usually consists of modulated light sources, transmission media, interconnection devices/networks, and optical receivers as illustrated schematically in Fig. 1. In general, each data stream or signal originally in electrical format is transformed into optical format by modulating either the driving current of a laser (or light-emitting diode) or the voltage across the transducer of an optical modulator. The modulated output is directed to an interconnection network via appropriate transmission media and to the designation, where a detector is used to convert the data back to electrical format. The potential advantages of optics, including an extremely high spatial and temporal bandwidth, immunity to electromagnetic interference, avoidance of impedance matching and ground loop issues, absence of frequency-dependent loss and crosstalk, low loss, and a lower fundamental limit in energy for communication of a digital logic level, have been studied extensively in recent years (Feldman et al. 1988; Goodman 1989; Goodman et al. 1984; Kostuk, Goodman, and Hesselink 1985; Miller 1989; Sawchuk and Jenkins 1986).

Holographic optical elements that diffract an incident beam into one or more components in specific directions play an important role in optical interconnection networks. The hologram can be recorded optically or generated by a digital computer. For example, holographic gratings for the connection of source $S1$ to detectors $D2$ and $D4$, and source $S2$ to detectors $D1$ and $D3$ [Fig. 2(a)], can be generated by using the recording configuration shown in Fig. 2(b) where the "*" denotes the phase-conjugate (i.e., the *time-reversed*) replica of the corresponding beams. The recording can be done in parallel provided that the sources are mutually incoherent. Some of the important issues that have been studied extensively include (1) the maximum number of holograms that can be superimposed in a given volume, (2) techniques to achieve uniformly high diffraction efficiency, and (3) minimization of crosstalk. High storage capacity, large angular and wavelength selectivities, and high diffraction efficiency of volume phase holograms offer tremendous potential for applications in programmable optical interconnections (Fainman 1989; Ford, Lee, and Fainman 1990).

Nonlinear optical phenomena such as optical phase conjugation, four-wave mixing, and two-wave mixing that involve dynamic volume holograms (Yariv 1978) are particularly attractive for real-time and adaptive optical storage and interconnection. Prior to the discovery of the photorefractive effect (Ashkin et al. 1966), demonstration and applications of these phenomena required optical intensities higher than 1 MW/cm^2 for efficient operation. These intensity levels are far too high for optical computing and interconnection. The discovery and develop-

Figure 1. A generic block diagram for optical interconnection.

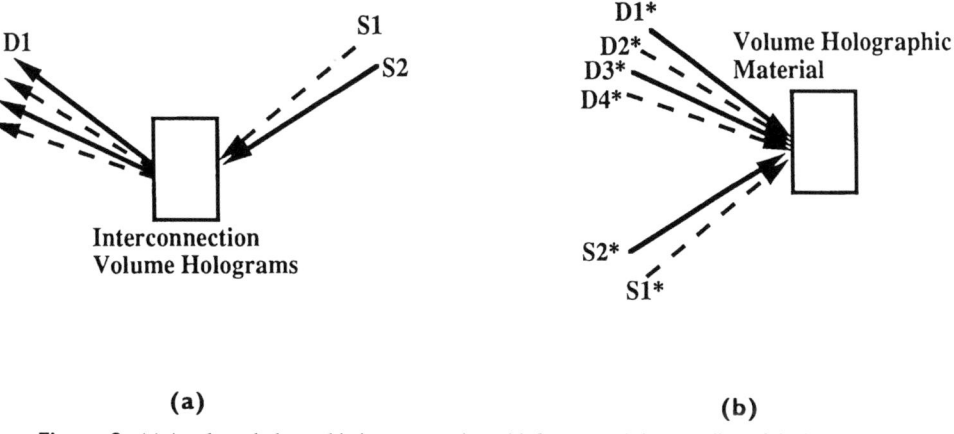

Figure 2. (a) A volume holographic interconnection with fan-out and (b) recording of the interconnection holograms.

ment of photorefractive materials (Valley *et al.* 1988) such as barium titanate, lithium niobate, strontium barium niobate, bismuth silicon oxide, and gallium arsenide, which exhibit these nonlinear optical phenomena at relatively low optical power (approximately a few milliwatts), completely change the story. The possibility of fixing the holograms (Amodei and Staebler 1971; Herriau and Huignard 1986; Kirillov and Feinberg 1991) further expands the boundary of their applications. A wide range of optical interconnection schemes using photorefractive holograms has been proposed and demonstrated worldwide. This chapter provides an overview of this new technology and discusses some of the highlights achieved and the technical challenges ahead.

Different types of optical interconnections are described briefly in Section 2 to show a perspective of how the photorefractive approach fits into the overall picture. Section 3 begins with a qualitative introduction to the photorefractive effect followed by a discussion of the phenomena and parameters relevant to applications in optical interconnection. For convenience, photorefractive phenomena are classified into three broad categories, namely, passive holographic storage, energy coupling, and optical phase conjugation. Optical interconnection schemes based on the nonlinear phenomena in each category are discussed separately in Sections 4, 5, and 6, respectively. Section 7 summarizes the key points and concludes with some thoughts on future research directions. To keep this chapter to a manageable size, some recent works involving photorefractive fibers (Hesselink 1990; Wu *et al.* 1990) and waveguides (Aronson and Hesselink 1990) have been excluded.

2. Classification of Optical Interconnections

Optical interconnection can be classified in a variety of ways (Goodman 1989; Hinton 1990) based on their functionality, architecture, network topology, or other features (Fig. 3). The interconnection network can be either fixed or reconfigurable. The transmission medium can be either free-space or guided structures such as optical fibers or waveguides. The distance involved can range from a few microns for intrachip gate-to-gate interconnection to several kilometers for machine-to-machine interconnection, and thousands of kilometers in telecommunications. The interconnection can be either one-to-one or one-to-many. The latter can be further classified into nonselective broadcasting, in which the signal from one source is broadcast to all the receivers without any discrimination, versus selective broadcasting, in which the signal from each source is distributed to a few selected receivers. Some examples of the interconnection functions described above are illustrated schematically in Fig. 4 where A, B, C, and D represent the sources; 1, 2, 3, and 4 represent the detectors; and the solid circles in the grid patterns indicate where the links are established. Optical configurations for the implementation of full broadcasting (b) and partial broadcasting (c) are illustrated in (d) and (e), respectively.

Functionally, the simplest interconnection network is a point-to-point fixed interconnect of which a fiber optic link is probably one of the most familiar examples. Point-to-point free-space fixed interconnection (Tsang 1990) has also been studied extensively. The key area of research in this approach is to improve the performance (mainly the speed) of the transmitter and/or receiver and the appropriate optics to reduce the signal-to-crosstalk ratio. Many of the advantages of using optics for communication listed in the previous section hold even at this simple functional level.

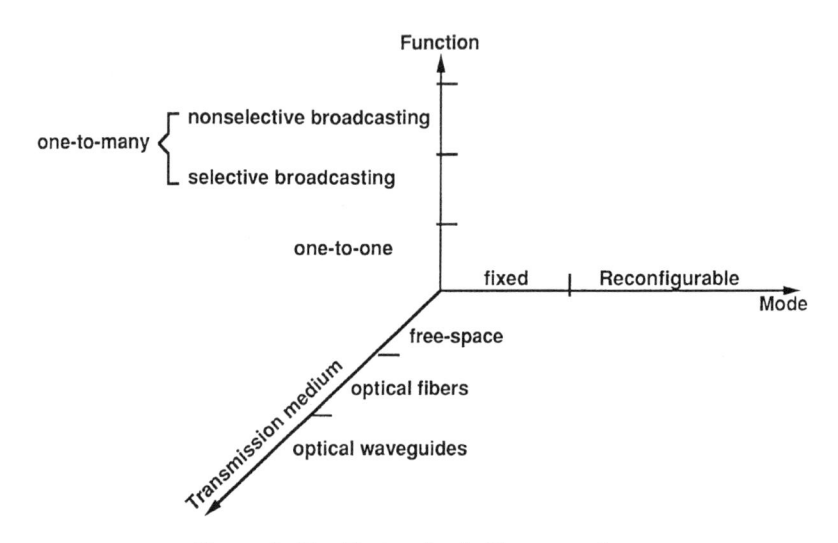

Figure 3. Classification of optical interconnections.

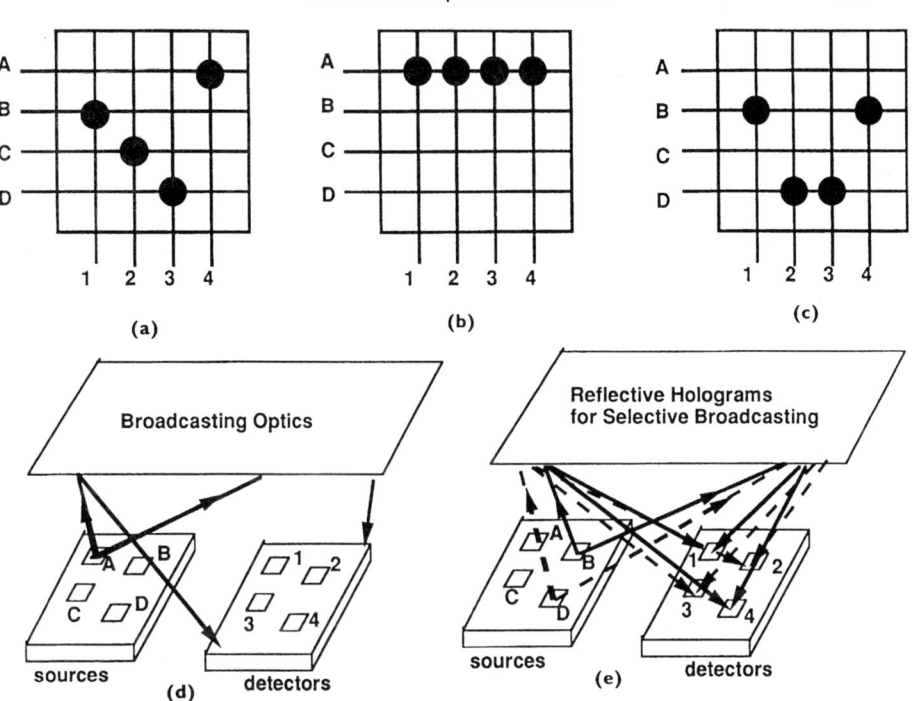

Figure 4. Some examples of different interconnection functions: (a) one-to-one; (b) and (d) full broadcasting; (c) and (e) selective broadcasting.

At a higher functional level, one-to-one reconfigurable interconnection networks (Joel 1968) that link an array of N sources to an array of N detectors in a permutation mode play a crucial role in many communication systems. Various network topologies (Hinton 1990), both single stage and multiple stage, that use a 2×2 switch as a basic building block to route the signal from each source to the designated receivers have been analyzed. The technology based on a lithium niobate switch (Voges and Neyer 1987) is probably the most advanced to date.

The most general and versatile reconfigurable interconnection network, normally referred to as a *generalized crossbar switch* (Sawchuk et al. 1987), can be formally represented by a matrix-vector multiplication scheme, as illustrated in Fig. 5. In this approach, the output from each source is equally distributed (fan-out) to all the detectors through a column (row) of a two-dimensional spatial light modulator (SLM). The transmitted beams from each row (column) of the SLM are then spatially integrated (fan-in) to each of the corresponding detectors. The interconnection pattern is reconfigurable by simply changing the interconnection matrix on the SLM. In principle, arbitrary interconnection with analog weight can be realized provided that the transmittance of each of the SLM windows can be

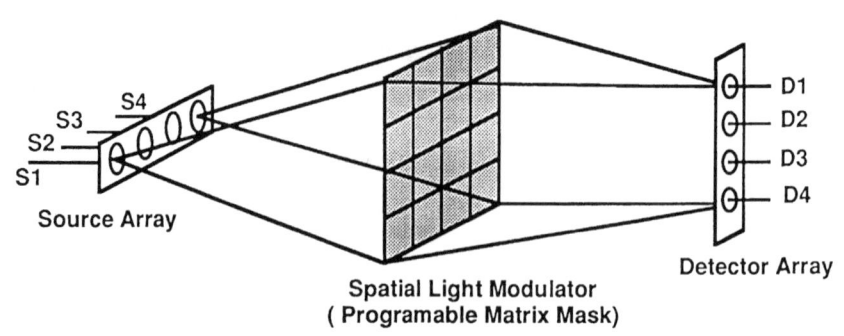

Figure 5. Optical matrix-vector multiplication scheme.

individually controlled and varied continuously over a certain useful range. Such an interconnection can be formally expressed as the following matrix-vector multiplication:

$$D_i = M_{ij} S_j, \tag{1}$$

where summation over the repeated index j is assumed. In Eq. (1), S_j is the strength (optical power) of source element j, D_i is the total signal power received by the detector element i, and M_{ij} is the analog weight linking S_j to D_i.

For interconnections of two-dimensional arrays of sources (input plane) and detectors (output plane), the vector-matrix multiplication scheme described above can be conceptually generalized to a tensor-matrix multiplication scheme represented by

$$D_{ij} = T_{ijmn} S_{mn}. \tag{2}$$

In practice, some kind of multiplexing scheme such as space-division multiplexing (SDM) or wavelength-division multiplexing (WDM) is required to achieve the four degrees of freedom required to represent a fourth rank tensor. A simple example of SDM in which a two-dimensional matrix is organized, into a submatrix to represent a four-dimensional tensor to implement the tensor-matrix multiplication is illustrated in Fig. 6 (Caufield 1987; Jang, Shin, and Lee 1988). Global interconnections of two-dimensional arrays of neurons with analog weight are critical to many image processing applications based on neural networks (Caulfield, Kinser, and Rogers 1989; Psaltis *et al.* 1990).

The high-capacity and high-resolution volume holographic storage in photorefractive crystals that can be recorded using a relatively low power source, together with the high diffraction efficiency and the real-time nature, make them very attractive as interconnection devices in free-space reconfigurable networks with massive connectivity. Nonreciprocal energy transfer in photorefractive multiwave

Photorefractive Optical Interconnects 255

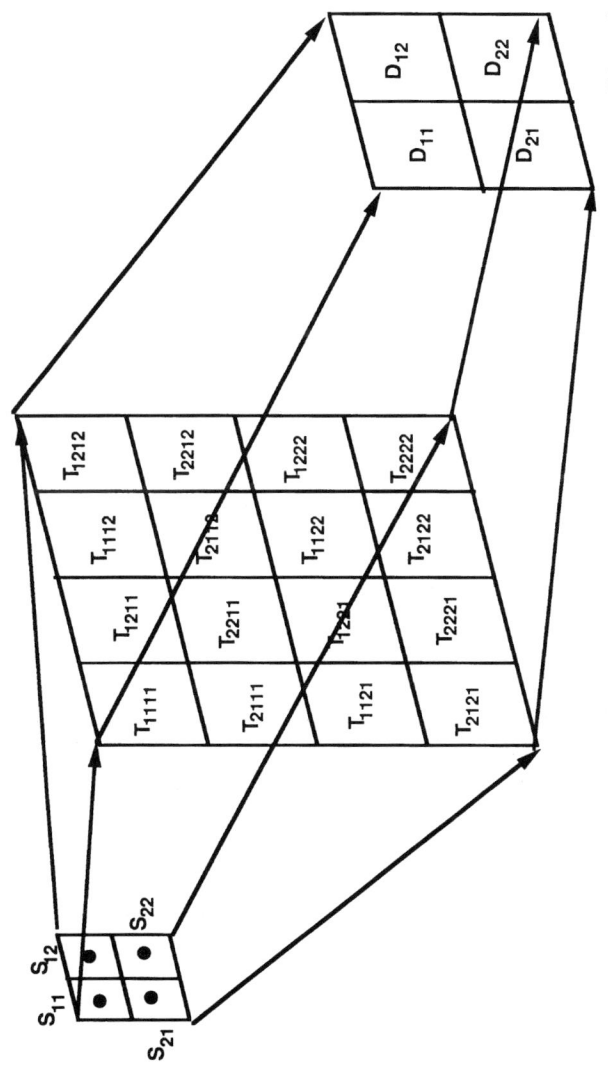

Figure 6. Optical tensor-matrix multiplication with N^4 parallelism via space-multiplexing (adapted from Jang, Shin, and Lee 1988).

mixing can be used as an adaptive optical amplifier to improve the energy efficiency of an optical crossbar network by one to two orders of magnitude (Chiou and Yeh 1990; Chiou *et al.* 1989). Efficient optical phase conjugation at relatively low optical power (approximately a few milliwatts) offered by many photorefractive materials (Feinberg and MacDonald 1989) facilitates self-aligned optical networks capable of aberration correction. The photorefractive phenomena and parameters relevant to these applications are discussed in the next section.

3. Photorefractive Effect

The photorefractive effect, the optically induced change in refractive index in electro-optic crystals, was first discovered in $LiNbO_3$ by Ashkin and coworkers in 1966 (Ashkin *et al.* 1966). They noticed that an intense blue or green laser beam focused into $LiNbO_3$ and $LiTaO_3$ crystals caused a change in refractive index at the focus. This phenomenon was first referred to as *optical damage* since it prevented the use of this class of materials for nonlinear optical applications such as harmonic generation and modulation. Subsequent investigations by Chen, LaMacchia, and Fraser (1968) revealed its potential for phase-only volume holographic storage. Since then, photorefractive materials have emerged as one of the most promising media for optical storage and information processing (Gunter 1982; Gunter and Huignard 1989; Rajenbach, Huignard, and Gunter 1990) because of their unique properties such as low-intensity operation, massive storage capacity, energy coupling (or optical gain), and real-time response.

The origin of the photorefractive effect can be explained by the following four-step process: (1) When a photorefractive material is exposed to a spatially varying optical intensity distribution (caused, for instance, by the interference of two or more mutually coherent beams) charge carriers from some bound states in the bright regions are excited to the conduction band. (2) The excited carriers migrate due to diffusion, drift, or the photo-voltaic effect to the darker regions where they are retrapped to fill the vacancies in the bound states. (3) The nonuniform charge distribution gives rise to a spatially modulated space-charge field. (4) The space-charge field induces a refractive index change via the linear electro-optic (Pockels) effect, giving rise to a volume phase grating. The hologram is dynamic and continuously adapts itself in a time-integrating mode to the change in intensity and phase of the writing beams.

A wide variety of photorefractive materials (Valley *et al.* 1988) has been studied to date. The approximate spectral range for some representative photorefractive materials is shown in Fig. 7. The boundary of the spectral range for each material is rather fuzzy. The boundary on the short-wavelength side is mostly limited by strong near-band-edge absorption whereas that on the long-wavelength

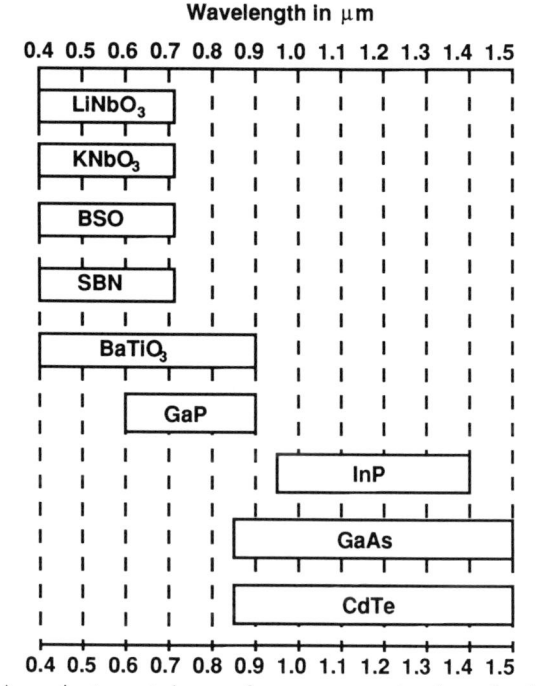

Figure 7. Approximate spectral range of some representative photorefractive materials.

side is practically limited by the slow response time due to inefficient photogeneration of charge carriers.

For convenience, we discuss the photorefractive phenomena in terms of three categories: (1) passive holographic recording, in which energy coupling does not play an essential role; (2) beam coupling, which involves energy transfer among the interacting beams; and (3) phase conjugation, in which the time reversal or phase-retrieving property plays a critical role.

3.1 Passive Holographic Storage

The illumination of a photorefractive material with two or more mutually coherent beams gives rise to a dynamic phase hologram. This aspect has been studied extensively for potential applications as an optical storage medium (Amodei and Staebler 1972; Burke *et al.* 1978). In contrast to conventional holography, the writing (recording) and reading of photorefractive holograms can take place simultaneously, although nondestructive read-out without the presence of the writing beams is also possible via some fixing process or by proper selection of the intensity and the wavelength of the reading beam (Delboulbe *et al.* 1989). Some of the most important parameters that are critical to passive holographic storage are:

1. diffraction efficiency
2. steady-state index modulation
3. photorefractive sensitivity
4. storage capacity
5. resolution
6. response time.

Each of these attributes is discussed in the following subsections. With the exception of the response time related to the dynamic nature of photorefractive holograms, parameters discussed in this section apply to other volume holographic materials as well.

3.1.1 Diffraction Efficiency

In holographic storage, one of the most important parameters is probably the diffraction efficiency, the ratio of the diffracted (output) intensity to that of the (input) reading beam. The condition for which diffractions from successive grating planes interfere constructively to give a maximum diffraction efficiency, known as the Bragg condition, is given by

$$\Lambda = \lambda \sin\theta_B/2, \tag{3}$$

where Λ is the grating spacing, λ is the wavelength, and the angle θ_B is known as the Bragg angle (Fig. 8). When the Bragg condition is satisfied, the diffraction efficiency η of a volume phase hologram is given by (Kogelnik 1969)

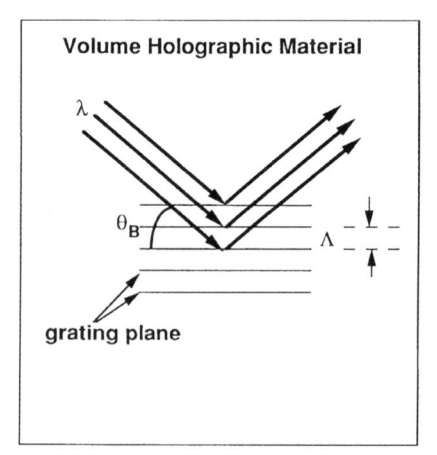

Figure 8. A schematic illustration of the Bragg condition in an unslanted geometry.

Photorefractive Optical Interconnects

$$\eta = \exp(-\alpha L/\cos\theta_B) \sin^2(\psi) \tag{4}$$

where

$$\psi = \frac{\pi L \Delta n}{\lambda \cos\theta}, \tag{5}$$

where α is the absorption coefficient, L is the thickness of the hologram, and Δn is the amplitude of the index modulation. The parameter ψ, defined by Eq. (5), is a measure of the dynamic range of the grating. Under certain conditions, a larger value of ψ may allow more holograms to be superimposed in a given volume of holographic medium (see Section 3.1.4).

Using a 514.5-nm argon-ion laser for writing and a 632.8-nm He-Ne laser for read-out, Hong *et al.* (1990) have measured the grating parameter ψ for a 4-mm-thick BaTiO$_3$ crystal and showed that its steady-state value can be as high as $5\pi/2$ (corresponding to $\Delta n \sim 10^{-4}$). The diffraction efficiency is measured to be about 25%, apparently limited by various loss mechanisms such as Fresnel reflection, absorption, and scattering. In principle, the diffraction efficiency of a volume phase hologram can approach 100% by eliminating the Fresnel reflection via an antireflection coating and by proper selection of the reading wavelength to minimize the absorption. Diffraction efficiencies as high as 86% have been reported for a photorefractive hologram recorded in an Fe-doped lithium niobate crystal (Amodei, Phillips, and Staebler 1971).

For applications where the reading and writing beams for the photorefractive holograms are constrained to be of the same wavelength, one can no longer select a wavelength based on minimum absorption because the absorption process is essential for the photogeneration of charges that contribute to the formation of the grating. In this case the maximum diffraction efficiency achievable is about 33% (Gunter and Huignard 1988a).

The dependence of the diffraction efficiency of a volume hologram on the reading wavelength and the reading angle when the Bragg condition is not satisfied can be derived from the couple-wave theory of Kogelnik (1969). A comprehensive treatment can be found in Chapter 9 of Collier, Burckhardt and Lin (1971). A measure of the angular (wavelength) sensitivity is the deviation of the incident reading beam angle $\Delta\theta$ (wavelength $\Delta\lambda_0$) from the Bragg angle (wavelength), which gives the first zero in diffraction efficiency. In the unslanted transmission geometry (see Fig. 8), $\Delta\theta$ and $\Delta\lambda_0$ are approximately given by

$$\Delta\theta = \frac{\lambda_0}{2nL \sin\theta}, \tag{6}$$

$$\Delta\lambda_0 = \frac{\lambda_0^2 \cos\theta}{2nL \sin^2\theta}. \tag{7}$$

High angular selectivity (i.e., small $\Delta\theta$) is useful for multiple storage. Recording and fixing of 511 simple gratings superimposed in a 0.02% Fe-doped lithium niobate crystal with a diffraction efficiency ranging from 2.5% for the last grating to 25% for the first grating (due to overcompensation in exposure) was reported by Staebler (1975). Recently, Mok, Tackitt, and Stoll (1991) have demonstrated the storage of 500 angularly multiplexed holograms of gray-scale images in a 0.015% Fe-doped lithium niobate crystal with an internal angular sensitivity (i.e., angle measured inside the material) of about 0.01 deg and with a fairly uniform diffraction efficiency of about 0.01 ± 0.001%. Multiple recording of eight simple gratings using angular multiplexing in a lithium niobate crystal and sequential read-out using a tunable dye laser has also been demonstrated by Wu *et al.* (1990).

3.1.2 Steady-State Index Modulation

The steady-state value of the amplitude of the index modulation (Δn_s) in a photo-refractive crystal is given by (Kukhtarev *et al.* 1979a)

$$\Delta n_s = \frac{1}{2} n^3 r_{\text{eff}} E_{sc}, \tag{8}$$

where n is the average linear index of refraction, r_{eff} is the effective electro-optic coefficient, and E_{sc} is the space-charge field. For the simplest case without an externally applied field and in the absence of the photovoltaic effect, the space-charge field E_{sc} can be expressed as

$$E_{sc} = \frac{imE_D}{1 + (E_D/E_Q)}, \tag{9}$$

where the imaginary unit i reveals the $\pi/2$ phase shift of the index grating with respect to the intensity fringes for the case of diffusion-dominant charge transport, m is the modulation of the intensity fringes, and the diffusion field E_D and the charge-limited field E_Q are given by

$$E_D = \frac{2\pi k_B T}{e\Lambda} = 1.6 \left[\frac{\text{kV}}{\text{cm}}\mu\text{m}\right]/\Lambda \tag{10}$$

$$E_Q = \frac{2\Lambda e N_A}{\epsilon} = 2.8 \times 10^{-14} \left[\frac{\text{kV/cm}}{\mu\text{m}}\text{cm}^3\right]\left(\frac{N_A}{\epsilon}\Lambda\right). \tag{11}$$

In Eqs. (10) and (11), k_B is the Boltzmann constant, e is the electronic charge, T is the temperature, Λ is the grating spacing, ϵ is the static dielectric permittivity, and N_A is the trap density. We have assumed that the donor density N_D is much larger than the trap density (i.e., $N_D \gg N_A$) so that the total charge available for contribution to the space-charge field is ultimately limited by the number of traps.

In this simple case, the space-charge field peaks at an optimum grating spacing Λ_0 with a numerical value of

$$\Lambda_0 \; [\mu m] = \frac{0.75 \times 10^7 \; \mu m \; cm^{-3/2}}{(N_A/\epsilon)^{1/2}}, \tag{12}$$

and the maximum value of the space-charge field E_{max} as limited by the trap density is given by

$$E_{max} \; [kV/cm] = 1.06 \times 10^7 \; kV \; cm^{1/2} \; (N_A/\epsilon)^{1/2}. \tag{13}$$

Because the value of N_A/ϵ is typically around 10^{14} to 10^{15} cm^{-3}, the maximum space-charge field E_{max} achievable without an externally applied field and in the absence of the photovoltaic effect is of the order of a few kilovolts per centimeter. The corresponding values of Δn_s, as given by Eq. (8), range from 10^{-3} to 10^{-6} for different photorefractive materials. The magnitude of the space-charge field $|E_{sc}|$ as a function of the grating spacing Λ, as described by Eqs. (9), (10), and (11), is illustrated in Fig. 9 for the special case of $m = 1$, and $N_A/\epsilon = 1.0 \times 10^{14}$ cm^{-3}. In principle, Δn can be increased by applying an external electric field to reach the saturation condition of $E_{sp} = E_Q$. Very high diffraction efficiency

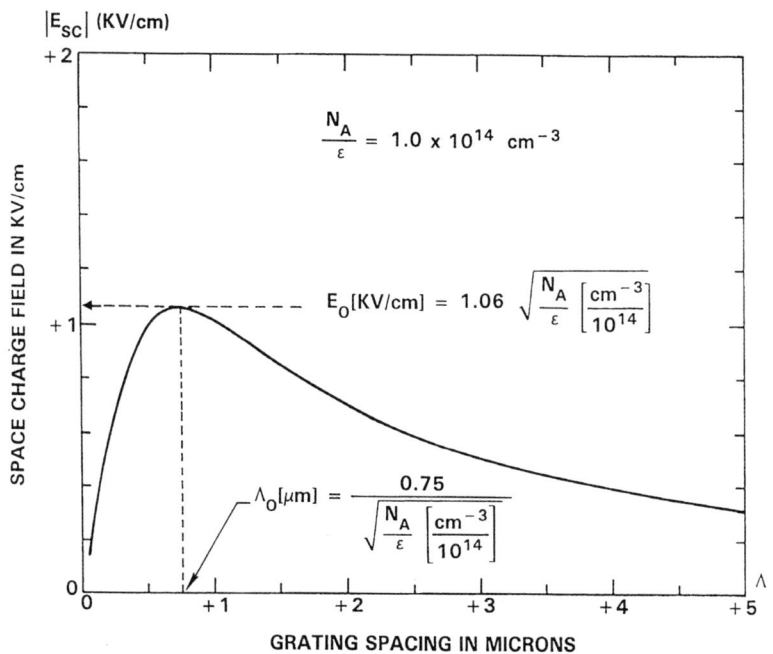

Figure 9. Dependence of the magnitude of the space-charge field on the grating spacing: a theoretical curve from a simple model.

(~95%) at an optimum grating spacing of 20 μm has been achieved in bismuth germanium oxide (BGO) with an external field of 12 kV/cm (Herriau et al. 1987).

3.1.3 Photorefractive Sensitivity

The photorefractive sensitivity S is defined as the refractive index change Δn per unit energy density absorbed:

$$S = \frac{\Delta n}{\alpha I_0 \tau}, \qquad (14)$$

where α is the linear absorption coefficient, I_0 is the input intensity, and τ is the response time. This definition allows comparison of different materials with a wide range of absorption coefficients and response times. Typical values of photorefractive sensitivity for some selected materials are listed in Table 1.

3.1.4 Storage Capacity

Holographic information storage by means of a volume phase hologram is of particular interest because of its extremely large storage capacity. The theoretical limit for optimal storage with wavelength λ is believed to be 1 bit per λ^2 area in a two-dimensional medium and 1 bit per λ^3 volume in three dimensions (Heerden 1963). The upper limit for storage density in three dimensions is therefore

$$C_{3D} = \frac{n^3}{\lambda^3}, \qquad (15)$$

where n is the background index of refraction of the medium. Equation (15) sets an upper limit for a storage density of about 9×10^{13} cm^{-3} for lithium niobate ($n = 2.27$) at 514.5 nm. In practice, the storage density is expected to be much lower than the theoretical limit given by Eq. (15) due to other practical limitations (Blotekjaer 1979; Gu et al. 1993; Lee 1988; Ramberg 1972). For either wavelength multiplexing or angular multiplexing, the number of holograms that can be multiplexed in the same volume is limited by the dynamic range of the amplitude

Table 1. Photorefractive Sensitivity (cm³/J) of Selected Photorefractive Materials

LiNbO₃	10^{-5} to 10^{-4}
KNbO₃:Fe	10^{-5} to 10^{-4}
KTN	10^{-1}
SBN:Ce	10^{-3} to 10^{-2}
InP:Fe	10^{-2}
GaAs:Cr	10^{-2}
CdTe	10^{-1}

of the index modulation. For example, if we assume that the minimum diffraction efficiency η_{min} required to achieve a reasonable signal-to-noise ratio (SNR) in the detection process is of the order of 10^{-5}, the corresponding grating parameter ψ_{min} calculated from Eq. (4) for the lossless case gives

$$\phi_{min} = \sin^{-1}(\sqrt{\eta_{min}}) \approx \sqrt{\eta_{min}} = 3.2 \times 10^{-3}. \qquad (16)$$

Taking the reported value ($\psi = 5\pi/2$) (Hong *et al.* 1990) as the maximum grating parameter ψ_{max} achievable from a 4-mm crystal, we can estimate the maximum number M of superimposed holograms per unit thickness t of the recording medium as

$$M = \frac{\psi_{max}}{\psi_{min} t} \approx 5 \times 10^2 \text{ mm}^{-1}. \qquad (17)$$

In a photorefractive crystal, the exposure of a new hologram partially erases previously recorded holograms. In general, it is desirable that all the multiplexed holograms exhibit equal diffraction efficiency. In a sequential recording scheme, the requirement of uniform diffraction efficiency modifies the expression for the number M given in Eq. (17) to (Psaltis, Gu, and Brady 1988)

$$M = \frac{\tau_e \psi_{max}}{\tau_w \psi_{min} t}, \qquad (18)$$

where τ_e and τ_w are the time constants associated with erasure and writing, respectively. Equation (18) agrees with the intuition that if we erase slowly, we can store more holograms. Interestingly, the estimated value given in Eq. (17) is about an order of magnitude higher than the experimental values reported independently by Staebler (1975) and Mok, Tackitt, and Stoll (1991); i.e., ~500 holograms in a 1-cm-thick lithium niobate crystal. The corresponding value of τ_w/τ_e is estimated to be 1.05 (Mok, Tackitt, and Stoll 1991).

Factors that may limit the storage capacity of a volume recording medium, including optical aperture effect, detector noise, *xy* addressing at the hologram plane by beam deflection, dynamic range, angular selectivity, and granularity of the recording medium, have been discussed by Gaylord (1979).

3.1.5 Resolution

The spatial resolution of a photorefractive volume hologram is fundamentally limited by the available charge density. For a typical experimental configuration, illustrated in Fig. 10, the plane of incidence containing the writing beams is approximately horizontal and the grating wave vector K is essentially along the horizontal x direction. The resolution along the x direction is therefore constrained by the grating spacing whose optimum value is dictated by the trap density N_A

264   Arthur E. Chiou

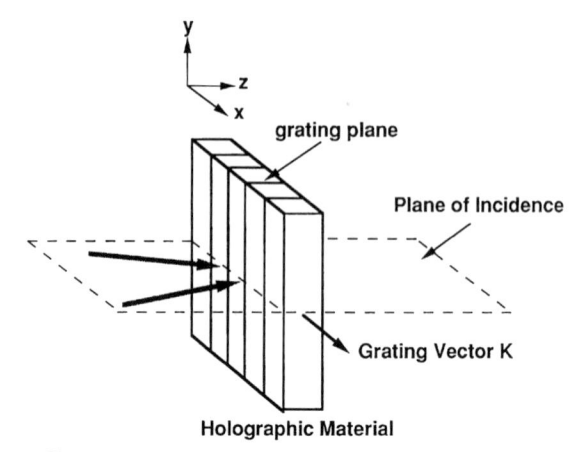

Figure 10. A typical geometry for holographic recording.

(for the trap-limiting case) as described by Eq. (12). If we assume that each smallest feature requires about five fundamental grating periods for acceptable diffraction efficiency, the horizontal resolution is approximately 5 μm for a typical grating period of 1 μm. In contrast, in the vertical direction, the resolution is limited solely by the fluctuation in trap density. For trap density of the order of 10^{17} cm^{-3}, the average distance between the traps is about 20 nm. Vertical resolution of the order of λ/n in the visible region is therefore feasible. The effect of the difference in horizontal and vertical resolutions requires further study.

3.1.6 Response Time

To the first approximation, the generation of a space-charge field in the photorefractive recording process (without an external electric field) can be regarded as the charging of a capacitor via optical excitation; the grating formation time τ is simply given by the well-known RC time constant of a capacitor

$$\tau = \frac{\epsilon \epsilon_0}{\sigma}, \tag{19}$$

where ϵ_0 is the free-space electric permittivity and ϵ is the static dielectric constant. The electric conductivity σ consists of two components, the dark conductivity σ_d and the photoconductivity σ_{ph}

$$\sigma = \sigma_d + \sigma_{ph} = \sigma_d + cI_0, \tag{20}$$

where the photoconductivity σ_{ph} is approximately proportional to the total intensity of the two writing beams ($I_0 = I_1 + I_2$).

Likewise, the storage time under dark conditions is given by the dielectric relaxation time ($\tau = \epsilon\epsilon_0/\sigma_d$). Typical storage times for some of the most common photorefractive materials and some relevant material parameters are listed in Table 2.

In the regime where $\sigma_{ph} \gg \sigma_d$, Eqs. (19) and (20) show that the hologram buildup time is inversely proportional to the total intensity of the recording beams. Although the photorefractive response time is typically very slow (approximately a few milliseconds to a few seconds at an optical intensity ~ 1 W/cm^2), recording of photorefractive holograms in BaTiO$_3$, using a single 30-ps pulse of 1 to 15 mJ/cm^2 at a wavelength of 0.53 μm, has been reported (Smirl et al. 1989). Other picosecond photorefractive effects have also been observed in GaAs (Valley et al. 1986), InP (Mao, Li, and Deng 1990), and CdTe (Petrovic et al. 1991).

Reading of the hologram will inevitably shorten the storage time due to the erasure effect caused by the second term in Eq. (20) where the total intensity of the writing beam I_0 should be replaced by that of the reading beam. The storage time in the presence of a read-out beam, however, can be much longer than the recording time by using a relatively weak reading beam or by using a different wavelength in the nonabsorbing spectral region of the material [i.e., by selecting a very small value for c in Eq. (20) for the reading beam]. Deviation (Klien 1988) from the simple model given by Eqs. (19) and (20) as well as the dependence of the response time on other parameters such as grating spacing, external electric field, and temperature have been studied and reported in the literature (Gunter 1982; Gunter and Huignard 1988; Valley and Klein 1983; Yeh 1987).

Photorefractive holograms can be fixed (Amodei and Staebler 1971; Bashaw et al. 1990; Delboulbe et al. 1989; Herriau and Huignard 1986; Kirillov and Fein-

Table 2. Dark Storage Time of Some Photorefractive Materials

	Dielectric Constant ε	Electron Mobility μ (cm^2/Vs)	Resistivity ρ (Ω cm)	ε/μ	Dark Carrier Density n_d (cm^{-3})	Dark Relaxation time τ_d (s)
KNBO$_3$	1000 50	0.5	10^{12} (10^9–10^{14})	2000 25	1.3 × 10^7	1 × 10^3
LiNbO$_3$	32	1	10^{15} (10^8–10^{19})	32	6.3 × 10^3	4 × 10^4
BaTiO$_3$	4300 1500	0.5	10^{12}	8600 3000	1.3 × 10^7	5 × 10^3 2 × 10^3
SBN:60	900 450	1	10^{12}	900 450	6.3 × 10^6	1 × 10^3 5 × 10^2
BSO	56	0.03	10^{15}	1.9 × 10^3	2.1 × 10^5	6 × 10^4
GaAs	12.9	8 × 10^3	10^8 (10^6–10^9)	1.6 × 10^{-3}	7.8 × 10^6	1.4 × 10^{-3}
InP	12.6	5 × 10^3	10^8 (10^6–10^9)	2.5 × 10^{-3}	1.3 × 10^7	1.4 × 10^{-3}
GaP	10.2	110	10^8 (10^6–10^9)	1.0 × 10^{-1}	5.7 × 10^8	1.1 × 10^{-3}
CdTe	9.4	10^3	10^8 (10^6–10^9)	9.4 × 10^{-3}	6.3 × 10^7	1.0 × 10^{-3}

berg 1991; Leyva, Agranat, and Yariv 1991; Micheron and Bismuth 1972) via electrical or thermal control to eliminate the unwanted erasure during read-out. Both methods are based on a transformation of the electronic space-charge distribution into an ionic-charge distribution, which is stable at room temperature under the illumination of the reading beams.

3.2 Photorefractive Two-Wave Mixing

When two mutually coherent beams interact inside a photorefractive crystal, non-reciprocal energy transfer takes place between the two interacting beams. This phenomenon is referred to as *photorefractive two-wave mixing* (or two-beam coupling) (Kukhtarev *et al.* 1979b). The energy transfer can be explained qualitatively by the self-diffraction of both beams by the grating written by themselves. Since the photorefractive grating is phase-shifted by $\pi/2$ (for the case of diffusion-dominant charge transport) with respect to the interference fringes, the diffracted component of one of the beams is in phase with the transmitted component of the other in one output port, resulting in a constructive interference with the output amplitude being the sum of the two components (Fig. 11). In the other port, the two components are opposite in phase, resulting in a destructive interference, which produces a transmitted beam with decreased amplitude. As a net result, one beam gains energy at the expense of the other. Photorefractive coherent amplifiers have found a wide range of applications including image amplification, logic operation, defect detection, laser beam steering, and energy-efficient optical interconnection.

Another unique property of photorefractive two-wave mixing is that the energy transfer takes place with virtually no phase crosstalk. This can be explained by the phase cancellation effect in the diffraction from self-induced dynamic grating. This unique property (energy transfer without phase crosstalk) has the potential of being used for laser beam cleanup (Chiou and Yeh 1985).

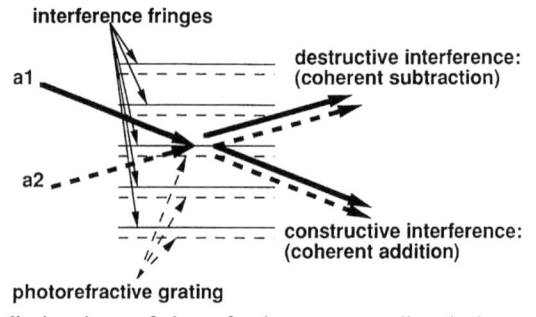

Figure 11. A qualitative picture of photorefractive energy coupling via the constructive (destructive) interference of the transmitted and diffractive components of the two interacting beams.

Energy coupling in two-wave mixing can be described by the following coupled-wave equations (Yeh 1989)

$$\frac{dI_1}{dz} = -\Gamma\frac{I_1 I_2}{I_1 + I_2} - \alpha I_1, \tag{21}$$

$$\frac{dI_2}{dz} = \Gamma\frac{I_1 I_2}{I_1 + I_2} - \alpha I_2, \tag{22}$$

where I_1 and I_2 denote the input intensity of two beams, α is the linear absorption coefficient, and the coupling constant Γ is given by

$$\Gamma = \frac{2\pi \Delta n}{\lambda m \cos\theta} \sin\phi, \tag{23}$$

In Eq. (23), λ is the free-space wavelength, 2θ is the full angle between the two beams inside the crystals, Δn is the amplitude of the index modulation (see equation), and ϕ is the grating phase shift (relative to the interference fringes). The values of Γ for various photorefractive materials and under different experimental conditions span over a range of about two decades from a fraction of a cm^{-1} to about 10^2 cm^{-1}.

The intensity (I_1' and I_2') of the two output beams can be calculated by solving the coupled equations with appropriate boundary conditions and can be expressed as

$$I_1' = \frac{I_1(0) + I_2(0)}{I_1(0) + I_2(0)\exp(\Gamma L)} I_1(0) \exp[-(\Gamma + \alpha)L], \tag{24}$$

$$I_2' = \frac{I_1(0) + I_2(0)}{I_1(0) + I_2(0)\exp(\Gamma L)} I_2(0) \exp[(\Gamma - \alpha)L], \tag{25}$$

In the example given here, energy is transferred from beam 1 (referred to as the *pump beam*) to beam 2 (referred to as the *signal beam*). A net gain is achieved provided that $(\Gamma - \alpha) > 0$. For the case of codirectional two-wave mixing, a photorefractive gain (g), independent of the absorption coefficient α, can be defined as

$$\begin{aligned} g &= \frac{\text{signal output with pump beam on}}{\text{signal output with pump beam off}} \\ &= \frac{[I_1(0) + I_2(0)]\exp(\Gamma L)}{I_1(0) + I_2(0)\exp(\Gamma L)} \\ &= \frac{(r + 1)\exp(\Gamma L)}{r + \exp(\Gamma L)}, \end{aligned} \tag{26}$$

where $r = I_1(0)/I_2(0)$ is the input pump-to-signal intensity ratio. In the special case where the conditions $[r \gg \exp(GL)$, and $r \gg 1]$ are satisfied, the gain g

becomes an exponential function of the interaction length L [i.e., $g = \exp(\Gamma L)$]. Image amplification with a gain of about 20,000 has been demonstrated (Yeh et al. 1989).

3.3 Optical Phase Conjugation in Photorefractive Materials

Optical phase conjugation (Fisher 1983; Yariv 1978) is a nonlinear optical technique to reverse the spatial phase (or wavefront) of an optical beam. The phase-conjugate beam retraces its original path faithfully in a time-reversed manner as if the propagation history of the beam was recorded and played back in a reversed order. The example on holographic recording for optical interconnection given in Section 1 (see Fig. 2) can be viewed as an example of generating phase-conjugate beams using a conventional holographic technique. One of the key advantages of nonlinear optical methods is the realization of real-time operation, which cannot be achieved by conventional holographic techniques. Photorefractive materials such as barium titanate and strontium niobate are among the most sensitive materials to date to perform optical phase conjugation using a relatively low-power laser beam (approximately a few milliwatts) (Feinberg 1983b; Feinberg and MacDonald 1989). Many different configurations for phase conjugation in photorefractive materials have been proposed or demonstrated for optical interconnection applications. They can be grouped into the following three categories: (1) four-wave mixing, (2) self-pumped phase conjugation, and (3) mutually pumped phase conjugation.

3.3.1 Photorefractive Phase Conjugation by Means of Four-Wave Mixing

Of the many methods used to achieve phase conjugation, degenerate four-wave mixing (DFWM), first proposed by Hellwarth (1977) and demonstrated by Jensen and Hellwarth (1978), has been demonstrated in numerous nonlinear optical materials including photorefractive materials. In photorefractive four-wave mixing (Feinberg and Hellwarth 1980), two counterpropagating pumping beams interact with a probe beam to generate an output that is the phase-conjugate replica of one of the pumping beams (Fig. 12). The process can be regarded as the recording of a hologram by the probe beam and one of the pumping beams, and the simulta-

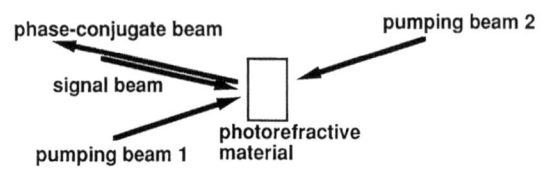

Figure 12. A schematic illustration of optical phase conjugation via photorefractive four-wave mixing.

neous read-out of the hologram by the other. Because of the counterpropagating geometry, the phase-matching condition is satisfied over a wide field of view. By proper selection of the intensity and the geometry of the three input beams, phase conjugation with a reflectivity larger than unity (i.e., phase conjugation with optical gain) can be achieved over a wide range of geometries and beam intensities. Having three input ports that allow independent spatial modulation in each input beams also facilitates its applications for image processing and optical computing such as real-time convolution and correlation (White and Yariv 1980), logic operations (Li *et al.* 1988), matrix-vector (Yeh and Chiou 1987) and matrix-matrix multiplications (Chiou, Khoshnevisan, and Yeh 1988), quadratic processing (Henderson, Walkup, and Bochove 1989), and interconnection (Ford, Bittner, and Lee 1989).

3.3.2 Self-Pumped Phase Conjugation

The strong beam-coupling coefficient due to the extremely large electro-optic coefficient in photorefractive materials such as $BaTiO_3$ and SBN gives rise to a unique phase-conjugate mirror that requires only one input beam. In contrast to the FWM process described above, a self-pumped phase conjugator (SPPC) (Feinberg and MacDonald 1989) generates the phase-conjugate replica of a single input beam via the combination of amplified scattering (in the volume) and some form of optical feedback. The optical feedback can be provided either by one or more external mirrors [Figs. 13(a), (b), and (c)] (Cronin-Golomb *et al.* 1983; White *et al.* 1982) or by the total internal reflection at the crystal-air interfaces [Fig. 13(d)]. The configuration of Fig. 13(d), known as the *CAT conjugator* (Fein-

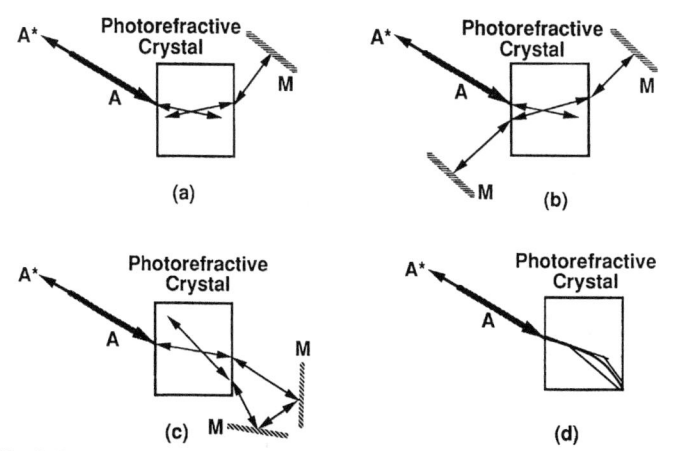

Figure 13. Self-pumped phase conjugation involving optical feedback via (a), (b), and (c) one or more external mirrors; (d) total internal reflection at the crystal-air interfaces.

Photorefractive Crystal

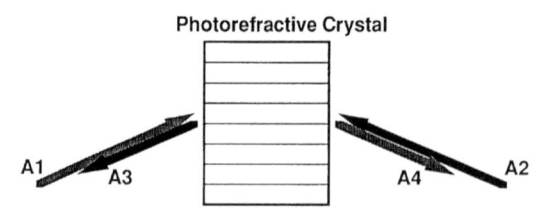

Figure 14. A schematic illustration of a mutually pumped phase conjugator.

berg 1982b), has become one of the most popular phase conjugators mainly because of its user-friendliness (simplicity), wide field of view, and very high fidelity. It can simultaneously phase conjugate more than one image-bearing beam with very little spatial crosstalk (Feinberg 1983a). A CAT conjugator with a strong (~10 to 100 mW) self-pumping Gaussian beam can be used to phase conjugate other image-bearing beams via four-wave mixing. As the counterpropagating pumping beams required for four-wave mixing are self-generated from the strong Gaussian beam, they are self-aligned and perfectly phase-matched to each other. This mode of operation is extremely attractive because of its fast speed, very large dynamic range, and very wide field of view (Chiou, Chang, and Khoshnevisan 1990).

3.3.3 Mutually Pumped Phase Conjugators

Mutually pumped phase conjugators (MPPCs) (Ewbank 1988; Fischer, Sternklar, and Weiss 1989; Smout and Eason 1987), also known as double phase-conjugate mirrors, or DPCMs, that use photorefractive materials represent another very interesting class of phase-conjugate devices with unique properties. In this case, two input beams incident on the opposite faces of a photorefractive crystal such as $BaTiO_3$ result in the phase conjugation of each beam (Fig. 14). The two beams can carry different spatial images and can be of different wavelengths (Fischer and Sternklar 1987; Sternklar and Fischer 1987). In this process, each beam writes its own grating by interacting with its scattered offsprings and erases the grating written by the other. Such competition causes the self-generation of a common grating shared by both beams in which read-out of the grating by one input represents the phase-conjugate replica of the other.

4. Interconnections Based on Passive Holographic Storage in Photorefractive Media

Holographic recording and subsequent read-out can be used to establish a massive interconnection network between an array of sources in an input plane to an array of detectors in an output plane. As discussed in Section 3.1, volume phase holograms are ideal for multiple storage because of their high diffraction efficiency, large storage capacity, and high Bragg selectivity. The dynamic and adaptive nature of photorefractive holograms makes them particularly attractive for reconfigurable interconnection in neural network applications. In this section, optical interconnection schemes based on passive holographic storage where photorefractive gain does not play an essential role are reviewed briefly.

4.1 Photorefractive Beam Steering

Any beam steering technique that directs a beam from a source to a designated detector establishes a point-to-point interconnection. The basic idea of photorefractive beam steering is illustrated in Fig. 15 in which an incident (reading) beam is diffracted by a photorefractive grating written by two mutually coherent writing beams (Henshaw 1984). The diffraction efficiency can approach 100% provided that the Bragg condition is satisfied (see Section 3.1.1). The dynamic nature of photorefractive holograms allows one to modify the holograms by changing the direction or wavelength (or both) of the writing beams. The writing of a new hologram automatically erases the old one previously recorded at the same location. A reading beam diffracting off the new holograms will be directed to different directions dictated by the orientation of the grating. In general, the reading beam and the writing beam can be of different wavelength. Writing with visible light where the photorefractive materials are highly sensitive (see Table 1) and simultaneous reading with Bragg-matched infrared beams have several advantages. Negligible infrared absorption in photorefractive material such as barium titanate or strontium barium niobate results in a higher diffraction efficiency and nearly nondestructive read-out. By means of a $Bi_{12}SiO_{20}$ crystal in an experimental configuration slightly different from that shown in Fig. 15, Herriau *et al.* (1986) have demonstrated a two-dimensional beam steering scheme of about 7 deg × 4 deg by moving one of the writing beams out of the original plane of incidence. A slightly different method was proposed and demonstrated by Wu

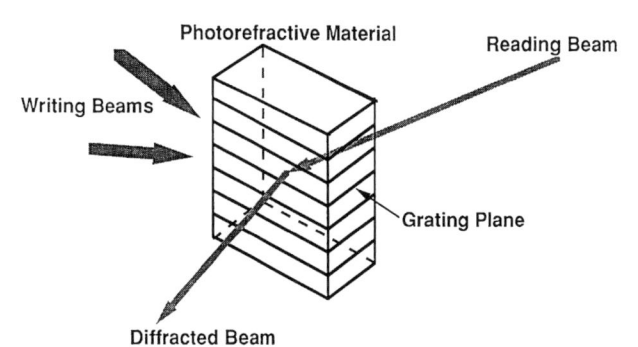

Figure 15. A schematic illustration of photorefractive beam steering.

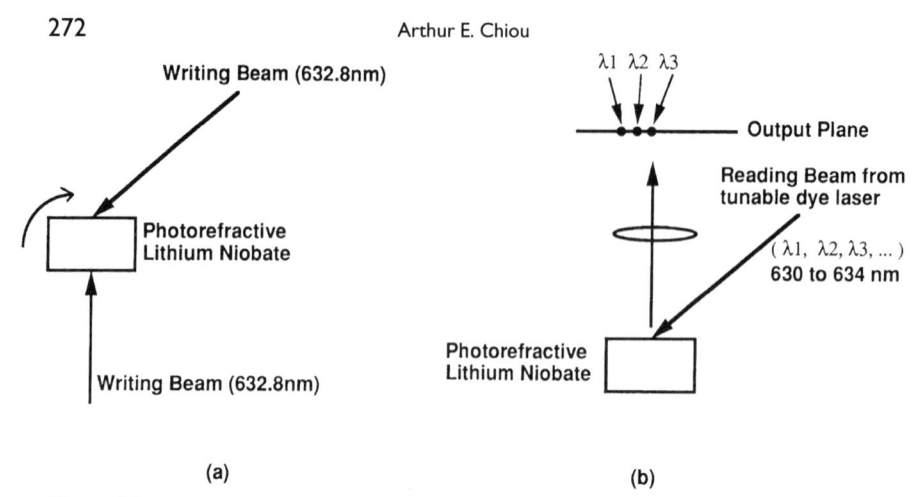

Figure 16. (a) Recording of angular multiplexed holograms and (b) selective read-out by wavelength tuning of the reading beam (adapted from Wu et al. 1990).

et al. (1990). In their demonstration, eight angularly multiplexed holograms were sequentially recorded in a lithium niobate crystal using a pair of mutually coherent 632.8-nm HeNe laser beams by rotating the crystal with an 0.8-deg step [Fig. 16(a)]. When the superimposed holograms are interrogated by a tunable dye laser (tuned from 630 to 634 nm), the diffracted (Bragg-matched) output from each grating appears sequentially along a line at the output plane as illustrated in Fig. 16(b).

The photorefractive beam steering methods described above can be viewed as *opto-optical Bragg cells* similar to beam steering that makes use of acousto-optic Bragg cells. Both can be used to connect a modulated source to a designated detector by diffracting the beam to the desirable direction.

4.2 Programmable Optical Interconnection by Means of Multiplexed Holograms

Programmable optical interconnection (Ford, Lee, and Fainman 1990) represents an attractive alternative for the more general and flexible reconfigurable optical interconnect networks for applications where the necessary interconnection can be predicted in advance. In this approach, all the interconnection patterns are prerecorded in some storage device and are selectively retrieved as required by the system. The reconfiguration rate is therefore limited only by the access time for the prestored patterns. Volume phase holograms offer large storage capacity and the potential for massively parallel fast retrieval (i.e., short access time) via any one of the multiplexing schemes such as wavelength multiplexing, spatial multiplexing, angular multiplexing, or their combinations. The possibility of *in situ* recording and fixing of holograms in photorefractive materials eases the problem associated with alignment. The technical challenges in this approach are (1) to maximize the number of interconnection holograms than can be superimposed with uniform (Brady, Hsu, and Psaltis 1990; Strasser et al. 1989; Taketomi et al. 1991) and sufficiently high diffraction efficiency and (2) to minimize the crosstalk noise (Gu et al. 1993; Shamir, Caulfield, and Johnson 1989). Because the recording of hundreds of holograms in a volume storage medium (using any one of the known or proposed multiplexing schemes) is very time-consuming, a third challenge is to be able to fix and duplicate the complete memory in one step (Piazzolla, Jenkins, and Tanguay 1991). Research activities addressing these important issues are critical to the advancement of this technology.

4.3 Parallel N^4 Weighted Optical Interconnections

Optical neural networks (Caulfield, Kinser, and Rogers 1989; Psaltis et al. 1990) typically require weighted global interconnection of two-dimensional arrays of neurons. Such an interconnection (of arrays of N^2 neurons) is formally equivalent to a tensor-matrix multiplication [see Eq. (2)] and therefore requires N^4 degrees of freedom. Without the aid of an additional degree of freedom (such as wavelength or phase), the N^3 degrees of freedom in a volume holographic medium can provide no more than N-to-N^2 or, $N^{3/2}$-to-$N^{3/2}$ interconnections (Psaltis, Gu, and Brady 1988). In other words, the total number of links cannot be greater than the total number of resolution cells (or degrees of freedom) in a given recording volume. If this criterion is violated, an attempt to establish the link between one pair of input and output points automatically generates the links for other pairs as well. A fractal sampling grid that selects $N^{3/2}$ points out of the N^2 points in the input and output planes to avoid this degeneracy problem has been proposed and demonstrated (Psaltis, Gu, and Brady 1988).

In the example given in Section 1 (Fig. 2), tensor-matrix multiplication was achieved at the cost of a large cross-sectional area required to accommodate the extra degree of freedom. By means of spectral hole-burning materials (Wild et al. 1990) and with wavelength as an additional parameter, the four-dimensional weight matrix can be implemented, in principle, in a compact three-dimensional volume. The implementation, however, requires cryogenic temperatures to achieve sufficiently narrow homogeneous linewidth.

5. Interconnections Based on Photorefractive Energy Coupling

The unique property of photorefractive beam coupling in which energy is transferred unidirectionally from one beam to the others can be used to implement an optical crossbar network with high energy efficiency. The photorefractive beam steering technique (Fig. 17) originally proposed and demonstrated by Rak, Le-

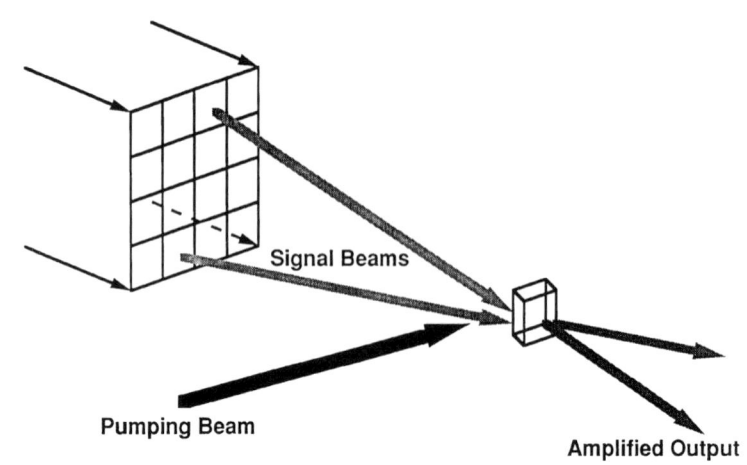

Figure 17. Optical beam steering based on photorefractive energy coupling.

doux, and Huignard (1984) can be viewed as a reconfigurable one-to-many interconnection. In this approach, a small fraction of the output from a laser beam is expanded to illuminate a two-dimensional SLM (a 2-D array of optical shutters). The beam components selected by the SLM (the signal beams) are allowed to interact with the main beam (referred to as the *pumping beam* in Fig. 17) inside a photorefractive crystal. Under appropriate conditions, the majority of the energy from the pumping beam can be transferred and equally distributed to the signal beams. The net result is a one-to-many reconfigurable interconnection network linking the source to the designated detectors with a high energy efficiency. Reconfiguration is accomplished by changing the pattern on the SLM. The dynamic and adaptive nature of the photorefractive hologram is responsible for the reconfigurability. A new hologram is formed and the old one is erased whenever the pattern on the SLM changes. The high energy efficiency is a consequence of the efficient energy transfer in photorefractive beam coupling, which allows a large fraction of the beam energy to bypass the inherent fan-out loss imposed by the SLM and a redistribution of the reserved energy to the designated channels in a later stage. With some modifications, this basic principle can be applied to an $N \times N$ crossbar switch, which is discussed in the following section.

5.1 Energy Efficient $N \times N$ Crossbar Network

As mentioned in Section 2, the $N \times N$ reconfigurable optical interconnection based on matrix-vector multiplication suffers from an intrinsic $1/N$ fan-out loss, which limits the maximum number of parallel channels N to no more than a few tens. One way to compensate for the fan-out loss is to use an array of semiconductor optical amplifiers or fiber optical amplifiers to provide sufficient gain. Another simple technique to circumvent the intrinsic fan-out loss is to use the efficient energy transfer in photorefractive wave-mixing similar to the beam steering technique described in the previous section.

5.1.1 Basic Principle

The basic principle of an energy-efficient photorefractive crossbar network (Yeh, Chiou, and Hong 1988) is illustrated in Fig. 18 for a 4 × 4 geometry. A beamsplitter (BS) is used to reflect a small fraction of the optical energy from the source array (V) to the signal arm where the output from each individual source is fanned out (via anamorphic optics) and is directed to a corresponding column of windows on an SLM. In contrast with the conventional approach illustrated in Fig. 5, the signal beams transmitted by the SLM are recombined in a photorefractive crystal with the pump beams transmitted by the beamsplitter prior to fanning-in to a detector array. Under proper conditions, efficient energy transfer from the pump to the signal beams takes place in the crystal due to photorefractive two-beam coupling. The transferred energy is equally distributed to the designated detectors prescribed by the interconnection pattern on the SLM.

For an $N \times N$ crossbar network incorporating a photorefractive crystal with coupling strength ΓL in conjunction with a SLM with transmittance t, the merit of the photorefractive approach is overwhelming when $t/N \ll 1$ and $[\exp(\Gamma L)](t/N) \gg 1$. In this most favorable regime (i.e., large fan-out and extremely strong coupling strength), the optimum beamsplitting ratio R and the maximum energy efficiency can be shown to be given by (Chiou and Yeh 1992a)

$$R_0 = \frac{1}{\{[\exp(\Gamma L)]t/N\}^{1/2}} \tag{27}$$

and

$$E_{max} = \exp(-\alpha L). \tag{28}$$

In this extreme case, only a very small fraction of the available energy is reflected into the signal arm. The maximum energy efficiency, which is limited only by the loss encountered in the photorefractive crystal, is independent of all the other experimental parameters! In practice, however, when the photorefractive gain is extremely high, additional measures may be required to reduce the noise (Joseph, Pillai, and Singh 1991; Rabinovich, Feldman, and Gilbreath 1991; Rajbenbach, Delboulbe, and Huignard 1989) due to stimulated scattering commonly known as *beam fanning* (Feinberg 1982a).

5.1.2 Crosstalk Noise Due to Nonuniform Amplification

To achieve maximum energy efficiency, it is important that the signal beam and corresponding pump beam overlap completely independently of the interconnection pattern selected by the SLM. This is accomplished by placing the SLM at the front focal plane of a Fourier transform lens with the photorefractive material at

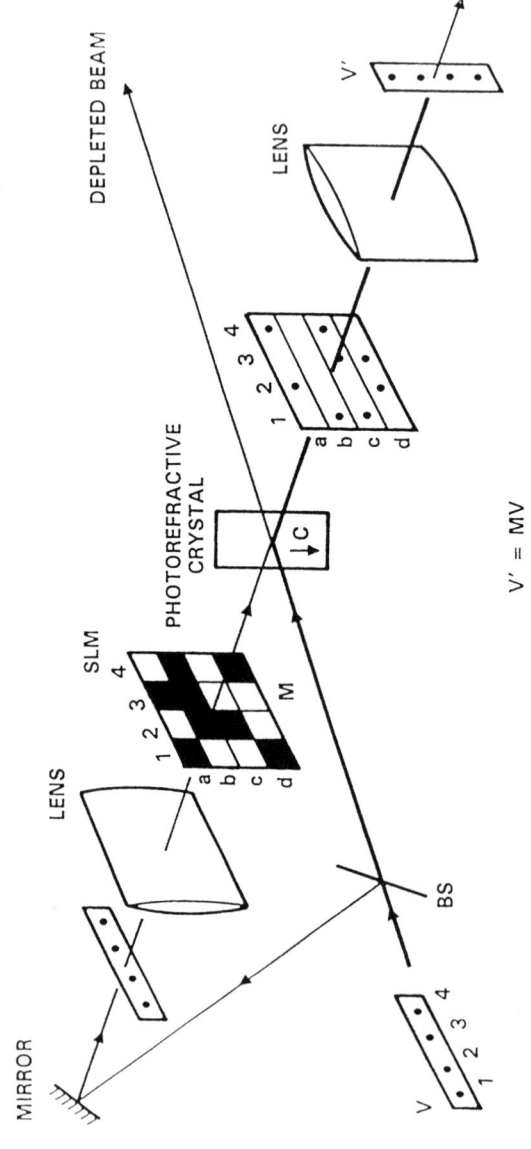

Figure 18. An energy-efficient optical crossbar network using photorefractive energy coupling (after Yeh, Chiou, and Hong 1988).

$V' = MV$

the back focal plane (Fig. 19) (Chiou and Yeh 1990). For one-to-one interconnection (or permutation), the shift invariance property of Fourier transformation ensures maximum beam overlap of any selected signal beam and the corresponding pumping beam inside the crystal. For one-to-many interconnection, more than one window in a column of the SLM will be switched "on." The Fourier transform of a column of the signal beam consists of a linear superposition of identical patterns, each with a different phase factor, which is dictated by the relative positions of the windows. As a consequence, the resulting intensity distribution of the signal beam consists of interference fringes at the Fourier plane. Nonuniform amplification in photorefractive two-wave mixing involving these interference structures in the Fourier domain can generate undesirable crosstalk noise at the output plane. This crosstalk noise can be minimized by moving the crystal slightly away from the exact Fourier plane (Gru, Chiou, and Hong 1993).

5.1.3 Reconfiguration Speed

A major drawback of this approach is the relatively slow reconfiguration time (~1 s), which is limited by the grating formation (and erasure) time of the photorefractive hologram at low optical intensity (~100 mW/cm²). In principle, the response time can be reduced by increasing the signal beam power since the photorefractive response time is approximately proportional to $1/I^x$, where I is the total beam intensity and the exponent x can range from 0.4 to 1 depending on the specific material. Photorefractive grating formation in barium titanate crystal on a time scale of the order of 100 ps using 43-ps pulses (~10 mJ/cm²) has been reported (Smith et al. 1987). The use of high-power signal sources for reconfigurable interconnects may be undesirable because of various constraints imposed by,

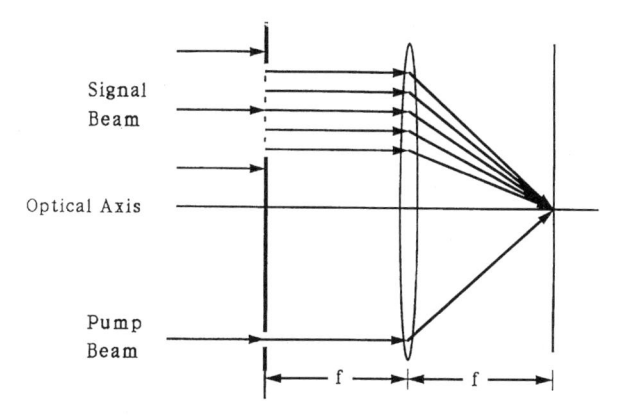

Figure 19. Overlap of the pump and the signal beams due to the shift-invariant property of the Fourier transform (after Chiou and Yeh 1990).

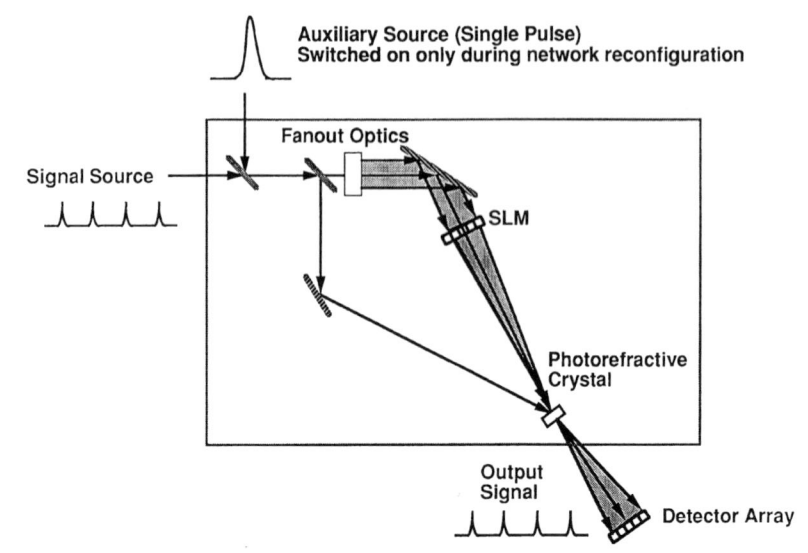

Figure 20. Schematic illustration of a photorefractive optical interconnection with a high-speed reconfiguration (after Chiou and Yeh 1992b).

for example, the data rate, duty cycle, and heat dissipation rate. A separate source, however, can be incorporated into a photorefractive reconfigurable interconnect (Fig. 20) to generate an auxiliary pulse, which is flashed momentarily only when reconfiguration is desired. Such an arrangement can, in principle, reduce the reconfiguration time by several orders of magnitude. Preliminary experimental results demonstrating the reduction in reconfiguration time are shown in Fig. 21 (Chiou and Yeh 1992b). The two oscillographs at the top show the long switching time (~6 s) without the aid of the auxiliary pulse. When the auxiliary pulse is turned on (for 500 ms) simultaneous to the switching of the SLM window, the

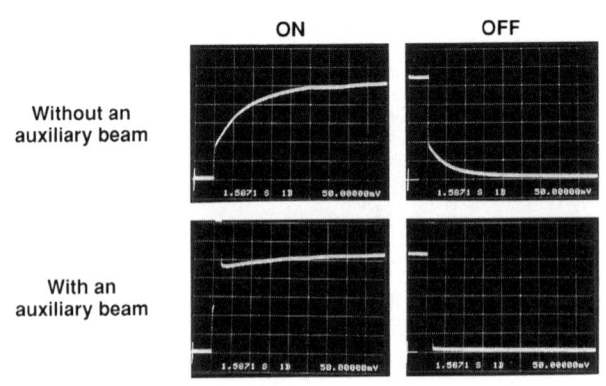

Figure 21. Preliminary experimental results demonstrating a high-speed reconfiguration (after Chiou and Yeh, 1992b).

switching time (for both on and off) is reduced to ~500 ms as shown in the lower oscillographs. Based on the response time of a fast barium titanate crystal reported recently (Garrett *et al.* 1992), we estimate that the reconfiguration time of the order of a millisecond or less should be feasible using an auxiliary nanosecond pulse of sub-mJ/cm^2.

6. Interconnections Based on Photorefractive Phase Conjugation

Optical phase conjugation offers high-resolution lensless imaging with unique features such as self-aligning and aberration correction. These attributes are critical to the implementation of optical networks linking a high density of sources and detectors. The three methods of phase conjugation using photorefractive materials discussed in Section 3.3, namely, four-wave mixing, self-pumped phase conjugation, and mutually pumped phase conjugation, have been applied to demonstrate different interconnection schemes.

6.1 Matrix-Tensor Multiplication Based on Four-Wave Mixing

Four-wave mixing geometry (see Fig. 12), which allows three independent input patterns, can be used to perform triple-products in real time. The phase conjugate output amplitude, under certain conditions, is proportional to the product of the three input amplitudes. Convolution and correlation of two-dimensional spatial patterns can be performed in real time when the photorefractive crystal is placed at the common Fourier transformed plane of the input images (White and Yariv 1980). Ford, Bittner, and Lee (1989) have shown that the correlation of a matrix (i.e., a two-dimensional spatial pattern) with a fourth rank tensor properly encoded into a two-dimensional format (see Fig. 6) contains the matrix-tensor product. An optical implementation using photorefractive four-wave mixing at the Fourier domain to perform the correlation was proposed, and a phase-code technique that can improve the output SNR at the cost of interconnection size and complexity was suggested and analyzed.

6.2 Interconnections Based on Self-Pumped Phase Conjugation

Since the first demonstration of the self-pumped phase conjugate mirror in the CAT configuration by Feinberg (1982b), simultaneous phase conjugation of more than one input has been studied for a wide range of applications including image subtraction (Chiou and Yeh 1986; Kwong, Rakuljuc, and Yariv 1985), novelty filters (Anderson and Feinberg 1989), and optical interconnections. For some input geometries, the two incident beams couple with each other inside the crystal via self-pumped phase conjugation, and the degree of coupling is very sensitive to the angular as well as the lateral position of the input beams. Sakamoto (1990) has demonstrated that the phase-conjugate output can be modulated by modulating the input beams, and that the output intensities depend on the duty cycles of the inputs in pulsed operation. This result is not surprising because for modulation rates much faster than the photorefractive response time, the crystal simply "sees" and responds to the average input intensity. A simple model of optical interconnection applied to neural networks based on simultaneous self-pumping of more than one inputs has been proposed. This approach, however, suffers from two major drawbacks: The number of inputs is likely to be limited to no more than a few, and control of the strength of connectivity is very difficult and slow.

A different approach for achieving global interconnection in optical neural networks based on a CAT conjugator at the Fourier plane (of an input image) has been proposed and demonstrated by Owechko and Soffer (1991). The global connectivity was demonstrated by first establishing a phase-conjugate image of a two-dimensional pattern (an array of random dots) and showed that the whole output pattern remains (for a short period ~ storage time) when the input was suddenly changed into one of the dots in the array. In other words, total recall of the original 2-D array of dots with partial input (one dot) was demonstrated. In addition, another experiment was carried out to demonstrate that the crosstalk caused by the conical Bragg degeneracy associated with a single volume grating can be greatly reduced by this approach because of the many angularly and spatially multiplexed gratings involved in a CAT conjugator. In the second experiment, a periodic 2-D array of dots in a square lattice was used as the input pattern. When the input was shifted laterally by half a period, the phase-conjugate output virtually disappeared and essentially recovered when the input was shifted by a whole period. In a subsequent paper, Dunning, Owechko, and Soffer (1991) demonstrated similar features (namely, global connectivity and reduction of crosstalk due to the conical Bragg degeneracy) using a mutually pumped phase conjugate mirror.

The claim that the conical Bragg degeneracy is removed due to multiplexed gratings in a CAT conjugator is true only for points along a horizontal line. In an experiment similar to the one described earlier, Chiou (1992) has demonstrated that when the periodic pattern was shifted vertically [instead of horizontally as was done by Owechko and Soffer (1991)] by half a period the phase-conjugate output did not disappear. For applications where many different holograms are superimposed, the interhologram crosstalk can be intolerable. The control of interconnection weight is also extremely difficult.

6.3 Interconnections Based on Mutually Pumped Phase Conjugation

Many different modes of operation and different aspects of dynamic optical interconnections based on MPPC have been proposed and demonstrated. As an example, a one-to-many interconnection that can be established by mutual phase conjugation of a signal source and a beacon source transmitting through a two-

Photorefractive Optical Interconnects 281

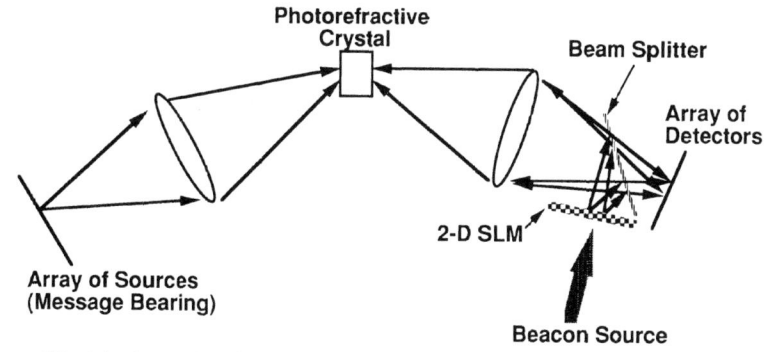

Figure 22. Adaptive optical interconnection by means of mutually pumped phase conjugation (adapted from Schamschula, Caulfield, and Verber 1991).

dimensional SLM is illustrated in Fig. 22 (Schamschula, Caulfield, and Verber 1991). A dynamically reprogrammable optical interconnect using temporally multiplexed writing beams in MPPC proposed by Cronin-Golomb (1989) to achieve arbitrary fan-out and fan-in is illustrated in Fig. 23. By cycling the lasers in the sequence (A1)–(B2, B4), (A2)–(B3), and (A3)–(B1), shown in Fig. 23(a), for example, the connections shown in Fig. 23(b) can be established when illuminated by A sources. A 2 × 2 interconnect of 488-nm beams using SBN was demonstrated and the problems of crosstalk and low energy efficiency associated with

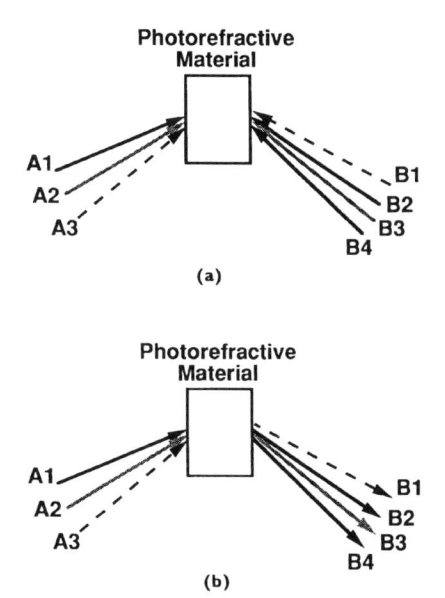

Figure 23. (a) Time-multiplexed recording of mutually pumped phase conjugating holograms for self-aligned interconnection with arbitrary fan-in and fan-out and (b) the resulting optical links (adapted from Cronin-Golomb 1989).

the coexistence of a large number of gratings were discussed. In addition to optical interconnection, an application for one-way imaging through thick optical distortions was also suggested.

In addition to the time-division multiplexing scheme described here, Weiss *et al.* (1988) have suggested the use of WDM and SDM in MPPC to achieve point-to-point interconnection, broadcasting, and crossbar switching.

7. Conclusion

In this chapter, various photorefractive phenomena have been described, including passive holographic storage, two-wave mixing, and phase conjugation, and their potential applications for optical interconnections have been reviewed. The key advantages of using photorefractive materials include their real-time adaptive nature, large storage capacity, high diffraction efficiency, and their unique property as a coherent amplifier or an efficient phase conjugate mirror at relatively low optical powers. Increasing applications of holographic techniques for one-to-many (fan-out) and many-to-one (fan-in) interconnections can be anticipated. Optical phase conjugation offers the additional advantages of self-alignment and aberration correction. For an $N \times N$ generalized crossbar network, however, crosstalk noise is a major issue that requires further study. In general, the relatively slow response time, nonlinear gain (or phase-conjugate reflectivity) with respect to input intensity, nonuniform gain with respect to input beam position and angle, and coherent noise introduced by these materials are some of the important issues that need to be overcome before photorefractive materials can be deployed into any practical systems. Evolutionary progress in many of these areas has taken place and will certainly continue.

Acknowledgement

I am grateful to John Hong, Pochi Yeh, Claire Gu, and other colleagues in the Optical Information Processing and the Applied Optics Departments at the Rockwell International Science Center for many discussions. My own research in photorefractive reconfigurable interconnection described in Section 5.1 was initiated by Pochi Yeh and has been supported by the Defense Advanced Research Projects Agency and Air Force Office of Scientific Research under contract F49620-90-C-0006.

References

Amodei, J. J., Phillips, W., and Staebler, D. L. (1971). *IEEE J. Quantum Electron.* **QE-7,** 321.
Amodei, J. J., and Staebler, D. L. (1971). *Appl. Phys. Lett.* **18,** 540–542.
Amodei, J. J., and Staebler, D. L. (1972). *RCA Rev.* **33,** 71–93.
Anderson, D. Z., and Feinberg, J. (1989). *IEEE J. Quantum. Electron.* **25,** 635–647.
Aronson, L. B., and Hesselink, L. (1990). *Opt. Lett.* **15,** 30–32.

Ashkin, A., Boyd, G. D., Dziedzic, J. M., Smith, R. G., Ballman, A. A., Levinstein, J. J., and Nassau, K. (1966). *Appl. Phys. Lett.* **9**, 72–74.
Bashaw, M. C., Ma, T.-P., Barker, R. C., Mroczkowski, S., and Dube, R. R. (1990). *Phys. Rev. B.* **42**, 5641–5648.
Berra, P. B., Ghafoor, A., Guizani, M., Marcinkowski, S., and Mitkas, P. A. (1989). *Proc. IEEE.* **77**, 1797–1815.
Blotekjaer, K. (1979). *Appl. Opt.* **18**, 57–67.
Brady, D., Hsu, K., and Psaltis, D. (1990). *Opt. Lett.* **15**, 817–819.
Burke, W. J., Staebler, D. L., Phillips, W., and Alphonse, G. A. (1978). *Opt. Eng.* **17**, 308–316.
Caulfield, H. J. (1987). *Appl. Opt.* **26**, 4039–4040.
Caulfield, H. J., Kinser, J., and Rogers, S. K. (1989). *Proc. IEEE.* **77**, 1573–1583.
Chen, F. S., LaMacchia, J. T., and Fraser, D. B. (1968). *Appl. Phys. Lett.* **13**, 223–225.
Chiou, A. (1992). *Opt. Lett.* **17**, 1018–1020.
Chiou, A., Chang, T. Y., and Koshnevisan, M. (1990). *OSA Annual Meeting Technical Digest 1990, OSA Technical Digest Series,* Optical Society of America, **15**, 40.
Chiou, A., Khoshnevisan, M., and Yeh, P. (1988). *Proc. SPIE.* **881**, 250–257.
Chiou, A., and Yeh, P. (1985). *Opt. Lett.* **10**, 621–623.
Chiou, A., and Yeh, P. (1986). *Opt. Lett.* **11**, 306–308.
Chiou, A., and Yeh, P. (1990). *Appl. Opt.* **29**, 1111–1117.
Chiou, A., and Yeh, P. (1992a). *Appl. Opt.* **31**, 5536–5541.
Chiou, A., and Yeh, P. (1992b). *Conference of Lasers and Electro-Optics 1992, OSA Technical Digest Series,* Optical Society of America, **12**, 60.
Chiou, A., Yeh, P., Campbell, S., and Hong, J. (1989). *Proc. SPIE.* **1151**, 24–32.
Collier, R. J., Burckhardt, C. B., and Lin, L. H. (1971). *Optical Holography.* Academic Press, New York.
Cronin-Golomb, M. (1989). *Appl. Phys. Lett.* **54**, 2189–2191.
Cronin-Golomb, M., Fischer, B., White, J. O., and Yariv, A. (1983). *Appl. Phys. Lett.* **42**, 919–921.
Delboulbe, A., Fromont, C., Herriau, J. P., Mallick, S., and Huignard, J. P. (1989). *Appl. Phys. Lett.* **55**, 713–715.
Dunning, G. J., Owechko, Y., and Soffer, B. H. (1991). *Opt. Lett.* **16**, 928–930.
Ewbank, M. D. (1988). *Opt. Lett.* **13**, 47–49.
Fainman, Y. (1989). *Proc. SPIE* **1150**, 120–141.
Feinberg, J. (1982a). *J. Opt. Soc. Am.* **72**, 46–51.
Feinberg, J. (1982b). *Opt. Lett.* **7**, 486–488.
Feinberg, J. (1983a). *Opt. Lett.* **8**, 480–482.
Feinberg, J. (1983b). Optical phase conjugation in photorefractive materials. In: *Optical Phase Conjugation.* Ed. R. A. Fisher. Academic Press, New York. 417–443.
Feinberg, J., and Hellwarth, R. W. (1980). *Opt. Lett.* **5**, 519–521.
Feinberg, J., and MacDonald, K. R. (1989). Phase conjugator mirrors and resonators with photorefractive materials. In: *Photorefractive Materials and Their Applications II: Survey of Applications.* Ed. P. Gunter and J.-P. Huignard. Springer-Verlag, Berlin, 151–203.
Feldman, M. R., Esener, S. C., Guest, C. C., and Lee, S. H. (1988). *Appl. Opt.* **27**, 1742–1751.
Fischer, B., and Sternklar, S. (1987). *Appl. Phys. Lett.* **51**, 74–75.
Fischer, B., Sternklar, S., and Weiss, S. (1989). *IEEE J. Quantum Electron.* **QE-25**, 550–568.
Fisher, R. A. (1983). Ed., *Optical Phase Conjugation.* Academic Press, New York.
Flannery, D. L., and Horner, J. L. (1989). *Proc. IEEE* **77**, 1511–1527.
Ford, J. E., Bittner, G., and Lee, S. H. (1989). *Proc. SPIE* **1151**, 220–230.
Ford, J. E., Lee, S. H., and Fainman, Y. (1990). *Proc. SPIE* **1215**, 155–165.
Garrett, M. H., Chang, J. Y., Jenssen, H. P., and Warde, C. (1992). *Opt. Lett.* **17**, 103–105.
Gaylord, T. K. (1979). Digital data storage. In: *Handbook of Optical Holography.* Ed. H. J. Caulfield. Academic Press, San Diego, 379–413.

Goodman, J. W. (1989). Optics as an Interconnection Technology. In: *Optical Processing and Computing*. Ed. H. H. Arsenault, T. Szoplik and B. Macukow. Academic Press, Inc., Boston 1–32.
Goodman, J. W., Leonberger, F. I., Kung, S. Y., and Athale, R. A. (1984). *Proc. IEEE,* **72,** 850–866.
Gu, C., Chiou, A., and Hong, J. (1993). *Appl. Opt.* **32,** 1437–1440.
Gu, C., Hong, J., McMichael, I., Saxena, R., and Mok, F. (1992). *J. Opt. Soc. Am.* A **9,** 1978–1983.
Guha, A., Bristow, J., Sullivan, C., and Husain, A. (1990). *Appl. Opt.* **29,** 1077–1093.
Gunter, P. (1982). *Phy. Rep.* **93,** 199–299.
Gunter, P., and Huignard, J.-P. (1988). Photorefractive Effects and Materials. In: *Photorefractive Materials and Their Applications I: Fundamental Phenomena.* Ed. P. Gunter, and J.-P. Huignard, Springer-Verlag, Berlin. 7–73.
Gunter, P., and Huignard, J.-P. (1989). Ed. *Photorefractive Materials and Their Applications II: Survey of Applications.* Springer-Verlag, Berlin.
Heerden, P. J. V. (1963). *Appl Opt.* **2,** 393–400.
Hellwarth, R. W. (1977). *J. Opt. Soc. Am.* **67,** 1.
Henderson, G. N., Walkup, J. F., and Bochove, E. J. (1989). *Opt. Lett.* **14,** 770–772.
Henshaw, P. D. (1984). *Proc. SPIE* **464,** 21–28.
Herriau, J.-P., Delboulbe, A., Huignard, J.-P., Roosen, G., and Pauliat, G. (1986). *IEEE J. Lightwave Technol.* **LT-4,** 905–907.
Herriau, J. P., and Huignard, J. P. (1986). *Appl. Phys. Lett.* **49,** 1140–1142.
Herriau, J. P., Rojas, D., Huignard, J.-P., Bassat, J. M., and Launay, J. C. (1987). *Ferroelectrics* **75,** 271–279.
Hesselink, L. (1990). *Int. J. Optoelectron.* **5,** 103–124.
Hinton, H. S. (1990). *IEEE Commun. Mag.* 71–89.
Hong, J., Yeh, P., Psaltis, D., and Brady, D. (1990). *Opt. Lett.* **15,** 344–346.
Jang, J.-S., Shin, S.-Y., and Lee, S.-Y. (1988). *Appl. Opt.* **27,** 4364.
Jensen, S. L., and Hellwarth, R. W. (1978). *Appl. Phys. Lett.,* **32,** 166–168.
Joel, A. E. (1968). *Bell Syst. Tech. J.* **47,** 813–822.
Joseph, J., Pillai, P. K. C., and Singh, K. (1991). *Appl. Opt.* **30,** 3315–3318.
Kirillov, D., and Feinberg, J. (1991). *Opt. Lett.* **16,** 1520–1522.
Klein, M. B. (1988). Photorefractive properties of $BaTiO_3$. In: *Photorefractive Materials and Their Applications I: Fundamental Phenomena.* Ed. P. Gunter and J.-P. Huignard. Springer-Verlag, Berlin. 195–236.
Kogelnik, H. (1969). *Bell Syst. Tech. J.* **48,** 2909–2947.
Kostuk, R. K., Goodman, J. W., and Hesselink, L. (1985). *Appl. Opt.* **24,** 2851–2858.
Kukhtarev, N. V., Markov, V. B., Odulov, S. G., Soskin, M. S., and Vinetskii, V. L. (1979a). *Ferroelectrics* **22,** 949–960.
Kukhtarev, N. V., Markov, V. B., Odulov, S. G., Soskin, M. S., and Vinetskii, V. L. (1979b). *Ferroelectrics* **22,** 961–964.
Kwong, S. K., Rakuljuc, G. A., and Yariv, A. (1985). *Appl. Phys. Lett.* **48,** 201–203.
Lee, H. (1988). *Opt. Lett.* **1,** 874–876.
Leyva, V., Agranat, A., and Yariv, A. (1991). *Opt. Lett.* **16,** 554–556.
Li, Y., Eichmann, G., Dorisinville, R., and Alfano, R. R. (1988). *Appl. Opt.* **27,** 2025–2032.
Mao, H., Li, F., and Deng, X. (1990). *Opt. Lett.* **15,** 888–890.
Micheron, F., and Bismuth, G. (1972). *Appl. Phys. Lett.* **20,** 79–81.
Miller, D. A. B. (1989). *Opt. Lett.* **14,** 146–148.
Mok, F. H., Tackitt, M. C., and Stoll, H. M. (1991). *Opt. Lett.* **16,** 605–607.
Neff, J. A. (1987). *Opt. Eng.* **26,** 2–9.
Owechko, Y., and Soffer, B. H. (1991). *Opt. Lett.* **16,** 675–677.
Petrovic, M. S., Suchocki, A., Powell, R. C., Valley, G. C., and Cantwell, G. (1991). *Phys. Rev. B* **43,** 2228–2233.

Piazzolla, S., Jenkins, B. K., and Tanguay, J. A. R. (1991). *OSA Annual Meeting Technical Digest*, Optical Society of America, **17**, 59–60.
Psaltis, D., Brady, D., Gu, X.-G., and Lin, S. (1990). *Nature* **343**, 325–330.
Psaltis, D., Gu, X.-G., and Brady, D. (1988). *Proc. SPIE* **963**, 468–474.
Rabinovich, W. S., Feldman, B. J., and Gilbreath, G. C. (1991). *Opt. Lett.* **16**, 1147–1149.
Rajbenbach, H., Delboulbe, A., and Huignard, J. P. (1989). *Opt. Lett.* **14**, 1275–1277.
Rajenbach, H., Huignard, J.-P. and Gunter, P. (1990). Optical processing with nonlinear photorefractive crystals. In: *Nonlinear Photonics*. Ed. H. M. Gibbs, G. Khitrova and N. Peyghambarian. Springer-Verlag, Berlin. 151–183.
Rak, D., Ledoux, I., and Huignard, J. P. (1984). *Opt. Commun.* **49**, 302–306.
Ramberg, E. G. (1972). *RCA Rev.* **33**, 5–53.
Sakamoto, A. (1990). *Jpn. J. Appl. Phys.* **29**, L2070–L2073.
Sawchuk, A. A., and Jenkins, B. K. (1986). *Proc. SPIE* **625**, 143–153.
Sawchuk, A. A., Jenkins, B. K., Raghavendra, C. S., and Varma, A. (1987). *Computer* **20**, 50–60.
Schamschula, M. P., Caulfield, H. J., and Verber, C. M. (1991). *Opt. Lett.* **16**, 1421–1423.
Shamir, J., Caulfield, H. J., and Johnson, R. B. (1989). *Appl. Opt.* **28**, 311–324.
Smirl, A. L., Bohnert, K., Valley, G. C., Mullen, R. A., and Boggess, T. F. (1989). *J. Opt. Soc. Am. B* **6**, 606–615.
Smirl, A. L., Valley, G. C., Mullen, R. A., Bohnert, K., Mire, C. D., and Boggess, T. F. (1987). *Opt. Lett.* **12**, 501–503.
Smout, A. M. C., and Eason, R. W. (1987). *Opt. Lett.* **12**, 498–500.
Staebler, D. L. (1975). *Appl. Phys. Lett.* **26**, 182–184.
Sternklar, S., and Fischer, B. (1987). *Opt. Lett.* **12**, 711–713.
Strasser, A. C., Maniloff, E. S., Johnson, K. M., and Goggin, S. D. D. (1989). *Opt. Lett.* **14**, 6–8.
Taketomi, Y., Ford, J. E., Sasaki, H., Ma, J., Fainman, Y., and Lee, S. H. (1991). *Opt. Lett.* **16**, 1774–1776.
Tsang, D. Z. (1990). *Appl. Opt.* **29**, 2034–2037.
Valley, G. C., and Klein, M. B. (1983). *Opt. Eng.* **22**, 704–711.
Valley, G. C., Klein, M. B., Mullen, R. A., Rytz, R., and Wechsler, B. (1988). *Ann. Rev. Mater. Sci.* **18**, 165–188.
Valley, G. C., Smirl, A. L., Klein, M. B., Bohnert, K., and Boggess, T. F. (1986). *Opt. Lett.* **11**, 647–649.
Voges, E., and Neyer, A. (1987). *J. Lightwave Technol.* **LT-5**, 1229–1238.
Weiss, S., Segev, M., Sternklar, S., and Fischer, B. (1988). *Appl. Opt.* **27**, 3422–3428.
White, J., and Yariv, A. (1980). *Appl. Phys. Lett.* **37**, 5–7.
White, J. O., Cronin-Golomb, M., Fisher, B., and Yariv, A. (1982). *Appl. Phys. Lett.* **40**, 450–452.
Wild, U. P., Renn, A., Caro, C. D., and Bernet, S. (1990). *Appl. Opt.* **29**, 4329–4331.
Wu, S., Meyers, A., Rajan, S., and Yu, F. T. S. (1990). *Appl. Opt.* **29**, 1059–1061.
Wu, S., Song, Q., Mayers, A., Gregory, D. A., and Yu, F. T. S. (1990). *Appl. Opt.* **29**, 1118–1125.
Yariv, A. (1978). *IEEE J. Quantum Electron.* **QE-14**, 650–660.
Yeh, P. (1987). *Appl. Opt.* **26**, 602–604.
Yeh, P. (1989). *IEEE J. Quantum Electron.* **25**, 484–519.
Yeh, P., and Chiou, A. (1987). *Opt. Lett.* **12**, 138–140.
Yeh, P., Chiou, A. E., and Hong, J. (1988). *Appl. Opt.* **27**, 2093–2095.
Yeh, P., Chiou, A. E., Hong, J., Beckwith, P., Chang, T., and Khoshnevisan, M. (1989). *Opt. Eng.* **28**, 328–343.

Chapter 11
Three-Dimensional Optical Storage Memory by Means of Two-Photon Interaction

A. S. DVORNIKOV, S. E. ESENER,* and P. M. RENTZEPIS[‡]

Department of Chemistry
University of California, Irvine
Irvine, CA 92717

1. Introduction 287
2. Persistent Hole Burning 292
3. Two-Photon Processes 293
4. Writing and Reading of Information in 3-D Space 297
    4.1 Writing 3-D Information 298
    4.2 Reading 3-D Information 302
    4.3 Erasing 3-D Information 304
5. 3-D Memory Materials 304
    5.1 Spiropyrans 305
    5.2 Other 3-D Materials 307
6. Sample Preparation and Spectra 309
    6.1 Sample Preparation 309
    6.2 Absorption Spectra 309
    6.3 Fluorescence Spectra 311
7. Durability of Written Form 313
8. Stabilization of the Written Form 316
9. Fatigue 319
10. Dependence of Stability on Polymer Host 321
11. Conclusion 322
    References 325

1. Introduction

Computer technology based mostly on semiconductor materials has progressed to such an extent that it has created an even larger than expected appetite for high-performance devices that must store, retrieve, and process huge volumes of data at extremely high rates (Gaylord 1972). Improvements in silicon technology are bringing computer usage to a critical point where the memory capacity and input/

---
*University of California, San Diego, Department of Electrical and Computer Engineering, La Jolla, CA 92093
[‡]To whom correspondence should be addressed.

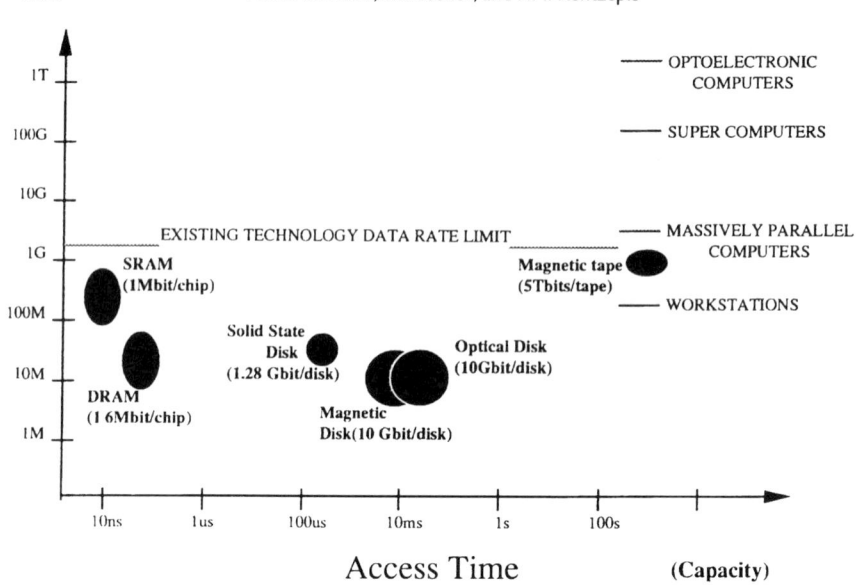

Figure 1. Access speed of existing memory technologies.

output (I/O) speed limit the performance (Figs. 1 and 2). Therefore, many researchers think that the major component that will modulate the practical limits of high-speed computing will be the memory. Because of the huge data storage requirements, the need for parallel execution of tasks, and the necessity of compactness, very high-capacity, low-cost memory is becoming almost mandatory.

The processing speed of today's high-performance computers is increasingly limited by data storage and retrieval rates rather than by processing power. The problem becomes exponentially more difficult for parallel computers, such as systolic arrays and array processors, because the number of data channels and the clock speed both grow simultaneously. Existing serial memory technologies are inadequate to meet these demands. Optical memories with two-dimensional parallel data access offer a fundamentally improved approach to data storage. Such memories can provide the gigabit data capacities with terahertz data rates necessary to meet and exceed the current system requirements. In addition, parallel optical memories are topologically compatible with the next generation of ultrafast parallel optoelectronic computers, which combine optical interconnections with electronic processing. Planar storage media, including magnetic disk, electronic random-access memory (RAM), and optical disk storage, are fundamentally limited by their two-dimensional nature. The data capacity is proportional to the storage area divided by the minimum bit size. Two-photon optical storage surmounts this limitation by extending the storage into the third dimension. Therefore, it offers the unique capability for both highly parallel access and large storage capacity.

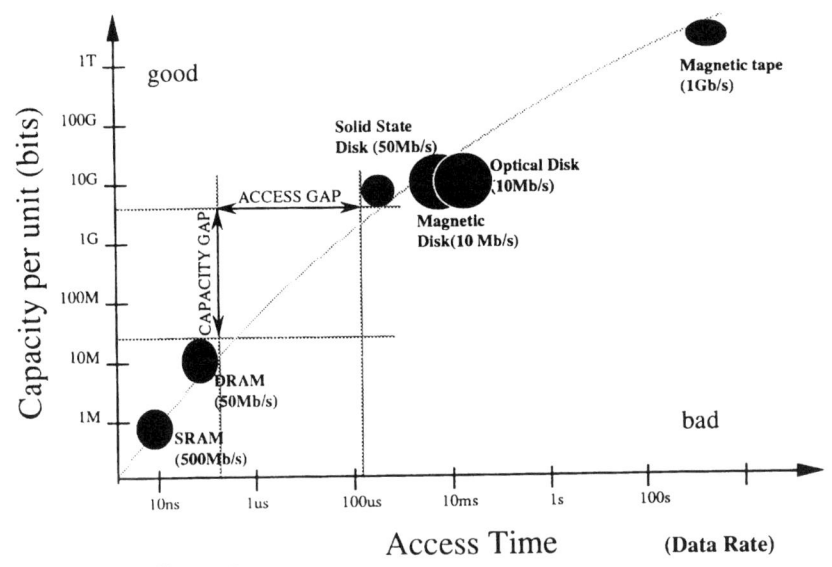

Three-Dimensional Optical Storage Memory by Means of Two-Photon Interaction 289

Figure 2. Data rates of existing primary storage technologies.

During the past 20 years, many memory technologies have been developed. Despite intense competition, several widely different approaches are in current use, including magnetic tape, magnetic disks (hard disks, floppies, and disk stacks), and electronic RAM and read-only memory (ROM). Why is there such a proliferation of technologies? Why isn't the best technology identified and used exclusively? Because each technology has strengths and weaknesses that make it suitable for certain specific applications. No single technology has achieved, to now, maximum performance in speed, capacity, and performance.

Modern computing systems use a *hierarchy* of memories rather than a single type. In the standard computer architecture, the three major levels of the storage hierarchy are secondary, main, and buffer storage (Fig. 3). Secondary storage holds a large capacity of data with a long storage lifetime. However, the access time to any particular piece of data is extremely long compared to the computer's clock cycle. For example, a hard disk stack may contain 100 TBytes of data with a 30-ms access time and an indefinite lifetime. Cache memories hold much less data, but the access time is comparable to the clock cycle. Electronic RAM is an example of cache memory where the capacity may be of the order of 100 MBytes, with a 100-ns access time and a 0.9- to 10-s lifetime. Finally, a buffer memory holds even less data, but the access time is equal to or less than the clock cycle. Local dynamic RAM circuits internal to a large VLSI chip may hold only a few bytes, but by providing temporary storage without delay, they play a critical role in many computing operations. A different type of buffer memory is a data acquisition unit, which accepts a limited amount information at an extremely fast data

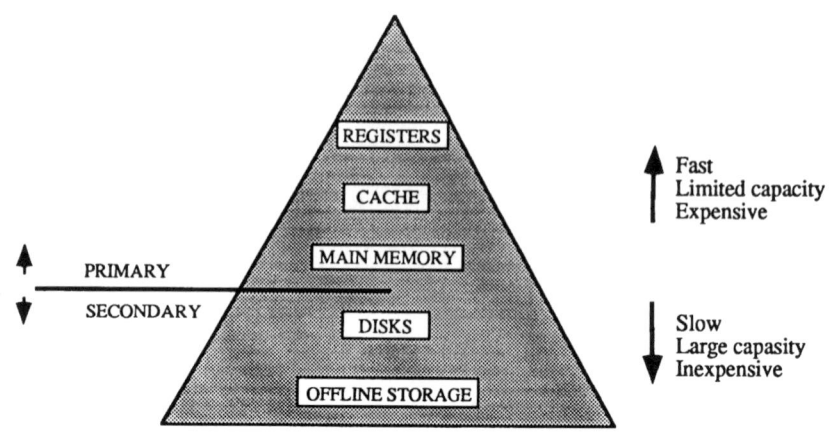

Figure 3. Memory hierarchy in existing computing architecture.

rate, holding the information only until it can be downloaded into more permanent storage. The memory hierarchy approach utilizes the strong points of each technology of the utmost extent, maximizing overall computer performance.

In Figs. 1 and 2 we show the current memory technologies in terms of their critical characteristics. Figure 1 shows that there is a four order of magnitude performance gap in access time between electronic RAMs and secondary storage devices such as disks. The width of this gap is doubling each year, forcing the development of new secondary storage systems. In addition, because the processing power doubles every year and the memory density every 2.5 years, a gap also exists in terms of memory capacity. This creates an increasingly dangerous mismatch between CPU power and current primary storage. Finally, Fig. 2 shows that the data rates of current primary technologies are significantly lower than required for parallel processors.

Existing serial memory technologies that use planar storage media, including electronic RAM, magnetic disk, and optical storage, are inadequate to bridge the gaps. The data capacity is fundamentally limited by their two-dimensional nature to the storage area divided by the minimum bit area. As the storage area increases for higher capacity, the access time grows. The data transfer rates are limited by their sequential nature to the I/O channel bandwidth.

Three-dimensional memories (3-DM) extend storage into the third dimension, enabling higher capacities and shorter access times (Parthenopoulos and Rentzepis 1989, 1990a, 1990b). Storing and retrieving the data in parallel using a 2-D format dramatically increases the achievable data rate. In addition, parallel-access optical memories are topologically compatible with the next generation of ultrafast parallel optoelectronic computers, which combine optical interconnections with electronic processing. However, one single 3-DM system cannot bridge all the gaps existing in current memory hierarchy, and there are trade-offs between high storage density, access time, and data transfer rates.

A terabit-capacity secondary memory system based on two-photon storage has been investigated with respect to optimization of materials, devices, data structures, and systems for ultrahigh density with millisecond access times and terabit per second transfer rates. In addition, dynamic random access storage systems with lower storage densities (Gbit/cm^3) but ultrafast response are being investigated. These systems can be optimized to bridge the memory access gap and will be used as main memory for future parallel optoelectronic computers as well as a transition memory between electronic RAMs and future two-photon secondary storage. With the necessary materials, device, and systems engineering, an entire parallel-access 3-DM hierarchy can be based on a common underlying structure of two-photon 3-D volume storage.

Our long-term goal is the development of a corresponding memory hierarchy of parallel-access optical memories. Such a memory hierarchy will enable the design and construction of efficient parallel optoelectronic computers by means of principles corresponding to existing computer architecture. It would be preferable if this family of memory technologies could all be based on a common underlying approach. This is, in fact, possible using the two-photon 3-D volume storage approach described in the following section.

The necessity, therefore, for the search to find means to store large amounts of information in small volumes cannot be overstated, nor can the requirement for these memories to be capable of large bandwidths and parallel access be overemphasized. Three-dimensional storage may provide a desirable solution to these needs. The various possible avenues that may lead to 3-D information storage include persistent hole burning (Moerner 1987), phase holograms (D'Auria et al. 1974), and two-photon processes. Especially promising is the use of organic materials (Parthenopoulos and Rentzepis 1989, 1990a; Stickler and Webb 1991; Hunter et al. 1990), semiconductors and biomolecules such as bacteriorhodorpsin (Birge 1990; Birge et al. 1990; Brauchle, Hampp, and Oesterhelt 1990; Thoma et al. 1990). In this paper we restrict our discussion to the last topic, namely, 3-D storage by means of two-photon absorption and particularly in the utilization of organic photochromic materials (Hunter et al. 1990).

The currently used magnetic and electro-optic disks are, to a large extent, one-dimensional devices providing for the input and output of information in a bit serial mode. To make a quantum increase in the information density available and to make the I/O information suitable for parallel processing, an all-optical storage device must be advanced and utilized and a means for storing more information per unit volume found (DeCegama 1989; Robinson 1989). In the case of optical systems, the density of information that can be stored depends on the reciprocal of the wavelength to the power of the dimension used to store information. Specifically, if the information is stored in a one-dimensional mode, then the density is proportionally $1/\lambda$. This relationship also suggests that the information storage density is much higher when ultraviolet (UV) rather than visible light is used. In a two-dimensional memory, the theoretical storage density is $1/\lambda^2$, and for a 2-D storage device that operates at 200 nm the maximum information storage is 2.5×10^9 bits/cm², while for a 3-D storage memory that uses the same light beam the density can be as high as 1.2×10^{14} bits/cm³. In previous communications we have presented experimental data that suggest there is a possibility for constructing 3-D volume memory devices based on a two-photon virtual excitation process (Parthenopoulos and Rentzepis 1989, 1990a; Birge 1990).

In the following sections we discuss briefly the theoretical requirements for a two-photon transition to take place and the means for writing and reading information within a 3-D volume memory. We also describe specific materials and methods utilized in our experimental studies in order to write and read information in a 3-D format by means of two-photon excitation, and we present the data that make it possible to understand the nonlinear and spectroscopic properties of these molecules. Based on these data the suitability of these molecules for 3-D devices is evaluated.

2. Persistent Hole Burning

The mechanism for the formation of persistent hole burning has been studied extensively both from the basic science point of view and its possible application to a frequency-domain optical storage device (Moerner 1987; Sild and Haller 1988).

In such a device, the spectral hole is burned at particular wavelengths and constitutes a 1 in the binary code with the normal nonburned region designated as 0 in the binary code. As in the case of two-photon 3-D storage, frequency-domain storage allows for a greatly increased random-access capability over the magnetic and optical disk devices. It is possible to achieve 10^{12} bits/cm² of information density if enough holes can be burned in the volume, which is irradiated by the writing laser. The materials to be utilized must be able to perform under the very strict conditions imposed by the engineering of the system. For example, the widths of the holes should be 100 to 500 MHz. Several materials have been found to yield holes of this width; color centers and phthalocyanine dye in polyethylene are two such examples. The temperature must usually be kept at near liquid helium temperatures to achieve these widths and even narrower widths have been detected at 0.3 K in porphine/polyethelene mixtures. To be of value, the hole should persist indefinitely and indeed several materials have been found that show a persistence limited only by the maintenance of liquid helium temperatures. However, spectral diffusion frequently leads to the broadening of the spectral holes and eventual loss of information. The materials should also be capable of hole reversibility to avoid being a write-once-only device. Such properties have been found in several organic materials of the phthalocyanine type dispersed in polyethylene. The mechanism responsible for the reversibility in these materials is believed to be proton transfer.

Another very important parameter for if hole burning is to be viable memory material is the irradiation time needed to write a hole. When the irradiation time is of the order of tens of nanoseconds, the burnt holes are shallow, which requires intense light for reading, which in turn may cause photochemical damage to the material. With advances in detection technology, it is rather appropriate to expect that very weak signals from a shallow hole will be easily detected with a high signal-to-noise ratio (SNR). There seems to be a classic cause and effect operating here. If the material lends itself to fast hole-burning formation, then the reading beam will probably also induce hole burning in the material. If the reading is efficient at relatively fast speeds, then most probably the writing, i.e., the hole formation, will require higher power lasers or longer times. The power of the laser may also influence the temperature of the system, which could result in erasure or loss of information at unacceptably short times.

Persistent hole-burning studies suggest that useful material for frequency-domain memory will probably be found in the foreseeable future. Progress has also been made in a material system that shows persistent hole-burning at higher temperatures and in holographic methods. Such advances in materials provide an impetus for research and promise for a memory device based on persistent hole burning. Holographic memories are not discussed because the technique is well known.

3. Two-Photon Processes

The theoretical bases for two-photon processes were established in the early 1930s (Goeppert–Mayer 1931). It was shown that the probability for a two-photon transition may be expressed as a function of three parameters: line profile, transition probability fit for all possible two-photon processes (see Fig. 4 for a schematic representation of four such processes), and light intensity. These factors are related to P_{if} by:

$$P_{if} \cong \frac{\gamma_{if}}{[\omega_{if} - \omega_1 - \omega_2 - \bar{v} \cdot (\bar{k}_1 + \bar{k}_2)]^2 + (\gamma_{if}/2)^2} \cdot \left| \sum_k \frac{\bar{R}_{ik} \cdot \bar{e}_1 \cdot \bar{R}_{kf} \cdot \bar{e}_2}{(\omega_{ki} - \omega_1 - \bar{k}_1 \cdot \bar{v})} + \frac{\bar{R}_{ik} \cdot \bar{e}_2 \cdot \bar{R}_{kf} \cdot \bar{e}_1}{(\omega_{ki} - \omega_2 - \bar{k}_2 \cdot \bar{v})} \right|^2 \cdot I_1 I_2. \quad (1)$$

According to this postulate, two-photon transitions may also allow for the population of molecular levels that are parity-forbidden for one-photon processes, such as $g \rightarrow g$ and $u \rightarrow u$, in contrast to the $g \rightarrow u$ and $u \rightarrow g$ transitions that are allowed for one-photon processes. In practice, however, when one is concerned with large molecules in condensed media, the density of the states is very large, the levels broadened by collisions, and the laser line bandwidth large enough to accommodate many levels. Therefore, there is little, if any, difference in the energy between the levels observed experimentally by one- or two-photon transitions in the large molecular entities used under the experimental conditions presented here.

Equation (1) is composed of three factors: the first factor describes the spectral profile of a two-photon transition. It corresponds to a single-photon transition at a center frequency ($\omega_{if} = \omega_1 + \omega_2 + \bar{v}\ \bar{k}_1 + \bar{k}_2$) with a homogeneous width γ_{if}. If both light waves are parallel, the Doppler width, which is proportional to $|\bar{k}_1 + \bar{k}_2|$, becomes maximum. For $\bar{k}_1 = \bar{k}_2$ the Doppler broadening vanishes and we obtain a pure Lorentzian line. The second factor describes the transition probability for the two-photon transition. This is the sum of products of matrix elements $R_{ik}R_{kf}$ for transitions between the initial state i and intermediate molecular levels k and between these levels k and the final state f. The sum extends over all molecular levels. Often a *virtual level* is introduced to describe the two-photon transition by a symbolic two-step transition $E_i \rightarrow E_v \rightarrow E_f$. Since the two possibilities,

$$E_i + \hbar\omega_1 \rightarrow E_v, \quad E_v + \hbar\omega_2 \rightarrow E_f \quad \text{(first term)} \tag{2}$$

or

$$E_i + \hbar\omega_2 \rightarrow E_v, \quad E_v + \hbar\omega_1 \rightarrow E_f \quad \text{(second term)}, \tag{3}$$

lead to the same observable result, the excitation of the real level E_f, the total transition probability for $E_i \rightarrow E_f$ is equal to the square of the sum of both probability amplitudes. The frequencies of ω_1 and ω_2 can be selected in such a way that the virtual level is close to a real molecular state. This greatly enhances the transition probability. Therefore, it is generally advantageous to populate the final level E_f by means of two different energy photons with $\omega_1 + \omega_2 = (E_f - E_i)/\hbar$ rather than by two equal photons. The third factor shows that the transition probability depends on the product of the intensities I_1 and I_2. In the case where the photons are of the same wavelength, then the transition probability depends on I^2. It will therefore be advantageous to utilize lasers emitting high-intensity light such as picosecond and subpicosecond pulses.

Four possible processes that may operate by means of two-photon excitation are shown in Fig. 4. The first corresponds to a stepwise or sequential two-photon absorption process [Fig. 4(a)] in which each photon absorption is allowed (i.e., two allowed one-photon sequential processes). Even though the final state reached by the two photons may be the same as by the simultaneous absorption of two photons via a virtual level [Fig. 4(b)], the effect toward a volume memory is overwhelmingly different. In the case of the sequential two-photon process, the first photon absorption takes place on a real level—by definition—by a molecule, or

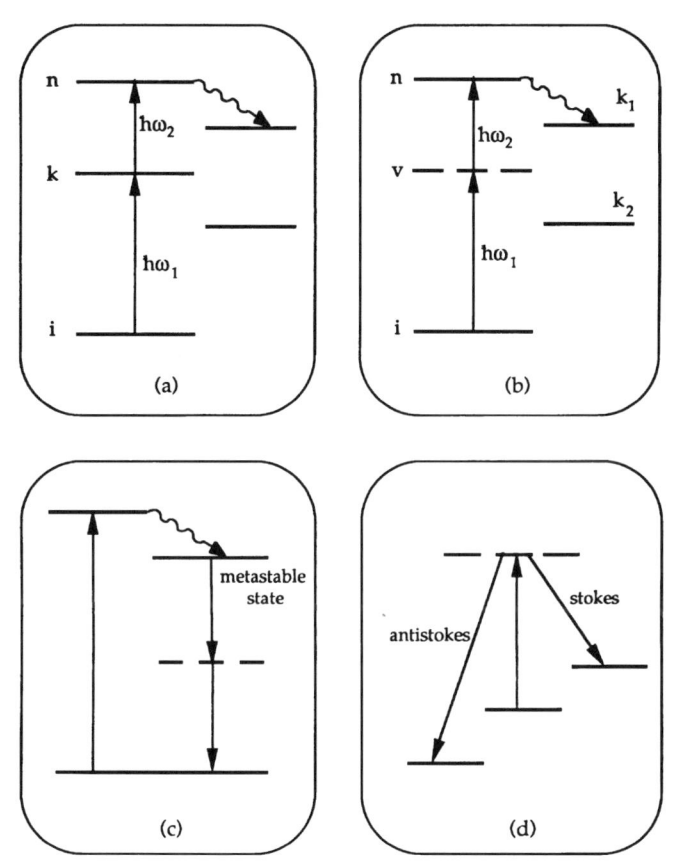

Figure 4. Schematic representation of two-photon processes.

atom, which has an allowed state at that energy. It will therefore be absorbed by the first such molecule or atom on its path, which is usually located on the surface. Subsequently, if sufficient photon intensity is available, several possibilities exist: (1) The photons from the same pulse may be absorbed by the same molecule, inducing a transition to higher electronic states; (2) populate an additional molecule further, inside the volume; or (3) after energy decay, populate a metastable level such as a triplet.

The second photon will encounter the same fate, namely, it will be absorbed preferentially by the molecules first encountered in its path, which are the molecules at or near the surface. Then with decreasing intensity, this beam will propagate and be absorbed by molecules further inside the volume. This second sequential beam may be delayed by a time interval equal to or slightly longer than the time required by the first excited state to decay to a low-lying metastable level. If the wavelength of this second beam is adjusted to be longer (smaller in energy) than the energy gap between the ground state and the first allowed state, (wavelength of the first beam), then the second light beam will populate only the upper electronic states of the excited metastable level. This is an interesting and important scientific aspect of nonlinear spectroscopy and photophysics; however, it does not result in true 3-D volume memory. This is because, as we mentioned earlier, there is no means possible by which light can interact preferentially with molecules located inside a volume without interacting first with at least equal efficiency with molecules residing on the surface.

The second scheme for two-photon absorption [Fig. 4(b)] makes it possible to excite molecules inside a volume in preference to the surface. This may be achieved because the wavelength of each beam is longer and has less energy than the energy gap between the ground state and first allowed electronic level. However, if two beams are used, the energy sum of the two laser photons must be equal to or larger than the energy gap of the transition. It is also important to note that there is no real level at the wavelength of either beam, therefore, neither beam can be absorbed alone by a one-photon mechanism. When two such photons collide within the volume, absorption occurs only within the volume and size defined by the width of the pulses. This is in sharp contrast to the sequential two-photon process where the first step involves the absorption of a single photon by a real spectroscopic level and hence is not capable of preferential volume storage.

The principal difference in the two cases as far as their suitability for 3-D volume memory is concerned is that the virtual case [Fig. 4(b)] avails itself to writing and reading in any place within the 3-D volume, while the sequential excitation is restricted in writing and reading first at the surface.

The other two processes shown in Fig. 4 show the possibility of two-photon emission [Fig. 4(c)] after single-photon excitation and the Raman effect [(Fig. 4(d)]. Neither of these last two cases is relevant to the topic under discussion and is not discussed further. We must note at this point that the same physics holds for all two-photon transitions regardless of the sequence by which they take place, whether via sequential steps between real levels or via virtual state interaction.

In the case presented here, we utilized a two-photon process; the photon energy of each beam was smaller than the energy gap between the ground state S_0 and the first allowed electronic level S_1. Therefore, such a beam of light propagates though the medium without observable absorption. When two such beams are made to intersect at a point within the memory volume, their effective energy is equal to the sum of the two photon energies $E_1 + E_2$. Therefore, absorption will occur if the $E_{S_1} - E_{S_0}$ energy gap is equal to or smaller than $E_1 + E_2$. At the point where the two beams interact, the absorption induces a physical and/or a chemical change, which will distinguish this microvolume area from any other part of the memory volume that has not been excited. These two molecular structures, i.e., the original and the one created by the two-photon absorption, are subsequently utilized as the write and read forms of a 3-D optical storage memory. For successful completion of this type of writing and reading, the light beams that perform either function must also be capable of propagating through the medium and be absorbed only at preselected points within the memory volume where the two beams intersect in time and space without any noticeable effect on other areas of the memory volume in which information may or may not be written.

4. Writing and Reading of Information in 3-D Space

The utilization of three-dimensional storage memory may provide several desirable characteristics that are not cumulatively found in today's electro-optic devices. The major advantages of such a storage device would be: (1) immense information storage capacity, $\sim 10^{13}$ bits/cm^3; (2) random and parallel access; (3) very fast optical writing and reading speed, nanoseconds and faster; (4) small size (i.e., ~ 1 cm^3) and low cost; (5) absence of mechanical or moving parts; (6) minimal crosstalk between adjacent bits; and (7) high reading sensitivity. The operations that enable one to store, retrieve, and erase information within a 3-D volume may be visualized as follows:

1. *Writing:* Information is recorded in any preselected position within the 3-D medium.
2. *Reading:* A process by which the medium is probed for the existence or absence of stored information in any place within the volume of the memory and then retrieved.
3. *Erasing* of the information recorded in any part of the memory thus the device may become available for recording new data.

Currently, information is stored in the form of binary code. The two states of the binary code, 0 and 1, may be thought of as photochemical changes, which lead to two distinct structures of the particular molecular species used as the storage medium. Such an example is provided by the changes in molecular structure occurring in photochromic materials such as spirobenzopyrans after the simultaneous absorption of two photons. The structure of some spirobenzopyran (SP) molecules is shown in Fig. 5. Spirobenzopyran has two distinct forms: the original, stable spiropyran form, which is converted to the merocyanine form after excitation with UV light. These two forms, which possess distinctly different structures and completely different absorption and emission spectra, provide the two states necessary

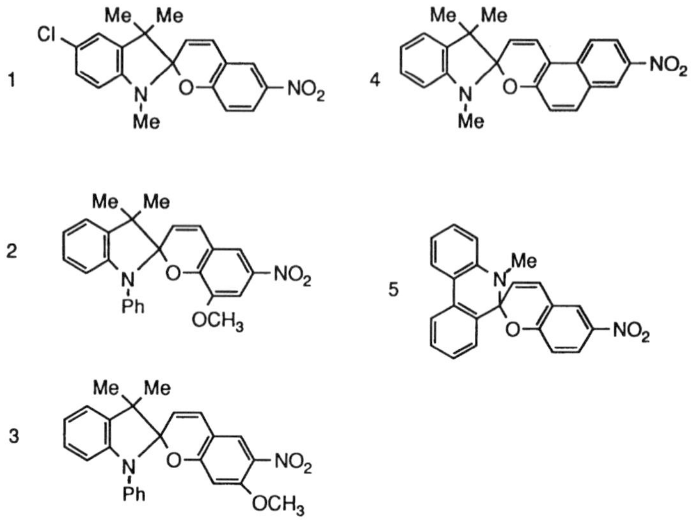

Figure 5. Structure of some spizopyrans used in 3-D memory studies.

for 3-D storage information in a binary format. Specifically, the original form is designated as 0 and the merocyanine form as 1 in the binary code. The spyro form has a closed ring structure and is referred to as the *closed form,* while in contrast the merocyanine structure is an open ring type and is referred to as the *open form.*

The essential elements of the 3-D information storage device described here are the molecule, the host matrix, and the two laser beams of the same or different wavelengths, which will provide the means for writing and reading by two-photon processes. Depending on material and process, the wavelength requirements are likely to be different, in which case the advantage of utilizing a dye laser or other tunable laser source becomes apparent. Another approach for wavelength tuning may involve second or higher harmonic generation in nonlinear crystals as well as stimulated Raman generated in gases and liquids.

4.1 Writing 3-D Information

To write information in a 3-D storage memory device that contains SP molecules as the recording medium requires excitation in the UV region of the spectrum because SP absorbs at that region, i.e., ~260 and 355 nm. This is shown in Fig. 6 where the absorption spectra of 1SP are reproduced. Excitation to this state is provided by the two-photon absorption of either a 1064-nm photon and a 532-nm photon, which is equivalent to a 355-nm photon, or two 532-nm photons, corresponding to a 266-nm photon energy, where 266 and 355 nm are the wavelengths

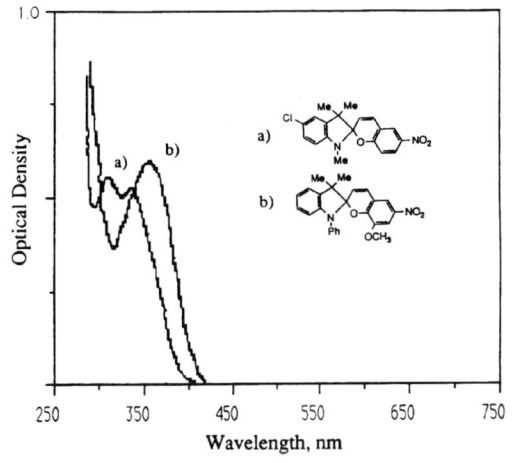

Figure 6. Absorption spectra of 1SP and 2SP in polymethylmethacrylate (PMMA).

of the two absorption maxima of the SP molecule. Note, however, that two-photon absorption induced by each beam separately may also occur. This will occur when the individual beams are sufficiently intense and will result in background noise. The background-to-signal ratio for two collinear beams propagating at opposite directions is 1:3. Since two-photon absorption is dependent on the square of the power, the effect of each beam will be approximately one-fourth that of the two beams combined, assuming two beams of equal power. This problem can be eliminated by utilizing two beams of different wavelengths such that one beam cannot induce any two-photon background noise, i.e., its wavelength is longer than necessary to induce a two-photon transition. Such, for example, is the case with a 1064-nm beam and the spyran molecule that absorbs at three and four times this energy but not at twice. However, when the 1064-nm beam is combined with a 532-nm beam, excitation of the spyran molecule to the first excited state at 355 nm is possible. The background noise maybe eliminated to a large extent by increasing the intensity of the 1064-nm beam and keeping the 532-nm pulses to as low an intensity as possible. In practice, the 532-nm beam intensity is reduced to such an extent that two-photon absorption of the individual 532-nm beam is not visible and the 1064-nm beam is increased proportionally so that the combined two-photon process, which is the product of the intensity of the two laser pulses, is sufficient to excite the molecule and consequently induce the structural change that constitutes writing.

Figure 7 displays an energy-level diagram of the two-photon process, a schematic representation of the write and read events and the molecular structures of the "write" and "read" forms of SP. By translating the beams along the axes of

300   A.S. Dvornikov, S.E. Esener, and P.M. Rentzepis

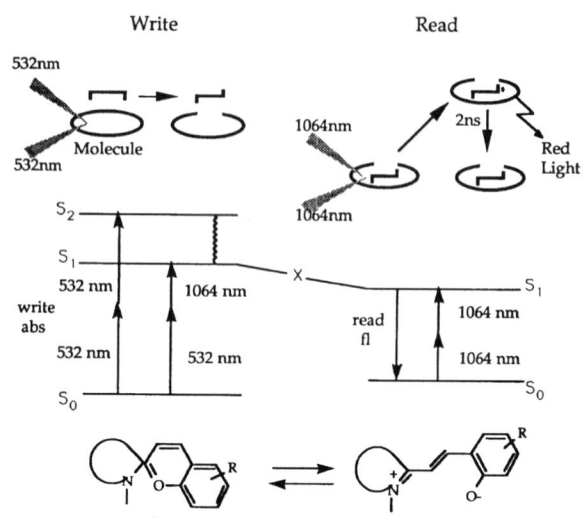

Figure 7. Energy-level diagram for 3-D writing and reading in spiropyran by means of two-photon absorption.

ORTHOGONAL BEAMS

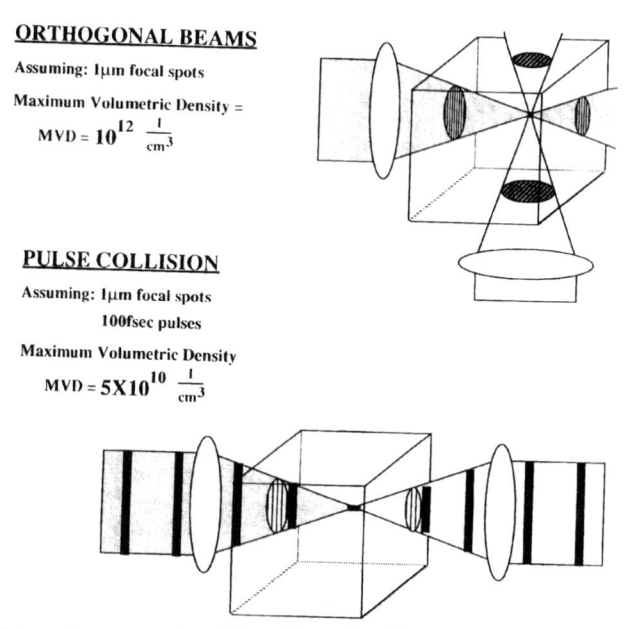

Assuming: 1μm focal spots

Maximum Volumetric Density =

$MVD = 10^{12} \frac{1}{cm^3}$

PULSE COLLISION

Assuming: 1μm focal spots
100fsec pulses

Maximum Volumetric Density

$MVD = 5 \times 10^{10} \frac{1}{cm^3}$

Figure 8. Schematic representation of the writing and reading processes by means of (a) orthogonal and (b) collinear beam interaction.

Three-Dimensional Optical Storage Memory by Means of Two-Photon Interaction   301

the sample volume (see Fig. 8), the required spatial pattern is achieved in the form of colored spots. The written volume appears colored because the read form spectrum shows an absorption in the 500-nm region. In this discussion the memory is in the shape of a cube but may be molded in any other form. Similarly most of the discussion presented is with written beams propagating orthogonally to each other. However, similar results may be achieved by two counterpropagating beams or, in fact, by any other colliding arrangement. Each configuration has advantages over the others, however, the physics is essentially the same. Figure 8 shows a scheme for orthogonal and opposite direction pulse interaction, while Fig. 9 displays a schematic representation of the experimental system used to write and read in 3-D space. The information can be stored not only a bit at a time but in a page format consisted of many megabits and with several pages superimposed within a memory volume. A complication can arise from the fluorescence of the written form, which if absorbed by an adjacent SP molecule will induce false information to be written or crosstalk. To avoid such deleterious effects, the molecules chosen must not fluoresce in the "write" form. No fluorescence from the "write" form of the spirobenzopyran molecules used in our experiments has been observed even at liquid nitrogen temperatures (Parthenopoulos and Rentzepis 1990a).

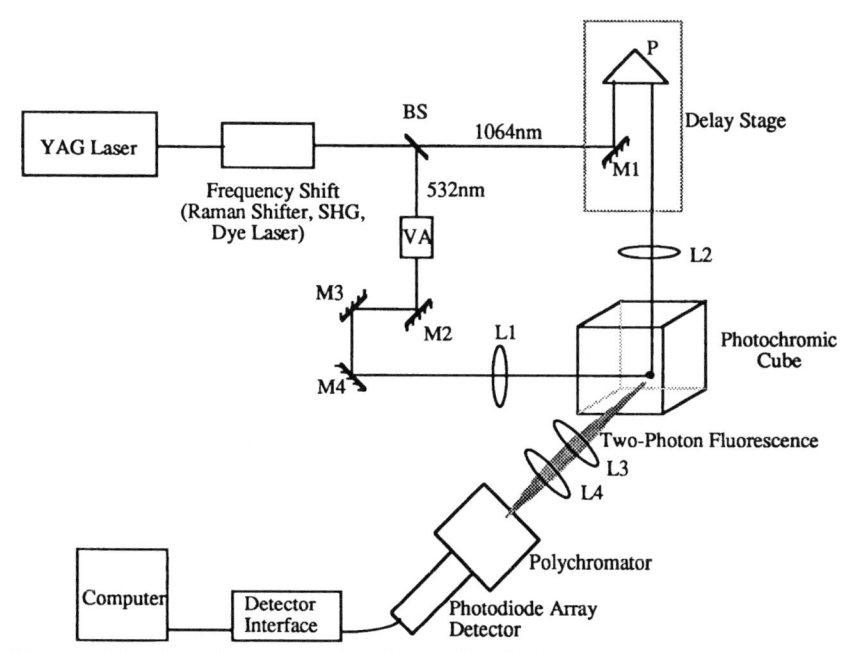

Figure 9. Experimental system used for writing and reading in a 3-D volume: *BS*—beamsplitter; *P*—prism; *M*—mirror; *L*—lens; *VA*—variable attenuator.

4.2 Reading 3-D Information

The procedure used to "read" the information written within the volume of the memory is similar to the write cycle except that the "reading" form absorbs at longer wavelengths than the write form, hence one or both laser beam wavelengths must also be longer than the ones used for writing. After the written molecule is excited by two-photon absorption, the molecule emits fluorescence with a lifetime of 5 ns at longer wavelengths than the absorption of both the write and read forms. This fluorescence is detected by a photodiode or charge-coupled device (CCD) and is processed as 1 in the binary code. The proper selection of materials that provide widely separated spectra are extremely important because they assure that only the molecules that have been written will absorb this radiation and consequently induce fluorescence to be emitted only from that part of the written memory that is being read.

The fluorescence emitted by the written form of SP is shown in Fig. 10. That the process indeed proceeds by two-photon absorption is verified in Fig. 11 where the slope of ~2 is obtained from a log plot of the laser energy versus fluorescence intensity. On the other hand, if the molecule has not been written, fluorescence will not be observed because the "read" two-photon energy is not sufficient to populate the closed form of the original, unwritten molecule, as shown in the energy level diagram of Fig. 7 and, in addition, because the closed form does not fluoresce. Self-absorption of the fluorescence by adjacent spirobenzopyran molecules that have been written does not affect the reading process because the largest

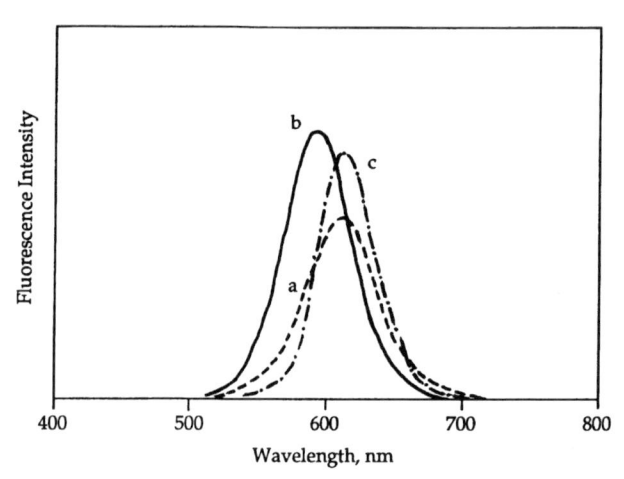

Figure 10. Fluorescence spectra of 1SP in liquid monomers and solid polymer matrices: (a) HEMA, (b) PHEMA and (c) PMMA.

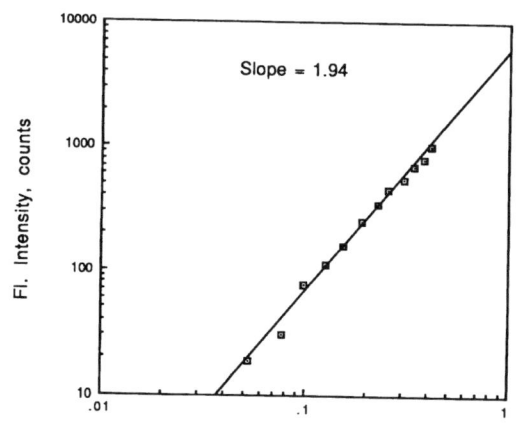

Figure 11. Plot of laser power versus fluorescence intensity.

segment of the fluorescence is emitted at longer wavelengths than the written form absorption band and consequently does not overlap considerably with the absorption of the written molecules. The small amount of fluorescence absorbed by adjacent written areas will yield signals that are either too weak in intensity to be detected or can be easily eliminated by means of electronic discriminators. Because the reading is based on fluorescence, a zero background process, this method has the advantage of a high "reading" sensitivity. Extremely low-level fluorescence measurements are possible by the use of photomultipliers or CCDs, which are capable of single photon detection. The fluorescence was found to decay with an ~5-ns lifetime, which in essence is the limiting speed of the reading

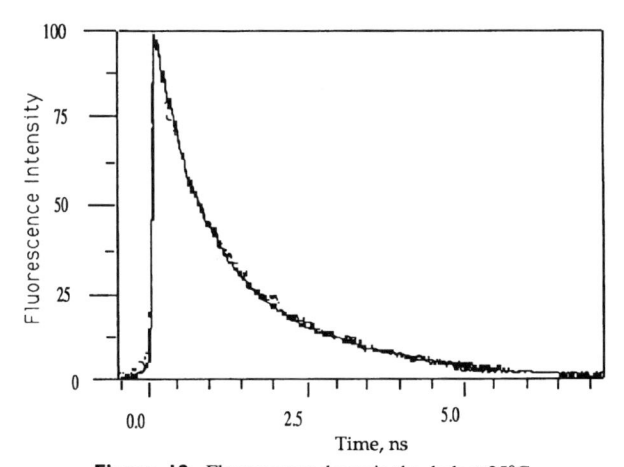

Figure 12. Fluorescence decay in the dark at 25°C.

process. Figure 12 shows the fluorescence lifetime of the 1SP written form after excitation with two 1060-nm photons.

4.3 Erasing 3-D Information

Erasing the information may be achieved either by increasing the temperature of the memory device to ~50°C or via irradiation by infrared light. By raising the temperature, the written molecules are raised above the energy barrier separating the write and read molecules, causing the written molecules to revert to the original form. The information is thus erased and the 3-D memory is ready for storing new data. By bleaching the sample with light (i.e., infrared), the duration of the "erasure" cycle can be shortened considerably. A limitation of the erasure by temperature is that it is not possible to erase selectively specific bits of the information stored in the 3-D memory volume. However, utilization of light for erasing circumvents this difficulty and makes it possible to erase specific, preselected bits of information without affecting any other areas of the memory.

We have described the means for writing, reading, and erasing information by means of two-photon processes. The description was for a single spot within the 3-D space; however, one of the very important strengths of this method is its capability of writing and reading a large number of bits simultaneously. Simultaneous or parallel writing and accessing of the information may be achieved by splitting the laser into a large number of beams, which propagate simultaneously through the memory volume either at opposite directions or at 90 deg to each other. Another possibility that is actively being pursued is the use of pulsed diode lasers located at opposite ends of the memory cube or orthogonal to each other. Even though it is rather difficult to mode-lock semiconductor lasers, the technology is progressing sufficiently well to expect high intensity at a reasonably short period of time. The availability of high-intensity short-pulse semiconductor lasers will decrease the size and power requirements of 3-D memory drastically and make these devices very attractive for many applications that require huge memory capacity and fast parallel access for either a primary or secondary memory.

5. 3-D Memory Materials

A vast number of molecules may be used as materials for 3-D devices. These include photochromic materials, phosphors, photoisomers, and semi-conductors. The above do not include materials for hole burning or holographic memory. Each of these materials has unique advantages. They also exhibit weaknesses that prevent or at least diminish their appeal for device utilization. Some materials such as phosphors are not yet available in clear, transparent form at thicknesses sufficiently large, i.e., 3 to 5 mm, to be of practical use as 3-D devices. Other materials must be maintained at very low temperatures in order to stabilize one of the forms; this is the case with some spyrans and photoisomers and to a large extent with hole-burning materials. Other materials exhibit such a low quantum yield for either the reading or writing process that they are rendered impractical. It is rather important therefore to select the molecules that have the possibility of improvement in all areas of importance for practical use.

5.1 Spiropyrans

One of the rather promising classes of molecules used in basic experiments for 3-D storage is the spiropyrans. These are molecules of the general structure shown in Fig. 5. The photochromism, namely, their change in molecular structure and color after light absorption, of spiropyrans is attributed to the photo-induced cleavage of the carbon-oxygen bond of the pyran ring and subsequent isomerization to the form referred to as *merocyanine* (Tyer and Becker 1970; Bertelson 1971). Spiropyran molecules are composed of two distinct molecular components linked by a sp^3 hybridized carbon. These two components are positioned orthogonally to each other. In such an orthogonal configuration the π-electron moieties of the molecule do not interact with each other. Therefore, the result is a molecule whose spectrum shows a strong band in the UV region and complete absence of absorption in the visible region.

The spectrum of this molecule, which is of the utmost importance for the writing process, can be thought of as a superposition of the spectra of the two orthogonally situated members (Tyer and Becker 1970). Designating this initial orthogonal structure molecule as 0 in the binary code, the device will show 0 for any light beam(s) propagating through the memory with a wavelength or sum of two photon energies, which is equal to or shorter than the absorption band of this molecule, i.e., 350 nm. Light at 350 nm or less induces absorption, which initiates the photochemical opening of the pyran ring (see Fig. 7), forming an isomer, which in turn rearranges to a planar form as a result of thermal isomerization. This planar form is colored in appearance and absorbs intensely in the 550-nm region as shown in Fig. 13. The intermediate time, between the orthogonal and planar species, has been identified by means of resolved spectroscopy (Krysanov and Alfimov 1982; Dvornikov, Malkin, and Kuzmin 1982). The final, colored species of an SP molecule is formed with a quantum yield, which varies from $\sim 10\%$ to 98%. This variation depends in part on the structure of the original molecule.

The energy levels of the chromene and heterocycle components depend on the substituents and the nature of the environment, i.e., on the solvent or polymer matrix. For example, spiropyrans with indoline as the heterocycle components exhibit high quantum yields for photoconversion to the colored forms because of the enhanced intramolecular energy transfer (Dvornikov, Malkin, and Kuzmin 1982) between the two constituent groups (Topchieu 1990). The choice of the

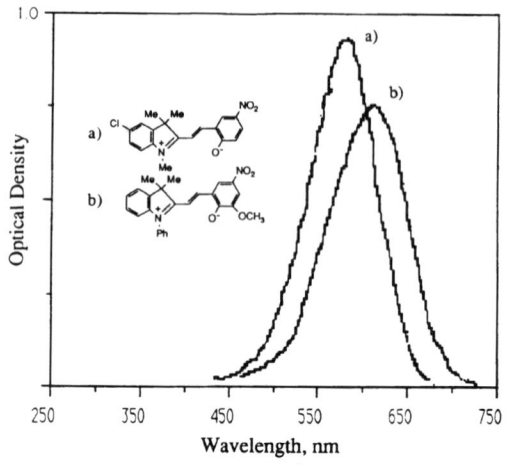

Figure 13. Absorption spectra of the open-writing form of 1SP and 2SP.

molecule used may, therefore, have a profound effect on the operation, speed, and performance of the overall memory device because it dictates the laser power requirements for writing and reading and in addition determines the lifetime of the photo process, which is in essence the limiting factor of the speed for the input and output of the information to and from the 3-D memory device. The polymer matrix usually decreases the rate of molecular transformation and its quantum yield compared to liquids because of an increase in viscosity and other considerations such as polarity and the dielectric constant. The hardness of the polymer matrix, however, may contribute to the stability of the written form and obviously solid material devices are quite often preferable to liquid form devices.

The mechanism that drives the write and read process in these photochromic molecules may be presented as follows:

$$\left.\begin{array}{l}(1)\ A \xrightarrow{2h\nu_1} A^* \\ (2)\ A^* \rightleftharpoons I \\ (3)\ I \rightleftharpoons B\end{array}\right\} \text{write}$$

$$\left.\begin{array}{l}(1)\ B \xrightarrow{2h\nu_2} B^* \\ (2)\ B^* \longrightarrow B' + h\nu_3\end{array}\right\} \text{read}$$

$$\left.B \xrightarrow{h\nu_4/\Delta} A \right\} \text{erasing}$$

where A represents the original closed form, 0 in binary code; A^* designates the electronic excited state of A; I is an intermediate species of very short lifetime; $h\nu_1$, $h\nu_2$, and $h\nu_4$ are photon energies; $h\nu_3$ is the fluorescence energy; $\nu_1 \neq \nu_2 \neq \nu_3$ and usually $\nu_1 > \nu_2 > \nu_3$; B is the colored mercocynine, open form binary code 1; B^* designates the excited state of B; and Δ = heat.

5.2 Other 3-D Materials

Fulgides are other molecules that are highly photochromic and may be used as materials for 3-D devices. Fulgides also exhibit ring opening and closure. The quantum yields for the read and write forms have been measured (Heller and Oliver 1981; Horie *et al.* 1988) and the lifetime of the process including intermediate states and kinetics (Parthenopoulos and Rentzepis 1990b) are shown in Fig. 14 in the form of ΔA versus λ. Because of a relative lack of fluorescence emission in the solid state and its very fast $\tau < 20$ ps fluorescence lifetime (Horie *et al.* 1988) in solution after picosecond excitation, these materials may not be considered useful for applications where the reading process is based on the detection of rather strong fluorescence emitted by written molecules.

Another distinct area of materials, which have some very interesting inherent

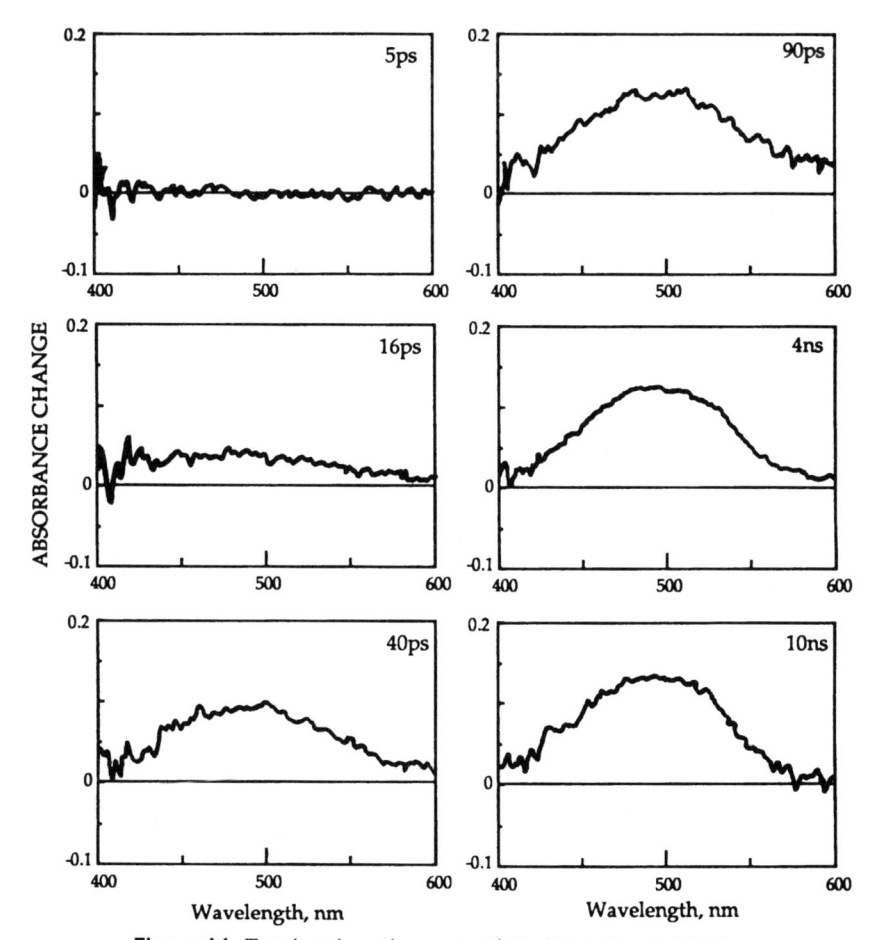

Figure 14. Transient absorption spectra (ΔA) of photochromic fulgides.

properties for optical memories, are the infrared phosphors. These materials emit in the visible region of the spectrum when irradiated with a near-infrared light. The phosphors we studied are semiconductor materials doped with particular electron trap atoms such as Eu^{+2}. The writing process is achieved by the promotion of an electron from the valence to the conduction band by means of UV irradiation. The electron is trapped by the Eu^{+2} "hole" and remains there indefinitely because the energy gap of the trap is much larger than kT.

Reading of the information is achieved by irradiating the phosphor with near-IR light (~1 eV), which is of sufficient energy to promote the electron over the hole energy barrier. Subsequently, the electron decays back into the valence band followed by visible light emission. Two disadvantages, at present, are associated with the commercially available phosphors: The information may be read only once and the phosphor is not soluble in any known to us polymer or other known to us matrix and, as mentioned previously, a 3-D block composed of these materials suffers from excessive light scattering. These materials, however, have the advantages of being stable at room temperature and since a very large number of

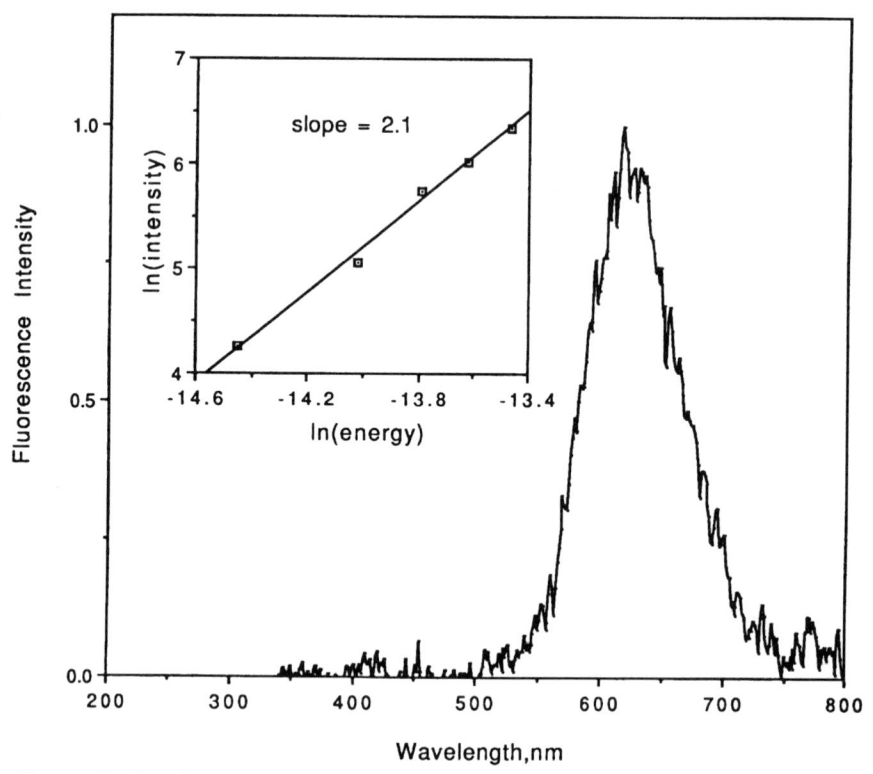

Figure 15. Two-photon fluorescence of Q-11 phosphor. Insert shows laser power versus intensity in log form.

electrons may be excited into the conduction band the storage of very large numbers of bits of information may be possible. To some extent, this diminishes the disadvantage of the read-once limitation. The two-photon fluorescence of a sample of Q-11 Quantex phosphor is shown in Fig. 15. The two wavelengths utilized for reading were either two 1.54-μm or two 1.9-μm beams. The second case is preferably because the photon energy sum corresponds to the maximum absorption wavelength of the Q-11 phosphor used for reading. At the present time, we favor the use of photochromic materials such as spiropyrans over other materials for 3-D memory devices because they possess most of the necessary characteristics needed for writing and reading. We are not suggesting that the materials as presented in this account are ready now for a practical application but rather show promise. Therefore, we use them as examples to discuss the progress that has been made in this field.

6. Sample Preparation and Spectra

6.1 Sample Preparation

The molecule 5'-chloro-6-nitro-1',3',3'-trimethyl-spiro-[2H-1-benzopyran-2,2'-indoline], 1SP (Chroma Chemicals), was purified by recrystallization from methanol and benzene. The polymer hosts polystyrene, PSt (Aldrich), polymethylmethacrylate, PMMA (Aldrich), polyethyleneglycol, PEtG (Sigma), as well as the solvents methanol (HPLC grade, Fisher), chloroform (HPLC grade, Fisher), and dichloroethane (HPLC grade, Aldrich) were used without further purification. Thin polymer films (100 μm) containing 1% SP by weight were prepared on glass slides by solvent casting from a dichloroethane solution, which contained 30% PSt by weight, or from a chloroform solution containing either 30% PMMA or 30% PEtG by weight. The films were placed in a vacuum for several hours to ascertain complete evaporation of the solvent. Solid blocks were also made by dissolving the SP molecule in a monomer such as methylmethacrylate then adding a sufficient quantity of a polymerization initiator. This homogeneous mixture was allowed to polymerize and then the solid block of PMMA/spyran was polished and stored at room temperature, at which SP is stable for indefinite periods of time.

6.2 Absorption Spectra

The absorption spectra were recorded by a double-beam spectrophotometer and fluorescence was also measured by means of a spectrofluorometer after excitation at its maximum absorption wavelength. We also measured the two-photon-induced fluorescence spectra using a 0.25-m monochromator with an intensified diode array coupled to a microcomputer attached to its exit slit. When needed, cw irradiation was achieved by a 150-W xenon lamp. Figure 4 shows the UV absorption spectrum of spyrobenzospyran in PMMA. The salient features of the spectrum are the two absorption bands with two maxima centered at approximately 325 and 260 nm, respectively. The 325-nm band is two to three times less intense than the 260-nm band. Therefore, 1SP may be a suitable material for two-photon absorption using a combination of the 1064-nm fundamental and 532-nm second harmonic of the Nd^{3+}/YAG laser.

Figure 13 shows the room temperature visible absorption spectrum of 1SP in PMMA after irradiation in the UV band with two photons. As is seen in Fig. 13, the absorption of the written form is centered at about 550 nm, which strongly red shifted from the original UV absorption band. This shift satisfies the criterion of band separation between the write and read forms of the molecule. The absorption spectrum of 1SP formed by two-photon excitation is found to be identical, as expected, to the one-photon spectrum. The two-photon photochromism is induced by spatially and temporally overlapping the 532-nm beam with the 1064-nm beam of the Nd^{3+}/YAG laser. The sum of the energies of the two photons equals the energy gap between the ground and first excited electronic state, which is located at 355 nm aboveground.

When the film is irradiated with either the 532-nm beam or the 1064-nm beam alone, photochromism is not observed. It is obvious that the two-photon method puts a stringent requirement on the simultaneous arrival of the two pulses since the intermediate virtual state has essentially no lifetime (Rentzepis 1968), and because the process is dependent on the square of the laser power. We use picosecond pulses because of their inherent high peak power. Since the PSt matrix shows a strong absorption at 266 nm, photochromism induced by two 532-nm photons in SP/PSt has not been observed probably because of the quenching by the PSt matrix. The absorption spectra of SP in PEtG after illumination by one photon or two photons are identical and are shown in Fig. 13. They appear to have a blue color, which is the consequence of absorption at 550 nm. If the irradiated films were kept at dry ice temperatures the color persisted for months. However, when the film was allowed to warm to room temperature the absorption shoulder at approximately 625 nm persists only for a few minutes. The appearance of different colored forms at different temperatures has been attributed to equilibrium between various isomeric species (Bertelson 1971).

The spectral peak is very similar to the absorption maximum of the merocyanine form of SP1 in PSt. In the less polar PSt matrix, aggregation is expected to be favored. Therefore, this new absorption shoulder can be attributed to aggregate formation. In PMMA, the absorption of the merocyanine written form, is also blue shifted relative to PSt. However, when the PMMA films are placed in dry ice ($-78°C$), a color change is not observed as is the case with PSt. It is possible that the more polar PMMA matrix prevents aggregation from occurring even at dry ice temperatures. Since the host polymer does not absorb at 266 nm and the absorption cross section of SP at 266 nm is higher than the absorption cross section at 355 nm, 266-nm two-photon absorption readily takes place in this system. A higher absorption cross section obviously allows for the decrease in the required beam intensity, which lowers the possibility of multiphoton photochemical decomposition of the sample and also permits the use of low power lasers. The absorption spectrum of the merocyanine written form of 1SP is blue shifted in the more polar PEtG matrix relative to the absorption spectrum in PSt. This indicates a possible shift in equilibrium and suggests a larger ground-state dipole moment.

6.3 Fluorescence Spectra

The fluorescence of the merocyanine, which corresponds to the written form, of the spirobenzoypyrans has received less attention than the fluorescence of the spiropyran form. However, this fluorescence has been observed previously (Becker and Roy 1965; Shabiya, Demidov, and Polyakov 1966; Horie *et al.* 1985). The spontaneous fluorescence spectrum of the merocyanine form of 1SP in PMMA and other matrices is shown in Fig. 10. The fluorescence of 1SP in PMMA follows at least the biexponential decay shown in Fig. 12. The lifetimes of the merocyanine fluorescence of 1SP in solution and in various solid matrices are summarized in Table 1 where the values of the biexponential components of the fluorescence decay are also displayed. The excited merocyanine molecule may decay by either isomerization to the original spiro form or revert to the ground state by emission of a photon (Shabiya, Demidov, and Polyakov 1966). This mechanism alone for the decay of the excited state will result in a biexponential decay lifetime curve. In addition, the written molecules within the polymer block and in solution may exist in various aggregate forms, each of which will decay from the excited state by a different lifetime. The presence of such aggregates in addition to the monomer is very probable considering the high concentration of SP in the films.

The rate of conversion of the merocyanine form to the original spiropyran form has been shown to be concentration dependent, suggesting the existence of various aggregate forms (Krysanov and Alfimov 1982). The fluorescence lifetime is also shown to be shorter in solution than in the polymer matrices. This may be

Table 1. Fluorescence Lifetimes of 1SP Dispersed in Various Polymer Matrices

Solvent/Matric	Concentration or % Weight	τ_1 (ps)	Amplitude	τ_2 (ps)	Amplitude
Methanol	2.9×10^{-5} M	40	0.75	300	0.25
PMMA	1%	1300	0.60	3300	0.40
PEtG	1%	500	0.62	2500	0.38
PSt	1%	1800	0.60	4000	0.40

attributed to viscosity effects in the rigid polymer matrices, in addition to the influence of the free volume that may be found in the solid polymer hosts. We find that the polar properties of the matrices used also influence the degree of aggregation so that analysis of the observed biexponential decays based on a simple model is not feasible. Fluorescence lifetime values of a different spirobenzopyran molecule have been reported previously (Horie *et al.* 1985) but these authors have reported only a single lifetime. However, the molecules studied and the concentrations are different than those we have investigated, therefore such discrepancies may be expected.

The disappearance of the ground-state, colored written form of SP in PMMA at room temperatures in the dark is displayed in Fig. 16, lower curve. The decay of this colored form is found to be biexponential. Two rate constants were measured: $k_1 = 0.00133$ s^{-1} and $k_2 = 0.00027$ s^{-1} with amplitudes of 0.2365 for k_1 and 0.489 for k_2, respectively. This biexponential decay is in reasonable agreement with the results presented previously (Krysanov and Alfimov 1982). In PEtG and in PSt, however, the decay constants are one to two orders of magnitude larger than in PMMA, and the colored form is found to fade with a much larger rate. Several studies on the fading rates of the colored form of spirobenzopyrans indicate that the bleaching rates depend on the distribution of the free volume in the polymer matrices (Smets 1983). In addition, the fading rates are strongly concentration dependent, because of the presence of different aggregates (Eckhard, Bose, and Krongauz 1987). Although the concentration of SP in the various matrices

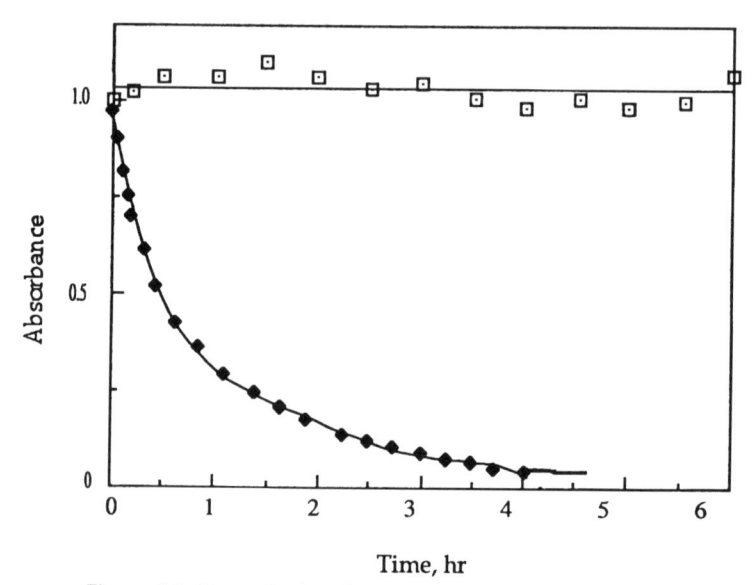

Figure 16. Decay of written form of 1SP; upper 77 K, lower 300 K.

was kept the same, differences in the bleaching rates still persist because of the varying polarity of the matrices. Several films of SP in PMMA kept at −78°C maintained the violet color of the merocyanine written form of SP for several months.

7. Durability of Written Form

Even though we have shown that we can write and read information in a 3-D format using photochromic materials, several critical characteristics must be examined before these materials may be considered as practical candidates for 3-D memory devices. These properties may include the stability of the written form at different temperatures, fatigue as a function of the number of cycles performed, laser power requirements for writing and reading, crosstalk, number of molecules per written bit, absorption cross section, and fluorescence quantum yield. Studies have been and are currently being performed in most of these areas. The spiro form of spyran materials, which correspond to 0 in the binary code or write form, is stable at room temperature, however, the written form is rather unstable and was found to revert to the original form within a few hours at room temperature. We have measured the decay kinetics and mechanism from 77 to 273 K with an accuracy of ±2 K keeping the sample in a cryostat, which allowed us to measure the stability of the written form as a function of temperature. The sample was kept at a particular temperature and irradiated with 532-nm photons. Then the fluorescence intensity of the written form was recorded as a function of the number of reading cycles.

The decay of intensity as function of laser irradiation, at 0.5 mJ, at various temperatures is shown in Fig. 17. When 1SP was dispersed in a PMMA solid block, the lifetime of the written form was found to increase as the temperature decreased. Similar behavior was observed in other polymer hosts. These data are presented in Table 2. A brief examination of the data displayed in this table makes it rather obvious that the rate of decay decreases as a function of temperature. Also, as we have shown before, when sufficiently low temperatures have been reached, i.e., −80°C, the written form becomes stable indefinitely. Activation energy parameters are, we believe, mostly responsible for the decay because to some extent they may prevent the isomerization process from occurring even though rapture of the C–O bond may still be possible at these low temperatures. In addition, spiropyrans behave differently depending on their structure. For example spiropyrans, which have the structures shown in Fig. 5 when dispersed in a solid polymer matrix (PMMA or PS), exist in a thermoequilibrium of two forms: a clear spiropyran form *A* and a colored merocyanine form *B*. The equilibrium concentration of either the colored or clear form depends on the specific molecular components of SP. Thus, SP 1–3 at room temperature exists almost exclusively in the

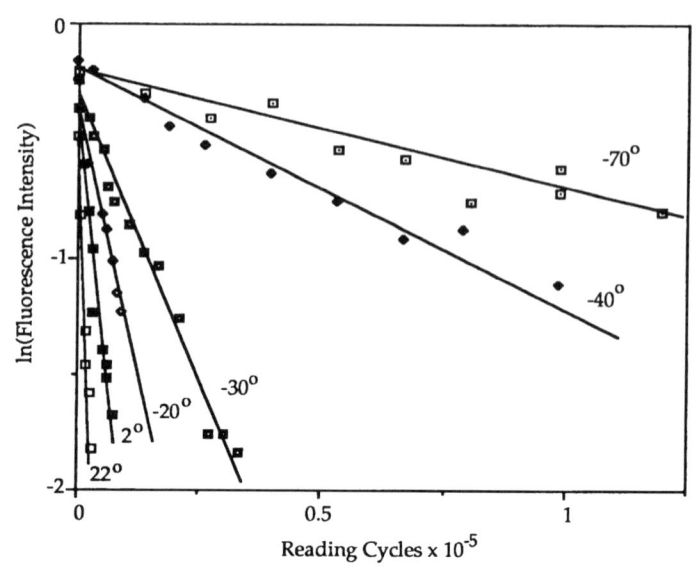

Figure 17. Fatigue of 1SP in PMMA as a function of temperature (shown as fluorescence intensity versus number of cycles at various temperatures at 0.5 mJ/cm^2).

spirocyclic form *A;* therefore, a solid polymer cube containing these molecules is colorless. SP 4 embedded in a polymer matrix exists in both thermoequilibrium forms *A* and *B*. The samples that contain SP5 are intensively colored due to considerably higher equilibrium concentration of the colored form *B* compared to form *A*. The absorption spectrum of the merocyanine form of 1SP and 2SP is blue shifted when the PS matrix ($\epsilon = 2.5$) is substituted by the more polar PMMA ($\epsilon = 3.7$) (Table 3). UV excitation of the closed form *A* results in the heterolitic cleavage of the C–O bond followed by isomerization to merocyanine from *B*, which leads to very strong coloration of samples. After irradiation, the samples encounter reversible rearrangement to the initial equilibrium form, which occurs at room temperature. The rate of thermal discoloration of merocyanine forms also depends on both the composition of SP and the polymer matrix.

Multiexponential thermal decay was observed in the photo-induced forms of SP molecules dispersed in the polymer matrices we studied. Such multiple exponential behavior is expected because of the many types of merocyanine isomers and the abundant nonequivalent sites present in a polymer matrix. These conditions lead to the difference in cyclization rates of SP molecules located in different sites of the polymer matrix. However, to the first approximation, thermal decay kinetics may be described as a sum of two exponentials. The decay constants calculated under this approximation are shown in Table 3. Note that replacement of one polymer by another polymer with higher polarity may cause the decrease in the rate of dark decay of the merocyanine forms. Apparently, this effect can be

Table 2. Photostability of Written Form of 1SP at Different Temperatures

Polymer					k, s^{-1} (τ, s)				ΔE, kcal/mol
°C	20	0	−20	−30	−40	−60	−70	−80	
PMMA	1.3×10^{-2} (76)	5.2×10^{-3} (190)	2.7×10^{-3} (370)	1.2×10^{-3} (850)	2.4×10^{-4} (4100)		1.2×10^{-4} (8400)		6.4
PS	4.9×10^{-3} (200)	6.1×10^{-3} (160)	7.2×10^{-4} (1400)		3.3×10^{-4} (3000)	2.7×10^{-4} (3700)			5.0
PVA	5.8×10^{-2} (17)	3.5×10^{-2} (28)	2.3×10^{-3} (430)		1.4×10^{-3} (715)	2.9×10^{-4} (3450)		2.5×10^{-5} (40000)	8.7

Table 3. Thermal Stability of Several Photochromic Molecules in Various Hosts

SP	Absorption Merocyanine Form, nm		Fluorescence Merocyanine Form, nm		$k_1;k_2$ (s^{-1})	
	PS	PMMA	PS	PMMA	PS	PMMA
1	609	580	645	625	$4 \times 10^{-3}; 2 \times 10^{-4}$	$1 \times 10^{-3}; 3 \times 10^{-4}$
2	630	615	690	670	$1 \times 10^{-2}; 6 \times 10^{-4}$	$5 \times 10^{-3}; 2 \times 10^{-4}$
3		580		620		$3 \times 10^{-2}; 2 \times 10^{-3}$
4		585		605		
5		565		610		

attributed to the relative stabilization of the polar structure of the merocyanine form by the polar environment of the matrix. The effect of the thermal decay processes on the stored information is obviously very detrimental to any device because it causes the information stored to be deleted. To alleviate this effect, the material is kept at low temperatures, i.e., −40°C or lower, where the decay of the written form is negligible. It is extremely important of course to find molecules that have both forms stable at room temperature. To achieve this, we are studying other types of photochromic molecules and also investigating means for the stabilization of the written form of 1SP and other spiropyrans.

8. Stabilization of the Written Form

The interaction of SP with light induces the formation of the written form, which is shown to be in an open-ended configuration. The two ends of the molecule are charged, forming what is known as *zwiterion* (see Fig. 7). At room temperature the two ends move closer and recombine, once again forming the closed molecular structure of the original molecule. In one study aimed at stabilizing the written forms, we investigated means by which one can chemically bind the two charged ends of the open form to another molecule or anchor them to the polymer matrix thus prohibiting the closure of the ring. This would result in the prevention of erasure of the written information, which occurs when the molecule reverts to the original structure, that of the closed form.

In view of the fact that the open form is essentially a di-anion with a positive charge located on the nitrogen and a negative on the oxygen (Fig. 7, lower right-hand molecular structure) an ionic species such as an acid could bind these groups and anchor the molecule permanently onto the open, written structure. This binding process was affected by the use of HCl and a variety of organic and inorganic acids. Reaction of 1SP with HCl resulted in shifting the equilibrium from the closed form to the open form, which rendered the open form stable indefinitely at room temperature. It was also possible to change this anchored form to the original, closed form again by irradiation with UV light.

The absorption and fluorescence spectra of 1SP in the presence of acid are shown in Fig. 18. The difficulty with this process is that the concentration of this bridged material dissolved in polymers is low, $\sim 10^{-5}$ M, and attempts to increase its concentration have resulted in the crystallization of the chromophore in the matrix and consequently the change of the cube from a clear to a translucent sample, which scatters very strongly and makes the utilization of this material as an optical memory device rather unacceptable. The use of polar type polymers such as polyhydroxyethyl methacrylate (PHEMA) for anchoring the two ends of written SP molecules has also improved the stability of the open form and resulted in a large increase in the lifetime of the written form. For example, while in the original molecule the information decayed to $1/e$ of its value within 70 min (Fig. 16, lower). At 20°C the bridged material was found to have a lifetime of 1.6×10^6 s or 3×10^4 min at 3°C (see Fig. 19). This constitutes a more than a hundred-fold increase in the stability of the written form and suggests to us that there is a good possibility that a stable room temperature material may be achieved by this type of chemistry; if not in this particular 1SP molecule, then in some of the other photochromic materials we are currently investigating.

As a consequence of the chemical binding described, the activation energy of the bridged species has increased to 40 kcal as shown in the Arrhenius plot of Fig. 20, where the rates at 321, 296, and 276 K (38, 23, and 3°C) are plotted versus $1/T$. The decay rate k (reciprocal lifetime) of the written form at 38, 23, and 3°C is given in Figs. 19(a), (b), and (c), respectively. Since the viscosity of the polymer

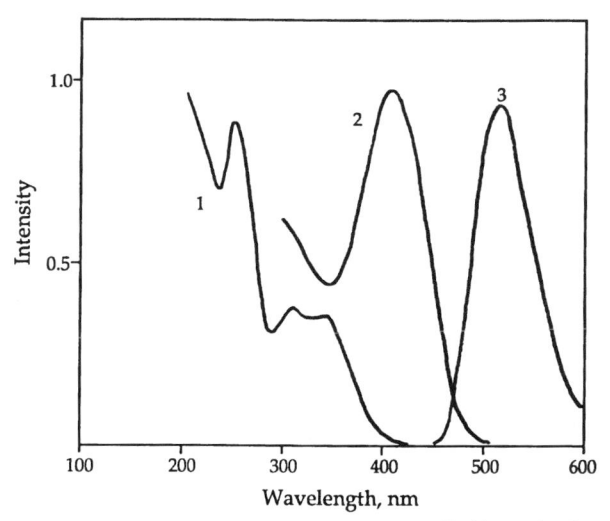

Figure 18. Absorption and fluorescence spectra of bridge molecules.

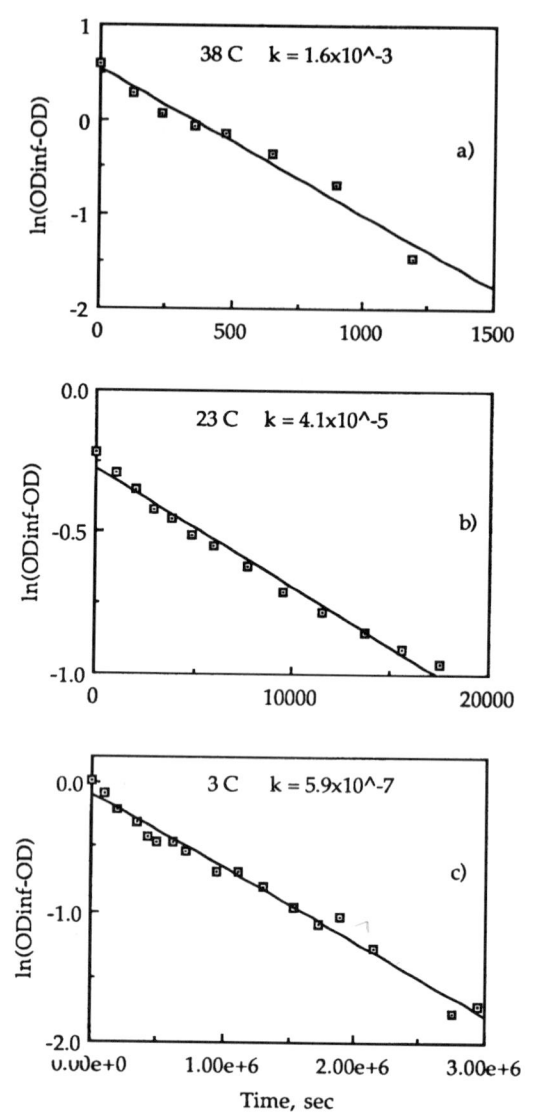

Figure 19. Decay of bridged written form of 1SP/PHEMA versus time: (a) 38°C, (b) 23°C, and (c) 3°C.

is practically the same at these three temperatures, the activation energy calculated from data in Fig. 20 must be influenced by the change in polarity and dielectric constant of the matrix with temperature. There are other means by which a material may have a stable room temperature written form. An obvious one is the design of a molecular structure which has equally low-energy minima in both the original and written forms of the molecule and where the activation energy re-

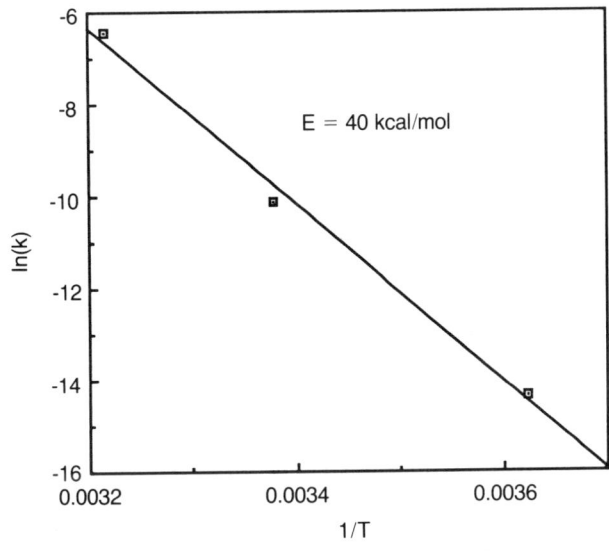

Figure 20. Activation energy plot of written form.

quired to shift it from one form to the other far exceeds kT. Such molecules are being formulated in our laboratories and details of these new systems will be presented in forthcoming communications.

9. Fatigue

Fatigue, which for a photochromic molecule is defined as the gradual loss of the ability to change color (write) after repeated excitation, or the gradual loss of color (reading) after a repeated number of fluorescence cycles is a very important parameter. Since these cycles correspond to the write and read cycles of the 3-D memory device, fatigue places a limit on the maximum number of write and read cycles that can be performed with a particular single 3-D memory unit. Fatigue therefore may be measured by the decrease in the fluorescence intensity of the written form as a function of the cycles performed. In addition, the influence of temperature and laser power on fatigue may also be important, so we have studied them extensively.

Most, if not all, materials that we know experience deterioration after a certain amount of use. Materials sometimes have an assigned lifetime even without use, but for the memory materials that we studied, the fatigue is, to a large extent, a function of the number of cycles performed and the energy per laser pulse used for reading and writing. In our fatigue studies we used a 1-cm cube PMMA polymer in which 10^{-2} M 1SP photochromic material was homogeneously dispersed by means of the procedure described previously in this paper. A set of information bits with a diameter of 30μm was written inside the PMMA/1SP cube. The material was maintained at ~77 K throughout the experiment. The reason for this low temperature was to ascertain that any decay measured was due to the reading process rather than temperature. As shown in the upper curve of Fig. 16, the decay of 1SP at 77 K is practically negligible, therefore the data presented in Fig. 21 may be attributed entirely to the laser beam energy and the number of cycles performed.

In these experiments, the written spot ($T \sim 77$ K) was irradiated with a laser beam with the preselected energy shown in Fig. 21, and the change in the fluorescence intensity of the written spot was measured as a function of reading cycles. The beam diameter remained constant in all measurements and the temperature did not vary by more than ± 2 K. The experiments were repeated several times and the data collected by means of three different laser energies are plotted in Fig. 21 in the form of intensity versus number of reading cycles. It is immediately evident, after even a cursory look at Fig. 21, that the energy of the beam plays a dominant role on the fatigue and the number of cycles that may be performed before the stored information fades. The fatigue expressed as a decrease in fluorescence intensity shows that half of the information is lost after 10^5 cycles when the beam energy is 1.25 mJ/cm^2, while the same intensity decrease occurs after $\sim 10^6$ cycles where the power of the reading laser was 0.5 mJ/cm^2. Practically no change is observed when a 0.05 mJ/cm^2 energy laser beam was used to read the stored information.

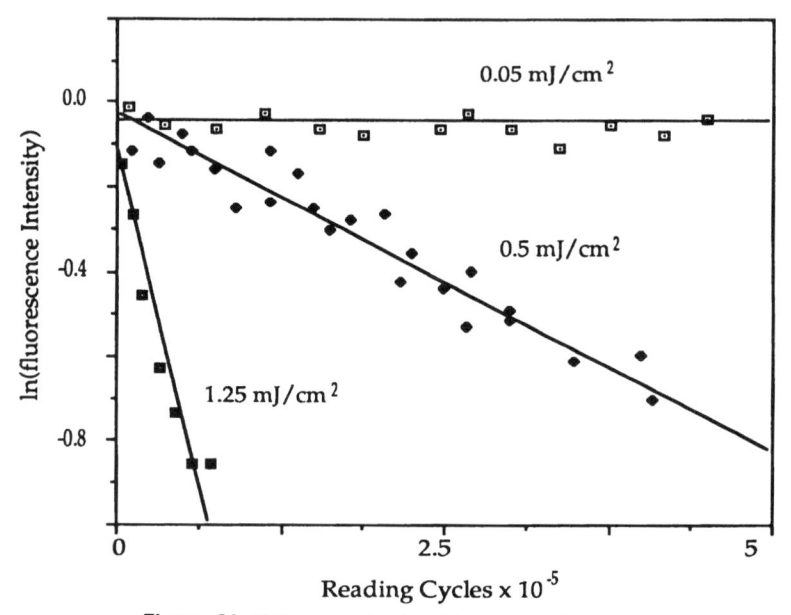

Figure 21. Fatigue as a function of laser energy for 1SP.

These results suggest that in order to utilize the 1SP material for the construction and utilization of a memory device, the energy of the laser must be of the order of 50 µJ if the information is to read more than 10^6. Because the low energy utilized for reading induces a small number of molecules to emit, the fluorescence intensity becomes very low, which imposes additional constraints on the 3-D fluorescence detection system. However, the single-photon measuring capability of CCD detectors may eliminate these constraints. Also, if the writing process is to be achieved by similarly low-power sources, then the absorption cross section and quantum yield for the conversion of the original form to the written form must be increased proportionally. At the present time we are investigating means for achieving these goals and also means for improving the fluorescence quantum efficiency of the written form.

It was shown previously that the written form decays with higher rates as the temperature increases. Therefore, the number of cycles is also expected to be highly dependent on the temperature. The effect of temperature on fatigue at constant laser power irradiation is shown in Table 2 where the fatigue rate of the written form presented is a function of temperature in several polymers matrices. It is evident that without further stabilization the 1SP material does not perform well at all at temperatures above $-30°C$. When stabilized, however, by a bridge or utilized at a low temperature a reasonable number of write/read cycles may be performed without substantial decay.

10. Dependence of Stability on Polymer Host

The 1SP molecule is usually dispersed homogeneously in a polymer, which provides the environment and, to a large extent, determines the stability of the written information. As discussed previously, although the original structure of 1SP is stable, the written structure whose red fluorescence is the means for reading the information is unstable and in PMMA, at room temperature, reverts to the original one with a rate of 7.2×10^{-2} s. Because the fluorescence intensity is a crucial parameter, we measured its intensity and its lifetime as a function of polarity and hardness of the host medium.

Two specific polymer samples were prepared by radical polymerization of MMA and 2-hydroxyethyl methacrylate (HEMA) in which 10^{-4} M of 1SP was dissolved. These polymer samples were cut to a 1- $\times$ 1- $\times$ 2-in. blocks and polished to optical quality. The fluorescence of rhodamine 6G with its known quantum yield of 0.9 was used as a standard for the measurement of the fluorescence efficiency of the two polymer blocks, PMMA/1SP and PHEMA/1SP, and the corresponding monomeric solutions, MMA/1SP and HEMA/1SP. Since both rhodamine 6G and our samples emit at the same 500- to 600-nm region, comparison of the data becomes more reliable. The fluorescence quantum yield Φ_{1SP} was calculated using the experimental data of the optical density of rhodamine 6G and

Table 4. Spectroscopic Constants of 1SP in Several Polymer Matrices

Solvent/Polymer Matrix	Fluorescence Quantum Yield	Thermal Decay Constant (s^{-1})	Lifetime (s)
MMA	$< 1 \times 10^{-3}$	7.2×10^{-2}	14
HEMA	3.0×10^{-3}	8.6×10^{-4}	1200
PMMA	1.6×10^{-2}	4.0×10^{-4}	2500
PHEMA	5.0×10^{-2}	3.0×10^{-5}	33000

the 1SP sample, designated as OD_{R6G}, and OD_{1SP}, respectively, and the fluorescence intensity rhodamine 6G, I_{R6G}, and 1SP, I_{1SP}, and the expression:

$$\Phi_{1SP} = \Phi_{R6G} \frac{OD_{R6G} \int I_{1SP} \, d\lambda}{OD_{1SP} \int I_{R6G} \, d\lambda}$$

The fluorescence quantum yields of 1SP calculated using the fluorescence spectra of 1SP n MMA, HEMA, PMMA, and PHEMA, are listed in Table 4. It is found that 1SP has a rather low quantum yield, 3×10^{-3} to 5×10^{-3} compared to the quantum yield for the fluorescence of rhodamine 6G. One of the reasons for the low quantum yield of the 1SP written form is isomerization, which occurs at a greater rate than the fluorescence decay lifetime and thus competes successfully with its fluorescence.

We have shown previously that polar solvents stabilize the written polar structure and attenuate the rate of isomerization. Similarly, hard polymer matrices limit the ability for molecular group movement, thus making isomerization slower and hence increasing the fluorescence quantum yield. The data in Table 4 show that the fluorescence quantum yield of 1SP increases by an order of magnitude from HEMA to PHEMA from 3.0×10^{-3} to 5.0×10^{-2}. A similar increase in the fluorescence quantum yield is found for MMA and PMMA. The higher fluorescence quantum yield for the written form of 1SP was observed in the PHEMA polymer matrix, which is both a hard and polar matrix. We must note that, even though the fluorescence quantum yield of 1SP in PMMA and PHEMA is low compared to rhodamine 6G, the 1SP written bits emit sufficient fluorescent light to be detected and used for information reading purposes.

11. Conclusion

It is evident that much more research and in-depth studies must be performed in order to understand the molecular characteristics of these materials and their influence on the stability of both the write and read forms. In addition, background

Three-Dimensional Optical Storage Memory by Means of Two-Photon Interaction   323

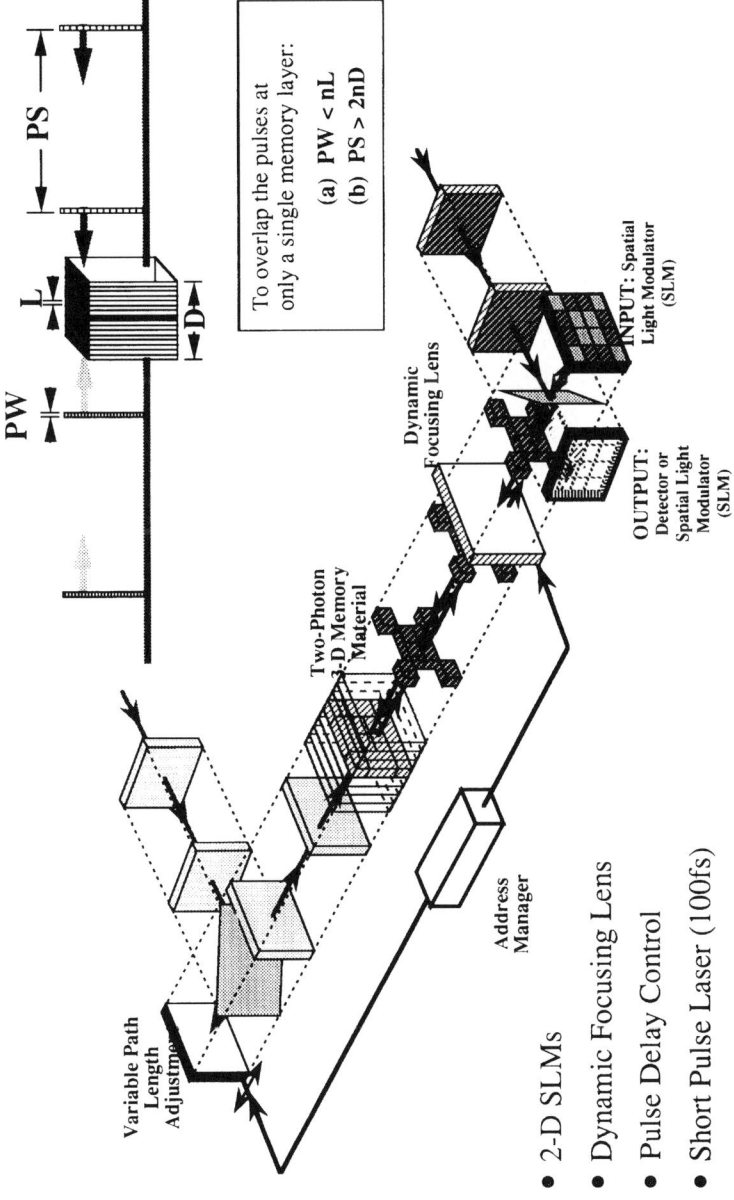

Figure 22. Schematic representation of a two-photon 3-D optical system.

noise during the reading and writing processes and the optical and engineering requirements for optical computers still need to be addressed. Many known serious difficulties are encountered when one attempts to construct—even conceptually—a 3-D optical system. Our studies on photochromics indicate that these are promising candidates for utilization in 3-D optical storage memory devices. We trust that continuing research pursued on 3-D memory devices by means of two-photon and the other promising areas mentioned briefly in the opening paragraphs of this chapter will result in a 3-D optical storage memory that will eventually make optical computing and large-scale parallel data processing a reality.

A possible configuration for a two-photon 3-D optical system is shown in Fig. 22. It represents a means for constructing an optical system capable of encoding and reading information to and from a 3-D volume memory in a parallel input/output mode.

In this chapter, we outlined the basic theory and experimental methods by which one may write/read and erase information within a 3-D volume memory. We have also described the molecular mechanisms that govern the write and read cycles and presented a brief description of the parameters that influence the stability and speed of the input and output of information. The materials described may not be optimum for device construction and practical utilization, but they are helpful in our intent to show the study and progress made in this field in the past two years and to point out some of the advantages and difficulties encountered.

Assuming that a practical 3-D memory may be constructed, the advantages of such a system are shown schematically in Fig. 2 where the access time of several conventional devices are compared to a 3-D two-photon device. The advantages in speed, density, and bandwidth become apparent, which, in combination with the other characteristics shown in Table 5, provide the impetus to continue the search for a 3-D memory material used in practical 3-D storage memory device.

Table 5. List of the Capabilities of Various Types of Computer Storage Memory Devices

Memory Type	Capacity	Access Time	Cost ¢/bit
Tape	10^{10} bits	100 s	10^{-5}
Disk	10^8 bits	300 ms	5×10^{-2}
Drum	10^7–10^8 bits	10 ms	10^{-2}
Core	10^6 bits	1 µs	2
Semi-conductor	10^5 bits	100 ns	20
Optical (2-D)	10^8 bits	10 ns	10^{-3}–10^{-4}
3-D	10^{13} bits	~1 ns	10^{-8}

ACKNOWLEDGEMENT

This work was supported in part by the U.S. Air Force Rome Laboratories and DARPA under contract F30602-90-C0014.

REFERENCES

Becker, R. S., and Roy, J. K. (1965). *J. Phys. Chem.* **69**, 1435.
Bertelson, R. C. (1971). *Techniques of Chemistry: Photochromism* (G. M. Brown, ed.), Wiley-Interscience, New York, Vol. 3, p. 45.
Birge, R. R. (1990). *Ann. Rev. Phys. Chem.* **9**, 683.
Birge, R. R., Fleitz, P. A., Gross, R. A., Izgi, J. C., Laurence, A. F., Stuart, J. A., and Tallert, J. R. (1990). *IEEE, FMBS* **12**, 1788.
Brauchle, C., Hampp, N., and Oesterhelt, D. (1991). *Adv. Mater.* **3**, 420.
D'Auria, L., Huignard, J. P., Slezak, C., and Spitz, E. (1974). *Appl. Opt.* **13**, 808.
DeCegama, A. L. (1989). *Parallel Processing Architecture and VLCI Hardware.* Prentice-Hall, Englewood Cliffs, NJ.
Demtröder, W. (1988). *Laser Spectroscopy.* Springer-Verlag, New York.
Dvornikov, A., Malkin, V. Y., and Kuzmin, V. (1982). *Bull. Ac. Sci. USSR, Div. Chem.* **31**, 1355.
Eckhard, H., Bose, A., and Krongauz, V. A. (1987). *Polymer* **28**, 1959.
Gaylord, T. K. (1972). *Opt. Spectra* **6**, 25.
Goeppert–Mayer, M. (1931). *Ann. Phys.* **9**, 273.
Heller, H. G., and Oliver, S. (1981). *J. Chem. Soc. Perkin Trans.* **1**, 197.
Horie, K., Hira, K., Mita, I., Takubo, Y., Okamoto, T., Washio, M., Tagawa, S., and Tabato, Y. (1985). *Chem. Phys. Lett.* **119**, 499.
Horie, K., Hirao, K., Keumochi, N., and Mita, I. (1988). *Macromol. Chem. Rapid Comm.* **9**, 267.
Hunter, S., Kiamilev, F., Esener, S., Parthenopoulos, D. A., and Rentzepis, P. M. (1990). *Appl. Opt.* **29**, 2058.
Krysanov S. A., and Alfimov, M. V. (1982). *Chem. Phys. Lett.* **91**, 77.
Moerner, W. E., ed. (1987). *Persistent Hole Burning: Science and Applications.* Springer, Berlin.
Parthenopoulos, D. A., and Rentzepis, P. M. (1989). *Science* **245**, 843.
Parthenopoulos, D. A., and Rentzepis, P. M. (1990). *J. Appl. Phys.* **68**, 814.
Parthenopoulos, D. A., and Rentzepis, P. M. (1990b). *J. Mol Str.* **22**, 2860.
Rentzepis, P. M. (1968). *Chem. Phys. Lett.* **2**, 117.
Robinson, B. (Sep. 18, 1989). Grand challenges to supercomputing. *Electron. Eng. Times.*
Shabiya, Ar., Demidov, K. B., and Polyakov, Yu. N. (1966). *Opt. Spect.* **20**, 412.
Sild, Olve, and Haller, K., eds. (1988). *Zero Phonon Lines.* Springer-Verlag, New York.
Smets, G. (1983). *Adv. Polym. Sci.* **50**, 17.
Stickler, J. H., and Webb, W. W. (1991). *Opt. Lett.* **16**, 1780.
Thoma, R., Hampp, N., Brauchle, C., and Oesterhelt, D. (1990). *Opt. Lett.* **16**, 651.
Topchiev, D. A. (1990). *Vysok. Soed. Ser. A* **32**, 2243.
Tyer, Jr., N. W., and Becker, R. S. (1970). *J. Am. Chem. Soc.* **92**, 1295.

Index

A

aberrations, 26–27, 194
  see also diffractive lens aberration properties of; planar microlens, aberration properties of
acceptance angle, 179
amplifier, 59–60, 62
  sense, 62
aperture
  numerical, 134, 172, 178, 195
    see also diffractive lens, numerical aperture and planar microlens, numerical aperture
  stop, diameter, 194
architecture, *see* optical computing, architecture
array
  device, 12, 220
    imperfect, 221
  focused, 199
  lenslet, *see* lenslet array
  optical gate, *see* optical gate array
  spot, *see* beamsplitter, multiple
array generation, *see* beamsplitter, multiple
array generator, *see* beamsplitter, multiple
array illuminator, *see* beamsplitter, multiple
asynchronous transfer mode (ATM), 92
ATM, *see* asynchronous transfer mode

B

backplane, 8
  optical, 163
banyan network, 21, 38, 160
  complete, 206
  optical implementation, 21, 160, 207–209
  permutation, 206–207
barrier
  conventional, 46
  ultrashallow, 62
beam combination, 28–30
beam separation, 28
beam shaping

anti-Gaussian, 233
  in array generators, 243
beamsplitter, multiple, 137, 154, 227
  applications of, 228
  beam shaping by, 243
  chromatic errors of, 244
  cascading of, 243
  compression ratio of, 230
  Fourier plane, 155, 237
  Fresnel plane, 157, 235
  image plane, 157, 231
  noise in, 244
  performance parameters of, 229
  splitting ratio of, 229
binary optics, 137–139, 238
bistability, 52–54
blazed grating, 148, 176
blazed structure, 181, 182, 184, 186
Bragg angle, 179, 258
Bragg condition, 258, 271

C

CGH, *see* hologram, computer-generated
chloromethylated polystyrene (CMS), 184–185
circuit design, 220
  fault-tolerant, 221
CMS, *see* chloromethylated polystyrene
computer aided design, 141
computer memory, 287
  access speed of, 288
  capacity of, 289
  hierarchy of, 290
  optical, *see* optical memory
computer-generated hologram (CGH), *see* hologram, computer-generated
contrast ratio, 47
coupled-wave equation, 267
critical distance, 198, 200
crossbar switch, 14, 253
  optical 14, 253
crossover network, 21, 207–209
  complete, 209

327

crossover network (*continued*)
  in logic circuits, 216
  optical implementation, 207–209
  permutation, 210–211
crosstalk, 21, 200–201

D

Dammann grating, 102, 155–157, 238–240
  array generation with, *see* beamsplitter, multiple, Fourier plane
dark conductivity, 264
DBR, *see* distributed Bragg reflector
depth of focus, 26
diffraction
  angle, 198
  efficiency, *see* diffraction efficiency
  grating, *see* diffraction grating
  pattern, 200
  spreading, 196, 199
diffraction efficiency, 143, 150, 176–180
  analytical method for calculation of, 176–177
  calculated results for, 150, 177–180
  experimental results for, 188, 190
  of volume holographic storage, 258
diffraction grating, 27–28
  see blazed grating; diffractive optical element
diffraction-limited spot size, 26, 195
diffractive lens, 151, 170–174, 187–191
  aberration properties of, 172–173, 190–191
  fabrication of, 180–187
  focal length of, 151
  focal spot profile of, 152–153, 188–190
  for normal incidence, 170–172, 187–188
  for oblique incidence, 172–174, 189–191
  numerical aperture of, 172, 178
  reflective, 170, 185, 187, 189
  replication of, 146
  transmissive, 170, 185, 187
  wavelength dependence of, 154
diffractive optical element (DOE), 137, 139
  fabrication of, 139–143
    errors in, 144–146
    lithographic, *see* lithography
  replication of, 146
diffusion, 116–119
  coefficient, 119
  equation, 117
dispersion, 33
distributed Bragg reflector (DBR), 79

distributed-index lens, *see* planar microlens, distributed-index
DOE, *see* diffractive optical element
donor density, 260
dual-rail logic, 215

E

electrical-to-optical power conversion efficiency, 88
electro-optic coefficient, 267
electron-beam lithography, *see* lithography, electron-beam
electron-beam resist, 182, 184–185
electron-beam writing system, 180–182
elliptical grating, 174
etching, 139, 142
exciton peak, 47

F

fan-in, fan-out, 16, 215–216, 228
fibers, optical, 213–214
field
  angle, 194
  extent, 194
  zero, 197
field of view, 16
flip-chip bonding, 9, 94, 161–163
flip-chip solder bump bonding, *see* flip-chip bonding
fly's eye lens, 231, 240
f-number, 30
  of a diffractive lens, 153–154
Fourier plane beamsplitter, *see* beamsplitter, Fourier plane
free-space digital optics, 9, 11
  limitations of, 34
Fresnel lens, 151, 170, 191
Fresnel number, 152
Fresnel plane beamsplitter, *see* beamsplitter, Fresnel plane
Fresnel zone plate, 151

G

gain, 56, 59–60, 62
  electronic, 59–60, 62
  time-sequential, 56

Gaussian elimination, 219
grating equation, 27

H

HOE, *see* holographic optical element, hologram
hole burning, 292
hologram
  computer generated (CGH), 138, 240
  multiple beamsplitter, 238
  multiplex, 238
  volume, 212, 238, 258–262
holographic optical element (HOE), *see* hologram
honeycomb condensor, 240

I

image plane beamsplitter, *see* beamsplitter, image plane
image relaying, 21
imaging system
  4f, 25, 160
  integrated, 160, 162
  telecentric, 25
index modulation, 230
integration
  device, 68, 77
  micro-optic, 137, 158
  system, 7, 163
interconnection, *see also* optical interconnection
  comparison of electronic and optical, 101
  design of, 30
  hierarchy of, 8
  in processing systems, 4
  irregular, 212
  network, *see* multistage interconnection network
  optical, parallel, 193
  reconfigurable, 217, 273
  topology of, 21
ion-exchange technology, 116

K

kinoform, 138

L

lateral magnification formula, 23
lens formula, 23
lenslet array
  circular-aperture, 174–175, 185
  diffractive, 159
  for multiple beamsplitting, 231, 240
  rectangular-aperture, 174–176, 183, 186
  refractive, 115, 121, 133
light coupling
  between laser diodes and PML, 134–135
light efficiency, 143, 230
linear absorption coefficient, 267
lithography
  electron-beam, 139, 180–187
  direct-write, 139
  optical, 139, 142

M

macro-optics, 194
MCM, *see* multichip module
memory, *see* computer memory
micro-optics, 194, 196
microlaser, *see* vertical cavity surface-emitting laser
microlens array, *see* lenslet array
MIN, *see* multistage interconnection network
minimum feature width, 153
modulator, 45–51
  array, 51
  Fabry-Perot, 49–50
  multiple quantum well, 50
  reflection, 48–50
  transmission, 48
MPPC, *see* phase conjugation, mutually pumped
multichip module (MCM), 8, 101
multiple quantum well, 46
  modulator, 50
    surface-normal, 48, 74
multistage interconnection network (MIN), 4, 202
  banyan, *see* banyan network
  complete, 204
  cost of, 203–204
  crossover, *see* crossover network
  latency of, 203
  perfect shuffle, *see* perfect shuffle network
  permutation, 202–203
  point-to-point, 203

N

network, *see* multistage interconnection network
numerical aperture, *see* aperture, numerical

O

optical computer, *see* optical computing
optical computing, 1, 74, 193, 214
  architecture, 13, 213, 217
optical gate array
  imperfect, 220
  yield
    effective, 221, 223
    fabrication, 220
optical interconnection, 22, 74–75, 100–101, 137, 139, 158, 193, 249
  2-D topology of, 22
  3-D topology of, 22
  advantages of, 250
  classification of, 251
  design considerations for, 30
  generic view of, 250
  implementation of, 24
  laser based, 102
  modulator based, 102
  network, *see* multistage interconnection network
  programmable, 217, 272
  reconfigurable, 92, 218, 273
  space-invariant, 201
  space-variant, 158, 201
optical logic device, 13, 64, 103
optical vector-matrix multiplication, 14, 253
optical memory
  three-dimensional, 287
    advantages of, 290
    capacity of, 291
    erasing of, 297, 304
    materials for, 304
      fatigue of, 316
      stability of, 313
    materials preparation for, 309
    means for creation, 291
    reading of, 297, 302
      wavelength for, 311
    writing of, 297, 298
      wavelength for, 309
optical programmable logic array, 40, 217

optical switch
  based on beam steering, 273
  prototype of SEED-based, 36–39
  self-routing, 92–93
optical switching energy, *see* self-electrooptic effect device, vertical to surface transmission electro-photonic device
optical tensor-matrix multiplication, 254, 273, 279

P

packaging, 4, 7, 158
pattern generator, 181–182
perfect shuffle network, 21, 204
  complete, 204
  optical implementation of, 205–206
  permutation, 205
phase conjugation, 268
  mutually pumped (MPPC), 279–280
  self-pumped (SPPC), 269, 279
phase contrast method, 231
phase grating, 141, 238
  binary, 238
  fabrication of, *see* diffractive optical elements, fabrication of
  multilevel, 141
photoconductivity, 264
photonic switch, *see* optical switch
photorefractive
  beam fanning, 275
  beam steering, 271, 273
  charge-limited field, 260
  CAT conjugator, 269, 280
  coupling constant, 267
  crossbar network, 274
    energy efficiency of, 275
    crosstalk noise in, 276
    reconfiguration rate of, 277
  diffusion field, 260
  effect, 256
    discovery of, 256
    origin of, 256
  energy coupling, 267, 273
  four-wave mixing, 268, 279
  gain, 267
  grating phase-shift, 267
  material, 256
    dark storage time of, 265
    response time of, 264

sensitivity of, 262
spectral range of, 256
optimum grating spacing, 261
reconfigurable interconnect, 218, 273
space charge field, 260
steady state index modulation, 260
two-wave mixing, 266
volume hologram, 257
  fixing of, 265
  erasure of, 265
planar microlens (PML), 113, 115
  aberration coefficients, 126
  aberration measurement, 123, 125
  aberration properties of, 125
  characteristics of, 120, 123
  distributed-index (DI-), 115, 120
  fabrication of, 115
  focal spot generated by, 122
  index distribution of, 121
  numerical aperture of, 134
  ray trajectory of, 122
  swelled (S-), 115, 131
  wavefront profile of, 125
planar optics, 24, 94, 139, 161, 172
planar optic system, *see* planar optics
planar reflection optical circuit, *see* planar optics
PML, *see* planar microlens
PMMA, *see* polymethyl methacrylate
POEM, *see* programmable optoelectronic multiprocessor
polymethyl methacrylate (PMMA), 182, 184
power dissipation, 18
programmable optoelectronic multiprocessor (POEM), 217–218

Q

quantum well, 46–49
  coupled, 62

R

ray trajectory, 120, 122
  of planar microlens, 122
reactive ion etching, *see* etching
reconfiguration
  architecture, 218–219
  interconnects, 217

regular interconnect computer
  assembly of, 221
  AT&T model of, 214
  design of, 221–223
Rent's rule, 5
replication, *see* diffractive optical element, replication of
responsivity, 15

S

S-SEED, *see* self-electrooptic effect device, symmetric
scaling
  lens, 195–196
SDM, *see* space-division multiplexing
SEED, *see* self-electrooptic effect device
self-electrooptic effect device (SEED), 51–69
  resistor-biased, 52
  diode-biased, 52
  diode clamped, 62
  logic, 64
  multistate, 58
  switching energy of, 60–64
    electrical, 61
    optical, 60–64
  symmetric, 36–39, 53–58
  transistor-biased, 59–60
    phototransistor, 59
    field effect, 59–60
  tri-state, 58
sense amplifier, *see* amplifier
serial-to-parallel data conversion, 91
shadowing effect, 145
shift register, 66–67
signal skew, 34
SLM, *see* spatial light modulator
smart pixel, 13, 64–69, 158
space-division multiplexing (SDM), 254, 282
spatial light modulator (SLM), 14
split-and-shift MIN, 209
splitting ratio, 229
spot array generation, *see* array generation
spot size, diffraction-limited, *see* diffraction-limited spot size
SPPC, *see* phase conjugation, self-pumped
stacked planar optics, 94, 113–114
stacked transmission optical circuit, *see* stacked planar optics

storage capacity
  of volume hologram, *see* volume holographic storage
  surface-normal optical device, 75
  switching energy, 60–64
  optical, *see* optical switching energy
  switching node, 65–67

T

TAB, *see* tape-automated bonding
Talbot effect, 234
tape-automated bonding (TAB), 9
telecentric imaging, 24
telescope array, 231
three-dimensional memory, *see* optical memory, three-dimensional
tradeoff
  micro-optics vs. macro-optics, 194
  device spacing vs. propagation distance, 199
trap density, 260
two-photon process, 291, 293
  schematic representation of, 295
  theoretical background of, 293

V

vector-matrix multiplier, *see* optical vector-matrix multiplication
vertical to surface transmission electro-photonic device (VSTEP), 73

applications of, 91
free-carrier absorption in, 80
LED-mode, 75
  switching energy of, 76
laser-mode, 78
  single lateral mode oscillation in, 80, 86
  specific contact resistance of, 88
  switching energy of, 89
vertical-cavity surface-emitting laser (VSEL), 79, 99
vignetting, 31
volume holographic storage
  angular multiplexing in, 260, 262, 272
  angular sensitivity of, 259
  critical parameters of, 258
  diffraction efficiency of, 258
  spatial resolution of, 263
  storage capacity, 262
  temporal multiplexing, 281
  wavelength multiplexing in, 262
  wavelength sensitivity of, 259
von Neumann bottleneck, 100
VSTEP, *see* vertical to surface transmission electro-photonic device

W

wavelength-division multiplexing (WDM), 254, 282
WDM, *see* wavelength-division multiplexing
wire-bonding, 9